HISTORY OF THEORY AND METHOD IN ANTHROPOLOGY

Critical Studies in the History of Anthropology

SERIES EDITORS

Regna Darnell
Robert Oppenheim

HISTORY OF THEORY AND METHOD IN ANTHROPOLOGY

REGNA DARNELL

University of Nebraska Press

LINCOLN

Acknowledgments for the use of previously published or copy-
righted material appear in each chapter's notes, which constitute an extension of the copyright page.

The University of Nebraska Press is part of a land-grant institution with campuses and programs on the past, present, and
future homelands of the Pawnee, Ponca, Otoe-Missouria,
Omaha, Dakota, Lakota, Kaw, Cheyenne, and Arapaho Peoples,
as well as those of the relocated Ho-Chunk, Sac and Fox, and
Iowa Peoples.

Publication of this work was assisted by the Murray-Hong Family Trust, to honor and sustain the distinguished legacy of
Stephen O. Murray in the History of Anthropology at the University of Nebraska Press.

Library of Congress Cataloging-in-Publication Data
Names: Darnell, Regna, author.
Title: History of theory and method in anthropology / Regna
Darnell, University of Nebraska Press.
Description: Lincoln: University of Nebraska Press, [2022] |
Series: Critical studies in the history of anthropology | Includes
bibliographical references and index.
Identifiers: LCCN 2021058923 | ISBN 9781496224163 (hard-
back) | ISBN 9781496231307 (paperback) | ISBN 9781496232243
(epub) | ISBN 9781496232250 (pdf)
Subjects: LCSH: Anthropology—North America—History. |
Anthropology—Methodology—North America. | Indians of
North America—Research—History. | BISAC: SOCIAL SCIENCE /
Anthropology / Cultural & Social | SOCIAL SCIENCE /
Ethnic Studies / American / Native American Studies
Classification: LCC GN17.3.N7 D3693 2022 | DDC 301.097—dc23
LC record available at https://lccn.loc.gov/2021058923

Set and designed in New Baskerville ITC Pro by Laura Buis.

CONTENTS

ILLUSTRATIONS

TABLES

ACKNOWLEDGMENTS

Chapter 1

Delivered at the annual meeting of the American Society for Ethnohistory, New Orleans, October 3, 2009. I thank Timothy Bisha, Jim Birckhead, Robert L. A. Hancock, Dean Jacobs, Bryan Loucks, and Dan and Mary Lou Smoke for ongoing conversations at many stages of this rethinking. The fine hands of Ray DeMallie, Ray Fogelson; and Tony Wallace, all now deceased, lie just below the surface and live in memory. I also thank the late Keith Basso, Neal Ferris, Walpole Island First Nation (Bkejwanong Territory), Driton Nushaj, the late Blair Rudes, and my late husband, György Ozöray, who was a geologist.

Chapter 2

I particularly thank Joshua Smith, Robert L. A. Hancock, and Craig Proulx for the nomination for the Weaver-Tremblay Award and their generous introduction and Liz Guerrier for the warm hospitality of Dave's Place. I am proud to have been a sometime and continuing mentor to each of them. It is impossible to enumerate all who have contributed to my thinking on the issues discussed in this chapter. I am grateful for so many opportunities to engage in wide-ranging dialogue. Anthropology is a collective enterprise of colleagues speaking respectfully to one another across permeable borders of culture, gender, academic discipline, and professional generation, then taking their insights out into the world. I acknowledge generous support from the Social Sciences and Humanities Research Council of Canada for many of the projects discussed here. I would like to single out the ongoing importance of CASCA to my thinking and to Sal Weaver and Adé Tremblay. I am grateful to my public health colleagues Jack Bend, Diana Lee, Courtney Hambides, Charlie Trick, Amardeep Thind, and the late Indigenous scholar and health practitioner Dana Winterburn.

Chapter 3

My thoughts on these debates at the time of writing owe much to Judith T. Irvine, the late Stephen O. Murray, and James M. Nyce, and Janice Boddy's comments on an earlier draft clarified my thinking about how to speak to an audience not immersed in Americanist matters. This chapter is about paralysis. It rejects the inevitability of the widening gulf polarizing disciplinary cultures. The American Anthropological Association was sorting out the relationships of sections to the larger organization at the time, which opened a window for an intervention to a cultural studies audience that I found most welcome.

Chapter 4

This essay approaches the relationship that J. Edward Chamberlin posits between stories and land from the standpoint of First Nations and Inuit narrative and reflects on the process by which outsiders may come to understand how Indigenous storytellers construct meaning and reflect on their present-day social and political circumstances. Such storytellers often employ traditional stories to establish cultural continuity and provide templates for contemporary reflexivity. I draw examples from more than four decades of fieldwork as a linguistic anthropologist (at the time of original writing), primarily among Plains Cree and Anishinaabeg (Ojibwe) peoples. I offer some proposals for establishing respectful relationships and transcending cross-cultural miscommunication. The essay both articulates and employs practices of First Nations and Indigenous pedagogical principles adapted from oral tradition. I attempt to mediate between conventional academic disciplines of the humanities and social sciences as well as between Indigenous and non-Indigenous discourses. Because cross-cultural differences in meaning making are deeply grounded in social practice as well as language in the narrow sense, careful attention to the underlying relational quality of philosophical thought in specific Indigenous traditions is required to calibrate narrative practices and the appropriate forms of interaction they entail. The stories themselves are the tip of a complex iceberg, and effective storytellers invite hearers or readers to interpret their words in terms of rich social and aesthetic conventions that differ greatly from those of mainstream Canadian society. "Common ground" is about traditional land in a literal sense, but it is also about the potential for discursive common ground. Ted Chamberlin graciously consented to remove the original context of presentation. The location of the symposium at Brantford, Ontario, made it impossible for me to secure permission to represent the territory as a participant invited at the behest of others. I also acknowledge the influence of Michael Asch, John Borrows, Rob Hancock, John Leavitt, Frederico Delgado Rosa, and Jim Tully. The text is considerably expanded from the time constraints of the original in ways that facilitate exploring the theorical implications of the relationship of method and theory.

Chapter 5

This chapter moves back and forth between the intersecting connections of engagements of Ray Fogelson and A. Irving Hallowell. They evoke different acknowledgments. For Hallowell, I thank Maureen Matthews, Jennifer Brown, and Laura Peers. For Fogelson, I acknowledge Sergei Kan, and Pauline Turner Strong, who prepared the volume in which this paper initially appeared. I am grateful to Karen Luckritz for sharing documents and insights. Their decade-long marriage brought a measure of serenity as Ray moved into retirement between Chicago and their place in Georgia. Joshua Smith and Grant Arndt facilitated plans to honor Ray at the American Society for Ethnohistory.

Chapter 6

This paper was originally presented in Montreal in May 2006 at a Plenary Session of the Canadian Anthropology Society on Human Nature and Human Identity. I thank Nigel Rapport and Katja Neves for the invitation to participate in these reflections on the conference theme and Margaret Lock for her complementary insights. The theoretical climate has changed greatly over ensuing years and for most anthropologists the landscape I lay out here is no longer as polarized as the one I describe. Enough time has elapsed to reveal underlying positions that persist in more muted form today if only because awareness of contrasting positions has increased. I have not attempted to update a debate that is now moot but rather to outline how I experienced it at the time. John Leavitt has been influential in my return to the question of universals. I also acknowledge Gaile McGregor, James M. Nyce, and Richard Preston.

Chapter 7

I thank Michael Harkin for the invitation to present at this conference in honor of Claude Lévi-Strauss (who was present at a number of the sessions), Marie Mauzé for the elegant local hospitality, and all of the editors for planning and executing this project. The problematic of transcending national boundaries in an ethnographic region was only partially resolved by the dampening effect of the functional monolingualism of many North American participants on local audience enthusiasm. Alexei Elfimov, Marjorie Halpin, Ira Jacknis, Frederico Delgado Rosa, John Leavitt, Sean O'Neill, and Michael Silverstein influenced my rethinking of the pitfalls of translation.

Chapter 8

An early version of this essay was presented at a symposium organized by Neni Panourgiá in 2011 in honor of the centennial of *The Mind of Primitive Man*. I draw on a related paper for the centennial conference organized at Yale by Isaiah Wilner (published as chapter 9, this volume). I am grateful for these opportunities to revisit the integration and ongoing relevance of Boas's thought. In addition, I thank Michael Asch, Lee D. Baker, Tim Bisha, Matt Bokovoy, the late Ray DeMallie, the late Ray Fogelson, Fred Gleach, Rob Hancock, the late Dell Hymes, Martin Levitt, the late Stephen O. Murray, Marc Pinkoski, the late Tim Powell, the late Michael Silverstein, Joshua Smith, the late George Stocking, and the late A. F. C. Wallace. That so many of these individuals are now deceased highlights the urgency of the historian's task.

Chapter 9

Conferences on the subject were organized at the University of Western Ontario by Regna Darnell, at the Wenner-Gren Foundation for Anthropological Research by Nene Panagourgiá, and at Yale by Isaiah Wilner. I am grateful to participants in these various events for invigorating scholarly reassessment of Boas's oeuvre. My own formulation of the Boasian paradigm relies especially on the insights of Lee D. Baker, Frederic W. Gleach, Robert L. A. Hancock, John Leavitt, the late Stephen O. Murray, Joshua Smith, and the late George W. Stocking Jr. There is considerable urgency of documenting anthropology's history.

Chapter 10

An early version of this paper was read at the American Anthropological Association meetings in December 1970, revised from Darnell (1969). I thank Margaret Blaker, Raymond DeMallie, Dell Hymes, Sydney Lamb, and William C. Sturtevant for their comments and encouragement. Linguistic classification is still a burning issue. I thank Michael Silverstein and Ira Jacknis for insights in revision. The American Anthropological Association and the Linguistic Society of America coordinated their resources to approach the same historical questions from different angles. I participated in both and found the audiences and perspectives quite distinct.

Chapter 11

A preliminary version of this paper was read at the meetings of the Linguistic Society of America in December 1969. The audience reaction made it clear that the lumpers and the splitters among Native American linguistics remain passionate in their positions. The question was not, for them, one of the history of linguistics relegated to the past. Because this chapter arose separately from different disciplinary roots, transition and some repetition have been inevitable. Darnell (1969, revised in Darnell 1998) constructed a more integrated analysis that found an afterlife in potential opposition for a more extensive version in this chapter. I am grateful to Dell H. Hymes and George W. Stocking Jr. for substantive and interpretive aid. I thank Stephen O. Murray and Michael Silverstein for insights in revision.

Chapter 12

This chapter highlights the complexity of forging international connections in light of pragmatic constraints. At the time of publication, it was an "aha" moment in my attention to the entangled mutual histories of national traditions. Several colleagues have contributed to retrieving its meandering history in the years since. The original invitation came from Alexei Elfimov, who translated my commentary in English for its appearance in Russian and provided the proper citation format. Emmanuel Désveaux graciously consented to my use of his material alongside my own and provided materials in French that supersede the original piece. Alex Pershai helped me navigate the languages and networks they crossed. I also thank John Leavitt, Sean O'Neill, Frederico Delgado Rosa, Michael Asch, Wendy Leeds-Hurwitz, Thierry Veyrié, and Michael Silverstein.

Chapter 13

The present version has not been previously published and appears here only in the parts that serve as a foil to other chapters linking French and American traditions through the ideas of Claude Lévi-Strauss and linguistic relativity. I thank Michael Asch for organizing the session that brought these papers together. My understanding of rationalism has been particularly enhanced in very different ways by John Leavitt and Marie Mauzé. It is critical that we think of these matters as theoretical.

Chapter 14

I thank Douglas Kibbee, whose paper titled "Durkheim, Language and Linguistics," read at the North American Association for the History of the Language Sciences (NAHOLS) in Philadelphia in January 1992, drew my attention to the absence of language in the work of both Lévi-Strauss and Durkheim. This led me to the intersection of potentially incommensurable positions across national traditions in anthropology and linguistics that I have discussed elsewhere in relation to the Boasian tradition in North America (Darnell 1991, 1992; see chapters 7 and 13, this volume). Konrad Koerner encouraged me to set out the parameters of the historiographic problem with reference to Lévi-Strauss, and the late

Stephen O. Murray commented on an earlier draft. My continuing reflections on Indo-European and how linguists think about it also draw on John Joseph, Henry Hoenigswald, Michael Silverstein, Christine Laurière, and Frederico Delgado Rosa.

Chapter 15

The role of Marie-Françoise Guédon has been crucial in preserving archival documents and locating them in appropriate repositories in Alaska and the United States. As executor of Frederica de Laguna's estate, her establishment of Frederica de Laguna Northern Books ensures a long-term legacy. Colleagues at Bryn Mawr College shared their memories.

Chapter 16

The reprinting of this obituary is problematic in the context of pending charges of long-term sexual harassment resulting in Hymes's shunning by the Graduate School of Education at Penn. I agonized over it but have chosen it include it despite my acute discomfort. I did not experience this myself during my long-ago interaction with Dell Hymes in the departments of anthropology and folklore. I left Philadelphia before he moved to the Graduate School of Education and have no direct knowledge of what transpired there. The chapter cites various of his actions of political activism on behalf of minorities that I admired at the time. Many of his students were women, and it seemed to me that their interests were facilitated. The genre of flagship obituary has a particular temporal status: it is directed toward generations to come as well as to contemporary readers. The slippery slope of who might be subject to contemporary opprobrium is one I consider myself unable to navigate to a consistent standard for the *longue dureé*. Many others discussed in this volume could also be singled out. The history of anthropology would be impossible if this were taken to its logical extreme. Adjustments to contemporary experience out of respect for privacy and the feelings of today's readers are quite another matter, and one that I take very seriously.

Chapter 17

The genre of flagship journal obituary does not lend itself to citation of acknowledgment or include archival sources because it contains within itself the sources of information on which it is based. Richard Handler, Ira Bashkow, and Fred Gleach facilitated access to documents at Chicago.

Chapter 18

A book review draws on existing knowledge and does not lend itself to citation of acknowledgments or archival sources. This review reflects the author's personal ambivalence about Stocking and his legacy and acknowledges its situated position in relation to this legacy. The genre of book review evokes a different voice than an obituary in a flagship journal. The contrast to the more measured and neutral tone of the *American Anthropologist* obituary is an object lesson in the need to consider the context in which words are written and for their author to acknowledge their situated position as well as their denotative content.

Chapter 19

The genre of flagship journal obituary does not lend itself to citation of acknowledgments or archival sources. My understanding of Anthony F. C. Wallace and his contributions owes much to the American Philosophical Society, Ray Fogelson, Charles Greifenstein, Robert S. Grumet, and Sol Katz. I also acknowledge Martin Leavitt, Adriana Link, Pat McPherson, Linda Mucumeci, Patrick Spero, Elinor Roach, and Ann Westcott.

EDITORIAL METHOD

The chapters have been edited for style, consistency, and relationship to the volume's overall story of method and theory in the history of anthropology as it has evolved to its present structure over the five-plus decades of the author's career. The narrative emphasizes the methodological and theoretical context out of which this anthropology has developed both in North America and internationally. I minimize the inevitable repetition across chapters covering similar background material by paraphrase, adding context, and occasionally telescoping parenthetical detail specific to its repeated citation presented elsewhere.

Some short quotes are set off in the text as they were in the original, and I have added few new ones. I retain much of the sentence structure, sequence, and subheads of the original, while at the same time smoothing out the flow of the prose and adding enough updates, clearly identified as such, to ensure that the chapters as they were first published remain in dialogue with the contemporary field. Original footnotes are included, but a few additional ones are added. Most are references to subsequent scholarship, most often my own, and reflect developments beyond the time frame of the reprinted chapter or signal more recent revisionist interpretations.

Some changes are stylistic: papers could not have used gender-inclusive language that did not yet exist although today its absence is offensive. When the early Boasians wrote in the late nineteenth and early twentieth centuries, terms such as "primitive" were common and are retained in quotes; quotation marks, [*sic*], and bracketed updates such as man[kind] call the reader's attention to these changes in the conventions of discourse. Conventions of academic writing have evolved. I follow an informal conversational style, for example, substituting "that" for "which" and inserting myself into the text by use of the first person and personal commentary about the subject of the chapter and the circumstances of its delivery. I minimize passive constructions and substitute active verbs for less effective ones.

Overuse of "of course," "however," and other hedges is common in the early writing of most scholars. Some infelicities are due to precomputer constraints on authorial ability to edit drafts. Editorial revision was more onerous before I acquired my first computer in 1985.

In expectation of an audience including students in interrelated disciplines who will be familiar with some but not all parts of the material, I have added some in-text expansions to orient readers unfamiliar with particular contexts, e.g., linguistics or physical anthropology.

The chapters are arranged thematically rather than chronologically to emphasize their approach to similar subject matter from more than one standpoint. I hope this approach will encourage readers to track the intertextual construction of academic arguments over time.

INTRODUCTION

Method and theory in the history of anthropology are defined in terms of ideas, institutions, and social networks for their implementation. Darnell (2021) addressed the question of institutions. This volume turns to theoretical questions of the history of anthropology, history, and historiography directed toward capturing the ongoing flow of scholarship in progress. The reader is invited to join in the reflexive exercise of deconstructing the process by which academic works are constructed. Readers who choose to skip this section will lack an explanation for the layers of overlying repetition that reveal the construction of a scholarly work and thereby find it pointless and disorderly. These notes constitute signposts that reveal how finished works produce later glosses that smooth over the vagaries of the emergence and thereby excise them from the documentary record. Documentary editing permits interlocutors to express themselves in the nuance of their own words, which are then subject to evaluation and framing in multiple contexts.

Many forms of normally undocumented interaction underlie the production of any integrated work. We might consider, for example, casual conversation that takes place at conferences or through professional associations. Intellectual links may arise when individuals meet in administrative roles and discover that they have common interests. For anthropologists who teach, regardless of the nature of their institution, its graduate or undergraduate status, in seminars or in lecture classes, or the nature of its student population, pedagogical feedback is a rich source of reflexive attention to ideas in the making. This creates a potential activist pedagogy in the world beyond the ivory tower. Such feedback is carried to other conferences where the rhetoric may be adjusted for a different audience and different aspects of the original idea. All of this goes into the final product. Practicing anthropologists, in or out of the academy, have access to unpublished material in the form of manuscripts and preprints in draft form. Colleagues ask for professional advice as well as feedback on their ideas; they require recommendations for jobs and promotions. Piecemeal publications cannot make a sustained argument because its pieces are developed over a series of efforts that cannot be found in the same place. That is why books are so important. Eventually, these things get integrated in a book. Darnell (2001) reflects a decade of such consolidation and integration. This sounds simpler than in the practice.

One train of thought in contemporary scholarship holds that reviews ought to be double blind. That is, fairness to applicants and their work is assumed to require a standard of objectivity in which personalizing the information requested is virtually impossible. Human resources personnel are trained to this standard. I am of the contrary view that "objectivity" is the wrong standard (not possible in any case) and that treating candidates generically cannot be fair. Once a short list has been arrived at, there must be a way to distinguish the uniqueness of what an applicant has to offer. Those who read such recommendations must expect to evaluate them beyond their face value, a question of self-conscious reflexivity about one's own potential sources of bias. Using one's experience to put in touch scholars and communities who ought to be requires a time-consuming commitment to maintaining connections. Rarely is this considered part of normal workload for an academic; nor is it likely to be highly valued by the institution in the allotment of activities to categories of research, teaching, and service. I contend in contrast that the three are inseparable and that the only way to balance a workload is to do the same things for more than one reason. This makes it impossible to balance a workload that must be reported relative to a forty-hour workweek. The academy is replete with double binds to which it is imperative that the social sciences and humanities call attention.

Establishment of stable relationships of collaboration with a publisher make it possible for colleagues to know where to look for the work of a scholar that interests them. Increasingly presses focus their lists in limited areas of specialization to market them effectively. I am the founding editor of a cluster of publication series in history of anthropology at the University of Nebraska Press that includes The Franz Boas Papers series, Critical Studies in History of Anthropology (with Stephen O. Murray until his death and more recently with Robert Oppenheim), and *Histories of Anthropology Annual* (with Frederic W. Gleach). Through the Murray-Hong Family Trust, Keelung Hong has endowed this research area. Under the prescient leadership of Matt Bokovoy, I have learned to balance the priorities of the publisher with those of the author in ways that allow flexible negotiation of long-term intellectual projects. The double vision, seeing from more than one point of view, is the key pedagogical point.

The process of academic production is rhizomatic and dynamic. My own work crosses and integrates interdisciplinary networks from international intersection of national traditions (e.g., through the Berose Encyclopaedia of the Histories of Anthropology), medical anthropology, and public health to linguistic anthropology to Anishinaabeg languages and cultures with language revitalization commitments in Ontario, Alberta, and British Columbia. Long-term connections with particular communities, individuals, and their homelands build momentum and establish trust over the course of a career that cannot be telescoped. It takes a long time to do good community-based research.

Because a dynamic history of anthropology requires that it remain open-ended, it is inevitable that one's work will be superseded. It remains valid as a document grounded in its own time and available as source material for future scholars. The work is on the record, and its standpoint is intelligible into the future. This understanding is counter to the definition of history employed by most historians, of whom George W. Stocking Jr. (1968), founder of history of anthropology as a separate subdiscipline within anthropology, may be taken as exemplar (cf. Cole 1999). Historians, by virtue of their professional training, are uncomfortable not knowing the outcome in advance when they describe and evaluate past events.

Historians of anthropology since the 1960s have had to come to terms with Stocking's hegemony over the field, which is still unquestioned in many quarters despite the passage of half a century, and establish their own credentials in divergence from his position. I have done so in publications from my MA thesis in 1967 and PhD dissertation in 1969 to the present (see additional Darnell references below). I argue that history of anthropology should not be distinct from the discipline of anthropology overall. Alternatives were already present at the time, in the work of Hymes and Hallowell as well as myself. Stocking relies heavily on the hermeneutic apparatus proposed by Kuhn (1962) and the terms he proposes and thus emphasizes the distinction between historicism and presentism. Kuhn's first edition excluded the social sciences from paradigmatic status because old theories often persisted alongside newer dispensations, factored along generational lines. Terms are critical to the needed evaluation (see King 2019), especially as they change over time because they highlight what is likely to be important in the long term for readers to assess the circumstances no longer present in living memory.

The genre of obituary provides an exemplar. Four are included in this volume. Obituaries, particularly in flagship journals, do not have sources in the normal sense of this term although they do reflect the relationship of the author to the biographical subject. Such a relationship is part of the decision to invite a scholar to prepare such a document and usually is reflected in personal details included in the obituary. Frederica de Laguna was my first teacher of anthropology as an undergraduate at Bryn Mawr College from 1961 to 1965, and we met often until I left Philadelphia in 1969 and later at conferences and on my visits there until her death. I came to know her better during these years when I was no longer her student. Dell Hymes supervised my MA thesis and PhD dissertation at Penn (1965–69); I was his research assistant during much of this time. We met thereafter largely at conferences after I moved to Canada in 1969; he and his wife Virginia visited Edmonton once as guest speakers at my invitation. I have an extensive file of personal correspondence with him that contains both professional and personal information about various colleagues and students. My disclaimers in the obituary clarify my unawareness of the censures that have surfaced more recently. My relationship to George W. Stocking Jr. was ambivalent. His scholarship defined history of anthropology as a subdiscipline. On the other hand, his gatekeeper role and personal temperament were such that I had to be very careful not to offend him. I avoided topics I knew he considered his preserve and continued to share my work with him in draft form for feedback. In retrospect I believe that he effectively plagiarized from this work and consequently did not acknowledge my role as his potential successor. Gender bias may also have been an issue. This is reflected minimally in the obituary and somewhat more so in the book review, included to emphasize the importance genre makes in what is said and how. Tony Wallace was department chair at Penn when I was there (1965–69). My research assistant office was just outside his on the balcony of the University Museum auditorium so I came to know him a bit. He shared documents from his files at the Eastern Pennsylvania Psychiatric Institute on matters of Iroquoian ethnohistory and served as a reader on my dissertation committee. I came to know him better in later years through the American Philosophical Society Philips Committee, and Iroquois Conferences; I visited him at Tuscarora several times while driving him to the APS meetings.

There is an ethical and methodological question about how much personal information should be shared in providing context. What anthropologists gleefully refer to as "gossip" adds verisimilitude that sociologists, for example, are socialized to omit in interests of "objectivity." Anthropologists draw readers (and reviewers) into their writing by including such tidbits. But self-discipline is needed to ensure that only biographical information necessary to make the point is included. The tell-all confessional must remain in the private domain; some anecdotes are germane and others are not. Dates are arbitrary, and the same rules must apply to all. The appropriate role of a senior scholar is to step back from contemporary events and facilitate the work of others, accepting that trends evolve. For example, I changed from the language of cybernetics (chaos and complexity) to that of materiality and vibration (resonance, rhizomes, and intersectionality) in order to communicate effectively with colleagues of other generations.

It is important not to read literally. The double meaning implicit in metaphor is critical. Chapter 4 reports an Apache elder's statement about hanging one's own clothes on the line to dry; the storyteller only puts the pegs on the line, leaving interpretation to the reader.

There are few citations of documents in this volume. Rather, the history of anthropology provides a lens or a point of view from which to assess contemporary materials. In this context, the circumstances of an invitation or the location of its presentation hold a salience that is not present in later published versions.

In sum, I am delighted to share some of my own "aha" moments with readers and to acknowledge once again the collaborative nature of my scholarship and the degree to which its boundary crossings may be instructive in terms of future practice beyond this volume. What I have called "transportable knowledge" underlies the ability to think well about anything.

The majority of my trusted assessors are thanked in the chapter acknowledgments, but some have a more pervasive impact on my thinking and are singled out here for particular or additional attention: Danielle Alcock, Michael Asch, Angie Bain, Lee D. Baker, Keith Basso, Matthew Bokovoy, M. Sam Cronk, Melanie Caldwell-Clark, Eva Cupchik, Jane Curran, Nathan Dawthorne, Tish Fobbin, Frederic W. Gleach, Janice Graham, Tracey Hetherington, Courtney Hambides, Keelung Hong, Andrea Laforet, Christine Laurière, Diana Lee, Wendy Leeds-Hurwitz, Andrew and Harriet Lyons, Gerald McKinley, Călin-Andrei Mihăilescu, Leif Milliken, Sarah Moritz, Neyooxet Greymorning, Robert Oppenheim, Bernard Perley, Bimadoska Anya Pucan, Ian Puppe, Frederico Delgado Rosa, Joshua Smith, Dan and Mary Lou Smoke, Heather Stauffer, Mark Turin, Rob Wishart, Elizabeth Zaleski, and Rosemary Zumwalt.

References

Baker, Lee D. 2010. *Anthropology and the Racial Politics of Culture.* Durham NC: Duke University Press.

Boas, Franz. 1911a. Introduction to the *Handbook of American Indian Languages.* Bureau of American Ethnology Bulletin 40. Washington DC: Government Printing Office.

———. 1911b. *The Mind of Primitive Man.* New York: Macmillan.

Darnell, Regna. 1967. "Daniel Garrison Brinton: An Intellectual Biography." Master's thesis, University of Pennsylvania.

———. 1969. "The Development of American Anthropology, 1880–1920: From the Bureau of American Ethnology to Franz Boas." PhD diss., University of Pennsylvania.

———. 1998. *And Along Came Boas: Continuity and Change in Americanist Anthropology.* Lincoln: University of Nebraska Press.

———. 2001. *Invisible Genealogies: A History of Americanist Anthropology.* Lincoln: University of Nebraska Press.

———, ed. 2015. *Franz Boas as Public Intellectual: Theory, Ethnography, Activism.* Franz Boas Papers series. Lincoln: University of Nebraska Press.

———. 2017. "Franz Boas as Theorist: A Mentalist Paradigm for the Study of Mind, Body, Environment, and Culture." In *Historicizing Theories, Identities, and Nations,* edited by Regnal Darnell and Frederic W. Gleach, 1–26. Vol. 11 of Histories of Anthropology Annual. Lincoln: University of Nebraska Press.

———. 2021. *History of Anthropology: A Critical Window on the Discipline in North America.* Lincoln: University of Nebraska Press. New York: Doubleday.

Darnell, Regna, and Frederic W. Gleach, eds. 2020. *Centering the Margin of Anthropology's History.* Vol. 14 of Histories of Anthropology Annual. Lincoln: University of Nebraska Press.

Hallowell, A. Irving. 1965. "The History of Anthropology as an Anthropological Problem." *Journal of the History of the Behavioral Sciences* 1:24–38.

Harrison Julia, and Regna Darnell, eds. 2006. *Historicizing Canadian Anthropology.* Vancouver: University of British Columbia Press.

Hymes, Dell H. 1962. "On Studying the History of Anthropology." *Kroeber Anthropological Society Papers* 26:81–86.

Irvine, Judith T., ed. 1994. *The Psychology of Culture: A Course of Lectures.* [Reconstructed from class notes of Edward Sapir.] Berlin: Mouton de Gruyter.

King, Charles. 2019. *Gods of the Upper Air: How a Circle of Renegade Anthropologists Reinvented Race, Sex, and Gender in the Twentieth Century.* New York: Doubleday.

Kuhn, Thomas S. 1962. *The Structure of Scientific Revolutions.* Chicago: University of Chicago Press.

Stocking, George W., Jr. 1968. *Race, Language and Culture: Essays in the History of Anthropology.* New York: Free Press.

Valentine, Lisa Philips, and Regna Darnell, eds. 1995. *Theorizing the Americanist Tradition.* Toronto: University of Toronto Press.

ABBREVIATIONS

Archival Documents

AAA	American Anthropological Association
APS	American Philosophical Society
BAE	Bureau of [American] Ethnology Institutional Abbreviations
SSHRC	Social Sciences and Humanities Research Council of Canada

HISTORY OF THEORY AND METHOD IN ANTHROPOLOGY

1

What Is History?

An Anthropologist's Eye View

The unofficial title of my 2009 presidential address to the American Society for Ethnohistory (ASE) is "What Would 'History' Look Like If You Did What I Do?"[1] It reflects my occasional musings about whether I really belong among the ethnohistorians. Many of my best friends are ethnohistorians. Over the years I have tried to speak to these colleagues from the dual perspectives of Native North American ethnographer and historian of anthropology— two essential pieces of "ethnohistory" but not combined in precisely the ways that are normative for the American Society for Ethnohistory.

Rarely does an academic get the opportunity to speak to colleagues at a modest remove from specific research results. So I am grateful for this opportunity to explore the potential of ethnohistory to realign the historian's craft in a more ethnographic, anthropological direction—by way of the metalinguistic nature of "history" as an analytical concept, with the caveat that the history I practice is often about the discipline of anthropology and its observational practices, rather than exclusively about purportedly exotic others. Whether based in archival research or fieldwork, my research subjects—academic colleagues or collaborating Native American and First Nations persons alike—are generally peering over my shoulder and engaging with my interpretations. This, in my view, is the proper work of anthropology.

I frequently recall the late Dennis Tedlock's evocative reading of the Popul Vuh over the shoulder of a contemporary Mayan medicine man who had received the "text" exclusively through oral tradition. His title, *The Spoken Word and the Work of Interpretation*, reflects the dual nature of the enterprise (Tedlock 1983). The traditional knowledge of the Popul Vuh first came to Tedlock as preserved in a codex accessible to invaders dependent on writing. Meanwhile, under the radar, subversively, Mayan oral tradition continued to record and transmit this history in customary ways. The coexistence of parallel written and oral forms attests to the survival of the Mayan point of view for both conqueror and Indigenous communities. Interpretation, in such a reciprocal, collaborative context, becomes an emergent property of dialogue, with reflexivity an inevitable although not necessarily intended consequence. Speaking to my own method in both fieldwork and academic discourse, I am wont to gloss this as "You think *what?* I never thought about it that way. We have to talk some more."

Combining insights derived from feminist-standpoint epistemology with the careful attention to the positioning and authority of speakers and actors whom I have learned to respect through engagement with First Nations and Native American cultures, I adhere to Hayden White's contention that "history" goes beyond the primary data of annals and chronicles *only* when at least two potential interpretations can be weighed against one another (White 1980). Any one interpretation, in this context, is partial and contingent.

At annual meetings I have often been nonplussed at the dis-ease [*sic*] with which many colleagues approach the question of oral history—some question whether it is "history" at all, and even more marginalize it as an unequivocally secondary form of evidence. Yet, if anything has changed during the history of the American Society for Ethnohistory, surely it is the emergence of an increasingly powerful compulsion to represent what Franz Boas called "the native point of view"—to transcend the absence of conventional written documents representing the other side of the story from the one that outsiders tell themselves.

The skeptics among us, and they include anthropologists as well as historians, contend that evidence from oral tradition is useful only when it confirms and fleshes out interpretations based on archival records. I draw a methodological rather than a disciplinary dichotomy. From what I have heard at this and other ASE conferences, perhaps I am flogging a moribund if not a dead horse. If so, let us congratulate ourselves on honoring both sides of our societal mandate—the "ethno" and the "historical." I worry, however, that insistence on convergent evidence in this limited sense entails an unconscious ethnocentric dismissal of the very position it purports to respect. There is nothing secondary about oral traditions for those who rely on them. The late Raymond D. Fogelson's cautionary words in his own ASE presidential address expand our understanding of history itself:

> All peoples possess a sense of the past, however strange and exceptional that past may seem from our own literately conditioned perspective. An understanding of non-Western histories requires not only the generation of documents and an expanded conception of what constitutes documentation but also a determined effort to try to comprehend alien forms of historical consciousness and discourse. (Fogelson 1989:134)

Oral traditions, in common with all forms of qualitative endeavor, have their own standards of reliability and validity and should not be evaluated in terms transposed wholesale from alien and alienating modes of historical imagination.

Reliability is assured by the repetition of historical stories, by acknowledging their sources and routes of transmission, and by calling on other members of an interpretive community to add their overlapping recollections to the corpus. For example, Plains Cree elder Freda Ahenakew and Algonquian linguist H. C. Wolfart (Ahenakew and Wolfart 1998) emphasize that the memory of the Treaty Six negotiation told to Jim Kâ-Nîpitêhtêw by his father was supplemented by transmitted recollections of others present at the same negotiation who were party to different scenes and events on that occasion. The amalgamation of their stories into a single narrative constitutes a community's history in terms of the experience of its most esteemed members. This history situates contemporary revisitings of treaty understandings in dynamic relation to ongoing land claims.

Templates from traditional knowledge (Cree *atayohkewina*, sacred stories)[2] also organize and locate individual narratives within the larger narrative that is the history of a people, a metahistory as it were. Julie Cruikshank (1990), for example, shows how life histories of three Yukon women deploy parallels between their unique personal experience and the experience encoded in traditional stories to establish a chain of historical and cosmological continuity that extends to their grandchildren and beyond. Angela Sidney, Kitty Smith, and Annie Ned realized that they were the last generation to have grown up in traditional ways. Each chose to index the change by the practices of puberty seclusion. Because young women today have a very different experience, these elders accepted responsibility to pass on their own experience of what they took to be the shared experience of women of their generation. Traditional stories of stolen brides are juxtaposed to give form to the experience of a young woman entering an arranged marriage. Such stories are both personal and generic. The similarities and differences of the three cases clarify both the pattern and its variability.

Another sort of what I call generic narrative (Darnell 2006) occurs when speakers emphasize their own difficult experiences and exhort younger community members to follow their example in overcoming obstacles of addiction and discrimination. Residential school narratives, long kept secret out of shame, are now framed in terms of community experience of intergenerational trauma alongside the graphic reports of individual residential school survivors. The stories place a burden and an obligation on those who hear them. The reliability of the genre arises from its repetition, from the independent construction of the residential school experience, in parallel though not identical ways by each narrator who now chooses to share their version of the collective history. Each story affirms the others, as evidenced by the public hearings of Canada's Royal Commission on Aboriginal Peoples (1996) and Truth and Reconciliation Commission (2015).

Like oral traditions, written histories of colonial encounter have their own tropes and metanarratives: terra nullius, eminent domain, white man's burden, the noble savage. Such tropes are widely shared and easily interpretable even if they are not accurate. They are repeated over and over again by different speakers or writers, in different contexts, and on different occasions. In *Do Glaciers Listen? Local Knowledge, Colonial Encounters, and Social Imagination,* Julie Cruikshank (2005) contrasts early Yukon explorers' narratives about the animacy, unpredictability, and power of glaciers with the more deeply embedded knowledge of their ways enculturated by Indigenous peoples who had lived alongside the glaciers through their long-shared history. Within the temporal reach of directly transmitted oral tradition, stories are told of how the people and the animals moved in relation to each other and to the movement of the glaciers. Interestingly, Indigenous people and early explorers identify virtually the same interactive features of glaciers, although they tell different and culturally specific stories about the whys and wherefores of their experience. Critically, however, the two traditions are not as far apart as Indigenous storied experience is from the observations of the contemporary scientist trained to recognize only the "objective" material features of the glaciers. Each narrative provides its own mode of historicizing the copresence of human communities and glaciers. European observers also differ in their opinions, although this is usually glossed over. From the perspective of multiple then-contemporary observers however, the science taken for granted today becomes the outlier and an inappropriate comparator for views that could not have been held by any observers at an earlier time.

Validity is assured in oral tradition because the audience present at every retelling always already has a history of hearing them from multiple narratives on multiple occasions and evaluating the alternatives in relation to one another. Further, startling though it may be to those of us socialized to read, memory can be trained, and those who live and work in a primarily oral tradition perforce learn to remember accurately. They foresee the possibility that others will call them out for inaccuracy or undue interpretive license. Can one speculate in such a tradition? Of course—the variability invites it. But interpretive speculation is exegesis, distinct from the raw data that are the "facts" of the history being transmitted. Keith Basso's Western Apache consultant Charles Henry, for example, tells the bare bones of a story that has come down to the Cibecue, Arizona, community in more than one version. He then elaborates the context that he imagines and emphasizes that "it could have happened that way" (Basso 1996:17).

Anishinaabeg (Ojibwe) listeners are implicitly enjoined by their responsibility to seven generations in each direction from the speaker to draw parallels across the inextricable continuum of past, present, and future. This time depth extends the direct reach of oral tradition and shades gradually into teachings transmitted from ancestors who are no longer remembered by name (Cree *nimosomipanak*, literally, "my grandfathers who are deceased"). People speak from their own experience—which includes knowledge transmitted to them directly through oral tradition. As long as the chain of transmission is unbroken, the experience becomes embodied in the receiver of a teaching or telling who, by receiving it, accepts a responsibility to pass it on. The persistence of the Indigenous Knowledge that these ancestors—both known and unknown—have passed on attests to its importance and ongoing validity for the community, tribe, or nation as a whole. Collective identity, with its entailments of continuity, persistence, and survivance, is the key to this historical imagination.

A history transmitted in this way carries an implicit sense of phenomenological presence. Moreover, the process is scarcely alien to Western philosophy: the uncertainty and doubt of St. Augustine, the orality of reading the Torah, and the face-to-face discipleship of the early itinerant Christian church all attest to the limitations of the written word and to the need for grounding semiotic principles of belief and tradition in the cultural processes that make them manifest. Such a history is emergent and contingent; it constitutes a powerful construction of both personal identities and communities of belonging (see Engelke 2007). It is akin to the evocative intimacy of the anthropologist's ethnographic present.

The customary separation of the methods of written history and unwritten "prehistory" has long bedeviled Americanist anthropology (Darnell 2001). The very concept of prehistory attests to the failures of an alternative historical imagination that would respect oral transmission of traditional knowledge and acknowledge the time depth of Indigenous traditions. Franz Boas (Valentine and Darnell 1999; Darnell 2001) distinguished between history and psychology, relegating oral traditions to the latter but mining them for insights about the elusive "native point of view" (although Boas appears to have considered this "psychology" to be timeless and ahistorical in ways that few would advocate today).

Boas's renegade student Paul Radin challenged the validity of a history external to the self-knowledge of his "informants" (in today's parlance, "interlocutors" or "consultants"). Radin's "history" was an ostensibly shallow one that drew on life history narratives that, albeit assembled from composite sources rather casually by contemporary standards, provide standpoint-based reflections on the experience common or generic to a community as well as particular to individual narrators. Despite their limited time depth, Radin rendered these "histories" as a revisionist alternative to the historicist methods imposed by Western anthropological scholarship. On this basis, he dismissed Boasian histories directed to reconstruction of culture history based on geography and culture traits as sterile and meaningless. I am not suggesting that we adopt this position but rather that we explore whether we might have our cake and eat it too. The historicist pendulum has shifted considerably since Radin's time, moving away from the "great man" (rarely including woman) theory of history to a less personalized and more socially contextualized "histoire de la longue durée." Rather, our challenge is to address *both* oral and written sources of historical reasoning without denigrating the legitimate insights of either. Not only the facts differ across accounts but also the modes of history making. In this respectful and open-ended sense, I elect to pursue convergent evidence for diverse historical purposes.

Judicious use of oral tradition on its own terms is commensurable in principle with the standards and goals of more conventional archival historical practice. My teacher and mentor, À. Irving "Pete" Hallowell, long ago defined the history of his discipline as an anthropological problem, to be approached in the same spirit and method as ethnographic fieldwork with an exotic other (Hallowell 1965). In my distant graduate student days, the late George W. Stocking Jr. deployed his credentials as historian to berate anthropologists for their "presentism" or Whiggish history in opposition to a purist "historicism" as the special preserve of his own discipline (Stocking 1968). Although Stocking's position evolved after the late 1960s, critics continue to cite him as though he maintained this static position throughout his career. I describe my own practice in contrast as "standpoint-based archival ethnography" (e.g., Darnell [1990] 2010:iv), a search for the point of view of another time and place.

Archival history itself has not stood still. For many practitioners, it also has become a moving interpretive target, as susceptible to evaluation as any other source of evidence. For example, Ann Stoler's *Along the Archival Grain: Epistemic Anxieties and Colonial Common Sense* explores the implicit social categories and "grids of intelligibility" (Stoler 2009:i) incorporated in colonial records of the Dutch East Indies Company that doubtless were considered unreflexively "factual" by the succession of bureaucrats who produced and interpreted them. Stoler approaches the genre of "archival form" as ethnographic data to be evaluated in much the same manner as field notes based on participant-observation immersion in contemporary cultures. The politics embedded in Stoler's documents reveal how this version of colonialism actually worked on the ground.

I cannot resist noting that Hayden White waxes ecstatic on the book's dust jacket, citing Walter Benjamin, about this "model of the new historiography rich in the historical, anthropological and psychoanalytical insights demanded by the newly theorized subjects of history." Anthropologists who habitually combine history and anthropology in our work have known how to do these things for a long time. Nor do I see Indigenous collaborators banging on the doors of the academy demanding to become "theorized subjects of [our, not their] history." Rather, they are asking us to hear and take seriously what they know about their own history and how it has intersected with our own.

Convergently, over recent decades, the discipline of history has increasingly incorporated the minutiae of the everyday into larger interpretations in a mode that I consider fully ethnographic. The new "microhistory" challenges its chroniclers to generalize from individual experiences, local contexts, and events, "across scales of space and time" (Brooks, DeCorse, and Walton 2008:3) to convey a sense of intimacy for readers far removed from the experience represented. What Clifford Geertz called "local knowledge" (Geertz 1983) constitute the working capital of the ethnohistorian, as should be the case for comparative social scientists and humanists alike. Anthropologists' case studies transcend their descriptive particulars to uncover qualitative patterns on a comparative plane.

Ethnohistory's palpable genealogy of applied research for the Indian Claims Commission, for example, lies alongside a less visible and still emergent cultural trajectory recognizing complexity, contingency, even fractally patterned chaos as intrinsic to the human condition. To take a single example of shift in the evolving paradigm, the Delgamuukw' decision of 1991 dismissed Indigenous oral genealogies encoding land claims as "primitive" and outmoded and consequently deemed anthropological expert testimony to be irretrievably flawed by advocacy and personal relationship. Blessedly, the Supreme Court of Canada overruled much of that British Columbia decision in 1997, recognizing oral history as a right of natural justice for peoples whose histories are contained solely therein. Direct narrative transmission could no longer be dismissed out of hand as mere hearsay. The court further and respectfully instructed evaluation of historical evidence based in oral tradition. It was to be treated simply as one among the possible sources of legitimate history presumably evaluated in its own terms. In such a context, ethnohistorians must embrace a further mandate to educate the institutions of both mainstream society and the academy to understand "history"—in its oral as well as its written forms—in more flexible, negotiable, and discourse-based ways.

So we have the archives and we have the things people say. Let's see if we can get them to come together. I take my examples from contemporary Americanist archaeology, a rich field of innovative historical interpretation at modest distance from my own field of practice that has increasingly foregrounded collaboration with the living inheritors of oral histories. T. J. Ferguson and Chip Colwell-Chanthaphonh's *History Is in the Land: Multivocal Tribal Traditions in Arizona's San Pedro Valley* (2006) learns alongside contemporary elders documenting different uses of "the same" landscapes by their respective ancestors. The Tohono O'odham, Hopi, Zuni, and Western Apache maintain "distinct oral traditions" (6) that create multiple and independent histories of a single river valley, each continuous to the present in cultural memories. The authors argue that traditional archaeologists have too easily dismissed ethnographic analogy and oral history alike as providing "a form of biased knowledge" (xv). Since contemporary tribal boundaries have shifted considerably and these groups did not inhabit the territory simultaneously, researchers "visited" the sites with field teams whose members held the requisite knowledge and were authorized by their communities to discuss their traditions of interaction with this land.

The use of landscape in stories tied to history, moral identity, and cultural continuity is now becoming well known, particularly through the contemporary Western Apache ethnography of Keith Basso. "Cultural landscapes" have "an intellectual component, reproduced through local practices and beliefs" (Ferguson and Colwell-Chanthaphonh 2006:27). That is, the landscape is interpreted by those who live alongside and within it as neither exclusively material nor fully observable. Memory intervenes in the construction of histories. Moreover, memory persists and is transmitted long after physical displacement from a landscape. "We remain part of every place we visit, . . . any place we breathe or leave our sweat" (31). Telling the stories enables contemporary people to "share this past with others" (31). Such a composite history, of course, thoroughly disrupts the NAGPRA (Native American Graves Protection and Repatriation Act of 1990) presupposition of exclusive "cultural affiliation." To further complicate the matter. Western Apache hold a concept of stewardship that teaches respect for "the ancient ones" whether their own direct ancestors or not (Basso 1996:225).

Archaeologists' artifacts were widely acknowledged as "living forces that shaped their sense of identity and world order" (Ferguson and Colwell-Chanthaphonh 2006:19). For an O'odham elder, the artifacts once "belonged to someone, though they're gone" (70). Zuni consultants describe a "memory piece" (i.e., mnemonic device) as "a marker left by the ancestors to mark their passing for contemporary people." "Sometimes they even broke things so they would not be taken away" (161). A Hopi consultant says: "It's important because it's ours" (121). "The old folks wanted to make history" and left the ruins and petroglyphs as evidence of their passing (124). "We don't write our history. . . . The artifacts are our documents. . . . I know it's Hopi because of our teachings" (135). That is, the primary historical purport of the ruins is ceremonial or spiritual. Contemporary elders know about places they have never visited and eagerly calibrate their historical traditions and prophecies with insights from geography and archaeology that are newly accessible to them.

These prescient archaeologists retain a distinction between "literal history" and "parable" or "metaphor" (Ferguson and Colwell-Chanthaphonh 2006:73) that I find troubling. "The O'odham we worked with did not claim that all such stories convey unconditional truth, that they portray absolute space and time. Instead, they emphasized that these stories 'often began with a real occurrence that was then elaborated with didactic motifs through generations of retelling'" (83). Consultants were undecided about the archaeologists' questions regarding the identification of contemporary peoples with specific archaeological cultures, but they remained adamant that "it's *history* they tell us through stories" (83, emphasis in the original). That is, these elders take their histories more seriously, though not necessarily more literally, than do the archaeologists.

Wesley Bernardini deploys oral tradition about Hopi migration histories "as a source of theory about the past, rather than as a source of raw historical data" (Bernardini 2005:7). "Serial migration" progressed through "discrete episodes" of abandonment and resettlement by clan and subclan groups. The village served as a heterogeneous "staging area" for successive movements between about 1275 and 1400, when various clan groups converged at the Hopi mesas. These "migration pathways" must be understood as nonlinear. Particular clan histories cannot be amalgamated into a single cumulative migration history of the Hopi people. Rather, Bernardini's "microhistories" focus on fine-grained ethnographic questions placing reciprocal interpretive value on traditional knowledge and archaeological evidence. The former attests to the crucial importance of clans being accepted for residence at Hopi mesas based on the ritual skills they could bring with them. The latter identifies material correlates of ceremonial practices and belief systems. Consequently, contemporary narrators are careful to specify that they can speak only for their own clans.

This model of ethnogenesis opens up vistas of historical imagination consonant with seminomadic subsistence practices and an oral tradition of overlapping experiential narratives grounding individuals and groups in particular territories and social relationships. Distance trade, intermarriage, and carefully maintained widespread kinship ties, for example, assured that there would continue to be accessible knowledge about places toward which one might move should future circumstances require (environmental crisis, warfare, population growth, and the like).

Archaeologists are not the only ones who theorize. Hopi consultants report what must be recognized as theories of history. Hopi *itaakuku*, "footprints," are interpreted as "historical metaphor" (Ferguson and Colwell-Chanthaphonh 2006:95) and employed in the stories of clan migration from the place of emergence to the Hopi mesas. Although oral tradition speaks of travel "in all directions" (109), contemporary Hopi consultants equate the clans who went to the northeast with Hohokam archaeological sites. Hopi tradition distinguishes *navoti*, "historical understanding derived from experiences handed down by ancestors to their descendants" from *wiimi*, "the sacred artifacts and the knowledge of how to use them properly in religious ceremonies and rituals" (121). For Hopi consultants, the archaeologists' artifacts are inseparable from the spiritual meanings necessary to their appropriate use. Although archaeological convention would have it the other way around, the artifacts are the material manifestation of and evidence for the validity of the stories.

Similarly, Zuni history is transmitted through religion, with different levels of esoteric knowledge conveyed to varying levels of initiates. These histories are respected for their "veracity" and recited on ceremonial occasions (Ferguson and Colwell-Chanthaphonh 2006:151). Multiple oral accounts of Zuni history are preserved by diverse ritual groups who transmit only what they have been taught as belonging to them. Zuni consultants are eager to acknowledge archaeological sites as "tangible evidence for anchoring oral tradition in a physical and cultural landscape" (155). The "powerful metaphoric and symbolic information of a religious nature" indeed goes beyond "literal history" (155). I argue in contrast that the literalism of "history" is itself a red herring and that we should be thinking about the intertwining of different kinds and purposes of history and historicizing. Perhaps traditional "history" is becoming an artifact of an outmoded historical imagination.

Bernardini nonetheless carries over assumptions from written history when he presupposes distortion of chronology at every stage in the chain of transmission (Bernardini 2005:24) and fails to identify peer-review mechanisms within a community. He equates the willingness of his consultants to derive new meanings or applications of received tradition as new information became available, on the one hand, with lack of attention to preserving the form and substance of what has been transmitted, on the other, rather than with creative adaptation.

Apache history in the San Pedro Valley is the most difficult to reconstruct because the Apache left few traces on the landscape to mark their passing. Thus, "Western Apache history is less contained in archaeological sites than in the landscape itself, where persistent places evoke memories of the ancestors" (Ferguson and Colwell-Chanthaphonh 2006:226). Elders worry that much of this knowledge is no longer being passed on and is restricted to segments of the community. Nonetheless, many Apaches still own land in the San Pedro valley, where their displacement has been incomplete and their seminomadic patterns of residence have rendered them invisible. They congregate in familiar places whether or not this ongoing presence is labeled by them or by others as living on traditional territory.

Nonetheless, Western Apache have a theory of history. Basso emphasizes that the closest term to the English "history" can be glossed as "that which happened long ago" (Basso 1996:154). Interestingly, however, they also speak about "the people's history," which they understand to be "history as-it-is-known" through accounts of the past events that have been transmitted through oral teachings (154). That is, the past is only accessible as mediated through narratives of human experience whose relevance must be renewed in each generation.

Ferguson and Colwell-Chanthaphonh make the tantalizing suggestion that all Western Apache bands define their homeland in relation to four sacred mountains, but that these mountains are identified with actual local landscapes depending on where the people are living at a given time (Ferguson and Colwell-Chanthaphonh 2006:193). Throughout a migration history, then, each band defines itself as sitting at the center of such a sacred landscape, in a new place, thereby constituted as "home." People came to new land already holding knowledge of their own history and movement. Basso reports that, according to elder Charles Henry, the types of descriptive place-names preserve different strata in the history of the community. The earliest ones reflect a time "when his ancestors were exploring the land and deciding to make it their home" (Basso 1996:30). Later, after the people had gathered in the area that remains their home today, deeper ties were established between the landscape and the experiences that people had on it. After a time, new names commemorated particular experiences and events. Names still are coined at least occasionally that add to the store of those binding Western Apache identity to their land.

Similarly, the medicine wheel heuristic with which I am more familiar maps spiritual and material geographies onto a widely shared cultural template that is employed to bring order to everything from directions to life cycles to colors to moral qualities. The template is, among other uses, a method to historicize individual and group experience over time. Although such locational devices are specific to particular cultural groups, we may expect other tribes to apply a comparable historical imagination to their own place-names and local environments, whether past or present. It follows, then, that identity, motives, and collective action must be understood at a finer-grained scale than the ones entailed by conventional archaeological taxonomies or culture-area classifications based on broad geographic proximity.

To this point, I have resisted the temptation to regale readers with exclusively Canadian examples of the expansion and enrichment of a Canadian notion of "history" for which recognition is overdue. I understand contemporary mobility as a two-way ongoing process and continue to explore what I call "nomadic legacies" of contemporary Anishinaabeg (Ojibwe) decision-making, with residential mobility following resources of employment, education, and social services rather than land-based subsistence resources. The reserve, as reservations are called in Canada, serves as a homeplace from which people go out and to which they return in what I characterize as an "accordion model" of Algonquian social organization (Darnell 1998). "The urban Indian," like the reserve itself, reflects a permeable category of trajectory in a course of movement between and among communities where social ties maintain rights to resources and community membership(s) in multiple locations (Darnell 2011). Contemporary life history narratives from London, Ontario, are consistent with the forms of historical imagination implicit in the collaborative archaeological projects discussed above (Darnell and Manzano Munguia 2005) and serve to constitute an interpretive community (Darnell 2008).

Returning to the archaeological context, my Western colleague Neal Ferris examines the three distinct aboriginal adaptations to colonialism in southwestern Ontario (Anishinaabeg, Delaware, and Haudenosaunee [Iroquois]) in a framework of cultural continuity from 1500 to 1750 that is "consistent with continuing expansion of Aboriginal-centric, sociopolitical community complexity" despite colonial incursion (Ferris 2009:xvi). "Territory" was not "singular, bounded, exclusive sociopolitical space" (6) but a balance of successive residences in relation to variable resources. Sites not utilized at a given moment were not considered "abandoned" but remained as resources for future return. Ferris further argues that classificatory categories such as "Ojibwe" function to mask the decision-making autonomy of smaller local groups with shifting or "recombinant" membership and territory (118, 35). "Multiple histories of the colonial experience" on a local scale often conflict among themselves as well as with the European-derived metanarrative, but such ethnographic microhistories more accurately reflect individual and community realities (25). Raymond Williams's "selective tradition" reinforces Ferris's analysis of Indigenous agency based on mobility (Williams 1979).

If colonial contact is read as a continuum of "place, time, local agency. and specific historical context," then archaeology offers the necessary time depth for what Ferris calls "deep history" (Ferris 2009:27, 115). Caches, which, like Bernardini's pottery, were traded over wide areas, provided "conceptual placeholders for imagining oneself within the communal home range" (50). Early reserves were located at traditional, usually summer, gathering places and did little to restrict seasonal mobility (62). "The cultural construction of these locales as fixed places" was European rather than Indigenous (65). Individual choice between "differing conventions and values over time" (65) maintained flexibility at the group level as an effective strategy of resistance against colonial hegemony. Documentary histories of immediate disruption of Indigenous cultural integrity upon contact and exclusive association of a people with a particular bounded piece of land simply do not fit the evidence.

Ferris emphasizes the role of ritual practices in signifying group membership: "Dispositions previously operating beneath awareness were overtly recognized as distinct from the world beyond the enclave and ascribed heightened meaning to reinforce self-referential notions of identity" (Ferris 2009:171). I suspect that such ritual practices have long come to awareness through contact with other groups, including anthropologists. Nonetheless, we are provided here with the ammunition to juxtapose "histories" in the sense of narratives chosen among possible interpretations. I draw here upon ongoing conversations with my colleague Bryan Loucks, who moves between the perspectives of academy and *Midewiwin*, the Anishinaabeg medicine lodge, in suggesting that history, for him, arises from "a sense of consciousness." It is meaningful insofar as it connects past, present, and future. Esoteric ritual components (accessible in degrees only after initiation and practice) open channels to sources of energy that link "the ancestors and their experience" to embodied identity (Loucks, personal communication with author, January 2007).

That such a history "belongs to" the people who use it as a tool to think with, heightens its status as history. This is Radin's history as it is experienced. As Fogelson long ago pointed out, ethnohistory has been *our* history of ethnic groups rather than an "ethnoethnohistory" respecting the validity of alternative historical imaginations. Historical accuracy requires specification of standpoint and context rather than premature metanarrative (Fogelson 1989). Understandings of time and space relationships are culture-specific and historicize the world in different ways. To compare them meaningfully we must first assess each in its own terms. The emergence of a discipline of Indigenous Knowledge attests to increasing recognition of the critical importance of not imposing our histories on those with whom we seek to sustain meaningful conversations, about history or anything else. Indigenous Knowledge requires of "history" a spiritual dimension that has been long excluded from the Western historical imagination. I propose to reinstate it and foreground its capacity to enrich our own "history."

Notes

1. Originally published as "What Is History? An Anthropologist's Eye View," *Ethnohistory* 58 (2011): 213–27.

2. I retain a Roman orthography devised as a transliteration from syllabics by an overlapping network of Plains Cree collaborators in northern Alberta in the 1970s and 1980s.

References

Ahenakew, Freda, and H. C. Wolfart. 1998. *Ana kâ-pimwêwêhahk okakêskihkêmowina: The Counselling Speeches of Jim Kâ-Nîpitêhtêw.* Winnipeg: University of Manitoba Press.

Basso, Keith. 1996. *Wisdom Sits in Places.* Albuquerque: University of New Mexico Press.

Bernardini, Wesley. 2005. *Hopi Oral Tradition and the Archaeology of Identity.* Tucson: University of Arizona Press.

Brooks, James, Christopher R. DeCorse, and John Walton, eds. 2008. Introduction to *Small Worlds: Method, Meaning, and Narrative in Microhistory,* 3–13. Santa Fe: School for Advanced Research Press.

Cruikshank, Julie. 1990. *Life Lived Like A Story.* Lincoln: University of Nebraska Press.

————. 2005. *Do Glaciers Listen? Local Knowledge, Colonial Encounters, and Social Imagination.* Vancouver: University of British Columbia Press.

Darnell, Regna. (1990) 2010. *Edward Sapir: Linguist, Anthropologist, Humanist.* Reprint, Lincoln: University of Nebraska Press.

————. 1998. "Rethinking Band and Tribe, Community and Nation: An Accordion Model of Nomadic Native American Social Organization." *Papers of the 29th Algonquian Conference,* 90–105. Winnipeg: University of Manitoba.

————. 2001. *Invisible Genealogies: A History of Americanist Anthropology.* Lincoln: University of Nebraska Press.

————. 2006. "Residential School Discourses and the Discourses of Self-Government: Changing Political Resonances of Land and Language in Algonquian Narrative." *Papers of the 37th Algonquian Conference,* 149–60. Winnipeg: University of Manitoba.

————. 2008. "First Nations Identity, Contemporary Interpretive Communities and Nomadic Legacies." *Arcadia* 43:102–13.

————. 2011. "Nomadic Legacies and Urban Contexts." In *Aboriginal Peoples in Canadian Cities: Transformations and Continuities,* edited by Heather Howard and Craig Proulx, 39–51. Waterloo ON: Wilfrid Laurier Press.

Darnell, Regna, and Maria Manzano Munguia. 2005. "Nomadic Legacies and Urban Algonquian Residence." *Papers of the 36th Algonquian Conference,* 173–86. Winnipeg: University of Manitoba.

Engelke, Matthew. 2007. *A Problem of Presence: Beyond Scripture in an African Church.* Berkeley: University of California Press.

Ferguson, T. J., and Chip Colwell-Chanthaphonh. 2006. *History Is in the Land: Multivocal Tribal Traditions in Arizona's San Pedro Valley.* Tucson: University of Arizona Press.

Ferris, Neal. 2009. *The Archaeology of Native-Lived Colonialism: Challenging History in the Great Lakes.* Tucson: University of Arizona Press.

Fogelson, Raymond. 1989. "The Ethnohistory of Events and Non-Events." *Ethnohistory* 36:133–47.

Geertz, Clifford. 1983. *Local Knowledge: Further Essays in Interpretive Anthropology.* New York: Basic Books.

Hallowell, A. Irving. 1965. "The History of Anthropology as an Anthropological Problem." *Journal of the History of the Behavioral Sciences* 1:24–38.

Stocking, George W., Jr. 1968. "On the Limits of Presentism and Historicism in the Historiography of the Behavioral Sciences." In *Race, Culture, and Evolution: Essays in the History of Anthropology,* 1–12. New York: Free Press.

Stoler, Ann. 2009. *Along the Archival Grain: Epistemic Anxieties and Colonial Common Sense.* Princeton: Princeton University Press.

Tedlock, Dennis. 1983. *The Spoken Word and the Work of Interpretation.* Philadelphia: University of Pennsylvania Press.

Valentine, Lisa Philips, and Regna Darnell, eds. 1999. *Theorizing the American-ist Tradition*. Toronto: University of Toronto Press.

White, Hayden. 1980. "The Narrativization of Real Events." *Critical Inquiry* 7:5–27.

Williams, Raymond. 1979. *Marxism and Literature*. Oxford: Oxford University Press.

2

Applied Anthropology
Disciplinary Oxymoron?

Introduction

Academics, sadly, have few opportunities to speak to their colleagues en masse, and I was delighted to address my fellow Canadian anthropologists on receipt of its Weaver-Tremblay Award, both directly at the annual meeting of the Canadian Anthropology Society/Société canadienne d'anthropologie (CASCA) at York University, Toronto, in May 2014 and in written form for its flagship journal.[1] I have added additional examples and elaborations for verisimilitude while attempting to retain the flavor of the spoken word. Although the award nominally recognizes achievements in applied anthropology, few have identified me primarily as an applied anthropologist, then or now. With the inevitable angst of an interdisciplinary scholar, I am simultaneously grateful for the honor and a tad defensive about whether I really fit its traditional mandate. I have thought a lot about the nature of applied anthropology and what might constitute excellence in pursuing it. While I applaud the recent revision of the award's description to recognize achievements in anthropology as a whole, it seems to me that the "applied" part persists implicitly, both in CASCA tradition and in the practice of Canadian anthropologists. I use this opportunity to reflect on what that might mean.

I am proud to stand in the genealogy of Sally Mae Weaver (1940–93) and Marc-Adélard Tremblay (1922–2014), each of whom I treasured as a colleague and friend. Both worked within the system, despite its limitations, providing yeoman labor to build a better world through dialogue, by understanding the standpoint of others who were and continue to be part of "us" rather than some unintelligible other. Sal mediated elegantly (and my goodness she was elegant) between Indigenous voices and Canadian public institutions. Her work tacked deftly between ethnography and theory or policy (Weaver 1972, 1981). She left us far too young. The loss of Adé in March 2014 was far more immediate at the time of original writing.

Adé devoted his career to building institutions through which the academy could serve society by applying anthropological knowledge. He founded the department at Laval explicitly around the principles and practice of applied anthropology and developed an interdisciplinary social science approach to the society surrounding the university. He reached out from region to province to a larger Canadian context, as his ethnographer's eye encompassed Indigenous peoples, rural farmers, and Quebec society. He was a diligent steward of the checks and balances entailed by a bilingual professional organization, both for the Canadian Ethnology Society (CES) and CASCA as its successor organization. In collaboration with New Zealand–born ethnologist and University of British Columbia Museum of Anthropology director Harry Hawthorne (1910–2006), the Hawthorne-Tremblay Report provided the first assessment of the status of Indigenous relationships to the Canadian state on a national scale in 1957. Although implementation of its recommendations was largely abortive, the report established a mandate in principle for the application of anthropological knowledge to emerging and ongoing political and policy dilemmas. Other recipients of the Weaver-Tremblay Award constitute an equally distinguished though somewhat motley crew, as anthropologists everywhere are wont to be. It is a legacy of distinguishing oneself from the crowd in which we may take pride.

Examination of the nature of applied anthropology begins with CASCA's own history and considers the degree to which it is generalizable to Canadian anthropology more broadly. When Julia Harrison and I exhorted our colleagues to define the singularity of Canadian anthropology in *Historicizing Canadian Anthropology* (Harrison and Darnell 2006), CASCA was the only available collective institutional framework at the national level; yet CASCA was and still is not representative of Canadian anthropology as a whole. Skewed access to a clearly defined collectivity aside, the results of the project's more or less systematic inquiries were neither definitive nor unambiguous. Canadian anthropologists were unable to define what they had in common with any great degree of consensus. Each contributor to *Historicizing Canadian Anthropology* took a different tack. Most favored a definition of professional identity so inclusive that its boundaries inevitably became blurred. Despite the variable responses, there was widespread agreement that applied anthropology held a more prestigious place here than in the United States and that more of us did it in Canada (whatever "it" was).

In the early CES years, applied anthropology provided a unifying umbrella for otherwise undifferentiated anthropologists to meet concurrently with separate associations of applied anthropologists and medical anthropologists, most of whom were also CES members. My recollection as a participant is that the term "ethnology" reflected the institutional support that Sal Weaver, Dick Preston, Adé Tremblay, and others negotiated with the Canadian Ethnology Service of the National Museum of Canada (now the Canadian Museum of History). The scope of the organization was not further clarified when the anthropologists split off from the Canadian Sociology and Anthropology Association (CSAA) in the early 1970s. At that time the linguists, archaeologists, and physical anthropologists declined to join the exodus, opting to remain in their more specialized autonomous associations. The failure of Sal's proposed "federation of anthropological sciences," on the model of the Canadian state, to capture the imagination of colleagues in other subdisciplines, none of whom had been active in the CSAA, mitigated against co-opting the term "anthropology" for the sociocultural anthropologists who remained to form the new organization. But ethnology failed to catch on as a term of self-identification because most members thought of themselves as anthropologists. Not until 1990, under the presidency of Michael Asch, did CASCA reclaim the holistic identifier "anthropology," unmarked in its potential scope and focus. Indeed, ethnographically inclined linguists and the occasional archaeologist or biological anthropologist have joined us.

I was not alone in conflating the medical and applied societies under the CASCA umbrella. The members tended to be the same people. Over the years CASCA has gradually absorbed the medical and applied anthropologists as simply anthropologists, except when we gather for the annual ritual to honor the "applied" legacy of Adé Tremblay and Sal Weaver. What is now the Weaver-Tremblay Award was established by the Society for Applied Anthropology in memory of Sal and adopted by CASCA subsequent to the merger. Although the applied anthropology part now lurks implicitly under the surface, the intentions of many of the founders continued to be reflected in the CASCA website affirmation of the "belief that professional associations need, where appropriate, to take public positions on matters of social and political concern, particularly in cases which impact directly on those who have been the traditional subjects of anthropological study" (CASCA n.d.). The distinction to be protected under the new regime was less of discipline or subdiscipline than balance between the francophone and anglophone anthropological communities. Both Sal and Adé were key figures in realizing this commitment. Applied anthropology in Canada, or in any other national context, does not operate in isolation from other variables that define the Canadian discipline.

I wonder how thoroughly "the Canadian anthropologist" has incorporated the applied and medical personae. Medical anthropology, one of my own more recent excursions into new territory by a very different interdisciplinary route, has always seemed to me an applied subfield, albeit with fascinating theoretical implications and immense practical importance to the well-being of Canadians. Yet most practitioners write primarily in a descriptive mode, focusing on the implementation of specific programs and models. Moreover, medical anthropology in Canada at the time of writing functioned under great duress—abandoned by the Social Sciences and Humanities Research Council (SSHRC), unintelligible to the Canadian Institutes of Health Research (CIHR), yet essential to Canadian society. I had recently read a set of grant proposals in which highly productive young medical anthropologists were retooling to represent themselves as anything else. A few devised ways to continue their health-related work by labeling it otherwise; more simply switched to other fields of specialization. CASCA members, especially Janice Graham and Jim Waldram, were articulate in leading the collective protest, with remarkably little effect. That effort is ongoing. Anthropologists do not speak from a position of power, perhaps not even a position of authority from the standpoint of the quantitative biomedical evaluators privileged by the medical sciences. Nevertheless, such interventions in public policy are integral to the practice of applied anthropology more generally. This is one important way to apply our expertise. When funding for urgent medical anthropology projects is unobtainable for many of our colleagues, it is difficult to see a way forward for this crucial segment of collective professional practice. The potential loss of a generation of young scholars threatens the continuity of this arena of application that Canadian anthropologists have nurtured. A similar cycle accelerates in momentum as I write these words in 2021.

Defining Applied Anthropology

Let me return to defining the beast. I suspect that Canada's mediating but autonomous role between Anglo and American anthropology persists because of the relative valuation that these national traditions place on the application of research results in the real world. British social anthropology, whatever its pragmatic efficacy (given that our British colleagues did not speak from a position of power either), self-consciously aspired to guide colonial administrators in shouldering what they perceived as the white man's burden. A. R. Radcliffe-Brown, whom I seldom quote since I am an unrepentant Americanist, nonetheless struck a resonant note for my own balancing act between the ethical and intellectual necessities of applying or practicing our discipline and a persistent fascination with ideas for their own sake, that is, with theory, a predilection I willingly acknowledge that I share. Radcliffe-Brown said this:

> The recognition of applied social anthropology has certain very definite advantages and certain equally definite disadvantages. To mention only one of the latter, theoretical social anthropology is still in the formative stage. The demand of social anthropologists to spend too much of their time on practical problems would inevitably reduce the amount of work that can be given to the development of the theoretical side of the science. But

without a sound basis in theory, applied anthropology must
deteriorate and become not applied science but merely empirical practice. (1958:105–6)

Despite the whiff of things I like less here—especially the patronizing edge of the senior scholar who knows best or the evocation
of civilizing the savage as the mandate of colonialism—Radcliffe-
Brown enjoins us to toggle between styles and methods of thinking from the theoretical to the methodological to the pragmatic
and political. I read Radcliffe-Brown as intending a reversible cir-
cuit rather than a stark binary choice. I do not think he meant
to suggest we should reconstitute the Victorian division of labor
between armchair and field.

Lest we conclude that this conundrum has long since faded
into disciplinary history, here is a 2014 version:

> The dominant narrative in academic applied anthropology is
> that we conduct research to solve practical human problems.
> The dominant practice in the field, however, seems to be that
> we do research but also engage with people to facilitate change
> to improve local conditions. . . . In applied settings with many
> variable conditions that affect outcome, it remains important
> to generalize from our practice to develop theories of applied
> social change so that we learn as we go. (Preister 2014:1)

By the mid-1930s, American anthropologists were talking about
applied anthropology in the context of "acculturation" as a pana-
cea to cure the purported ills of a salvage ethnography increasingly
accused by born-again functionalists from the other side of the
pond of being insulated from the realities of then contemporary
Native American lives. A. Irving Hallowell, an American anthropologist already a veteran of extensive field research in Canada
with the Berens River Ojibwe, chaired the U.S. National Research
Council Committee on Acculturation. This initiative largely fiz-
zled after the Rockefeller Foundation stopped funding the social
sciences around 1933.

How applied anthropology, in its current avatar of practicing or
public anthropology, became the fifth subdiscipline of the four-
square Americanist tradition within the American Anthropolog-

ical Association is another, distinctly un-Canadian story. In the American usage, applied anthropology serves largely as a euphemism for someone who couldn't get a job in academia and was forced to settle for a non-academic position and likely to be embittered by their lack of agency in a demoralizing job market. The American Anthropological Association intended to legitimate non-academic employment, but to my ear, the overtone is patronizing. The legitimacy of applied anthropology was recognized primarily when academic anthropologists also did such things in their spare time, whereas non-university-based full-time applied anthropologists were tacitly excluded from engaging in theory, an endeavor that remained a jealously guarded prerogative of the academy.

I do not much like any of these ways of thinking about applied anthropology, nor do I think they capture the quintessence of the Canadian anthropological experience. My institutional home away from home, the American Philosophical Society (APS), was founded in Philadelphia by Benjamin Franklin in 1743 "for the promotion of useful knowledge" (APS n.d.b). The gentleman scholars [sic] of American colonial society (Thomas Jefferson, Albert Gallatin, John Pickering, and Peter Stephen Du Ponceau among them) were men of affairs well-endowed with the financial resources and cultural capital to pursue the sciences. They valued progress, technology, innovation, and, in an odd sort of way, democracy. Theirs was a strangely populist elitism. Useful knowledge, after all, had to apply to someone or something. They sought practical knowledge as a basis for evidence-based policy and aspired to forge a new kind of polity that entailed coming to terms with the Indigenous societies in whose midst they had settled. Though our standards of utility and the social good have changed, to be useful to society remains not a bad objective for applied anthropology.

I worried that the discomfort with the label "applied anthropology" expressed in my title would be provocative for some colleagues, especially those impatient with theory. My intention was to evoke reflection rather than irritation or outright dismissal. To state the matter baldly, I was and remain acutely uncomfortable with the term "applied anthropology" because I believe that all anthropology is or ought to be applied—otherwise why bother? It follows that everything anthropologists do either is, or potentially becomes, simply anthropology. I conclude that the applied part must be an oxymoron. How, after all, can we purport to study human life without engaging it? To engage the world inevitably has consequences, whether for good or ill. These consequences may be either conscious and empathetic or unintended, a consequence of carelessly playing ideas off against one another as though they could exist in isolation from society and its members. This is my first objection to the term as normally used.

My second objection is that application has the potential to become an end in itself, an excuse not to engage with the dynamic debates at the core of our discipline. This is the sense in which applied is often opposed to theoretical, as though one precluded the other. I argue, in contrast, that each has value, depending on the circumstances and the question under consideration. When they enrich one another, the whole becomes greater than its parts. The urgency of the short-term project holds a legitimate priority in much applied research. But it behooves us to recall the mutual entailment of these processes that requires ongoing commitment to an issue, a group of people, or a set of social institutions with an evolving presence in time and space. Anthropology is at its very heart a comparative discipline in which our case studies, our ethnographies, reciprocally highlight the insights of the particular.

All this may seem rather abstract, more theoretical than applied. Let me turn to some of the projects and preoccupations, many of them interdisciplinary, albeit in a characteristically anthropological way, that underpin my claim to be an applied anthropologist. I cite my personal experience not out of egomania but because I know it best and can thus tease out the underlying threads of motivation and integration, in the same way that I often choose to teach ethnographies written by people I know so that I can add a dimension of the personal that underlies any text.

Reflexivity is a powerful tool in the hands of the anthropologist as analyst of both self and society. I have jousted, with varying degrees of success, with linguists, historians, literary critics, demographers, and medical clinicians and researchers. Isaiah Berlin's contrast between the hedgehog with one great idea and the fox who jumps from one idea to another has long fascinated me. Like most of us, I have deployed both strategies, sometimes simultaneously. My several, mostly sequential, career specializations suggest at first glance the flightiness of the fox. Such repositionings arose naturally with a recurrent element of serendipity over the course of my career. I have rarely planned to move from this point to that one. The contingency of what I actually ended up doing at any given time has taught me not to project the future in great detail but to take up each opportunity because it is there, because something needs to be done, I know a little bit about it, and, paraphrasing my public health colleague Charlie Trick, "if I didn't do it, it might not get done." We applied anthropologists also have a habit of charging into doing the things that ought to be done and working out the details as we go along.

What in the moment appears to be a series of happenstances develops over time an underlying logic, a hedgehog-like continuity that, for me, resides in the application of anthropological knowledge. This is what the subtitle of my fourth-year capstone seminar in theory called "how to think like an anthropologist" regardless of the subject at hand. Anthropology is a lens, a way of seeing the world. Applied anthropology, as I understand it, is the glue uniting the larger enterprise that I still prefer to call simply anthropology. Or perhaps they are coterminous in magnitude, distinguished primarily by the standpoint from which we view our own work at a given conjuncture or in a given context. Such a standpoint is not static; application in one context becomes theory in another and vice versa.

I am not alone in taking such a position. An aesthetic moment, signaled by Johannes Fabian, evokes the beauty as well as the truth of seeking and applying knowledge (Fabian 1983). Sir Isaac Newton epitomized such a view of science when he said, "I don't know what I may seem to the world, but as to myself, I seem to have been only like a boy playing on the sea-shore and diverting myself in now and then finding a smoother pebble or prettier shell than ordinary whilst the great ocean of truth lay all undiscovered before me" (Partington 1996:494). Or if you prefer, Bruno Latour portrays the Janus faces of science, contrasting the fascinating, messy business of doing the work with the much tidier presentation of results, the task-based pedagogy that so often stifles the transmission of anthropological knowledge in the classroom (Latour 1987). The pleasure, the opening for creativity, is in the doing.

The second source of my narrative tools for thinking about the world is my fieldwork. It takes place far from the ivory tower (even when meeting Indigenous collaborators on campus when guided by non-academic protocols and priorities).

The Plains Cree of northern Alberta say, "peyak esa," once upon a time, the culture hero-trickster-creator Wisahketchak was walking—and the most amazing things began to happen (Darnell 2020). He[2] cocreated the world with those who lived in it. This was not exactly a dialogue. Wisahketchak was not forthcoming about his intentions or inner motives; he was and remains a creature more of impulse than of thought, with frequent awkward if not fully tragic consequences. The meaning of the cautionary tales about his antics resides in the eye and ear and imagination by which the hearer imbibes and applies the object lessons of the stories told and retold about the things they say that "that one, that Wisah-ketchak," did and how his applied creative energy made the world in the form that we know it today. I employ the trickster's lens to the stages of my experience as an applied anthropologist.

The Alberta Years

As I was walking, I found myself in Edmonton in 1969, trained (at least in a retrospect focused in response to the test of real-world experience in eerily abstract versions of linguistic anthropology and the history of anthropology), looking for some Indians (as they called themselves and the still preferred term for many individuals and communities) to study who had a language I could learn or at least learn to analyze. The local ones turned out to be Plains Cree about whom I had no presuppositions, and they found the city girl from down east endlessly amusing. Things began to happen, and many of them were, by any definition, applied anthropology, albeit without conscious intention or even acknowledgment on my part at the time.

Hanging out with a kindergarten class in a community where most children still came to school speaking only Cree led, in due course, to language revitalization projects with teachers from a dozen northern Alberta communities and preparing community-specific curriculum materials with them. Today I would call this "collaborative anthropology." Language was not yet a burning political issue in the Harold Cardinal years at the Indian Association of Alberta, so I worked with women and children pretty much under the radar. In retrospect, that benign neglect was a blessing, a window for creativity.

I especially enjoyed a project to adapt Sesame Street for Plains Cree (with the late Barbara Burnaby, who was then working for Saskatchewan New Start). We incorporated culturally appropriate forms of etiquette as well as direct translation of pedagogical content (Darnell and Vanek 1972). Our sponsors insisted on a script, which I dutifully wrote and, as expected, the actors chose to ignore. We borrowed an old man (a generic term of respect) as storyteller for some Cree kids from a boarding school in Prince Albert while their parents were on the trapline. He confidently told the children he would tell the story again in Cree: "You'll like it better that way." One child declined to draw Wisahketchak because the traditional hero was the eye through which the story could be seen, not an actor to be observed in it—a clear standpoint theory of access to traditional knowledge.

I got angry when I learned soon after my arrival in 1969 that the University of Alberta taught Ukrainian but not Cree. So I found some fluent Cree speakers and taught the language and culture alongside them. Over the next few years, the course moved from noncredit adult education to an anthropology reading course to a calendar course for which I negotiated departmental teaching credit every second year. Again, it was a collaborative enterprise, with Indigenous students sharing their knowledge and experience and going home on weekends to consult grannies or occasionally other relatives when we were uncertain about something or to resolve conflicting information. The Cree language program model, developed with the advice and participation of several communities in the region, had at least a part in the establishment of a Faculty of Native Studies at the University of Alberta in 1985. After fifteen years, I had proudly put myself out of a job, handing over the course to the son of a woman who had been one of my own early Cree language teachers. Capacity building is a major tenet of applied anthropology.

In those years I often found myself mediating with social services on behalf of women trying to keep or reclaim their children, appearing in court as a character reference for language consultants. I could assure the court that they were professors at the university or would provide transportation for collaborators who wanted to visit friends and relatives in more or less nearby communities. "It's just over there," they would say, gesturing vaguely, and we were off on another unpredictable excursion. Participant observation is a methodology that has a tendency to relegate the "research" part of doing anthropology to the interstices of the ongoing flow of everyday life. But that's how you stumble across the things you'd never have thought to ask about. Not until later do you mull over the meaning, often in stages over many years. I learned to say, staring politely into undifferentiated midspace, "I've always wondered about . . . ," while interlocutors solemnly acknowledged my wondering. Then I waited until they raised the subject again, usually satisfying my curiosity, although sometimes only years later.

Ontario Defamiliarization

When I moved to Ontario in 1990, I had no idea what to expect on the Indigenous front. But I took it for granted that I would again seek research and collaboration with local First Nations communities. I wanted to live and work in the same place as I had been privileged to do in Alberta. More things were familiar than I expected, although others proved new and profoundly local. The copresence in southwestern Ontario of Anishinaabeg, Lenape, and Haudenosaunee traditions and the relative proximity of these communities to urban centers lent an initially peculiar contrastive character to my internalized sensibilities. By now I too had become a storyteller, and I carried stories across Canada as I added new ones. Interlocutors in southern Ontario wanted to know what things were like out there in the Prairies. Because I worked extensively with language consultants generations older than myself, I carried stories of spiritual teachers whose names were known and highly respected in my new home. Although they contributed immensely to how I understand things that I am authorized to share, I have chosen not to write about many of the things I learned while facilitating these early revitalization programs. The ethical stance of nondisclosure for reasons of privacy is an application of anthropology.

I got angry again, this time because Indians who lived in the cities of Edmonton, Alberta, and London, Ontario, spoke English and ate pizza more often than moose were dismissed by academics, the media, and the general public alike as assimilated, therefore no longer legitimately Indigenous. With my then colleague Lisa Philips Valentine and later Allan McDougall, I spent the next fifteen years trying to understand and catalog the forms of discourse that carried over from traditional languages, mostly Anishinaabemowin (Ojibwe), into English. We documented multiple Indian Englishes, a catchall term rarely exploring local variants that differed in systematic ways from so-called Standard English, which we also documented as variable in practice. Variability arose from both the structures of traditional languages and the etiquette underlying their use in interaction across a variety of genres. Cross-cultural miscommunication, too often unrecognized, is a rich and largely untapped field for applied anthropology.

In the course of trying to make explicit why and how the ten thousand or so Indigenous people living in London, Ontario, in the 1990s maintained their sense of identity, I moved gradually from a textual discourse-centered approach to a more ethnohistorical one, and my fieldwork relied increasingly on explicitly collaborative methodologies. Oral tradition presupposes a time dimension for the transmission of traditional knowledge. It constitutes history from "the native point of view" [*sic*] the phrase a recurrent mantra in the writing of Franz Boas.

What I came to call "nomadic legacies," the cultural patterns of relationship between people and resources, particularly land, developed out of a hunter-gatherer mode of subsistence but persist in contemporary practices of residential mobility (Darnell 2004, 2006, 2008, 2011; Darnell and Manzano Munguia 2005). I argue, contra most of my erstwhile colleagues in demography, that the numerically stable urban Indigenous population in London is dynamic, reflecting a continuous movement of Indigenous individuals and families back and forth between the city in search of education, employment, and social or medical services and the reserve, the home place to which people retain the right and usually the expectation to return. Mobility in this context is a nonrandom flow, an effective strategy and a mechanism of community strength, a pattern of redistributing disparately located resources, a mode of circulation rather than an obstacle to ongoing membership or participation. Such a sustainable pattern of resource exploitation is applicable beyond the bounds of the Indigenous community (Darnell 1998). It is transportable knowledge.

Over half the members of a given reserve community may not be in residence at any given moment; this does not mean they have ceased to be active members of the community (though some have). "Where are you from?" is the first step to establishing relationship, the appropriate question to initiate an encounter with an Indigenous person. "Where do you live now?" is irrelevant. My ongoing work in this area integrates nomadic resource exploitation with the flexible and personalized strengths of oral tradition, producing a relational ontology of face-to-face interaction of living beings that conflicts with the mainstream privileging of literacy when settlement is accepted unproblematically as the sine qua non of civilization.

Medical Sciences

In 2003 I joined colleagues in Western University's Schulich School of Medicine and Dentistry to develop a research program in ecosystem health featuring a distinct Indigenous engagement centered in southwestern Ontario. A memorandum of understanding (MOU) with Walpole Island First Nation set out to document the human health effects of pollution from Sarnia's chemical valley upstream from the community. This partnership remains ongoing across multiple generations of community members, graduate students, and faculty. The MOU proved increasingly superfluous as relations of trust solidified. The core personnel (Jack Bend, a toxicologist from Schulich; Charlie Trick, an oceanographer from the Department of Biology; and me, an anthropologist from the Faculty of Social Science) were senior faculty who could afford to invest time, skills, and energy in a long-term program. Graduate students and untenured faculty members rarely have this luxury. To draw them into ongoing projects constitutes another variant of applied anthropology as capacity building.

My collaborative work with colleagues in the medical and health sciences has been the most challenging fieldwork I have tackled over my career; it draws lessons from all previous periods. The assumptions of biomedicine often fail to mesh with traditional Indigenous understandings of well-being. Medical practitioners, whether researchers or clinicians, find it difficult to hold in abeyance the entitlement of privileged access to "truth" acquired unreflexively as part of their socialization to medical "science." I do not criticize particular colleagues; the issues are systemic. The Ecosystem Health team has come a long way together, and we have all stretched our understandings of what we do and how it relates to those with whom we work, both within and beyond the university. Nonetheless, a gulf remains, and constant vigilance is necessary to maintain an accessible crossing.

Some recurrent sticking points in conceptualizing well-being include:

1. Algonquian traditions privilege a time perspective of seven generations in both directions from the speaker. This time frame transcends the proximate health status of the individual medical patient and embeds the individual within a biographical and inherently social context of family and community. Ethnographic research projects rarely have the luxury of a longitudinal perspective that allows them to understand local history through the perspectives of those who live it.

2. The inclusion in many contexts of plants, animals, and the environment as a whole on a par with human persons is taken for granted by Indigenous people but often greeted with snorts of impatience from colleagues trained in biomedicine: "Don't tell me about that stuff. I am only interested in people."

3. Incorporation of traditional healers in medical practice is increasingly common, but rarely is such practice given the respect of equal validity in a domain of its own. Medicine plants are rarely acknowledged by medical personnel for their therapeutic efficacy as attested by community experience. For Indigenous consultants, however, efficacy requires establish-

ing a relationship to the medicine plants. This is incomprehensible within the biomedical model of cause and effect.

4. Continued access to traditional foods not contaminated by externally introduced pollution over which communities have limited control is a high priority. The most common question in public presentations of our results has been "How much fish can I feed my family?" The answer requires locally relevant parameters. One need not pause to wonder how many people a five-pound fish will feed. At Walpole Island First Nation the culturally appropriate answer is "one." Local control of the food supply is paramount. Carrots and potatoes, as well as medicine plants, were described as "traditional" foods when grown in a community garden regardless of their introduction by settlers (Bekeris 2012).

5. Local control of resources in relationship to the environment is also at stake in the parallel established in authoritative discourse between endangered species and language revitalization, illustrated by a Walpole Island First Nation translation of biological and botanical research results into Anishinaabemowin (Ojibwe language) (Darnell 2006; Darnell and Stephens 2007; Jacobs 2006). Our preliminary epidemiological study based on biomonitoring of hair and blood samples for heavy metals, mercury, and cortisol as a measure of stress combines well with ethnographic investigation of traditional knowledge, given a respectful attention to local protocols. There is enormous potential for synergy in the amalgam of knowledges.

6. Medical colleagues have had trouble understanding why blood samples do not bother people who deal with blood matter-of-factly in everyday life, between diabetics' needles and the dressing of fish and game. They consider hair unproblematic and find it difficult to take seriously the widespread Indigenous belief that hair, with its capacity for growth, is a living being and holds the essence of a person that can be used against them by someone who intends harm.

The applied anthropology in this series of projects has been twofold: on the one hand, it constructs a tentative bridge between two very different traditions that share goals of health and well-being. It valorizes the local, experiential, and longitudinal knowledge of the community alongside the more formal "scientific" methods of biomedicine. On the other hand, the results of such collaboration are available for community use in ongoing land claims and resource management negotiations with federal and provincial governments and industry. (The third hand requires considerable adjustment of medical education. But that is a challenge for another occasion and requires a long-term commitment of resources.)

Western's Interfaculty Master of Public Health (MPH) program, established in 2013, engaged many of the same colleagues but with considerably expanded institutional resources and pedagogical infrastructure. The medical school has resources undreamed of by social science programs. As the pet social scientist in the program, I have sometimes felt severely marginalized. Nonetheless, my cross-appointment and participation have ensured that cultural and social questions would remain salient. In 2013–14 my anthropologist colleague Gerald McKinley and I co-taught "Social and Cultural Determinants of Health," using World Health Organization (WHO) criteria, and "Aboriginal [now Indigenous] Health." The substantial international background of our first cohort facilitated sharing of students' cross-cultural experience as practicing health professionals and greatly enriched the case-based pedagogy.

At least part of the culture of the medical school is moving in the direction of what to me is a more anthropological appreciation of culture, context, and history or time depth. I had to do some fancy scrambling to learn to communicate in the medical language, and not to be embarrassed by asking naive questions (to which I almost always received serious clarifications in response). This applied anthropology has been rewarding both for the MPH program and for the participants, even though every head in the room still swivels to me whenever the word "culture" is mentioned. Western University showcased the Indigenous health prong of the curriculum as an important form of institutional branding for the nascent program. Both pedagogically and in the development of interdisciplinary and cross-cultural research, this is a richly productive applied anthropology. Although readers from other disciplinary backgrounds may frame similar insights in terms of familiar disciplinary vocabulary and reference points, for me anthropology is the umbrella that pulls it all together.

The Applied Anthropologist in the Academy

Wisahketchak must have figured out that someone needed to take the university in hand. Since I was there, I found myself applying my ethnographic experience to my workplace. There are good reasons so many effective administrators have been anthropologists: we know how to attain consensus, depolarize, take account of underlying agendas and motivations, treat our partners with respect, and construct a workable plan with others. I consider my two bouts as president of Western's Faculty Association, along with work on faculty workload and pay equity studies, the Research Ethics Board, University Strategic Plan Task Force, Board of Governors, and so on, to be part of my applied anthropology. Some of these in-house commitments have been closer to my professional expertise: founding director of First Nations (now Indigenous) Studies (where putting myself out of a job only took me three years this time); facilitation of language programs in both Ojibwe and Mohawk; hiring local cultural and linguistic experts to teach in the interdisciplinary First Nations Studies (as it was then called) program; donation of my personal Indigenous library to the program on behalf of students who were compelled to spend their book allowance on groceries. Most anthropologists have done these things or their equivalents. Most of us have also served beyond the university in various professional organizations, building infrastructure for the training of anthropologists and the dissemination of anthropological knowledge. Although universities largely devalue such activities as merely "service," I believe that we apply our professional skills in service to the world around us across the domains of research, teaching, and service—with the same activities ideally and often in practice contributing simultaneously to all three.

History of Anthropology

History of anthropology has remained the constant thread in the work I have done over the last five-plus decades. But I do it in a different way than when I began, largely because I have learned the political importance of this knowledge, individually for friends and collaborators and for communities, to transcend artificial boundaries of culture, gender, status, economic or educational background, and so on. The late George W. Stocking Jr., on my dissertation committee during his single semester at the University of Pennsylvania, is still widely quoted for his unflattering early-career characterization of anthropologists as incapable of historicism, of separating themselves from their own standpoint (Stocking 1968). He changed his mind, gradually, after he joined the anthropology department at Chicago, but the early dichotomy remains for many a convenient straw target. Even then, I already wrote self-consciously for an audience in anthropology with a desire to articulate disciplinary history and practice. Teaching archival methods to anthropologists seemed to me easier than teaching historians to think from non-mainstream standpoints.

The dangers of refusing to separate standpoint from research results are considerable, when we venture to apply our anthropological knowledge beyond the academy. It is a two-step process in which the distinction must be maintained. Justice Allan MacEachern concluded in Degamuukw'l in 1991 that anthropologists could not be "objective" if they followed the ethical imperatives of their professional association, the American Anthropological Association. CASCA did not then, and still does not, have its own code of professional ethics, out of characteristically Canadian deference to the lack of consensus among internally divergent positions on the consequences of an advocacy position for our scientific credibility or the potential of "taking sides" to generate conflict with powerful political and economic pressures beyond the boundaries of our fieldwork sites. Both for reading our own history for its applications and cautions in the present and for listening to the positions of others grounded in different relational ontologies, perspective or subjectivity or standpoint, when applied judiciously, provides an invaluable tool rather than an obstacle. We must adapt our pedagogical practice to educate interdisciplinary colleagues as well as judicial, political, and educational institutions.

The Language and Method of Science

Anthropologists must reclaim the language and prestige of science for our qualitative and ethnographic methodologies and for the theories that arise from them. I have identified "generic narratives" in which Native speakers, even in English, relate personal experience so that it resonates effectively with generational, family, or community experience (Darnell 1998, 2013). What is unique is less reportable. The stories are not all the same, but nor is the variation random. When one reaches a point of saturation where new types of stories do not appear, the "sample" is large enough. This is reliability; it turns to distinctive features—including gender, both my own and the speaker's, in residential school stories, and others—that explain the variability among types of what I call "generic narratives." Validity in qualitative research is attested by internal consistency, historical trajectory, feedback from research collaborators, and convergent evidence from as many sources as possible. There is a considerable difference between the merely anecdotal and what literary critic Kenneth Burke (the father of anthropologist Eleanor Burke Leacock) called the "representative anecdote," the story that makes it all make sense.

Even among anthropologists, many do not know how to listen to a carefully chosen story. I once gave an invited lecture in which I chose a single narrative to illustrate the organization of traditional stories in Plains Cree (published as Darnell 1974). The first question, from a senior colleague who should have known better, was, "Is that the only story you've ever heard?" How could one choose a representative story without drawing on a reservoir of shared stories? To identify the proper story, the persuasive one to tell, is to capture the generalization embedded in the particular. Such narratives, ideally framed alongside more formal evidence, are the things that persuade, that are remembered, that make a difference in the world.

The Boas Project

The project with which I have been most thoroughly preoccupied for the past decade is also applied anthropology. I hold a SSHRC Partnership Grant as general editor of The Franz Boas Papers:

Documentary Edition with the American Philosophical Society (APS), the University of Nebraska Press, the University of Victoria, the Musgamakw Dzawada'eneux Tribal Council, and multiple descendant community collaborators. At first glance, this might seem to be a research-for-its-own-sake sort of enterprise. On the contrary, it has integrated disparate threads of practicing and applying anthropology over my career—history of anthropology, narrative analysis, oral tradition, language revitalization, residential mobility, resource sustainability, collaborative fieldwork—and has provided resources to support both Indigenous and academic personnel (increasingly they are the same people) to do the research.

Boas was a man for whom science held paramount value and justified ethical positions acceptable in his time that would be utterly unacceptable today. Despite these obvious limitations when evaluated by contemporary standards, Boas was an applied anthropologist, although he was other things too. The first volume of the Franz Boas Papers stands as the framing document for a revisionist history and practice implicit in Boas's stature as public intellectual (Darnell et al., 2015). The subtitle identifies theory, ethnography, and activism as three arenas in which Boas has been misread by self-interested successors attempting to replace the mentalist elements of his paradigm with a more positivist and objectivist stance (Darnell 2001, Darnell et al. 2015). The documentary project returns to his original words in professional correspondence, contextualizes them for a new generation, and aspires thereby to set the record straight by letting him speak for himself—at least in relation to the contemporary anthropology of the early twenty-first century.

The Canadian research team (as of CASCA 2014, Michael Asch, Robert L. A. Hancock, Sarah Moritz, Brian Noble, Joshua Smith, and Peter Stephenson) is augmented by an international advisory board, primarily American and German. Boas crossed national traditions with a vengeance. That he did his fieldwork in Canada has been virtually invisible in Boas scholarship; this in turn has deepened the rift, with a consequent lack of access for Indigenous community descendants of those who produced them to the original documents.

The Boas Papers (APS n.d.a) were digitized by the American Philosophical Society (APS). Both digital repatriation and community capacity building are fundamental goals of the Indigenous Advisory Council (IAC), designed to advise on the proper treatment and dissemination of culturally sensitive materials. The Boas Project applies endangered language protocols developed at the APS under the leadership of the late Timothy Powell, founding director of the Center for Native American and Indigenous Research, and his successor, Brian Carpenter. By requiring researchers to seek the advice and approval of descendant communities, the APS breaks new ground for archival stewardship of First Nations[3] and Native American documents in collaboration with communities to interpret and make them accessible to a variety of publics and useful to source communities.

The synergy across interrelated projects, institutions, and national traditions already adds up to more than its constituent parts. The work continues beyond the formal life of the grant (which ended in 2021). I return to the metaphoric nonlinear resilience of the rhizome, epitomized by the (short-lived, now sadly defunct) Crabgrass Collective, with solid roots in CASCA, a scintillating amalgam of theoretical volatility and pragmatic commitment to applying anthropology in a broadly defined political sphere. We live in interesting times. The Chinese proverb bills this as a curse. But it is also a challenge in which I believe anthropologists of wildly diverse stripes are well situated to intervene, to apply our knowledge. I invite all of you to join me.

Notes

1. Originally published as "Applied Anthropology: Disciplinary Oxymoron," *Anthropologica* 57 (2015): 1–11.

2. Wisahketchak, and the trickster generally, is understood among Indigenous Canadians to be male, a response to gendered division in roles. My usage here is a conscious turning of that expectation.

3. "First Nations" is the term habitually used in Canada, but "Native American" is customary in the United States.

References

American Philosophical Society (APS) n.d.a. *Boas Papers.* Mss.B.B61. Philadelphia.

———. n.d.b. *About the APS.* http://www.amphilsoc.org/about. Accessed March 15, 2014.

Bekeris, Leanne. 2012. "A Seat at the Table: A Nonconformist Approach to Grassroots Participation in the Articulation of Health Standards." Master's thesis, University of Western Ontario.

Canadian Anthropology Society (CASCA). n.d. CASCA: A Brief History. https://www.cas-sca.ca/about/history-of-casca. Accessed March 15, 2014.

Darnell, Regna. 1974. "The Social Context of Cree Narrative." In *Explorations in the Ethnography of Speaking*, edited by Richard Bauman and Joel Sherzer, 315–36. Cambridge: Cambridge University Press.

———. 1998. "Rethinking Band and Tribe, Community and Nation: An Accordion Model of Nomadic Native North American Social Organization." *Papers of the 29th Algonquian Conference*, 90–105. Winnipeg: University of Manitoba.

———. 2001. *Invisible Genealogies: A History of Americanist Anthropology*. Lincoln: University of Nebraska Press.

———. 2004. "Persistence of Nomadic Habits in Urban Rural Migration: Towards a Qualitative Demography." *Proceedings of the 35th Algonquian Conference*, 75–89. Winnipeg: University of Manitoba.

———. 2006. "Residential School Discourses and Discourses of Self-Government: Political Resonances of Language and Land in Algonquian Narrative." *Proceedings of the 37th Algonquian Conference*, 149–60. Winnipeg: University of Manitoba.

———. 2008. "First Nations Identity, Contemporary Interpretive Communities and Nomadic Legacies." *Arcadia* 43:102–13.

———. 2011. "Nomadic Legacies and Urban Contexts." In *Aboriginal Peoples in Canadian Cities: Transformations and Continuities*, edited by Heather Howard and Craig Proulx, 39–51. Waterloo ON: Wilfrid Laurier Press.

———. 2013. "The Nature of Knowledge: Calibrating Discourses across Cultures and Finding Common Disciplinary Ground." *Journal of Canadian Studies* 46:20–44.

———. 2020. "Walking alongside Wisahketchak: Fieldwork, a Retrospective Experience That Takes a Long Time." *Journal of Anthropological Research* 76:44–50.

Darnell, Regna, and A. L. Vanek. 1972. *Two Trails: A Proposal for Cree Educational Television*. Prince Albert: Saskatchewan New Start.

Darnell, Regna, and Christianne Stephens. 2007. "Species at Risk: Reflections on Translation from Walpole Island First Nation." *Proceedings of the 38th Algonquian Conference*. 129–42. Winnipeg: University of Manitoba.

Darnell, Regna, and Maria Manzano Munguia. 2005. "Nomadic Legacies and Urban Algonquian Residence." *Papers of the 36th Algonquian Conference*, 173–86. Winnipeg: University of Manitoba.

Darnell, Regna, Michelle Hamilton, Robert L. A. Hancock, and Joshua Smith, eds. 2015. *Franz Boas as Public Intellectual: Theory, Ethnography, Activism*. The Franz Boas Papers: Documentary Edition, vol. 1. Lincoln: University of Nebraska Press.

Fabian, Johannes. 1983. *Time and the Other: How Anthropology Makes Its Object.* New York: Columbia University Press.

Harrison, Julia, and Regna Darnell, eds. 2006. *Historicizing Canadian Anthropology.* Vancouver: University of British Columbia Press.

Jacobs, Clint. 2006. *Species at Risk on Walpole Island First Nation.* Bkejwanong Territory [ON]: Nin.Da.Waab.Jig Heritage Centre.

Latour, Bruno. 1987. *Science in Action: How to Follow Scientists and Engineers through Society.* Cambridge MA: Harvard University Press.

Partington, Angela, ed. 1996. *The Oxford Dictionary of Quotations.* Rev. 4th ed. Oxford: Oxford University Press.

Preister, Kevin. 2014. "Using Our Field Experience to Build Theories of Applied Social Change: Why Do We Not Do More?" *Journal of Northwest Anthropology* 48:1–10.

Radcliffe-Brown, Alfred. R. 1958. "The Meaning and Scope of Social Anthropology." In *Method in Social Anthropology: Selected Essays by A. R. Radcliffe-Brown,* edited by Mysore N. Shrinivas, 96–107. Chicago: University of Chicago Press.

Stocking, George W., Jr. 1968. *Race, Culture, and Evolution: Essays in the History of Anthropology.* New York: Free Press.

Weaver, Sally M. 1972. *Medicine and Politics among the Grand River Iroquois: A Study of the Non-Conservatives.* Ottawa: National Museum of Man.

———. 1981. *Making Indian Policy: The Hidden Agenda, 1968–1970.* Toronto: University of Toronto Press.

3

....

The Anthropological Concept of Culture
at the End of the Boasian Century

Introduction: Situating the Critique of Culture

A critique of culture at the turn of a millennium is legitimate, perhaps even inevitable; in accordance with social constructionist standards of evidence; however, such a critique cannot escape the situated perspective of the late twentieth century.[1] The dominant processes of globalization, ethnonationalism, and multiculturalism all seem in the light of the moment to create new and unique circumstances that gainsay the traditional conceptual and geographical boundaries of what anthropologists have long called culture. Even in the fleeting span of a century of anthropology's history as a professional science, the culture concept has changed in response to the contexts in which anthropologists have applied it. Responding to the disciplinary cultures of its users, the concept has not remained static. There has never been and can never be a single homogeneous anthropological concept of culture.

A critique of the concept of culture has arisen simultaneously from multiple directions, both internal to the discipline and imposed upon it from without. On the one hand, external challenges have emanated from other social sciences and humanities disciplines and, on the other hand, from the increasingly recalcitrant "Others" once relatively unproblematically studied by hegemonic anthropologists who continued to control the parameters of the encounter. If the identity of the discipline is to be understood as how anthropologists have responded to such challenges, then its contemporary posture must too frequently be characterized as defensive rather than constructive.

Challenges arising from academic turf wars abound from the even more recently emergent discipline of cultural studies; these are often dismissed from a view within anthropology with a jaundiced internal eye as mere bastardizations of the discipline. In this view, cultural critics, especially those based in literary studies, tend to undermine the very basis of doing social science (without much anxiety that something important is being conceded). Such cavalier dismissal of accumulated anthropological practice and theory fails to attend to the actual complexity and variability of definitions of culture and ongoing revisions of related dynamic theoretical positions now a century old.

Let us formulate, for the sake of setting them against the contemporary culture concept, some exemplary planks of the cultural studies critique:

1. Colleagues in cultural studies accurately point out that the primitive "Other" no longer acquiesces to being studied. Rarely do they go on to examine the range of responses of contemporary anthropologists to these challenges from the subjects of study or acknowledge that they are accepted as well founded in both history and current practice.

2. Cultural critics correctly note that cultures cannot be bounded for tidy study as separate entities; indeed, the very notion of cultural community seems to break down, with diaspora increasingly frequent. Critics reify the culture concept in its most simplistic form without attention to the subtleties with which it has actually been applied. Anthropologists argue for the continued utility of their traditional theoretical tool kit and take umbrage at the superficiality of the cultural studies version of anthropology. Many anthropologists challenge the adequacy of their fieldwork.

3. The term "ethnography" has been appropriated almost as widely as "culture," usually without attention to microanalysis of the viewpoint of the "Other" that is so crucial to the sense of professional identity of anthropologists.

4. The relativist epistemology employed by many cultural critics, whether implicitly or explicitly, denies the realism at the core of social science research: the assumption that there is a world out there, both natural and social, and it matters

to "get it right." Some cultural critics dismiss these commitments as holdovers from an outdated positivist social science.

5. The emphasis on commodification and mass culture or popular culture endangers counterbalancing acknowledgment of the agency of individuals to change their culture(s).

6. Postcolonial theory has reconfigured the history of anthropology as exploitative, fatally flawed at its point of origin because of its links to imperialist hegemonies. Feminist theory, applying a parallel logic, charges an irreparable complicity with Western patriarchal culture. Therefore, it is never legitimate for anthropologists to speak about, never mind for, cultural others.

As a result of these and other critiques, ethnography remains paralyzed between irresolvable ethical dilemmas and persistent epistemological uncertainties. At the core of these challenges, however, lies the purported inadequacy of the anthropological concept of culture itself. Based on three decades of fieldwork (at the time of the original writing) among the tribe of anthropologists, based on oral history and archival documentation, I suggest that a reflexive history of anthropology provides us with the capacity to reframe a contemporary critique of culture and rehabilitates a viable praxis in response to the epistemology of postmodernism.

The Boasian or Americanist tradition contains two discrete strands of culture theory: a more sociological mainstream position associated with the work of Alfred L. Kroeber, Robert H. Lowie, Leslie Spier, and perhaps Franz Boas himself, and a maverick, more psychological stance foregrounded in the work of Edward Sapir, Paul Radin, and Alexander Goldenweiser. The latter strand of Boasian culture theory provides effective counters to the contemporary critiques of the culture concept. We do not need to throw out the cultural baby with the reified imperialist bath water. The concept of culture still works if updated and refined in response to contemporary issues.

The definition of culture has evolved considerably since Franz Boas's critique of the comparative method of classical evolutionism called for detailed ethnographic attention to the histories of particular cultures without a prior assumption of unilinear development (Boas 1896). Boas's ethnographic practice does not meet the standards of the turning millennium. In the context of their own day, however, his principles of ethnographic research cleared the way for contemporary attention to culture as a symbolic form expressed in the words of native speakers of native languages[2] and written down as a direct result of collaboration and division of labor between anthropologists and members of culture. Boas's unswerving commitment to recording culture as seen from the native point of view continues to be foundational to resolving contemporary ethical debates about appropriation and power.

Boas and his first generation of students were in fundamental agreement that the anthropological concept of culture distinguished their discipline among the emerging social sciences of the late nineteenth and early twentieth centuries. The trend toward professionalization across American science rigidified disciplinary boundaries and motivated claims to conceptual autonomy that would justify institutional arrangements. For anthropology, this meant alliances of universities providing professional training with museums providing fieldwork opportunities and publication outlets (Darnell 1969, 1998).

The conceptual justification for an autonomous discipline of anthropology rested on the assertion that every normal human being living in community with others possesses a culture and utilizes it in the ongoing construction of individual and group identity. This "culture" was to be understood independently of "'civilization," which was narrower in scope, the possession of a cultured individual or of a logocentric worldview defining itself as the epitome of human achievement. Whether or not civilization was a homogeneous entity emerging from a single historical tradition, cultures (including our own) were plural, diverse, and of equal validity and value, in principle if not always in practice. Cultural relativism, in this sense of respect for diverse social arrangements and symbolic constructions of reality, had an inverse side: commensurability was assumed to result from shared membership in the human species, what the classical evolutionists called "the psychic unity of mankind."

Despite of this shared baseline, the Boasian position was not monolithic. Hindsight reveals an obvious methodological caution: although for an observer located outside the Boasian inner circle, the Boasians appear very much alike, their apparent similarities dissolve in the context of their own times and points of view. Biography, understood as cultural history approached from the standpoint of a single individual, leads rapidly to idiosyncratic but nonetheless nonrandom positionings (see Darnell [1990] 2010). Boasian arguments about the nature of culture were highly individualized and passionately defended. The concept of culture functioned to unify the Boasian discourse precisely because it was a fuzzy, undefined category to which different interlocutors could attach different meanings that facilitated dialogue with a semblance of consensus as a rigid definition could not have done.

At the most sociological reach of the ostensibly shared concept, Kroeber argued at length in the *American Anthropologist* that anthropology dealt with a level of phenomena not recognized by the sciences dedicated to studying organic or inorganic phenomena (Kroeber 1917). He identified "culture" as the crucial distinctive feature of the superorganic. Despite links to both the natural sciences and the humanities, often existing in uneasy tension, this distinctiveness required its own methods of analysis. Kroeber was determined to establish anthropology as a legitimate social science based on its conceptual autonomy, earning it a legitimate place in the academy despite its parvenue status there. Culture superseded biological evolution, with the intersection of history and society lending it a unique cumulative character and potential for more rapid adaptive change than was possible at the organic level. Kroeber attributed group differences to culture rather than race, insisting that "genius" appeared with equal frequency regardless of cultural conditions (though the resulting expression depended on the social environment in which the ability was realized).

Kroeber's argument for the nonbiological basis of the superorganic entailed that society did not operate at the level of the individual, even though it was a product of human mental activity:

When we cease to look upon invention or discovery as some mysterious inherent faculty of individual minds which are randomly dropped in space and time by fate; when we center our attention on the plainer relation of one such advancing step to the others; when, in short, interest shifts from individually biographic elements, which can be only dramatically artistic, didactically moralizing, or psychologically interpretable, and attaches whole heartedly to the social, evidence on this point will be infinite in quantity, and the presence of a majestic order pervading civilization will be irresistibly evident. (1917:200–201)

The study of the individual, therefore, lay beyond the domain of anthropology. History (employing a methodology distinct from that of the natural sciences) rather than psychology (defined as the science of the individual in isolation) represented the causal dynamic of the social at the superorganic level.

Although Kroeber devoted most of his essay to the inapplicability of methods of organic or biological evolution to the study of social phenomena, his notion of culture as superorganic became the focal point of a different critical theoretical debate in Americanist anthropology, with unintended consequences that persist today albeit with somewhat different terminology. Boas (1887) had distinguished the methods of the sciences and the social or human sciences according to much the same logic employed by Kroeber. This logic remained unacknowledged in the backlash against Kroeber's position from fellow Boas students (Darnell 2015, 2017).

Edward Sapir was the paramount spokesperson for the opposition. Sapir was not particularly interested in the disciplinary autonomy of anthropology; his own work spanned linguistics, anthropology, psychology, sociology, folklore, and belles lettres—without any particular sense that the boundaries or their labels mattered.

Although Kroeber's argument for the analysis of culture as distinct from the methods of the natural sciences was efficacious for his purposes in 1917, it has not weathered well in the theoretical climate for which it cleared the ground. Kroeber himself took care not to reify culture but to define it as a nuanced level of patterning accessible through rigorous application of historical methodology. Ironically, however, he is most often attacked in contemporary critiques, particularly those originating outside anthropology, for the reification of culture.

Sapir's critique of the Kroeberian position reveals the actual complexity of Boasian positions on the nature of culture and entails a definition of culture that is both continuous with this persistent strand of the Americanist tradition that Boas spearheaded and germane to contemporary theorizing of the culture concept as a basis for cross-cultural research.

Sapir's Rejection of the Superorganic

Sapir, in sharp contrast to Kroeber, rejected the necessity of a link between accepting "culture" as the core concept of anthropological analysis and the autonomy of the cultural level of analysis from the actions and awareness of its individual members. Writing to fellow Boasian Robert Lowie (July 10, 1917: UCB) soon after Kroeber's paper appeared, Sapir opined that Kroeber was depending on "dogmatism and shaky metaphysics." His "excessive undervaluation" of the role of the individual in history was mere "abstractionist fetishism." Sapir hoped that other Boasians would rally round him to pose an alternative.

Lowie was the wrong person to ask. His own work emphasized social structure and shared cultural beliefs, especially religious beliefs. Next to Kroeber, he was the most sociological of the early Boasians. Sapir, however, considered him a safe interlocutor who would not challenge his preliminary musings. Sapir did not long stand alone on the substance: he co-opted Alexander Goldenweiser to join him in public response. By 1917 Paul Radin also weighed in on the role of the individual in the histories of particular cultures.

Crucially, none of these arguments rested on the claim that the so-called primitive was qualitatively distinct from so-called civilized society. Sapir, Goldenweiser, and Radin all dabbled in belles lettres and attributed the same creative impulses to ethnographic subjects as to their own colleagues, at least in principle. The cultural relativism with which Boasian critique superseded classical evolutionary theory further cemented the utility of recognizing a single panhuman process of individual adaptation to cultural environment.

Sapir's published rebuttal was more muted than the personal

criticism of Kroeber's position that appears in his correspondence. To his own rhetorical question "Do We Need a Superorganic?" the answer was a resounding "no." For him, free will, religion, philosophy, and aesthetics were all excluded by the determinism implicit in Kroeber's model. Sapir rejected the analogy of superorganic to organic as inherent properties of phenomena and deemed the organic to be an objective reality. The social, in contrast, was a symbolic reality, constituted by self-conscious human action. It was not content but form, a place from which to see, a space for reflexivity.

Following (albeit without citation) Boas's argument on the study of geography, Sapir argued that the uniqueness of historical phenomena necessitated different methods for the social and natural sciences (Sapir 1917). A superorganic level of culture to account for the uniqueness of individuals was superfluous. Sapir could envision no other motivation for Kroeber's theorizing of the superorganic. Conversely, the uniqueness of the individual was a question in which Kroeber was singularly uninterested. Thus, he failed to see the effectiveness of Sapir's critique, although the relation of culture and individual would become the core of the latter's culture theory over the ensuing two decades.

Alexander Goldenweiser, whose brief critique appeared alongside Sapir's in the *American Anthropologist* later in the year, attributed the "superorganic" to Kroeber alone rather than to shared Boasian culture theory. Like Sapir, he argued that the particularities of history invalidated Kroeber's cultural determinism in any particular case. The events of history could not be predicted, in part because of the role of individual agents in history. "Civilization," a term Goldenweiser preferred to "culture," was "not only carried but also fed by individuals" because "the biographical individual" constituted a "historic complex sui generis . . . composed of biological, psychological and civilizational factors" (Goldenweiser 1917:448). "Sui generis" is a Kroeberianism for the autonomy of the superorganic. Goldenweiser's challenge in elevating the unique individual to a similar position of theoretical centrality and determinism had dramatic impact.

Goldenweiser's argument necessitated inserting the individual into history, which posed a challenge for the anthropologist because societies without written history did not record biographical documentation for historical events. Undaunted by the problem of access to individual actions in the societies normally studied by anthropologists, Goldenweiser took it as axiomatic that the processes of cultural change operated through the actions of individuals the same way in an American Indian tribe [*sic*] or a modern nation-state. Boas, in contrast, grounded his approach on trait element diffusion reflecting the past history of the group; he did not attempt to reconstruct the individual agencies underlying cultural events not recorded in writing. Sapir, Goldenweiser, and Radin, in contrast, developed a culture theory centered around the individual as a creative force in group history. Their methodology was drawn from oral tradition and included collective history as passed down through family and tribal lines.

Kroeber, justifiably, considered the public critique of his paper an unfair attack. He complained to Sapir (July 24, 1917: UCB) that he had merely codified established Boasian practice in a way that he considered commensurable with Sapir's position:

> I've left absolutely everything to the individual that anyone can claim who will admit to the social at all. . . . What misleads you is merely that you fall back on the social at such occasional times as you're through with the individual; whereas I insist on an unqualified place, an actuality, for the social at all times.

Sapir conceded that "our common tendency is away from conceptual science and towards history. Both of us want to keep psychology in its place as much as possible" (Sapir to Lowie, October 29, 1917: UCB). They were operating with incommensurable binary oppositions: for Kroeber, culture and history; for Sapir, culture and the individual (not, for him, equated with psychology).

Kroeber considered it imperative that Boasians present a public face of disciplinary unanimity, whatever their private differences. In his view, Sapir was indifferent to the urgent need to defend the legitimacy and autonomy of Boasian anthropology, especially in claiming a legitimate place in the academic hierarchy:

> I don't give a red cent whether cultural phenomena have a reality of their own, as long as we treat them as if they had. You do, most of us do largely. . . . If we're doing anything right, it deserves

a place in the world. Let's take it, instead of being put in a corner. That's not metaphysics: it's blowing your own horn. (Kroeber to Sapir, November 1917: UCB)

The debate resurfaced periodically throughout Sapir's lifetime, underscoring that Sapir and Kroeber were perceived by their peers as constituting the two poles within Boasian anthropology. Both remain authoritative in at least some parts of the contemporary discipline (although the polarization is far less extreme today than at the time of original writing). Sapir wrote to Kroeber (May 24, 1932: UCB) that "the dichotomy between culture as an impersonal concern and individual behavior" could never be more than a useful fiction "for the preliminary clearing of the ground." But it was dangerous to take it too seriously because it had no explanatory power at the level of either culture or personality. Only months before his death, Sapir wrote to Kroeber:

> Of course, I'm interested in culture patterns, linguistic included. All I claim is that their consistencies and spatial and temporal persistences can be, and ultimately should be, explained in terms of humble psychological formulations with particular emphasis on interpersonal relations. I have no consciousness whatsoever of being revolutionary or of losing an interest in what is generally phrased in an impersonal way. Quite the contrary. I feel rather like a physicist who believes that immensities of the atom are not unrelated to the immensities of interstellar space. In spite of all you say to the contrary, your philosophy is pervaded by fear of the individual and his reality. (August 25, 1938: UCB)

It was a poignant and passionate defense of a theoretical position he had sustained over the intervening two decades without changing his fundamental premises about the importance of the individual in relation to culture. The language of culture and personality was new, as was the reference to interaction, but the concept persisted. The terminological changes reflected Sapir's encounters with Chicago sociology and Harry Stack Sullivan's interactional psychiatry in the context of the interdisciplinary social science of the 1920s and 1930s (Murray 1986).

Without appreciable disjuncture from the concept of culture

he had acquired as a student in the first decade of the twentieth century, Sapir arrived at a mature theory of culture built on Boasian foundations (Darnell 1986). His theory of symbolic interaction from the standpoint of the individual member of a given culture employed a methodology of cross-cultural research through life history and texts recording the knowledge transmitted by Native American oral traditions. Its fundamental premises included the symbolic and aesthetic or expressive nature of culture, its basis in social relations, its locus in the individual, a cultural relativism that focused on the commonsense intelligibility of the everyday world for the actors within it, and cultural meaning without exoticism imposed by the ethnographic gaze of the anthropologist.

Fine-Tuning the Sapirian Position

After his calls to the University of Chicago in 1925 and to Yale University in 1931, Sapir became a prestigious and sought-after member of the interdisciplinary jet set. He systematically rejected the role of purveyor of the exotic that his colleagues from sociology and psychiatry attempted to impose upon him. In his theoretical articles and in his classes on the "psychology of culture" (Irvine 1994; Darnell et al. 1999), the majority of Sapir's examples were simple ones from his own society that were already familiar to his audience. The nature of culture depended on the intelligibility of symbolic forms shared by the anthropologist and their subjects of study, not on the reification of the culture of the so-called primitive. Sapir argued that the goal of ethnography was to remove the exotic from the study of the cultural "Other" in the course of the ethnographic encounter through fieldwork. "The exotic" was an inadvertent by-product of the anthropologist's failure to construct meaning in local terms at the onset of their research; it was firmly entrenched in the eye of the beholder.

"Culture, Genuine and Spurious," originally written for a literary audience, puzzled many of Sapir's colleagues when it appeared in the *American Journal of Sociology* (Sapir 1924). His initial intention was to explicate the anthropological usage of the culture concept for an educated popular audience. The nontechnical language and choice of metaphors and examples from everyday life in North America reflect that original audience as well as his own excursions into literary and artistic circles from around 1917 to 1925 (Darnell 1986).

Whereas Kroeber rejected the popular usage of culture as cultivation in favor of one focused around tradition or societal heritage, Sapir retained both senses of the term "culture" and played them off against one another. The older connotation, while inadequate in isolation, enriched the anthropological conception so as to encompass individual variability among the members of a culture through the expressive values motivating individual creativity, thereby rendering a given cultural tradition meaningful for its individual members.

Sapir's "genuine" culture satisfied the intellectual (cognitive), emotional (affective), and aesthetic (expressive) needs of individuals. He was adamant that genuine culture could exist at any level of social complexity. For an audience that equated the primitive with the absence of civilization, Sapir focused on demonstrating the satisfaction available to the individual in a small integrated community. His prime exemplar was the salmon fisherman of the Northwest Coast, a choice that reflected his own extensive fieldwork among the Nootka (now Nuu-Chah-Nulth).

Sapir contrasted genuine culture with the spiritual malaise of his own society in the aftermath of the First World War. The "spurious" quality of this culture did not, however, depend on a contrast between the civilized and the so-called primitive. Instead, Sapir assumed that individual diligence in pursuit of intellectual and aesthetic excellence could create genuine culture at a personal level even in what he saw as the wasteland of contemporary North America. After about 1916 Sapir felt increasingly isolated in Empire Loyalist Ottawa as a Jewish immigrant, an intellectual, and a pacifist. His career was derailed by wartime cutbacks of funding for scientific fieldwork and publications, and his personal life was disrupted by the long-term illness and death of his first wife. His critique of the human cost of North American robber baron economics, urbanization, and industrialization foreshadows that of Ruth Benedict's *Patterns of Culture* (1934) a decade later. His exemplar for the spuriousness of the brave new American world was the telephone operator who worked all day at a switchboard in a mechanical and impersonalized job, lacking creative adhesion to a community, the genuine, holistic, personally satisfying culture of the Northwest Coast fisherman.

In light of these concerns, it is ironic that Sapir's argument has been interpreted within the noble savage paradigm rather than in relation to his actual argument that the relationship of the individual and culture was the key issue in anthropological theory. For Sapir, they were sides of the same coin; the same piece of social behavior could be interpreted either from the point of view of society and culture or from that of the individual.

The response to "Culture, Genuine and Spurious" was considerably more positive in literary than in social science circles, where a superorganic concept of culture was dominant. Sapir's argument was too humanistic for many of his colleagues. Even those who wrote poetry in their spare time kept it separate from their social science. For Sapir, however, the forms of culture were aesthetic and available for creative expression and use by the individual to change culture. Ironically, the value attached to a genuine culture in Sapir's humanistic sense is more compatible with the contemporary theoretical climate than it was at the time of its formulation.

Sapir followed the Boasian party line in arguing that the anthropologist as analyst was necessary because the meanings of cultural forms to individuals were held unconsciously and therefore were not directly observable. Normal social interaction virtually demanded lack of attention to the meaning of behavior. Sapir did not pursue the idea that if the anthropologist could learn to make explicit cultural patterns held below the level of consciousness, including those of their own society, then so could the "Other."

In practice, Sapir (for whom language was always the cultural form par excellence) relied on the grammatical intuitions of his most effective "informants" for their native languages and set a standard of "psychological reality" for adequacy of grammatical analysis (Sapir 1925, [1933]1949). I have argued elsewhere (Darnell [1990] 2010, reprinted in Darnell 2021) that intensive linguistic work with a limited number of speakers led Sapir, more than other Boasians, to view culture through its verbal expressions by particular individuals. Thus, his theoretical grounding of grammar in individual unconscious knowledge linked his psychology of culture with its concomitant emphasis on individual standpoint.

Sapir challenged the hitherto unexamined anthropological and sociological assumption that individual members of Indigenous societies were unproblematically typical of their communities. All fieldworkers learn to cross-check their data from a variety of individuals, but Sapir noted that the resulting ethnographic accounts filtered out such embarrassing ambiguities in favor of a simplified impersonal statement of cultural pattern. The problem was epistemological as well as methodological, its dynamic element being the interaction of the individual and their culture. The danger lay in reification of the heuristic fiction of culture, obscuring the variability of individual interpretations of symbols with their complex mixture of personal and institutional components. Sapir was less concerned to jettison Kroeber's superorganic than to explore in particular cases its intersection with individual sensemaking.

Individual personality had a dynamic integration not unlike that of cultural patterning itself. By the 1930s Sapir understood socialization as an interaction of the child with culturally patterned experience. In the process, personality integration held the potential for creative action to modify cultural patterns. Neither culture nor the individual could be understood in isolation. This is a very different position from what later came to be known as a culture-and-personality approach. Sapir's fellow Boasians Ruth Benedict and Margaret Mead were concerned primarily with the typological comparison of whole cultures. Sapir's emphasis on the individual precluded such facile generalization. He frequently cited J. Owen Dorsey's report that Omaha elder Two Crows denied an ostensibly factual statement made by another Omaha elder. No fieldworker could take for granted that any given individual would or could represent "the culture." Variability around cultural norms did not invalidate ethnographic research. Rather, it held ethnographers accountable for explaining the causes of differences in beliefs and behaviors among individuals. Although Sapir did not explore this position in his own fieldwork, his successors did.

Sapir's cultural theory, despite its continuities with the mainline Boasian argument, fundamentally reconstitutes both terms: he approaches culture in terms of the individual and individual psychology through cultural values and societal interactions. This position is remarkably contemporary in its attention to the relations of individuals and groups, the consequences of the leap from observation to generalization in ethnographic writing, the acknowledgment of intracultural variability and conflict as the normal states of cultural affairs, the grounding of cultural meanings in social interaction, the need to assess cultures according to the satisfaction they provide to individual members, the absence of exotica in cross-cultural variability, and the epistemological basis of cultural relativism.

Revisiting the Critique of Culture

These Sapirian insights clear the way for an affirmative response to the self-defensiveness with which anthropologists have often approached contemporary theoretical debate. Returning to the exemplary critical attacks cataloged at the outset allows us to conclude that a coherent theory of culture is emergent in anthropology in North America at the millennium, with an even more recent resurgence well underway as I write. Cultural critics to the contrary, many anthropologists believe that their concept of culture has always been sufficiently nuanced to reflect these variations in the circumstances of human communities and their inhabitants.

1. Anthropologists now have "consultants" or "collaborators" rather than "informants." Research agendas and reflexive analyses are two-way processes, dialogic rather than monologic. Whether in the field or the academy, the "Other" now studies us. There are Boasian precedents. The Americanist tradition has always had to deal with the presence of critics within communities studied—"they" are literate and live among us, after all. The line between anthropologist and "Other" can no longer be clearly drawn, if indeed it ever could.

2. Models of culture grounded in individual agency and adaptiveness can be extended to the study of urban communities, subcultures of our own society, and communities in diaspora. Individuals may move among communities, as member or outsider, and reconstitute communities in new circumstances. The need for shared norms for symbolic interaction will apply in all such communities, even temporary ones. Bor-

der crossings are not new, and communities have never been homogeneous.

3. The symbolic forms of an unfamiliar culture cannot be derived from theoretical premises in an ivory tower; they are genuinely alternative and accessible only through extended and intensive exposure to words, texts, behaviors, interactions. Anthropologists call this characteristic fieldwork method participant observation. "Genuine" ethnography in Sapir's sense assumes that familiar surface forms are likely to mean something dramatically different at first but become reasonable once the underlying meaning reveals itself in situ. There is no shortcut. The emphasis of the Boasian tradition of conducting research in Indigenous languages is particularly notable here.

4. We can claim realism about the world without claiming to know that reality in a simple or direct way. What we can know is grounded in a particular point of view. The more points of view we have, whether they be those of individuals or of cultural communities, the more the overlaps lend credibility to a description of "reality." Consensus is a powerful tool to frame epistemological relativism and set the stage for political action.

5. The spuriousness, in Sapir's terms, of contemporary culture has foregrounded a subcurrent of local knowledges and political positionings, a synergy of individuals and communities to create a more genuine culture. Resistances to homogenization may be interpreted as yearnings for genuineness. Local knowledges have persisted in the face of globalization.

6. Postcolonial theory demonstrates the inescapable consequences of the past actions of our forebears. Neither paralysis nor guilt is a constructive response. Acknowledgment of power relations and effort to structure conversations across their barriers is a legitimate goal both across and within cultures.

Some years ago I was invited for a guest lecture to an undergraduate English class in popular culture. I accepted the invitation to explain how I, as an anthropologist, used the term "culture" in a different way than it had been used throughout the course. After considerable self-reflection, I decided to begin: "Culture is something that belongs to people. It is about personal identity and community membership." Being an Algonquian linguist, I turned to the grammatical distinction known as "inalienable possession." In Cree, you just can't talk about "someone's" culture; there's a way to say it, but one almost never does, and it always sounds funny. I went on to talk about standpoint theory and situated knowledge and the capacity of individual agents for complex symbolic conceptualization and interaction. Some students were responsive to the expansion beyond written texts, and others were not.

Without denying the pitfalls, I continue to believe that it is possible to establish conversations across cultural boundaries. This requires refusing to concede moral and actual agency sufficient to initiate communicative interactions; to speak with rather than for others, and to report that such conversation is possible, though not always successful; and to evoke the quality of the learning. For example, the reader may think through an alternative way of seeing the world differently by reading over the shoulder of the far-from-omniscient ethnographer. The process is ongoing.

Notes

1. Originally published as "The Anthropological Concept of Culture at the End of the Boasian Century," *Social Analysis* 4 (1997): 42–54.

2. The term "native" (also "native languages," "native linguistics," "native speaker") is conventional in the literature and established Boasian usage. It would distort the discourses as written to change it to the more contemporary term "first language"; "heritage language" is also used in some contexts. I retain the terms for Boas's use but use more contemporary language when speaking in my own voice.

References

Benedict, Ruth. 1934. *Patterns of Culture*. Boston: Houghton Mifflin.
Boas, Franz. 1887. "The Study of Geography." *Science* 9:137–41.
———. 1896. "The Limitations of the Comparative Method of Anthropology." *Science* 4:901–8.
Darnell, Regna. 1969. "The Development of American Anthropology, 1879–1920: From the Bureau of American Ethnology to Franz Boas." PhD diss., University of Pennsylvania.

————. 1986. "The Emergence of Edward Sapir's Mature Thought." In *New Perspectives in Language, Culture, and Personality*, edited by William Cowan, Konrad Koerner, and Michael K. Foster, 553–88. Amsterdam: John Benjamins.

————. (1990) 2010. *Edward Sapir: Linguist, Anthropologist, Humanist.* Berkeley: University of California Press.

————. 1998. *And Along Came Boas: Continuity and Revolution in Americanist Anthropology.* Amsterdam: John Benjamins.

————. 2015. "Mind, Body and the Native Point of View: Boasian Theory at the Centennial of The Mind of Primitive Man." In *The Franz Boas Papers, Volume 1: Franz Boas as Public Intellectual—Theory, Ethnography, Activism.* Franz Boas Papers Documentary Edition Series, edited by Regna Darnell, Michelle Hamilton, Robert L. A. Hancock, and Joshua Smith, 3–18. Lincoln: University of Nebraska Press.

————. 2017. "Franz Boas as Theorist: A Mentalist Paradigm for the Study of Mind, Body, Environment and Culture." In *Historicizing Theories, Identities, and Nations, Histories of Anthropology Annual*, edited by Regna Darnell and Frederic W. Gleach, 1–26. Vol. 11 of Histories of Anthropology Annual. Lincoln: University of Nebraska Press.

————. 2021. *The History of Anthropology: A Critical Window on the History of Anthropology.* Critical Studies in the History of Anthropology series. Lincoln: University of Nebraska Press.

Darnell, Regna, Judith T. Irvine, and Richard Handler, eds. 1999. *Culture: Collected Works of Edward Sapir.* Vol. 3. Berlin: Mouton de Gruyter.

Goldenweiser, Alexander. 1917. "The Autonomy of the Social." *American Anthropologist* 19:447–49.

Irvine, Judith T., ed. 1994. *The Psychology of Culture: A Course of Lectures.* [Reconstructed from class notes of Edward Sapir]. Berlin: Mouton de Gruyter.

Kroeber, Alfred L. 1917. "The Superorganic." *American Anthropologist* 19:163–213.

Murray, Stephen O. 1986. "Edward Sapir and the Chicago School of Sociology." In *New Perspectives in Language, Culture, and Personality*, edited by William Cowan, Konrad Koerner, and Michael K. Foster, 241–92. Amsterdam: John Benjamins.

Sapir, Edward. 1917. "Do We Need a Superorganic?" *American Anthropologist* 19:441–47.

————. 1924. "Culture, Genuine and Spurious." *American Journal of Sociology* 29:401–29.

————. [1933] 1949. "La realité psychoogique des phonemes." *Journal de Psychologie Normal et Pathologique* 30:247–65. Reprinted in English translation as "The Psychological Reality of Phonemes" in Sapir 1949:46–60.

————. 1949. *Selected Writings of Edward Sapir in Language, Culture, and Personality.* Edited by David G. Mandelbaum, 46–60. Berkeley: University of California Press.

4

Calibrating Discourses across Cultures in Search of Common Ground

This essay explores the relationships and dialogic potentials among linguistic anthropology, literary studies, and First Nations ethnography in light of my personal negotiations of these often-slippery boundaries over more than five decades.[1] I explore the need to ground theory or philosophy in the experience of the speaker or actor, so that listeners or readers can assess its relevance to their own experience at the moment of telling and as it evolves over a lifetime. I draw heavily on my personal experience not because it is unique or emblematic but because it enables me to refract conclusions in relation to the experiences from which they arose, to exemplify the process I advocate.

I employ a First Nations[2] pedagogy as I have come to understand it, as an outsider and learner, and to value its scope from analytic distance. Emergence in the process of interaction is the essence of oral tradition. In the widely shared story cycles characteristic of the Algonquian linguistic family, the trickster (Cree Wisahketchak, Ojibwe Nanabush) was walking, and his actions caused things to happen in the world that gave the world its present form (Darnell 2020). Contemporary Indigenous experience is structured around narrative progression, establishing continuity with the past, using the traditional stories as a template for how things happen and their consequences. I adopt such a pedagogy both on grounds of ethical engagement with First Nations communicative economies and as an exemplar of qualitative social science methodology at its most powerful. The poles of pedagogy and theory reveal convergent methodologies when I approach cross-cultural encounter as an ongoing series of communicative events within highly contextualized processes.

Anthropology as a discipline rests upon the alternation of theory and ethnography (cultural description) and integrates its commitment to taking seriously the minutiae of individual lives with the pursuit of a comparative dimension of an empirical science of humankind. On the one hand, such a science would be impossible if all societies and cultures did not share an essential human nature; on the other hand, particular realizations of that shared human heritage (both cultural and biological) differ quite dramatically in their surface forms.

The overlap between the social sciences and humanities perhaps reaches its most potent conjuncture in literature, particularly comparative literature; its multiplicity recapitulates strategies of awareness of contrast that for me arise from fieldwork and its incumbent encounters. Stories act in the world to create and sustain the identities of those who tell them and those who listen to them and to enable effective communication across cultural boundaries. Stories about land inevitably become stories about Indigenous encounters with colonial newcomers. The newcomers brought stories from many elsewheres that resonate with the prior and ongoing experiences of Indigenous storytellers in Canada. Literature and anthropology share a common project here, although their modi vivendi differ. Anthropological method bases generalizations across culture and language on firsthand fieldwork, usually extensive and in initially unfamiliar cultural settings, although an increasing number of anthropologists use native speaker or member-of-culture insight and access to study their own communities of origin. Such auto-ethnography is close to the methodology of two-eyed seeing employed by some Indigenous scholars. Participation in local life and observation of what people actually do (that is, what anthropologists call participant observation) overlap and intersect to produce a reflexive account to which the standpoint of the anthropologist is the indispensable key. The trick in literature is to speak to both insider and outsider audiences simultaneously—to find different common ground that may eventually allow them to talk to one another. Very few writers manage this. Tom King, Drew Hayden Taylor, and Thomson Highway are among them.

Although positivist social scientists of varying persuasions decry the purported lack of objectivity and replicability of such a methodology, I argue that the carefully chosen anecdote and meticulous attention to what interlocutors from elsewhere actually say about how they make sense of their experience are more likely to produce effective cross-cultural communication than a superficial calibration of the exotic and unintelligible with the unexamined preconceptions of the investigator. Good ethnography is similar to literature in its capacity to invite suspension of disbelief and empathy instead of prejudgment outside the structure of the narrative. Like the new criticism of my long-ago English major, I believe the text must be taken seriously even though I also want to go beyond it. The important thing is to know the difference between the text and its interpretation. The social scientist differs in accepting an obligation to report accurately what is observed; the "what if?" of literary imagination is curtailed in description if not in interpretation. Nevertheless, "the truth about stories" (King 2003), in both literary and ethnographic modes, transcends the chronicling of events to engage what Chamberlin calls "ceremonies of belief," the concurrent strands of story that are true in a presuppositional or cultural sense beyond and discrete from the literal facticity of their content (2003:227).

The most fundamental human knowledge is held largely below the level of conscious thought, but it can be articulated in the context of ongoing experience as needed. One way is by entering into dialogue with an outsider who needs to have things explained that can be taken for granted among the members of a culture where everyone knows them. Anthropologists and other social scientists are not the only ones to think about the meaning of life under particular cultural conditions or the nature of social order; ordinary people everywhere do it all the time. If nothing else, there is the universal need to formulate such knowledge in the socialization of children, a habit often drawn on in socializing the anthropologist to local ways (Briggs 1986). The dialogue inherent in such a process reorients the culture concept, ridiculed by some critics as static and reified, toward process. What Dennis Tedlock and Bruce Mannheim call "the dialogic emergence of culture" (1995) takes seriously what others articulate about their lives and experiences.

Prima facie, the anthropologist is a partner in the dialogue rather than an objective observer positioned outside the interaction.

The ethnographer enters into a different kind of dialogue on return from the field, because the writing of ethnography calibrates knowledge acquired in the field with forms of being and speaking that are intelligible to an audience back home. Shifting between dialogue away and dialogue at home has a stereoscopic impact that further hones insight. Anthropologists attempt to capture the particularity of their fieldwork experience while also providing a lens for others to share something of what it means to live elsewhere and try to learn to think about the world as people do there. Good ethnography allows the reader to peer over the shoulder of the anthropologist and observe him or her learning to dissolve surface exoticism into comprehensible social action geared toward making sense and living in society. The commonalities underlying dialogue ideally create a shared space of discourse, unique to that interaction that presupposes all parties begin with mutual respect and willingness to consider other points of view. Regardless of the relations of power that apply in the larger world external to the discourse, effective communication requires an implicit social contract in which two or more persons agree to interact, to speak together, and to negotiate an acknowledgment of the legitimacy of one another's positions if not consensus on what to do about it. Interlocutors need not agree in order to remain in dialogue. They only agree to speak together about the positions they hold.

Consideration of language leads inexorably to land. Language is the mode of stories, and stories are the way to claim that one belongs in a place. The emplacement of an anthropologist matters, not just in terms of the fieldwork site but also in terms of the scholarly and public venues in which our conclusions are presented. That is why land acknowledgments have become salient in public gatherings in recent years. The Indigenous community whose land is shared with speakers from elsewhere potentially facilitates a calibration of knowledge traditions that is diametrically opposed to the long-standing cross-cultural miscommunication of interlocutors destined to remain forever strangers.

Indigenous ties to land are not interchangeable. I am a relative stranger in this land, but since moving to southern Ontario in 1990, I have been taught much about how to be a guest who would be welcomed back. The manners appropriate to a guest are widely shared across Indigenous territories in Canada and the United States, and I brought to potential dialogue here what I had learned elsewhere; therefore I am obligated by good manners to acknowledge my own embeddedness in place and community. Although my examples of knowledge calibration are drawn from a broader range of cultures and territories, I interpret what I know of other places and peoples based on personal experience of living and working alongside First Nations communities in Canada, primarily the Plains Cree of northern Alberta from 1969 to 1990 and the Anishinaabeg of southern Ontario since 1990. To live and work in the same place opens a rich dimension of ongoing engagement. At a purely pragmatic level, it is easier to maintain close contact with individual collaborators and their communities, but it also allows me to absorb the feel of the land and the ways different cultural traditions, including my own, have lived on it over time. I sustain relationships to land as well as people. Part of the continuity in my work results from the difficulties of switching languages of interest in midcourse for a linguistic anthropologist. I have acquired a modest and respectful acquaintance with Ojibwe (like Cree, a language of the far-flung Algonquian language family that includes both Cree and Ojibwe), southern Slavey (an Athabascan language of the Mackenzie Delta), and Mohawk (an Iroquoian language of the Haudenosaunee Confederacy spoken at Six Nations of the Grand River and elsewhere), in addition to the Plains Cree with which I began. The domains of land and language are inextricable, though the precise nature of the relationship responds to local conditions and changes over time.

By the mid-1980s in Alberta I began to worry that I too easily elided the particularity of Plains Cree ways of understanding the world with Algonquian grammatical categories and inadvertently conflated them with those of First Nations in general. Like the Plains Cree, the Slavey of the Northwest Territories were hunters, trappers, and gatherers, many still living primarily off the land despite "permanent" settlement and other rapid and quite dramatic changes to their traditional practices, but their language belongs to the Athabascan language family. I proposed to hold traditional lifeways constant and compare their linguistic encodings. I found similarities in ties to land and ways of moving around on it and a subsistence pattern grounded in locality. Although the grammatical categories of Algonquian and Athabascan languages divided experience differently, the languages within these language families also expressed attitudes and practices reflecting the common experience of their speakers who inhabited similar environments. For example, the animate grammatical category in Cree classifies much of the living world as alive in the same degree that human persons are alive, whereas Slavey speakers are more concerned with what linguists call "hierarchies of animacy"; for them, some things are more alive than others. Concern with the interactive capacity of living beings or entities that are considered objects in Indo-European languages is a generalization that crosses linguistic boundaries and underscores the interdependence of hunter and prey, land and its human use, nature and culture. Such linguistic patterns are deeply rooted. They persist and continue to structure experience even when speakers are no longer, or no longer primarily, hunters and trappers.

Language is a significant route to growing roots in a new place. Accordingly, when I came to the University of Western Ontario as chair of anthropology in 1990, one of my first acts was to hire David Maracle, Kanatawahkon, to teach Mohawk; I audited the course the first year he offered it, on the grounds that I was now living in a region with two very distinct Indigenous traditions—Haudenosaunee and Anishinaabeg—and therefore had an obligation to know something about both. Nearly a decade later, I audited Anishinaabemowin (Ojibwe) with Eli Baxter, who grew up on a trapline on the Albany River before attending residential school and becoming a language teacher. I hoped to increase my capacity to transpose some of what I knew about Cree to a closely related Algonquian linguistic and to some extent cultural tradition. This time, it was not primarily subsistence pattern that motivated my sense of apposite comparison but linguistic relationship. Western's First Nations [now Indigenous] Studies program, of which I was founding director in 2003, aspired to reflect the cross-linguistic and cross-cultural complexity of the region. Sharing of the same land over time, rather than a language or traditional subsistence pattern, has linked the Anishinaabeg and Haudenosaunee traditions, now also embracing a commitment to the third distinct founding tradition of the Lenape (Delaware).

Early experiments with Cree honed my sense of the intimacy that sharing a language creates for its speakers. A speech community is both constituted and sustained by its common forms of expression and interpretation. Speakers who have never previously met come into contact already sharing an orientation to the world, a form of knowledge that is both linguistic and cultural. Language learners use their growing fluency as a tool to think differently about relationships and the world in which they are embedded. I did not become a fluent speaker of any of these languages or a near-insider to the communities of their speakers. Some of the members of these communities agreed to share their knowledge with me. As a result, I experienced glimmers of concepts and grammatical constructions that were virtually impossible to express in fluent English, despite awkward paraphrases and examples encoded in the stories my language teachers used to express their experience in terms I could understand. This leisurely process of transmission imbued me with an appreciation of the expressive elegance of the Cree language, an aesthetic precision that I could not possibly have dreamed up by any kind of linguistic thought experiment. Rather, it revealed itself gradually over a *longue durée* of resocialization and recalibration of knowledge traditions.

Classrooms are not good places to learn about languages, because they are isolated from the speakers of the languages they attempt to teach. I knew this, but nevertheless I taught Plains Cree language and culture for fifteen years at the University of Alberta, with native speakers doing the speaking while I did the semantic bridging to English and the course management. In the early days of this course, the local community wondered if there was anything to worry about and sent around an elder to observe the class and report whether we were appropriating traditional knowledge, representing it outside of the experience that validated it in the eyes of community members. To my simultaneous relief and disappointment, the elder concluded that what we were doing was acceptable, mostly because it was harmless; we were not talking about anything of great importance in these elementary language classes. Indeed, elementary language classes are remarkably similar across languages despite dramatic differences in the languages they introduce. To go deeper is not an elementary matter. Rather, it is as much a matter of language use as of linguistic structure, of what Dell Hymes (1974) called "communicative competence" or "competence for performance." For example, the class once had a guest who talked about hunting moose the week after we covered kinship terms. After he agreed that he liked (the taste of) moose meat, one of the students proudly asked him in grammatical Cree if his son liked moose meat. He replied that his son *eats* moose meat, answering the polite question that should have been asked. The student failed to perceive the gentle correction intended to teach the proper use of kinship terms by example. One does not speak for others even on matters of little apparent significance or controversy. It is a question of personal autonomy rather than of privacy, with good manners requiring circumspection and self-discipline.

My encounters with these languages and their speakers have changed my thinking, feeling, believing, and capacity to interpret my own experience in ways that I could not have predicted in advance. I still consider myself a monolingual speaker of English. I have too much respect for these languages to claim fluency, linguistically or in terms of the inaccessible (to me) knowledge that Cree persons acquire through childhood socialization and accumulate over a lifetime of experience. Matters that lie beyond the narrowly linguistic are an integral part of the language.

Fieldwork remains the quintessential rite of passage for academic or disciplinary qualification, yet anthropologists rarely receive explicit training in how to do it. Oral tradition passed on by anthropological elders is anecdotal but highly prized because it has succeeded for the raconteur in her or his fieldwork and because it establishes an intellectual genealogy of continuity across generations of anthropologists. I had an enormous advantage over the usual fledging fieldworker because my dissertation on the history of Americanist anthropology was completed before I first encountered the Plains Cree. Therefore, I could hang out and purport to be learning the language without the pressure of having to pester people for knowledge that I could deploy in short order toward some grand theoretical synthesis designed to establish my professional credentials. I suspect that I seemed relatively harmless until I became a known person and could be judged on the basis of my own actions.

Anthropology's oral tradition suggests that fieldwork should begin with a community census (how people position themselves on land) and learning the language, because these things are straightforward and ethically unproblematic. Late in 1969, I thought my provisional census of the first Alberta Cree community where I worked was in pretty good shape when an elder died suddenly. The population quadrupled for the funeral, and many of the returnees stayed for months; a few simply came home and stayed. Horrified, I asked who these new people were. My teachers assured me that all of these people lived here and belonged in the community; they had been away for unspecified periods of time that were irrelevant to their right to return home. Over two ensuing decades of visiting this community frequently and working with them on language revitalization projects, I came to expect that these and other community members would come and go as the circumstances of their lives dictated. I too was sometimes there and sometimes not. So much for the idea that a census has easy boundaries—the ties of people to the place are not directly observable and cannot be held to a static model of residence or continuous presence. People were known to each other through the stories of their lives and their ties to the place.

Learning the language was an equally complicated point of entrée to ethnography. Teachers assumed that I wanted to learn about the lifeworld encoded in the language and thereby absorb the moral virtues of the stories articulated in it. Why else would anyone want to learn a language? Initially my language teachers taught me more about how to behave as a proper Cree person than about the language as such. Earning the trust of potential teachers necessarily preceded the decision to share something as intimate as *their* language.

In a project to videotape traditional activities for the elementary school Cree language classes, another community I came to know well during these years decided it was acceptable to record these things because the elders had spoken about traditional matters exclusively in Cree. They believed that the rare outsiders who learned enough Cree to understand them were likely to be trustworthy. Despite the urgency of passing this knowledge to a generation of Cree-speaking children in the community, speakers remained concerned to protect the privacy of the language, as though it were a living being. To receive such instruction was a primary motivation for children to become fluent speakers of their traditional language. Even elders who spoke quite good English did not feel that traditional matters could be discussed respectfully in English. What for a mainstream Canadian speaker of English would be a matter-of-fact documentary about traditional activities was for these Cree curriculum producers a way of transmitting spiritual values alongside traditional practices unique to the Cree and properly retained under their control for their sole use.

The late Farley Mowat, who held a master of arts in anthropology, tells in *People of the Deer* (1975) about learning Inuktitut during a winter he spent camping with an Inuit extended family on their trapline. He found Inuktitut much easier than he had expected based on dire warnings in the anthropological literature. When they came out to the trading post in the spring and he proudly tried out his skills, no one understood what he said. His hosts unabashedly explained that they knew their language would be too hard for him, so they taught him baby talk. It was polite to indulge his wish to learn their language, but they declined to teach him more than what they thought he was prepared to learn. This is one reason fieldwork takes a long time. Briggs (1986) describes parallel experiences of "learning [being taught] how to ask" and to behave like a proper person in Mexicano culture before he could address his research questions.

I was privileged to have access to much of this superficially leisurely and indirect pedagogy of oral tradition because I worked with elders who were fluent speakers to record their words in writing and prepared audio and video tapes for family and community use in a future beyond the time of their own passing. My travels to consult elders about curriculum materials and technologies of transmission recapitulated the traditional process whereby young people who wish to learn are encouraged to sit with different elders over a considerable period of time. I was not the primary target of the teaching but the conduit through which it could be organized for most effective use in maintaining the language by transmitting traditional knowledge in it. As an unobtrusive listener, I was welcome to learn to the extent of my capacity.

Many Canadians believe that Aboriginal peoples have been so thoroughly assimilated that they are no longer collectively distinct from the mainstream or indeed that they constitute a collectivity at all. Sadly, this failure to comprehend the differences, never mind the fervent wish of many Native individuals and communities to maintain a distinct identity into the indefinite future, has become a political and ideological, as well as a linguistic and cultural, issue. Many politicians and engaged citizens have forgotten that treaties with the First Nations peoples promise them a legal and moral status different in kind from that of any other inhabitants of the country now called Canada. The Canadian Constitution Act of 1982 recognizes but does not define Aboriginal rights.

This political context entails spiritual dimensions of Indigenous identity and identification with traditional territory that strike few chords for most mainstream Canadians. The indelible spirituality of the political in First Nations thought perpetuates the cross-cultural miscommunication at the heart of interactions between an entrenched system of settler colonialism and the beleaguered victims of often well-meaning but ultimately destructive impositions from outside. An obvious exemplar is the ongoing work of the Truth and Reconciliation Commission on the transgenerational legacy of residential schools that grew out of the work of the Aboriginal Healing Foundation, which in turn grew out of the scathing indictment of Canadian Indian policy and its outcomes in the reports of the Royal Commission on Aboriginal Peoples (1996). In ensuing years First Nations political leaders have acted, with increasing success, to redress the balance of power and authority sadly inherent in the encounter of Native and non-Native across the Americas. Strategies of resistance and what Anishinaabeg writer Gerald Vizenor (1994) calls "survivance" strive to prevail, for individuals as well as communities.

A widespread belief still prevails in Canadian society that cultural difference has to be exotic and by implication that the exotic is not to be found at home. Anthropological scuttlebutt has it that Margaret Mead, the anthropologist who did the most to break down the cultural isolationism of North America between the two world wars of the last century, said that Canada was the hardest country for her to study because, on the surface, everything seemed quite familiar—and then a startlingly fundamental difference with immense consequences, hitherto masked from view and intractable from conscious articulation, never mind formal analysis, would sneak up on her.

Something similar occurs when mainstream Canadians encounter First Nations peoples. I never had to go far away to encounter profound difference underlying superficial similarity. In southern Ontario, the majority of Native peoples live in cities rather than on reserves, eat pizza more often than moose, and speak English as their first, often only, language. What makes them distinct is far deeper than these surface markers of cultural identity. I have characterized one of the prevailing patterns of First Nations distinctiveness as a "nomadic legacy," a habit of moving people to resources rather than bringing resources back to a homeplace (Darnell 2008). This strategy, in which people come and go purposefully, evolved to maximize traditional subsistence strategies; it persists in the residential decision-making of contemporary Indigenous peoples seeking employment, education, or services away from home. By maintaining ties to home while they are away, they reserve the right to return there. The reserve itself is a significant resource even, perhaps especially, for those who are not residing there at any given time. Its ongoing existence in one's absence maintains continuity of life experience and identity for individuals, families, and the home communities.

Though other factors are also involved, this preserves traditional patterns of subsistence on the land as an option for some community members. For example, the James Bay and Northern Quebec Agreement of 1975 specified trapper subsidies, not because the James Bay Cree intended to return en masse to the ways of their forebears but because the continued existence of a few hunters and trappers served as exemplar that such a lifestyle remains integral to what it means to be Cree within modernity. A few people still continued to live off the land, and through them, those who chose other means of livelihood retain a tie to traditional practices. The possibility of pursuing them persisted as an option at the level of the community as a whole.

"Home" is a reference point, the "spiritual logic" of this tie to land, to home territory for the members of a community (Chamberlin 2003:70, 106). To maintain such ties, it is necessary only that *someone* maintain the homeplace in what I call an accordion model of Algonquian social organization (Darnell 1998). Just as small extended family groups used to hunt together in the winter and come together with other such families at traditional gathering places in the summer, reserves have become gathering places for many contemporary people. Decontextualized media reports that over half of Canada's Native population (including First Nations, Métis, and Inuit) live off-reserve have created an alarming public and political response that the reserves are no longer necessary, that the future of Aboriginal peoples lies in cities, physically and spiritually isolated from traditional territories that they understood as land-based home places. Such myopia about how people come and go endangers the collective sovereignty as well as the personal identity of former hunters and gatherers who still move around as a strategy of living well in the contemporary world.

A significant stereotype that still bedevils the relations of contemporary First Nations peoples to outsiders is that "civilization" requires people to be settled permanently on bounded chunks of land. Traders, missionaries, and government officials alike deplored what they judged to be the random and unpredictable movement of the First Nations peoples in search of resources; they failed to comprehend the importance placed on experience-based knowledge of specific land and environment rather than on accumulation of material manifestations of culture. The documentary record shows that the roles of settler and former nomad differ from this stereotype. Settlers are constantly seeking new places to establish their farms, while nomads exploit the same broad range of territory over long periods of time. Nomads adapt to the land as they find it rather than modifying it to meet their needs (Chamberlin 2003:30; Brody 2000). Traditional First Nations patterns of land use and stewardship allow hunters to utilize parts of their land some of the time, over time, and entail their intimate ties to the familiar resources of a particular home territory. Movement took place within a known territory according to a seasonal cycle; hunters and their kinfolk established ongoing relationships to the land, including to the plants, animals, and other beings with whom they cohabited.

The question of the beings living alongside humans on the land is both linguistic and cultural. The puzzling distinction, for speakers of English or French, between animate and inanimate codifies the underlying assumptions of Algonquian culture and history. In Plains Cree, living things include human persons, animals, birds, fish, many plants (especially those with capacity to defend themselves, as with thorns, and those useful to humans), spirits, tobacco that moves to the spirit world and links people to it, the bow that powers the movement of an arrow, male genitals and female breasts (both for their life-giving capacity), and containers that give form (e.g., spoon or lake bed). Anything with capacity for self-propulsion or purposeful movement is alive. The third-person pronoun for "that living person" does not distinguish gender; being alive trumps being male or female in grammatical hierarchy. In this context, it is unsurprising that Anishinaabeg who speak of "all my relations" do not separate out human persons from other kinds of living beings. These beings share a property of being alive and participate actively in the body of stories that created relationships for the world and its denizens and sustain its continuance by their retelling. When Anishinaabeg envision land stewardship, for which human persons hold a special responsibility by virtue of the particular gifts or talents given them by the Creator, they are enjoined to plan for seven generations into the future and to draw on the wisdom of seven generations into the past. The time depth of oral tradition often attains this ideal in practice: me (1), my parent (2), my grandparent (3), my grandparent's parent (4) as the neutral alternating generation, my grandparent's grandparent (5) who spoke to my grandparent about what his or her grandparent (7; 6 is neutral) told of what he or she as a small child had been told by his or her own grandparent. The alternating generations in the sequence of seven are already deceased, mature adults earning a living and gaining the experience to become elders in due course, or not yet born. The inevitable succession of grandparent/elder and grandchild/learner creates a flow that maintains the connection of community, land, and traditional knowledge. The individual for whom such a genealogy remains accessible is truly well educated and embodies the knowledge directly transmitted through such an unbroken line. Plains Cree poet, artist, and academic Neal McLeod illustrates such a genealogy and generalizes its ideal manifestation in what he calls "Cree narrative memory" (2007). Age, experience, and embedded relationship to tradition are highly valued. The transmission of knowledge is utterly dependent upon them. Life-long learning continues throughout a life cycle and entails performing one's knowledge in successive ways appropriate to one's age and stature. A child may be identified as a potential apprentice to acquire such a body of knowledge at a very young age and encouraged to hang around with grandparents or elders and assist them with the tasks of everyday life and with their duties in the community. Often these young people will be encouraged to travel around and to sit with other elders whose experiences and understanding are different but complementary. Each teacher and learner is expected to access and integrate knowledge uniquely. This protracted learning process takes as long as it takes. The young person learns how to listen and to observe and absorbs the knowledge that, on the death of a teacher, will permit them to sustain the knowledge chain into the future through their own performance. Unfortunately, of course, things do not always happen in the appropriate sequences and completions. Much is lost when an elder dies prematurely or unexpectedly before the knowledge held in stewardship has been transmitted. Moreover, some elders deliberately choose not to pass on what they know, because they deem it irrelevant to present-day circumstances, and young people do not want to learn in this way.

Many contemporary communities are committed to revitalizing traditional languages and to recording orally transmitted knowledge in nontraditional technologies precisely because this knowledge is the collective intellectual property of the community, and its transmission is endangered by human frailty. Anthropology's distinctive contribution to the staking out of common ground is that their recorded texts often provide contemporary communities with critical sources to recover and reintegrate such knowledge.

The contribution of the fieldworking anthropologist to understanding the reciprocal entailments of land, language, and identity arises from ethnographic contextualization, what Bronislaw Malinowski, working in Melanesia, called the "imponderabilia of everyday life" (Malinowski 1922) and what Franz Boas, on Canada's West Coast, called "the native point of view." Ethnographic verisimilitude relied heavily on the stories people told about themselves in the early days of professional anthropology, primarily on texts in native languages produced by Native speakers.[3] Stories told by First Nations peoples themselves have blurred the lines between at least some genres of ethnography and literature over the last century. Standpoint, voice, and the power of narrative are the keys.

The question of whether cultures are ultimately commensurable, that is, whether it is ever possible to understand the thought world of someone whose knowledge is acquired through socialization of a dramatically different kind or, more abstractly, whether it is possible to calibrate ways of knowing across cultural boundaries. Many Western philosophers (among my favorite targets is the early work of the late Richard Rorty [1980]) have argued that we civilized Western folks are forced to constrain ourselves to a conversation among thinkers who share a historical genealogy, and that moving outside this established conversation inevitably results in unintelligibility. Such a view imprisons both parties to potential learning in their own thought traditions and profoundly underestimates the fundamental human capacity for empathy and imagination. Lamentably some contemporary philosophers, for example, post-Chomskian linguists, rarely move outside their monocultural comfort zone. What linguists long called "the Theory" is impervious to counterevidence and, thus, from an ethnographer's eye view, is not very interesting. Post-Enlightenment rationalism has been taken prematurely as universal, resulting in dismissal of profound differences across languages as trivial on a priori grounds. Such variability must be construed as an empirical question.

Stereotyped presuppositions based on the language of the powerful have created a frustrating intellectual climate for those of us who work with languages and communities that do not share these assumptions and whose differences have been deemed trivial in light of larger issues external to their experience and celebration of their own distinctiveness. It is all too easy to dismiss as savages those whose speech, communicative forms, and lifeways we do not understand. Such a blatant generalization would remain premature until or unless it can be demonstrated that English, perhaps supplemented by reference to other languages of the Indo-European linguistic family, embodies the universal properties of human language in some privileged fashion. The underlying assumption is remarkably arrogant. There are, of course, some honorable exceptions. For example, the late Kenneth Hale collaborated with Albert Alvarez to produce a grammar of his native Papago (now called Tohono O'odham) in Papago (Alvarez and Hale 1970). The point is not that all grammars should be written in Papago (although some should be) but rather that Papago provides analytic categories that do not distort the patterning of the language being described and that its resources are fully adequate to the task of writing a grammar even though no Papago intellectual has previously attempted to do so. This is what we mean by the productivity of natural languages (Hockett 1960), with or without the intervention of a linguist.

A continuous anthropological tradition that I have defined as "Americanist" (Darnell 2001), is perhaps regaining modest ascendency, of seeking out "the native point of view" and analyzing unfamiliar languages in their own terms. Franz Boas, the central founding figure of this tradition, as editor of the Bureau of American Ethnology's Introduction to the *Handbook of American Indian Languages* (1911, 1922), aspired to present a model or template for the grammar of any Indigenous American language or language type. Boas jettisoned the familiar categories of Latin, Greek, and Sanskrit grammar in favor of categories arising from the structures of the languages being described. He was willing to risk initial incommensurability across languages, at least prior to exegesis, in order to preserve patterns of both grammar and discourse unique to each language and culture. The grammatical sketches in the first volume of the *Handbook*, intended for emulation by nonprofessionals, were accompanied by brief texts (that is, stories and teachings) elicited from native speakers. Ideally, for a language to be considered adequately described, a dictionary and more extensive texts would be required. The texts were important on methodological grounds because they were elicited from native speakers and thus constrained the unconscious importation of categories from the linguist's own linguistic background.

Boas's most talented linguistic student, Edward Sapir, and Sapir's protégé Benjamin Whorf further developed the idea that grammatical categories had considerable influence on what Whorf called "habitual thought" (1956). One *could* get beyond the incommensurability of the things it was difficult to say or to translate in a particular language, but to do so would require considerable effort by the anthropologist/linguist or by the native speaker or, more commonly, by a dialogue between them. Further complexities arose when the would-be grammarian wrote up the results for an audience that had not shared the experience of linguistic immersion or been exposed to the cultural context in which the language was spoken. In sum, the ethnographer's experience seemed to confirm Whorf's insight that language, thought, and reality are inextricably linked, mutually entailed. The strongest form of this argument would be deterministic and leave no room for personal agency, bilingualism, or translation. Later critiques to the contrary, Whorf proposed no such reading. His comparisons of Hopi and what he called Standard Average European were geared to revealing underlying trains of thought that did not make sense to participants in cross-linguistic encounters because they did not share each other's presuppositions or experiences. Each language had to be treated respectfully in its own terms before adequate translation or comparison could take place. Whorf talked about "multilingual awareness" as the capacity linguists developed to think outside the categories of their natal language.

Critics of the so-called postmodernist anthropologists (for example, Clifford and Marcus 1986) fail to recognize the power of reflexivity and dialogue to provide reliability and validity to storied insights about language, land, culture, and identity. Ethnographic writing is more than an imaginative exercise without checks on the poetic instincts and political convictions of the observer as writer. The more transparent the role of the narrator or author, the clearer the capacity of the audience to judge for themselves the situated and partial truth of the stories. The purported subjectivity of narrative analysis is balanced in such a perspective by the ability of the research subject to speak back in response to the analysis. Collaboration in this sense has been growing at both individual and community levels over recent decades in the relationship between anthropology and linguistics on the one hand and First Nations [or Indigenous] Studies on the other.

Whorf's fellow Boas student Paul Radin (1927; see Darnell 2001) asserted that every society had its philosophers, people who liked to think about things. Anthropologists specialize in finding such philosophers and establishing conversations with them. These conversations have a tendency to lurch, in the metaphor of Clifford Geertz, from one astonishment to the next (1973, 23). It may take a whole book or article to explain a concept labeled by a single term in the language being experienced (e.g., "Kula" in the Trobriand Islands, "potlatch" or "hamatsa" on the Northwest Coast, "mana" in the Pacific, "shaman" from Siberia, or "karma" from Buddhist teachings). Once one has grasped the range of meaning and the context of application for such a term, it can be used with the clarity of its entailed meaning. Many such words have come into settler colonial languages and persist in contemporary use without speakers' awareness of their original contexts from elsewhere. The knowledge contained in a good etymological dictionary is not part of everyday language awareness.

Whatever the theoretical possibilities of effective cross-cultural communication, such truncated and awkwardly emergent constructions of meaning are not satisfying when they arise in everyday communication. My Cree friends tell me that they do not like to tell stories to most white people because it takes too long. What every self-respecting Nehiyaw (Cree person) knows by virtue of socialization has to be painstakingly explained. It ruins both the humor and the flow of a story. Widely across Indigenous North America, the aesthetic of Cree storytelling is minimalist; it invites elaboration and interpretation by the listener or reader in light of their own experience. An elder once told my late friend Keith Basso, who worked with the Western Apache in the American Southwest for more than half a century, that telling stories is like stringing a clothesline. The storyteller's job is to string the line (choose the story appropriate to the audience and context), hang the pegs (the characters and the events of the plot), and trust each hearer to hang their own clothes on the line. The listener is expected to go away and think about the story and how it applies to personal life experience as it emerges over time. Every learner should hear the same story differently at different times and continue to apply it differently to make sense of their experience.

The capacity to imagine, to respond to a story and its teller, perhaps with another story, is at the core of being human. Anthropologists, like literary scholars, share our stories in ways not different in kind from those shared with us by the people we come to know in other places and through other story lines. The links between land, language, community, and identity are intelligible everywhere. Stories reach across barriers of culture and history, memory and experience, with the potential to create new, shared stories.

Notes

1. An earlier form of this chapter appeared in J. Edward Chamberlin's *If This Is Your Land, Where Are Your Stories? Finding Common Ground* (Toronto: Knopf Canada, 2003). It is substantially expanded here and framed more widely to emphasize method and theory in the work discussed.

2. The term "First Nations" was ubiquitous at the time of this research, and its scope persists in names, programs, and self-identifications. In reference to my own work, I retain "First Nations" where it reflects the end point of my personal experience and thereby avoid overgeneralization. I substitute "Indigenous" when speaking in my own voice. This chapter pertains to specific North American traditions that recognize their geographical, sociopolitical, and ecological commonalities. I retain [*sic*] in such contexts.

3. Lowercase "native speakers" is conventional among linguists and distinguished from uppercase "Native peoples," also a potentially problematic term when all others are lumped as "non-Native." Alternatives are "first language," "natal language," and in some contexts "heritage language." The terms "Aboriginal" and "Indian" as in Indian Act persist in Canadian contexts because they are enshrined in legislation.

References

Alavarez, Albert, and Kenneth Hale. 1970. "Toward a Manual of Papago Grammar: Some Phonological Terms." *International Journal of American Linguistics* 36:83–97.

Boas, Franz. 1911. Introduction to the *Handbook of American Indian Languages: Vol. 1*. Washington DC: Smithsonian Institution.

———. 1922. Introduction to the *Handbook of American Indian Languages: Vol. 2*. Washington DC: Smithsonian Institution.

Briggs, Charles. 1986. *Learning How to Ask: A Sociolinguistic Appraisal of the Role of the Interview in Social Science Research.* Cambridge: Cambridge University Press.

Brody, Hugh. 2000. *The Other Side of Eden: Hunters, Farmers and the Shaping of the World.* Vancouver: Douglas and McIntyre.

Chamberlin, J. Edward. 2003. *If This Is Your Land, Where Are Your Stories? Finding Common Ground.* Toronto: Knopf Canada.

Clifford, James, and George Marcus, eds. 1986. *Writing Culture: The Poetics and Politics of Ethnography.* Berkeley: University of California Press.

Constitution Act. 1982. Schedule B to the Canada Act 1982 (UK), 1982, c. 11.

Darnell, Regna. 1998. "Rethinking Band and Tribe, Community and Nation: An Algonquian Model of Native North American Social Organization." In *Papers of the 29th Algonquian Conference,* 90–105. Winnipeg: University of Manitoba.

———. 2001. *Invisible Genealogies: A History of Americanist Anthropology.* Lincoln: University of Nebraska Press.

———. 2008. "First Nations Identity, Contemporary Interpretive Communities and Nomadic Legacies." *Arcadia* 43 (1): 102–13.

———. 2020. "Walking Alongside Wisahketchak: Fieldwork, a Retrospective Experience That Takes a Long Time." *Journal of Anthropological Research* 76:44–50.

Geertz, Clifford. 1973. *The Interpretation of Cultures.* New York: Basic.

Hockett, Charles F. 1960. "The Origins of Language." *Scientific American* 203:89–97.

Hymes, Dell H. 1974. *In Vain I Tried to Tell You.* Philadelphia: University of Pennsylvania Press.

James Bay and Northern Quebec Agreement. 1975. Grand Council of the Crees (of Quebec), Northern Quebec Inuit Association, Government of Quebec, James Bay Energy Corporation, James Bay Development Corporation, Quebec Hydro-Electric Commission, and the Government of Canada. November 11, 1975.

King, Thomas. 2003. *The Truth about Stories: A Native Narrative.* Toronto: House of Anansi.

Malinowski, Bronislaw. 1922. *Argonauts of the Western Pacific.* London: Routledge and Kegan Paul.

McLeod, Neal. 2007. *Cree Narrative Memory: From Treaties to Contemporary Times.* Saskatoon SK: Purich.

Mowat, Farley. 1975. *People of the Deer.* Toronto: McClelland & Stewart.

Radin, Paul. 1927. *Primitive Man as Philosopher.* New York: Dover.

Rorty, Richard. 1980. *Philosophy and the Mirror of Nature.* Princeton: Princeton University Press.

Royal Commission on Aboriginal Peoples. 1996. Report. Chairs René Dessault and Georges Erasmus. Ottawa: Queen's Printer.

Tedlock, Dennis, and Bruce Mannheim, eds. 1995. *The Dialogic Emergence of Culture.* Urbana: University of Illinois Press.

Vizenor, Gerald. 1994. *Manifest Manners: Narratives on Postindian Survivance.* Lincoln: University of Nebraska Press.

Whorf, Benjamin Lee. 1956. *Language, Thought and Reality: Selected Writings of Benjamin Lee Whorf,* edited by John B. Carroll. Cambridge MA: MIT Press.

5

....

"Keeping the Faith"

A Legacy of Native American Ethnography, Ethnohistory, and Psychology

This chapter was written to introduce a volume in honor of Raymond D. Fogelson.[1] Like the Native American elders with whom many contributors honor his work, Ray's nuggets of wisdom were often delivered cryptically, embedded in the discourse of the moment, frequently at a very late party at the annual meetings of the American Anthropological Association (AAA). When I was invited by a contingent of Ray's former students to contextualize his intellectual genealogy as a context for their own, I sought a metaphor that would draw us all into a single extended lineage. Unsurprisingly, I found that metaphor in Ray's own practice. When I tried out this metaphor on some of his former students, it became clear that I was not alone in treasuring accumulated hand-scrawled notes breezily signed "Gardez le Foi, Ray." Ray died in January of 2020, but the chapter continues to be otherwise apropos, and his legacy lives through our collective memories of him.

I found myself musing, not for the first time, "What are the tenets of this faith we are keeping together?" and "Who are the 'we' who are keeping them?" To guard an unspecified faith presumably involves standing alongside various equally unspecified others. Any attempt to overspecify the tenets of the faith would foreclose the open-ended possibilities for overlap and cross-fertilization that might bind us together in webs of mutual significance. The network of the potentially faithful is almost infinitely expandable in principle. That Ray chose this inclusive and nondyadic image for the ritualized closing of many personal letters is thoroughly consistent with his tenacious sociability, which has brought together and sustained many of us in this faith over the years. We have something in common: membership in a vital and ongoing tradition of research and scholarly civility—of which knowing Ray is more symptom than cause.

I reflect here on the Americanist heritage that Ray and I shared. The two of us were, in somewhat different senses, the last students of A. Irving "Pete" Hallowell—Ray at the University of Pennsylvania and me at Bryn Mawr, where Pete taught a seminar in the history of anthropology in 1964–65 after his mandatory retirement from Penn at the age of seventy. He wasn't old, and he didn't want to retire. We persuaded him that Bryn Mawr classes always met on the lawn in nice weather. This was more or less accurate, although as option rather than imperative. Reassured that no one would harass him if we were caught, he spearheaded our migration to the cloister. We brought him a chair, thinking it a courtesy. He was crushed at his exclusion and sat with us on the grass, cross-legged, bolt upright, for two hours without squirming while ten young women sprawled, wriggled, and fidgeted. Through his practice, I began to understand that Pete was a fieldworker and that the Ojibwe had taught him well. He could sit and listen respectfully, to students as well as to Indigenous consultants.

Ray received his PhD from Penn in 1962, three years before I began my graduate program there. I received my PhD seven years after his, having followed in his decisively planted footsteps. Although we never overlapped directly at Penn, many of our experiences of professional socialization did. Now and again, I heard the name Fogelson mentioned with the approval the elders show for a young man whom it is already clear will carry on the tradition, "keep the faith." Pete mentioned casually, leaving the possibility open-ended to my discretion, that I had to talk to this Fogelson character, that he knew a lot about several of the things I was interested in: history of anthropology, psychology and culture, and Indians, as they were then called, for example. None of these interests were bizarre in themselves, but the combination was sufficiently rare to forge friendships rapidly. Although Pete never made it explicit, I inferred in retrospect that he considered Ray a dynamic younger example of his own dictum that anthropologists studying their own history should apply the methods of their discipline (Hallowell 1965). That is, they should produce ethnographies from their own position in the professional tribe. It required no grand leap to use archival documents in addition to or even instead of field notes. After all, the ethnohistorians in our midst, among whom Ray was already prominent, had been doing so for a long time. This combination of methods, for me, remains the link between my own work in the history of anthropology and my praxis as an Americanist linguist, ethnohistorian, and symbolic anthropologist.

Although the larger faith is that of Americanist anthropology, with Franz Boas as its prophet, the University of Pennsylvania, like all major institutions that have trained substantial segments of the national profession, had its own unique, local, particularistic version of that tradition. Hallowell was prescient about the significance of such local intellectual genealogies:

> Anthropology at large has not yet developed an acute historical consciousness. As I see it, the history of anthropology in Philadelphia is only a small segment of a larger whole. I hope that I have said enough, however, to indicate that anthropological activities here, when viewed in historical perspective, have been an integral part of a wider flow of events elsewhere and have influenced them as well. Awareness of past events should lead to a more rational appraisal of contemporary aims and achievements, as well as a sounder evaluation of our future goals and the best means to achieve them. (Hallowell 1964:7)

Despite two decades of intervening scholarship, we still know too little about the institutional particularities of our major departments (Darnell 2002). Hallowell did his part, writing about his own career in Philadelphia anthropology as well as about the intellectual roots of what we now call anthropology. The latter articles were replete with footnotes and exhaustive in detail. His year-long seminar in history of anthropology did not emerge from the Middle Ages in Europe until after Christmas. Near the conclusion of his final lecture, Malinowski and Radcliffe-Brown were about to burst upon the scene. He did not attempt to integrate the dual modes of his history making.

Those few who choose to explore their own genealogies, whether professional or personal, usually emphasize origins and founders, dates and "epitomizing events" (Fogelson 1989) that condense actual historical context and process into forms that are easily grasped precisely because they are highly simplified symbolic constructs. I too have been guilty of stopping at this point. Historians of anthropology, however, ought to be prepared to extend our genealogies to situate ourselves in the larger discipline. Our innovative contributions do not arise full blown from a vacuum. Let us begin, then, by rendering visible the shared genealogy that grounds Ray Fogelson's work in Philadelphia Americanist continuities.

In the good rabbinical fashion from which much of our Americanist-Boasian standard for scholarship derives, let us review some relevant begettings. Franz Boas begot Frank Speck, who begot Hallowell. Together, Hallowell and Speck produced Anthony Wallace. Speck's death in 1950, the year of Wallace's PhD, left Hallowell and Wallace to beget Fogelson. In the latter two cases, the Americanist psychology and culture tradition was transmitted at the University of Pennsylvania through professional socialization by two generations of mentors working together to train their successors and future colleagues. This dual-generation pattern was an unintended consequence of hiring practices rather than a conscious ideology. Mid-career and senior scholars have the stature and local authority to insist on hiring someone they can talk to. This is one reason departments often choose to hire their own graduates. The expansion of American anthropology in the years after World War II encouraged this kind of generational collaboration and local specialization. At Penn, Hallowell began as the younger partner to such a line of pedagogical transmission and became its senior member in due course. This is how generational succession maintains institutional continuity. Ray was the last student at Penn in that mold and the natural successor to his teachers. But his career led him away from Philadelphia to pursue elsewhere the faith transmitted to him through Speck, Hallowell, and Wallace.

At Pennsylvania the result was a partial discontinuity. Hallowell's position was filled by Dell Hymes, a linguist whose work overlapped with that of Wallace and Ward Goodenough in ethnosemantics rather than in culture and psychology. Although he shared Hallowell's commitment to history of anthropology, Hymes came to it through a very different genealogy, grounded in overlaps with linguistics rather than psychology. By the time I arrived at Penn, Pete was already emeritus, although for me he remained both mentor and friend to the end of his life. I thought of him as my grandfather, not my uncle, as Ray suggested the kinship read for him. Eventually I became comfortable calling him Pete because he made it clear that anything else made him feel old.

Meanwhile, away from the home ranch, Ray returned from the University of Washington to the University of Chicago at the behest of Melford Spiro who was, not incidentally, a student of Hallowell as well as of another Boasian, Melville Herskovits, at nearby Northwestern. Spiro received his PhD in the same year as Wallace, recreating with Ray at Chicago the earlier Pennsylvania pattern of dual-generation mentors in psychology and culture. The tendrils of the Penn tradition were extended by way of this highly productive Chicago grafting. Or, to employ a more ethnographically grounded metaphor, the Penn tradition migrated or diffused to Chicago. Another Penn transplant was James VanStone, who also had worked with Speck and Hallowell. Based at the Field Museum in Chicago, VanStone shared Ray's interests in ethnohistory and world's fairs. He was just older enough than Ray to provide a link to Speck in the Penn version of the Boasian tradition.

That's about the time that I went job hunting at the AAA meetings in Seattle (where Ray introduced me to many of his friends) and just after George Stocking moved from Berkeley to Chicago by way of a semester at Penn—perfect timing to reinforce and legitimate my work in history of anthropology. This discontinuous genealogical line extended from Hallowell to Hymes. Hymes and Stocking were contemporaries and had been colleagues at Berkeley.

Although there is no necessary connection between an interest in psychology and culture, ethnohistory, history of anthropology, and ethnosemantics, my experience of them at Penn, and in Philadelphia anthropology more generally, was closely linked. Similar theoretical positions developed at Yale and Berkeley in the same period but without the intensely Americanist emphasis characteristic of the Philadelphia variant of ethnosemantics. The American Indian commitments and resources of the American Philosophical Society, going back to the society's founding by Thomas Jefferson and Benjamin Franklin, may well have influenced the university and its museum to sustain this ethnographic specialization when the discipline elsewhere was increasingly characterized by overseas ethnography.

To return to the Chicago transplant, when George Stocking arrived, Ray Fogelson's heritage from Hallowell predisposed him to reinforce Stocking's work in the history of anthropology. Ray and George already had a lot in common: George was a historian, whose formal training in anthropology consisted of two courses in anthropology with Hallowell as a Penn graduate student in American civilization. Their subjects—psychology and culture and the history of anthropology—constituted the poles of the genealogical transmission, this time factoring along disciplinary rather than institutional lines.

Since I was a student of Hallowell and Wallace but never of Fogelson, I have a certain hesitation in adding my own name to this genealogy. Instead, I emphasize direct continuity through Ray's students and former students at Chicago. My own adventures in Canada form an interrelated grafting that also shares a link to Hallowell. When I told Pete I was going to Edmonton in 1969, he reported learning to ride a horse there in 1925. After a pause, he observed "it's cold up there." This was as close as I got to instruction in how to undertake fieldwork. Nonetheless, the fieldwork was reasonably successful, and the grafting was reinforced in my own scholarship despite the quite different direction taken by the anthropology program at the University of Alberta. I do not attempt to trace the ultimate origins of these genealogies. Post-Boasian Americanists acknowledge that origins are ultimately unrecoverable. In this case, they recede into a disciplinary prehistory of German idealism that Boas brought to North America (see Stocking 1996). When Frank Speck came to Penn in 1907, George Byron Gordon, the new director of the museum, was scrambling to revive the abortive academic anthropology nominally associated with the honorary professorship of Daniel Garrison Brinton, who died in 1898 and was not replaced. Having completed his MA with Boas at Columbia, Speck moved to Penn to take up a prestigious Harrison Fellowship. Although he received his PhD from Penn, he continued to maintain close ties to New York anthropology. Speck vacated the Harrison Fellowship just in time for it to be taken up by Edward Sapir in 1908 (Darnell 1970, 1988, 1990). In retrospect, such serendipities seem virtually inevitable because the outcome is known to the contemporary observer. For those living in the moment, however, uncertainties abounded.

Speck and Sapir formed the two poles of the anthropology Hallowell acquired at Penn. They were peers in a founding generation that had divided up the wide-ranging interests of Franz Boas. In conversation with Ray Fogelson (reported in Fogelson 1976a), Hallowell recalled: "Boas had said the last word. What one strove for was to follow Boas in his ubiquitous interests." None of the students fully attained the scope of their teacher, but Speck and Sapir between them encompassed the ethnographic approaches of Boasian anthropology. Speck was immersed in the point of view of the northeastern Algonquian and Iroquoian hunters and gatherers and was particularly intrigued by their theories and practices regarding what his own society classified as ecology and natural history. Sapir was more interested in symbolic culture, with an emphasis on language and the verbal articulation of culture in texts from native speakers of Native languages (Darnell 2001).

Speck and Sapir were also mirror images in personality, completing and balancing one another. Sapir's review of Carl Jung's *Psychological Types* in 1923 lyrically articulated his lifelong sense of alienation from North American mainstream culture; Speck anchored him in that normalcy. Although Sapir left Penn in 1910 to organize Canadian anthropological work along Boasian lines, his two years at the University of Pennsylvania were formative for Hallowell's anthropology, particularly insofar as both men later turned to culture and personality. The movement from Sapir's locus of culture in the individual to Wallace's mazeway within an "organization of diversity" model of cultural transmission is fundamentally continuous, despite its mediation through Speck with a consequent loss of Sapir's focus on language as the methodological entrée to the point of view of the individual.

Tony Wallace was Speck's last student and one source leading him to embrace a commitment to northeastern ethnography. Wallace was the son of historian Paul Wallace, whose biography of Conrad Weiser remains a classic for anthropologists working in the Northeast. The position of both Wallaces is consistent with

Boasian insistence that anthropology ought to move between the explanatory poles of history and psychology, with the former a necessary prelude to the latter (Darnell 2001). Speck's specialization in both Iroquoian and Algonquian cultures fell on fertile ground with Wallace. He also inherited a Boasian commitment to exploring the native point of view. Wallace's 1950 dissertation on modal personality and the persistence of Indigenous worldview among the contemporary Tuscarora built on this foundation. He demonstrated that history and psychology are inseparably linked in particular cases and, in the process, operationalized Sapir's notions of intracultural variability. His biography of the Delaware chief Teedyscung, based on his MA thesis, applied an equally Sapirian life-history method.

Speck wasn't around by the time Ray arrived at Penn, but his influence persisted indirectly, mediated by the continued reliance of both Hallowell and Wallace on his place in their genealogies. Fogelson became a specialist in Iroquoian but focused primarily on the Southeast, again following precedents in Speck's work, writing his MA on the role of the conjurer among the Eastern Cherokee and his PhD on the Cherokee ball game. His fieldwork with both the Eastern Cherokee and the Oklahoma Cherokee bands was augmented by extensive archival work for both Cherokee communities. Ethnohistory and multisite fieldwork formed a continuum.

Fogelson developed the ethnohistoric tradition along a range of theoretical dimensions in combination with contemporary consultants. History was not linear, static, or merely antiquarian. The past became meaningful alongside its ongoing resonances in the present; "the sunny chunks of memory culture" refused to stay in separate temporal compartments (Fogelson and Kutsche 1961:109). Fogelson's early interest in magic, medicine, sorcery, and witchcraft (1961, 1975) led to consideration of how traditional materials were incorporated into contemporary religious practices. The Keetowah Society, which originated to protest long-defunct land allotment policies, persists today as "traditional religion," reworked by the Cherokee in line with their pragmatic worldview (Fogelson 1977:189). It is a revitalization movement without the rhetoric of revolution that Wallace's typology of revitalization movements predicted. Links between gender and politics emerged from Fogelson's discussion of eighteenth-century Cherokee women and their "petticoat government" (Fogelson 1990).

Fogelson's early efforts to locate the Cherokee in relation to northern branches of the far-flung Iroquoian language family remain standards for theoretically sophisticated ethnohistory. For example, he documented that the Cherokee booger mask tradition (Fogelson and Bell 1983:54) involved features of form, function, and meaning similar to those attested among the five nations of the Iroquois Confederacy (for example, begging, disease connection, speaking in whispers or exotic languages, the carrying of weapons, facial expressions, and, among old people, walking with bent gait or using canes). A genetic relationship among the masking complexes emerges despite major surface differences.

This symbolic-interpretive work has been significant for Iroquoian studies. William Fenton's monumental synthesis on Iroquois masks frequently cites Fogelson's proposed interpretations (Fenton 1987:463, 488, 507). "Fogelson reminds us," Fenton writes, of patterns that "no Iroquois has ever suggested . . . as an explanation, to the author's knowledge." Fenton was an empiricist who stuck close to his evidence. Some of Ray's connections involve "a speculative leap," although they are grounded in ethnohistorically attested practices. This is "a deep level of analysis" of the meaning of symbols that brings "startling results." Fogelson's more theoretical work creates a symbolic anthropology grounded in ethnohistoric and ethnological detail, giving it a verisimilitude that neither theory nor descriptive data alone can begin to match. Fenton was a mentor for Ray's ethnographic work and encouraged theoretical open-endedness even though his own inclinations remained closer to the analytic perspective of his Iroquois consultants.

"The native point of view" is crucial to Fogelson's version of the Americanist tradition. His presidential address to the American Society for Ethnohistory explored the implications of the prefix "ethno" when applied to any semantic domain insofar as it is understood in terms intelligible to members of the originating culture. An ethnohistory that met this standard would have to be called "ethno-ethnohistory" (Fogelson 1989). He generalized the argument building on earlier parallel constructions. Cherokee disease beliefs involved an "ethnospecificity" that cannot be generalized easily across cultures (1961:221). Fogelson called for an "ethnopersonality theory" (1975:127) and for an "ethnopsychology which involves working through native languages to gain insights into world view and knowledge of the localized behavioral environment" (1985:5). This latter language directly evokes Hallowell. Fogelson suggests that "the American Indian psyche" can be understood through Western eyes but should also be approached in terms of the psychological ideas of various American Indian groups (l985:4).

The native point of view is significant in its own right, but its insight is enhanced when privileged alongside that of anthropological science. Fogelson speculates that prophecy is the appropriate genre for Indigenous history and that its continuous adaptation permits contemporary survival (1985:23). Such survival is rooted in the stabilities of Native American cultures in "the internal strengths of Indian societies as expressed through the idiom of kinship, in the abiding sense of community, in the adaptive significance of what we derogatively view as factionalism, and in the political and legal effectiveness of native advocates" (1989:139).

A "highly developed level of historical consciousness" (Fogelson 1989:139) functions as a survival mechanism. Moreover, having attempted to understand the native point of view, the ethnohistorian must also acknowledge that their work is grounded in "bi- or multicultural frames of reference" where points of view must be juxtaposed and balanced (1989:141). The Native American tribes studied by ethnohistorians do not exist in isolation from contact and adaptation; their cultures cannot be studied without acknowledging the complex borrowings and merging of shared history by groups in contact.

Some of the members of this Philadelphia-based anthropological extended family have reflected on their articulations with these genealogies. My evidence is who cites whom and how ideas and problems are related in terms specific to the Penn tradition. When I reread Tony Wallace's *Culture and Personality* (1962) in preparing this essay, I was struck by how often he cited (albeit sometimes only implicitly) people who also were part of my own professional socialization. Ward Goodenough, Loren Eiseley, Carleton Coon (albeit before my time), John Alden Mason (whom I met through

Hallowell), John Witthoft, and Dell Hymes were all Wallace's colleagues at Penn that he used as sounding boards for his own ideas and cited as authorities to substantiate his arguments.[2]

The Penn version of "culture and psychology" (Wallace's preferred term) was clearly distinguishable from what Ruth Benedict and Margaret Mead called "culture and personality." The latter focused on how socialization produced differences in national character (Mead) and holistic cultural pattern (Benedict). Both grounded their work in Americanist anthropology, assuming that culture rather than biology would explain variations in human personality. Their contacts with psychologists were particularly with John Dollard, Karen Horney, and Erik Erikson, neo-Freudians who modified Freudian psychoanalysis in terms of cultural context (cf. Darnell 1990). With a somewhat different twist, this is the crux of the challenge posed to Mead's work by the late Australian sociobiologist Derek Freeman, who charged inaccurately that all Boasians ignored the biological basis of cultural diversity and similarity.

Hallowell was more interested in the psychoanalytic basis of psychology and culture, which, he asserted in retrospect, "had nothing to do . . . with personality studies as they later developed" (Hallowell 1967:4). Both Hallowell and Wallace explored the relationship of mind and body in the context of human and primate evolution and applied physical anthropological expertise not available when Sigmund Freud and his colleagues wrote. Hallowell identified Sapir as the model for his early involvement with psychoanalysis (Hallowell 1972:8). The decline in popularity of culture and personality in the "narrow sense" did not bother him because his own view of "psychological anthropology" had always been broader (Hallowell 1967:8).

For both Hallowell and Wallace, a broadly defined psychology and culture involved the relationship of mind and body in the context of human evolution. Fogelson contextualizes Hallowell's concern with "the behavioral environment of the self" as a way of reconciling Darwin and Freud. The link between social evolution and ecology came by way of Speck (Fogelson 1976b:xii). Interestingly, Wallace's use of the term "ethnoecology" follows Fogelson's lead in his combination of other "ethno" terms (probably without being aware of the influence) (xiii). "The native point of view" was a piece of the Boasian program that was particularly emphasized at Penn. Hallowell (1964:5) believed that "Speck's self-involvement with the study [of] a people and their problems was perhaps greater than that of other anthropologists of the period. . . . And I imitated my mentor for a long while. I too identified myself with the Indians, and tried to avoid serving on university committees." (Others will have to report whether the latter also characterized Wallace or Fogelson). The identification was not entirely positive. In retrospect, Hallowell believed it had prevented him from recognizing the complexity of Indian[sic]-white relations and the continuing multicultural character of contemporary cross-cultural interactions.

The native point of view never fully replaced that of the analyst. Hallowell's early work with the St. Francis Abenaki documented changes in the kinship system "unknown to the Indians themselves" (Hallowell 1964:6). He saw no contradiction between this analytic standpoint and his concurrent efforts to seek out and report the theorizing of social life as formulated by his consultants. For example, when he asked hesitantly if people ever married their cross-cousins, Chief William Berens replied: "Who the hell else would they marry?" (8). The expletive highlighted both the absurdity of the anthropologist's question in local terms and the unmistakable conviction of the consultant that they understand their own culture.

The perception of the individual actor surfaces repeatedly in Hallowell's ethnography, as Wallace noted (Fogelson 1976a:159). Spiro (in Fogelson 1976a:3, 53) described this as the phenomenology of the self as understood by the actor. Spiro also emphasized (3, 5) that ethnography was not studied solely for its own sake but for the light it could shed on social behavior. This fits my sense of what ethnoscience was about in the late 1960s at Penn better than criticisms from other quarters that it was mere description with no possibility of closure or generalization. It is also consistent with the emphasis on the need for anthropology to be a science in Hallowell's introduction to Wallace's *Culture and Personality*. Culture cannot be explained in terms of itself. Only the move to another level of structure, in this case the psychological, has the potential to lead from description to explanation.

Hallowell's fascination with Ojibwe ontology, that is, with things that are believed by the Ojibwe to exist in the world, also reflected his interest in folk science and Western science. In line with the relativistic turn that began in the mid-1980s, however, I then preferred to speak of his ethnography as setting a standard for cross-cultural epistemology.[3] Hallowell's later work (brought together in Fogelson 1976a) evinces a similar intertextuality. Section introductions by specialists in diverse areas of Hallowell's expertise both document the scope of his interests and add evaluative reflexivity that reinforces the unity of the continuous and continuing genealogy traced in this chapter. These essays include Wallace on cognition and culture, Washburn on transculturation, Spiro on phenomenology, and Fred Eggan on social structure and what Hallowell called "the behavioral environment of the self."

This exploration of Ray Fogelson's professional roots in the Penn tradition raises as many questions as it answers. To date, the history of anthropology has produced few examinations of the intellectual, institutional, and social interactional networks of individual scholars. Conference sessions and thematic volumes honoring particular scholars come closest to facilitating such historicist reflexivity. Yet, the identification of our own individual and collective genealogies is an important part of what we do both as practicing anthropologists and as historians of our discipline. I take pride in acknowledging ancestors and relations among my contemporaries and descendants, treasuring the situated continuities emanating from our overlapping experiences. Although the Americanist tradition has not produced a "school" in any rigid sense, it has produced an inclusive open-ended group of scholars who talk productively to one another, to the considerable enhancement of the discipline (Valentine and Darnell 1999). Ray Fogelson is among the scholars standing at multiple crossing points in such genealogies and thus holds a position of considerable ongoing and wide-ranging influence.

Ray might have been the last of the latter-day Boasians who seemed to know everything. Few of us still aspire to talk intelligently across the subdisciplines, and even fewer read the specialized literature with any enthusiasm or consistency. Ray prided himself on being the last book review editor of the *American Anthropologist* to deal with all four subdisciplines. It was hard to find a topic he didn't know a lot about. Usually he had read something about whatever it was very recently. And then there were the piles of books on his coffee table, desk, and every other visible surface. It was more fun than a good bookstore because every item was selected by Ray's wonderful quirky intelligence. I could entertain myself browsing in those stacks indefinitely. Anthropology isn't supposed to be narrow, and Ray reminded us that it is not.

Ray was a teacher who didn't need hierarchy or formality to maintain his authority. He was so approachable and unpretentious that some people, more fools they, have been known to underestimate him. I have known many of Ray's students over the years—for the simple reason that he has always introduced me to them and made sure they were at conferences to meet people like me. None of his students ever failed to acknowledge his breadth of intellect, his wealth of knowledge, or his careful attention to students and colleagues as whole persons whose professional socialization surpasses library, classroom, and keyboard or foolscap (the last option gestures to respect for Ray's conscientious resistance to technological interference with the life of the mind).

Pete's students, and Ray's, and some of mine, continue to transmit the legacy, keeping the faith in a continuously emergent and revitalized set of interpretive practices and ethnographic engagements. Our collaborations have led us to redefine, through Ray's career and my own, the kinds of values toward our scholarship and our colleagues including students and Indigenous consultants, often and increasingly the same people that we take with us in our fieldwork. Otherwise, our research subjects will tell us to go back where we came from. In Ray's words:

> As Indian sovereignty has been re-affirmed, as movements for self-determination have gained momentum, and as formerly mute Indian voices become more strident, native confrontations with anthropology and anthropologists become inevitable. For many, these developments herald the death of the Americanist tradition. . . . If there is to be a resurrection of Americanist studies, and I think there will be, anthropologists will have to become wards to the people they study. They will have to pledge allegiances to new nationalisms. They will have to face the challenges of transmitting and translating the past and continuing results of Americanist research to new audiences in new contexts. (Fogelson 1999:82–83)[4]

This, I believe, is a powerful commentary statement of the legacy we share, of the faith we continue to keep with Ray Fogelson.

Notes

1. Originally published as "Keeping the Faith: A Legacy of Native American Ethnography, Ethnohistory and Psychology," in *New Perspectives on Native North America: Cultures, Histories, Representations*, ed. Sergei Kan and Pauline Turner Strong, 1–13 (Lincoln: University of Nebraska Press, 2006).

2. Hallowell declined to criticize the inherent racism of Carleton Coon's position that was already recognized by then. I chose not to discuss this with him.

3. I wonder now if Pete would have been interested in talking about epistemology and situated knowledge or if the ontological claim made by the Ojibwe would have seemed to him quite a different matter. There is no reason to expect the Ojibwe to accept alternative epistemologies as equally valid that are patronizing to those for whom they represent ontological truth. I have changed my mind alongside the shifting anthropological climate and now recognize Pete's prescience in a point made well before its time though not on grounds of this distinction.

4. The language in this quotation is outdated but was correct and respectful at the time it was written. This chapter also uses "Native American," "native language," "Indian," and "Indian sovereignty" in ways that would be phrased differently today.

References

Darnell, Regna. 1970. "The Emergence of Academic Anthropology at the University of Pennsylvania." *Journal of the History of the Behavioral Sciences* 6:80–92 (reprinted in Darnell 2021).

———. 1988. *Daniel Garrison Brinton: The 'Fearless Critic' of Philadelphia*. University of Pennsylvania Publications in Anthropology, no. 3. Philadelphia: Department of Anthropology, University of Pennsylvania.

———. 1990. *Edward Sapir: Linguist, Anthropologist, Humanist*. Berkeley: University of California Press.

———. 2001. *Invisible Genealogies: A History of Americanist Anthropology*. Lincoln: University of Nebraska Press.

———. 2002. "Departmental Networks and the Cohesion of American Anthropology." Centennial Address, American Anthropological Association, Washington DC.

———. 2021. *The History of Anthropology: A Critical Window on the Discipline in North America*. Critical Studies in the History of Anthropology. Lincoln: University of Nebraska Press.

Fenton, William. 1987. *The False Faces of the Iroquois*. Norman: University of Oklahoma Press.

Fogelson, Raymond D. 1961. "Change, Persistence, and Accommodation in Cherokee Medico-Magical Beliefs." In *Symposium on Cherokee and Iroquois*, edited by William Fenton and John Gulick, 213–25. Bureau of American Ethnology Bulletin 180. Washington DC: Government Printing Office.

———. 1975. "Analysis of Cherokee Sorcery and Witchcraft." In *Four Centuries of Southern Indians*, edited by Charles Hudson, 113–31. Athens: University of Georgia Press.

———, ed. 1976a. *Contributions to Anthropology: Selected Papers of A. Irving Hallowell.* Chicago: University of Chicago Press.

———. 1976b. General Introduction. In *Contributions to Anthropology: Selected Papers of A. Irving Hallowell*, edited by Raymond D. Fogelson, ix–xvii. Chicago: University of Chicago Press.

———. 1977. "Cherokee Notions of Power." In *The Anthropology of Power*, edited by Raymond D. Fogelson and Richard M. Adams, 185–94. New York: Academic Press.

———. 1985. "Interpretations of the American Indian Psyche." In *Social Contexts of American Ethnology, 1940–1984*, edited by June Helm, 4–27. 1984 Proceedings of the American Ethnological Society. Washington DC: American Anthropological Association.

———. 1989. "The Ethnohistory of Events and Non-Events." *Ethnohistory* 36:133–47.

———. 1990. "On the 'Petticoat Government' of the Eighteenth-Century Cherokee." In *Personality and the Cultural Construction of Society*, edited by K. Jordan and M. J. Swartz, 161–81. Tuscaloosa: University of Alabama Press.

———. 1999. "Nationalism and the Americanist Tradition." In *Theorizing the Americanist Tradition*, edited by Lisa Philips Valentine and Regna Darnell, 75–83. Toronto: University of Toronto Press.

Fogelson, Raymond D., and Amanda Bell. 1983. "Cherokee Booger Mask Tradition." In *The Power of Symbols*, edited by N. R. Crumrine and Marjorie Halpern, 48–69. Vancouver: University of British Columbia Press.

Fogelson, Raymond D., and R. J. Kutsche. 1961. "Cherokee Economic Cooperatives: The Gadugi." In *Symposium on Cherokee and Iroquois Culture*, edited by William Fenton and John Gulick, 83–123. Smithsonian Institution Bureau of American Ethnology Bulletin 180. Washington DC: Government Printing Office.

Hallowell, A. Irving. 1964. "Anthropology at the University of Pennsylvania." *Proceedings of the Philadelphia Anthropological Society*: 3–7.

———. 1965. "The History of Anthropology as an Anthropological Problem." *Journal of the History of the Behavioral Sciences* 1:24–38.

Jung, Carl Gustav. 1923. *Psychological Types.* New York: Harcourt, Brace.

Stocking, George W., Jr., ed. 1996. *Volksgeist as Method and Ethic.* Madison: University of Wisconsin Press.

Valentine, Lisa Philips, and Regna Darnell, eds. 1999. *Theorizing the Americanist Tradition.* Toronto: University of Toronto Press.

Wallace, Anthony F. C. 1962. *Culture and Personality.* New York: Random House.

6

....

Anthropological Approaches to Human Nature, Cultural Relativism, and Ethnocentrism

This chapter revisits what may seem to many to be an old-fashioned kind of anthropology, one grounded in but not identical with the Americanist tradition that grew up around Franz Boas and his first generation of students in the early decades of the twentieth century (Darnell 2001).[1] It is a commentary rather than a research paper in the traditional sense and reflects my long-term interest in what makes an anthropologist and how some aspects of professional identity have maintained continuity over time. My tracing of this genealogy is necessarily personal, since my own amalgam of linguistic and cultural anthropology with history of anthropology has emerged from my experience in ways that will not apply in precise details to anyone else's.

The critical research strategies of Boas's resolutely anti-evolutionist paradigm ranted against premature generalization and built a cross-cultural comparative database over his six-decade career.[2] Postwar positivism in North America has obscured the theoretical coherence of this paradigm to a point where heroic historicist efforts are now necessary to restore its meaning. Such a reassessment is well underway. I have chosen exemplars for this coalescence of revitalized Americanist perspectives who are not conventionally understood to share a single intellectual project. Many are not anthropologists in the narrow sense of disciplinary training or employment. Most have moments of thinking like an anthropologist and of addressing issues on which anthropologists have long been recognized as experts within the humanities and social sciences.

The strand of Boasian thought that intrigues me most is not the mainstream of this tradition in its heyday, or at least not as that mainstream is often caricatured. Rather, I propose to confront similar trajectories toward simple answers that still cry out for resistance from ethnographers and theorists alike. The question of human nature has been foreshortened in the social sciences and humanities, with a consequent lack of nuanced attention to the culturally specific. Ethnography, particularly in cultural studies, has been dismissed as mere detail rather than as real-world verisimilitude that documents the plasticity of human nature. Anthropologists, more than other social scientists, deploy their ethnographic skills to characterize human nature as simultaneously diverse and uniform. The distinctive identity of the human resides in personal and cultural agency (what Edward Sapir called "the impact of culture on personality") and on the species-wide capacity for reflexivity. I believe that our discipline urgently needs, at present, to move in tandem between theory and ethnography, between the universal and the culture-specific, the biological and the cultural. We are uniquely poised to avoid the broader culture's predilection toward renewed speculative and premature generalization based on rigid dichotomization of what are, in the real world, continuous phenomena with overlaps and ambiguities.

One significant fracture line in contemporary anthropology revolves around the binary causality attributed by many to culture and biology, with the apparent corollary that anthropologists must choose between the two traditional ends of this continuum. Dan Segal and Sylvia Yanagisako (2004) argue that the North American discipline should jettison its long-established commitment to the multiple perspectives of the four traditional subdisciplines. Their exhortation to "unwrap the sacred bundle" implies that American anthropologists have accepted the inevitability of the traditional quadratic structure passively and unreflexively. They present no evidence for the purported mental state of their colleagues.

Segal envisions the American Anthropological Association (AAA) umbrella of professional identity and socialization devolving to the presumably incommensurable specialized positions of the association's thirty-four constituent sections (though more have been added since).[3] Yanagisako apparently takes pride in having presided over the dismantling of the Stanford University Department of Anthropology into two bitterly opposed camps, roughly divided around the oppositions of culture versus biology and cultural analysis versus science (Segal and Yanagisako 2004). More recently, the Stanford program has been reunited, if not fully reintegrated.

My own position is that if the scientists and the humanists within our discipline decline to communicate with one another, we have ceded the science of anthropology's strongest claim to provide a unique critical edge on getting at the essence of human nature and identity. Neither perspective in isolation is complete or autonomous. Anthropology is not, of course, the only social science discipline to have struggled with such internal diversities of method and interpretation. The polarization between experimental and social psychology, human and physical geography, or clinical practice and experimental medicine, for example, is long-standing. Anthropology alone has insisted—until quite recently and even now only in limited quarters—that the two approaches are conceptually inseparable. In my view, Robert Borofsky (2002) sets such a high standard of evidence for meaningful collaboration across the subdisciplines that he fails to capture the more generalized professional ethos of awareness that the specialized problems of culture and human nature attacked by particular anthropologists do not, or at least should not, exist in a vacuum.

This position has seemed obvious to me since my first encounters with anthropology. In a long-ago undergraduate theory course, the Boas-trained instructor threw out two alternative approaches to the question of human nature: psycho-biological universals or comparative ethnography. Most students found the former more titillating, but in retrospect I acknowledge that we have gotten further with the latter. Universals have proved elusive, given the need to satisfy the standards of our ethnographic methods and predilections. Over the past four decades, many have overemphasized the universals, or at least assumed they could be formulated directly, unmediated by surface diversities. I explore some of these arguments in anthropology and related disciplines and hypothesize that they constitute instances of premature generalization, much like the ones that concerned Boas in his critique of the paradigm of classical evolution. Today's universalists ask, for the most part, the right questions about human nature and identity, but the answers may well prove to be more complex.

Linguistic Theory and Universals

Since my own career began in linguistic anthropology, I begin by exploring the (usually ethnographically uninformed) obsession of contemporary linguistic theory with universals. For most of my professional career, the science of language has abrogated responsibility for the description and explanation of the real languages around whose study it crystallized as a professional discipline. Noam Chomsky focused on Saussurean "Langue," "the competence" of "the ideal speaker-hearer in a perfectly homogeneous speech community" and cavalierly dismissed as "mere performance" the real speech on which analyses of unwritten languages have traditionally been based (Chomsky 1965:1). Chomsky argued that any linguistic feature turning out not to be universal is thereby excluded from the universal grammar he aspires to formulate. Such a theory is nonfalsifiable, since counterexamples can be rejected as mere "butterfly collecting," to adopt his favorite metaphor. This rather crude position changed little after the 1960s. In 1987 Chomsky asserted that the study of language is not actually about languages in the plural at all. Rather, it explores the human capacity for language, understood to be replicated everywhere with trivial variations that are uninteresting to theory as he conceives it. The equally unfalsifiable corollary is that since most theoretical linguists speak English, English will serve as well as any other language or languages as a metalanguage for the statement of linguistic universals. Linguists who continue to work on real languages, alongside their speakers, are reduced to apologizing for the particularity of their work; many have acceded to its categorization as nontheoretical. Sadly, this has been the price of a place at the edges of the mainstream. Cognitive science, for all its breakthroughs in framing language alongside other modes of human neurological and cultural-communicative complexity, has, I believe, prematurely adopted the overvaluation implicit in the Chomskian universalist baggage.

From an anthropological standpoint, we urgently need the ethnographic verisimilitude provided by examining how speakers of particular languages accomplish social order. Polish-born linguist Anna Wierzbicka, long-based in Australia, offers an elegant methodological contrast to the Chomskian approach through her meticulous attention to the content and context in which particular languages (usually Polish, English, and various Australian Aboriginal[4] languages that are still spoken) have developed their characteristic features (Wierzbicka 1972). Wierzbicka calls her putative universals "semantic primitives." These basic conceptual categories are defined at the lexical rather than at the grammatical level. Universal concepts are combined in language-specific ways, facilitating translation by paraphrase into a metalanguage of underlying componential forms. Thus, for example, seeing is a universal capacity or concept, whereas color is one form it takes in many, perhaps even most, human societies. Particular colors identified in the lexicon vary with culture and language (Wierzbicka 1972). Ethnoscience in 1960s anthropology developed a parallel ethnosemantic logic, albeit largely independently based on the componential study of kinship.

Giles Deleuze and Felix Guattari's equally elegant critique of contemporary linguistics concurs that we (philosophers, linguists, and, by extension, anthropologists) ought to be working from the languages and their speakers to the universal theory rather than the other way around. They privilege pragmatics, which they define as "a politics of language." In Deleuze and Guattari's terms, Chomsky is a theorist of the arbor; his model is abstract and linear, excluding what it cannot incorporate tidily. Their own contrasting "rhizomatic" standpoint emphasizes the mutual entailment of language and its social field. They aspire "to make Chomsky's trees bud and to shatter linear order" through such an applied pragmatics (Deleuze and Guattari 1987:157). They differ from the cognitive scientists in considering the human mind more like a grass than a tree, in another favorite metaphor.

Social scientists are not immune to classificatory aspirations for grand generalization. As a long-ago student of Erving Goffman, I was constantly frustrated by the disarticulation between his elegant holistic approach to communicative behavior, moving beyond language to interaction, and the facile assumption that his interactionist framework applied universally. Therefore, he did not consider it necessary to distinguish his metalanguage from everyday language. Concepts such as tie-signs, stigma, impression management, or the presentation of self in everyday life manifest themselves in diverse forms that Goffman himself failed to explore across cultural borders. Although his arguments doubtless contained a modicum of the devil's advocate, a position he often adopted with glee, Goffman appeared to hold a genuine belief that ethnographers of speaking could never learn about other societies the kinds of things he thought he already knew intuitively about his own by virtue of childhood socialization. The complexity of his own society, moreover, was unproblematized across research projects that subjected mental patients, homosexuals, compulsive gamblers, and Shetland Islanders to the vagaries of his personal member-of-culture intuitions (Goffman 1967). Goffman's unparalleled ethnographic intuition remained strangely unreflexive, lacking the defamiliarization provided by anthropological fieldwork. The method of introspection, especially in its reflexive guises, provides important insight. Contemporary understandings of reflexivity acknowledge its partiality, the status of any single introspection as one among many possible standpoints that can be evaluated relative to one another. Goffman's definition of sociology as a science (Goffman 1981) never acknowledged the contingent character of his own position—for example, that being born Canadian affected his standpoint. Gaile McGregor (1985) argues persuasively that his lurking cynicism about human relations fraught with danger injects a peculiarly Canadian mindset into his version of Chicago sociology. The kind of reflexivity entailed by the work of ethnography seems to me infinitely more interesting than taking intuition in isolation at face value. Goffman died suddenly in 1982, so we cannot know if he would have changed his mind.

Members of culture often respond to our discovering of the shared patterning underlying surface incommensurability with a hearty "so what?" to the explicit formulation of that which every civilized person always already knows. Nonetheless, once one establishes that there is more than one way to do anything, the search is on for a level of generalization that facilitates meaningful comparison. Intracultural variability provides one such level. Anthony F. C. Wallace, for example, contrasts the overfacile attribution of homogeneity to all members of a culture, reproducing itself by "replication of uniformity," to the "organization of diversity" in which the actions of the members of a culture complement one another without necessarily acknowledging their differences (1962). In such a model, the organization or attainment of social order precludes premature glossing over of functional complexity.

At another level of generalization, structuralism as formulated by developmental psychologist Jean Piaget (1970) recognizes patterns as significant only when they occur across structural levels, for example, from physics to chemistry to biology, or from species capacity to cultural pattern to individual action. Within levels of structure, he considers information to be merely descriptive rather than explanatory or theoretical. Chomsky's (1957) distinction between descriptive and explanatory adequacy adopts a similar logic.

Sometimes the anthropologist responds to theory generated from a culture-specific, Western, or logocentric standpoint by rendering it cross-cultural, by applying the generalization to alternative data, without necessarily critiquing the limitations of premature generalization inherent in the project; the source is merely the primary data. Theoretical linguistics made much of language philosopher H. Paul Grice's (1963) universal maxims for linguistic interaction, the pragmatics as opposed to the grammar of speaking. Significantly for ethnographers, Grice formulates a "cooperative principle" that entails interaction and collusion to create effective communication. Despite their generalized formulation, however, the specific maxims are not universal in application; ethnographers have found no such magic formula. To illustrate, I present Grice's maxims and contrast them with some First Nations and Native American versions of the need for more nuanced and culture-specific formulations:

> 1. The Maxim of Quantity: speakers must provide as much information as required but no more than this.

> First Nations/Native American speakers assume that background information is shared. Thus, the interpretive task of the unprepared listener may be insurmountable. In every culture, private behavior among known persons shares this property of eliding what is already known. Most North American Indigenous peoples elaborate this maxim as an aesthetic prin-

ciple underlying valued speech. Minimalism reigns, even at the cost of effective information transfer.

2. The Maxim of Quality: speakers must not present statements they believe to be false or for which they lack adequate evidence.

First Nations speakers are much more concerned than mainstream Canadians to know where information comes from so they can judge how reliable it is. This preoccupation arises naturally when important cultural knowledge is transmitted through oral tradition.

3. The Maxim of Manner: speakers should avoid obscurity and ambiguity, be brief and orderly.

Anyone who has ever heard a First Nations elder in pedagogical mode will need no elaboration of the challenges to expectation of interpretive universality. Relevance is in the ear and mind of the listener. Judgment of relevance is deferred and often is not understood fully at the time of speaking.

4. The Maxim of Relation: Grice takes for granted that conversations have beginnings, middles, and ends, and that they respond to the transitory and immediate needs of interlocutors.

In First Nations communities, conversations ideally evolve across occasions, relationships, and lifetimes. The speech event is not bounded in time or space.

My somewhat belabored point is that ethnographers cannot just plug in Grice's maxims or Goffman's interactional frames as purported universals. They are useful insofar as we ought to be searching for things like them, but the universality of their detailed realizations cannot be taken for granted. The level at which the maxims are general or universal remains an empirical or ethnographic question. Functional universals such as Grice's cooperative principle have proven more robust than substantive ones.

Ethnographic Standpoints

Whether we begin inductively or deductively, the challenge is how to move between the external analysis and what Boas called the native point of view, from the etic to the emic. What Edward Sapir ([1933] 1949) labeled "the psychological reality of the phoneme" applies beyond meaningful units of sound to meaning within culture more generally. Sapir (1916) was also the Boasian anthropologist who formulated more abstract ways of getting at "time perspective" in American aboriginal culture. But he never got both trains of thought into the same argument. This is the characteristic Boasian toggle between science and history (Darnell 2001), between universal human nature and the impact of culture on human social identity. One involves individual agency, intracultural variability, and member awareness, whereas the other privileges analytic distance and aspires to objectivity.

Claude Lévi-Strauss (1964) evokes vast vistas of myth diffusion, adaptation, and reintegration patterned in ways that could not possibly be formulated by the member of culture situated at a single point in time or local area within a continental cultural and ecological region. In a delightful National Film Board of Canada teaching film titled "Behind the Masks," Lévi-Strauss explicates the universal symbolism of mask designs while the carver tugs on his sleeve trying to dispute his imputed meanings. Lévi-Strauss brushes off the artist's interjections as irrelevant. His grand rhetoric about the universal products of the human mind aspires to generality, to "a view from afar" (1985) of culture and identity that has little to do with the perspective of the language speaker. In another side of Lévi-Strauss's oeuvre, however, he remains stubbornly attracted to the well-chosen ethnographic comparison as a method of articulating the universal. When he turns to ethnography to make his case, his meticulously detailed comparisons reveal similar "deep" or underlying patterns in social structure, political organization, village settlement pattern, myth, art, language, and so forth, particularly for the South American societies he studied firsthand. Part of this quintessential French intellectual longed to concentrate the universalist argument on the culture of the Parisian intellectual (as did Pierre Bourdieu). Darnell (2004, chapter 7, this volume) argues that the historicist side of the Boasian argument is recapitulated in this analyst-based, external perspective on the meaning of culture in terms inaccessible to its members. Lévi-Strauss is, therefore, a Boasian as well as a structuralist.

The historical manifestations of his structuralist universals navigate among and across intersecting cultures, perhaps drawing on an implicit structuralism in Boas's historicism.

The key to the significance of the ethnographic standpoint is that the validity of the counterexample holds utterly different significance in inductive and deductive research. A scientific theory that fails to account for a single counterexample is, at most charitable reading, limited in its applicability. I am more interested in the scientific status of what Prague School linguist Roman Jacobson called "near-universals." These are the kind of patterns that may be derived from comparative ethnography. There are reasons some things almost always occur together. The linguistic model has been widely borrowed by anthropologists. Roman Jakobson (1968) identified similar patterns of "markedness" in the phonological patterns in child language acquisition, aphasic patterns of loss and regaining of speech, and putatively universal laws of sound change. In all three domains, some things were found to be more basic, more common, than others. Many languages lack phonemic (meaning-changing) voiced stops (b/d/g), but if there is no contrast of voiced and voiceless, the language will almost always have the voiceless series (p/t/k). Glottalized series appear only alongside a prior contrast of voiced and unvoiced, that is, as a third level of phonological contrast. Further, a language that distinguishes voiced and voiceless stops will be likely to have a similar distinction at other points of articulation. Occasional exceptions do not invalidate or falsify this "near-universal" statement about universals. Interpretation and contextualization necessarily abound in such a model. It generates explanations of particulars in relation to generalizations based on the collective weightiness of many cases. Comparative linguists turn to historical contact as a mechanism to explain anomalies and to show patterned change in progress. The generalizations make it possible to formulate specific questions across cases.

In "The Study of Geography," Franz Boas contrasted science in the narrow sense with history-geography-cosmology and asserted the necessity of employing alternating methods according to the problem at hand (Boas 1889). In the intervening years, more of us have come to question the idea that science itself lies beyond interpretation and to realize that we cannot do science without grounding our knowledge in interpretation. Many of us, especially under stimulus from feminist theory, deem the standpoint of the investigator to be inseparable from phenomena observed (see Haraway 1991).

British social anthropology also wrestled with the question of whether our "science" is universal. A collapsed Azande granary roof led E. E. Evans-Pritchard (1937) to muse on what we would now call the social construction of science. In the field, Evans-Pritchard suspended the judgments of his natal culture and concentrated on getting his head around how the Azande interpretative system uses witchcraft to explain the apparently random consequences of termite-driven collapse. He acknowledges the superior explanatory power for Azande survivors of witchcraft as the source of harm, relative to the depersonalized random chance taken for granted by Western science.

Bronislaw Malinowski (1922) made similar points about the inseparability of spells and practical knowledge in the construction and use of sailing canoes in the Trobriand Islands. I suspect that this debate has suffered in intervening years because "we" are hung up on the word "science." In our hubris, we assume it has no precise equivalent outside the European Enlightenment legacy (although Chinese, Indian, and Arabic "sciences" share many of its distinctive features). Because of the prestige of science, however, non-Western peoples around the world understandably attempt to valorize their own forms of "Indigenous Knowledge" by claiming for them the prestige of "science." Human inquiry, both naturalistic and philosophical, is a universal. Again, substantive content and its degree of systematization differ dramatically, and we would be hard put to understand the alternatives on the basis of categories derived from our own tradition(s).

Clifford Geertz (1988) contrasts the "eye/I-witnessing" strategy of Malinowski with the ostensibly objective journalism of Evans-Pritchard, the universalizing and homogenizing elegy for the so-called primitive in Lévi-Strauss, and the moralizing cross-cultural critique best known through the work of Ruth Benedict. National traditions in anthropology have conceptualized the cross-cultural in remarkably parallel ways.

Returning to North America, Benedict elegantly problema-tized the ethnocentricity of the normal and abnormal designa-tions across cultures. Her relativism rested on tolerance rather than nihilism. Although this methodology now seems naively eth-nocentric in its borrowing of terms from Western abnormal psy-chology (the megalomaniac Kwagiuth [now called Kwakwaka'wakw] and the paranoid-schizophrenic Dobuans) and Greek mythology (the Dionysian Plains and the Apollonian Zuni), Benedict (1934) provided a surprisingly unsensationalized treatment of these con-trasts, which she deployed in her musings about where the Amer-ica of the interwar years had gone off track. Cross-cultural contrast provided a method for her reflexivity and enabled a critique of American society and its discontents. Benedict's later work (1946) moved "beyond relativism" to explore universals on which judg-ment, subsequent to ethnographic effort to understand phenom-ena in their own terms, could and should be made.

Edward Sapir's "Culture Genuine and Spurious" (1924), written a decade before Benedict's classic work, had been virtually unin-telligible to his cronies in Rockefeller-sponsored interdisciplinary social science. His colleagues confidently assumed the inevitabil-ity and desirability of "the American way." Margaret Mead's sev-enteen years of *Redbook* magazine columns that she coauthored during the 1960s and 1970s would hone this critique, through eth-nographic contrast, to its fullest elaboration. As the United States moved inexorably out of its isolationism in pursuit of manifest destiny beyond the continental frontier, anthropologists provided guidance to both politicians and the general public. Even in the immediate aftermath of the Second World War, Benedict (1946) managed to move beyond the naive cultural relativism with which she is usually associated today to advise on how to reincorporate Japan into the civilized world, as civilization was defined by the victors. Benedict's images of cultural diversity are grounded in an unarticulated, and therefore unquestioned, assumption of univer-sals located not all that far from the surface of human behavior. Selection from her "arc of cultural possibilities" presupposes a con-tent and internal logic for the selections and adaptations made by unique cultures (Benedict 1934). Something like this model is implicit in all comparative ethnography, whether or not its critical cross-cultural implications are drawn explicitly. Not all cultures have such clear patterns. Rapid culture change was responsible for Benedict's poignant quotation of a California Digger Indian that the cup of his culture was broken (Benedict 1934:33). She recognized that such change often caused disintegration of traditional cultures, but she did not theorize further what interwar Americanist anthropology called "acculturation."

In a latter-day resuscitation of the Benedictine strategy, Eric Wolf (1999) accepts her implicit expectation of seeking out interesting patterns, selecting three "extreme" cultural elaborations from different levels of social organization (the Benedictine version of the Kwakiutl (Kwakwaka'wakw) cannibalism among the Aztecs, and whatever one might want to call Hitler's National Socialist genocide campaigns). Discussion of these diversities is only interesting, I argue, insofar as it entails underlying universals and a method for pinning down their nature. The point of Wolf's attempted resolution of the impasse is that relations of power operate in all societies but manifest themselves differently depending on the complexity and specific culture history and political economy of the society in question.

I have argued elsewhere (Darnell 2001) that Benjamin Lee Whorf's (1956) efforts to correlate language, thought, and reality through the study of grammatical categories followed a preexisting Benedictine labyrinth. He contrasted the grammatical categories of what he called Standard Average European (SAE) with those of Hopi, a language whose encoded way of seeing the world seemed better suited for explicating Einstein's relativity theory than for devising the physics on which it was based (Whorf 1956). But in Whorf, as in Benedict, "multilingual awareness," reflexivity, opens the potential of becoming (dialogically) bilingual and bicultural, of negotiating multiplex identities.

I address one final example of an important theorist whose ideas would be so much more interesting after a good introductory course in anthropology. The late Richard Rorty (1979) in his early work deconstructs the "mirror of nature" paradigm that has enmeshed Western philosophy in metaphysics and argues that all we are left with is the possibility of "edifying conversations" and perhaps the history of science (a suggestion he does not pursue). That is, he gives up on the idea of "truth" or even of closer approximation to something(s) in the real world. We can merely talk to each other. Even more sadly, he rejects the edifying potentials of ethnography and argues that the conversation he envisions can only be intelligible within the bounds of Western philosophy itself (Rorty 1979). Edification is divorced from the capacity for empathy.

Following a precedent long ago set by Boasian maverick Paul Radin (1927), I argue to the contrary that dialogic interaction (i.e., conversation) is both possible and edifying across cultural boundaries. We anthropologists have been doing that for a long time. Radin's exegesis of Winnebago philosophy was arrived at through edifying conversation. His precedent attests to the anthropological capacity to imagine communities other than our own. We have the capacity to talk to others and to arrive at levels of abstraction where the questions we ask emerge despite the difficulties of getting to their culture-specific answers. We can learn new categories, acquire new tools to think with. We do these things all the time within our own society. The possibility of ethnography rests upon the same communicative potentials across human communities.

Conclusion

Ethnography is necessarily an enterprise for the bricoleur. But we must not fall into the trap of thinking that precludes generalization about human nature and personal or group identity. Too often, we have allowed the larger world beyond disciplinary boundaries to restrict anthropology to the study of disappearing exotica with limited recognition of its capacity to integrate increasingly broad communities in thinking together about the discontents and resistances of a globalizing world. Globalization, like human nature, is not as simple as it seems on the surface, and we must take care that productive concepts lead us not to premature conclusions but to careful generalization that does not mask underlying diversity, whether cultural or biological.

Notes

1. Originally published as "Anthropological Approaches to Human Nature, Cultural Relativism and Ethnocentrism," *Anthropologica* 51 (2009): 187–94.

2. Boas and his contemporaries used terms that both they and their Indigenous collaborators considered respectful, although usage has changed since.

Terms such as "Indian," "American Indian," "First Nations," and "Native American" are to be understood in this context of analyzing Boasian work. More contemporary terms are substituted when I speak in my own voice.

3. In contrast, the Canadian model of national confederation as an umbrella for more diverse provincial interests and perspectives facilitates moving back and forth between federal and provincial jurisdictions that need not signal incommensurability even when the positions are not identical (Harrison and Darnell 2006).

4. "Aboriginal" is the accepted term for Indigenous Australians.

References

Benedict, Ruth. 1934. *Patterns of Culture.* Boston: Houghton Mifflin.

———. 1946. *The Chrysanthemum and the Sword.* Boston: Houghton Mifflin.

Boas, Franz. 1889. "The Study of Geography." *American Anthropologist* 2:47–53.

Borofsky, Robert. 2002. "Four Subfields: Anthropologists as Mythmakers." *American Anthropologist* 104:463–80.

Chomsky, Noam. 1957. *Syntactic Structures.* The Hague: Mouton.

———. 1965. *Aspects of the Theory of Syntax.* Cambridge MA: MIT Press.

———. 1987. *The Chomsky Reader.* Edited by James Peck. London: Serpent's Tail.

Darnell, Regna. 2001. *Invisible Genealogies: A History of Americanist Anthropology.* Lincoln: University of Nebraska Press.

———. 2004. "Text, Symbol, and Tradition in Northwest Coast Ethnology from Franz Boas to Claude Lévi-Strauss." In *Coming to Shore: Northwest Coast Ethnology, Traditions, and Visions,* edited by Marie Mauzé, Michael Harkin, and Sergei Kan, 7–21. Lincoln: University of Nebraska Press.

Deleuze, Giles, and Felix Guattari. 1987. *A Thousand Plateaus: Capitalism and Schizophrenia.* Minneapolis: University of Minnesota Press.

Evans-Pritchard, E. E. 1937. *Oracles, Witchcraft and Magic among the Azande.* Oxford: Clarendon.

Geertz, Clifford. 1988. *Works and Lives: The Anthropologist as Author.* Stanford: Stanford University Press.

Goffman, Erving. 1967. *Interaction Ritual.* Chicago: Aldine.

———. 1981. *Forms of Talk.* Philadelphia: University of Pennsylvania Press.

Grice, H. Paul. 1963. "Logic and Conversation." In *Syntax and Semantics.* Vol. 3, *Speech Acts,* edited by P. Cole and N. Morgan, 41–58. New York: Academic Books.

Haraway, Donna. 1991. *Simians, Cyborgs and Women: The Reinvention of Nature.* New York: Routledge.

Harrison, Julia, and Regna Darnell, eds. 2006. *Historicizing Canadian Anthropology.* Vancouver: University of British Columbia Press.

Jakobson, Roman. 1968. *Child Language, Aphasia, and Phonological Universals.* The Hague: Mouton.

Lévi-Strauss, Claude. 1964. *Mythologiques.* Vol. 1, *Le Cru et le Cuit.* Paris: Plon.

———. 1985. *The View from Afar*. New York: Basic Books.

Malinowski, Bronislaw. 1922. *Argonauts of the Western Pacific*. New York: Dutton.

McGregor, Gaile. 1985. *The Wacusta Syndrome: Explorations in the Canadian Landscape*. Toronto: University of Toronto Press.

Piaget, Jean. 1970. *Structuralism*. New York: Harper Colophon.

Radin, Paul. 1927. *Primitive Man as Philosopher*. New York: Dover.

Rorty, Richard. 1979. *Philosophy and the Mirror of Nature*. Princeton: Princeton University Press.

Sapir, Edward. 1916. *Time Perspective in Aboriginal American Culture: A Study in Method*. Canada Department of Mines, Geological Survey, Memoir 90, Anthropological Series no. 13. Ottawa: Government Printing Bureau.

———. 1924. "Culture, Genuine and Spurious." *American Journal of Sociology* 29:401–29.

———. (1933) 1949. "La realité psychologique des phonémes." *Journal de Psychologie Normale et Pathologique* 30:247–65. Reprinted in English translation as "The Psychological Reality of Phonemes," in *Selected Writings of Edward Sapir in Language, Culture and Personality*, edited by David G. Mandelbaum. Berkeley: University of California Press.

Segal, Daniel, and Sylvia Yanagisako, eds. 2004. *Unwrapping the Sacred Bundle: Reflections on the Disciplining of Anthropology*. Durham NC: Duke University Press.

Wallace, Anthony F. C. 1962. *Culture and Personality*. New York: Random House.

Whorf, Benjamin Lee. 1956. *Language, Culture and Reality: Selected Writings of Benjamin Whorf*. Edited by John B. Carroll. Cambridge MA: MIT Press.

Wierzbicka, Anna. 1972. *Semantic Primitives*. Frankfurt: Atheneum-Verl.

Wolf, Eric. 1999. *Envisioning Power: Ideologies of Dominance and Power*. Berkeley: University of California Press.

7

....

Text, Symbol, and Tradition in Northwest Coast Ethnology from Franz Boas to Claude Lévi-Strauss

The Americanist anthropology that I practice has evolved to its present stature and structure in great part as a result of the intersection of a culture area—the Northwest Coast—with the work of two seminal scholars, the German-turned-American Franz Boas and the Frenchman Claude Lévi-Strauss.[1] The latter mined the broad ethnological fields of the Americas with a theoretical range not entirely incompatible with a characteristically Americanist historical particularism. To be sure, there is a degree of perversity in this reading. These two intellectual giants are hardly the only scholars to have worked on the Northwest Coast, as evidenced by the number of distinguished scholars, both French and North American, who contributed to the volume in which this chapter first appeared. Despite dramatic and fundamental differences in the paradigms of historical particularism and structuralism, there are also similarities and continuities that transcend the usual rhetorics of revolution and discontinuity (Darnell 1998). In this context, I argue that Lévi-Strauss becomes a Boasian of sorts (Darnell 2001). These border crossings between the French and Americanist traditions come into focus on the Northwest Coast, thereby providing a veritable microcosm for the history of anthropology and the salience of the national traditions that are one way to organize its diversity (Darnell 2000). Americanist anthropology has been remarkably insular, a myopia reflected more in superficiality of historicist consciousness than in actuality. Recognition is long overdue that European colleagues (particularly French and Russian colleagues in the case of the Northwest Coast) have contributed to the peculiar mélange of ethnological insight that constitutes our disciplinary heritage.

My own work as a historian of anthropology has focused primarily on the Americanist tradition because it seems to me to have been submerged without intellectual justification in a wave of post–World War II enthusiasm for overseas fieldwork (already practiced by Lévi-Strauss in Brazil a decade earlier) and British colonialist functionalism becoming degraded into implicitly ethnocentric interpretation, perhaps best exemplified by E. E. Evans-Pritchard's conclusion that the Azande were capable of rational thought but mistaken because of the tools their culture provided them with which to think. More adequate scientific tools were presumably deployed exclusively by post-Victorian gentlemen [*sic*] in the field. I exaggerate, of course—in an attempt to highlight and reevaluate the fluidity of the Americanist position developed by Boas and his students during the first half of the past century.

The distinctive features of the Americanist tradition, as I have argued elsewhere (Darnell 2001, 1999), are mentalist, products of the human mind. Despite contrasts of the inductive and deductive methods that give a dissimilar surface appearance to ethnographically based arguments, I suggest that these distinctive features characterize the work of Lévi-Strauss as well as that of Boas and his students.

In sum: culture is a system, a structure if you prefer, of symbols contained in human minds situated in the context of particular social traditions. Language, thought, and reality are inseparable, their forms colored indelibly by categories learned through socialization. The database that provides access to these products of the human mind is encapsulated for study in texts, preferably volunteered in an interactional context in the speaker's first language. Such texts reveal what Boas called "the native point of view" or "the culture as it appears to the Indian himself" (Berman 1996).[2] The downside of the Americanist commitment to recording texts so that the accumulated knowledge preserved in oral traditions would not be lost to human civilization lies in its potential ethnocentric nostalgia for the formerly primitive that denies the contemporary vibrancy of First Nations (as Native Americans are called in Canada) communities and traditions. My own anthropological predilections lead me to treasure what Helen Codere (1966) called Boas's "five-foot shelf of Kwakiutl ethnography" and to believe that this corpus has contemporary use-value in the communities that legitimately and inalienably own this irreplaceable intellectual property. Whatever we might want to say about the intractability of anthropologists in so recognizing it, First Nations traditions are far from static. It follows that First Nations communities and individuals are not objects to be studied. Rather, at least ideally, and varying across individuals, communities, and contexts, they are collaborators and consultants, embodying the possibility of respect coexisting with, perhaps even mutually reinforcing across, dimensions of difference. My final suggestion for a fundamental characteristic of this Americanist tradition is that the fieldwork takes a long time. Northwest Coast ethnologists tend to devote a lifetime to a single nation or at least to a culture area. My own mentors, Frederica de Laguna as an undergraduate at Bryn Mawr and Dell Hymes as a graduate student at the University of Pennsylvania, ensured that I would remain immersed in this tradition. Over my more than three decades in Canadian anthropology at the time this chapter was initially written, the presence of the Northwest Coast has been inescapable in my anthropology.

If the history of anthropology is reflected in this culture area, conversely, a personified Northwest Coast has contributed to the history of anthropology by imposing its particular characteristics on visiting ethnologists. Richard Fardon (1990) assembled reports of the area-specific attitudes and practices of anthropologists working in culture areas around the globe, albeit Native North America is represented in his collection only by Eskimo (called Inuit in Canada) hunters. Over a professional lifetime, scholars absorb many forms of habitual thought from the peoples with whom they work, and they come to share without conscious effort much that must be explained to colleagues who have worked elsewhere. Sense of humor provides a telling example. My colleague the late Keith Basso, whose work on Western Apache jokes about white men pioneered in this area, was himself a masterful raconteur. We have often been able to finish one another's stories from the field; they arise from a similar set of cultural assumptions that are widely found across Indigenous North America (Basso 1979).

If we are to understand this process of interaction between a field site and a particular anthropologist, or a succession of anthropologists, it behooves us to identify what is unusual about the Northwest Coast. Indeed, we must consider why the concept of the culture area still seems to work for ethnologists trying to delimit the purportedly "natural" scope and boundedness of their investigations. "Franz Boas worked there" is insufficient explanation for the significance of Northwest Coast examples in theoretical and comparative work across national anthropological traditions, especially the French (including Marcel Mauss as well as Claude Lévi-Strauss) and the Americanist (e.g., Ruth Benedict's use of Boas's Kwakiutl (Kwakwaka'wakw) ethnography in *Patterns of Culture* in 1934).

For both Boas and Lévi-Strauss, the Northwest Coast provided a convenient laboratory for controlled comparisons, in contrast to the casual absence of context in classical evolutionary reasoning. The Northwest Coast environment was relatively constant, with rich maritime and riverine resources permitting cultural fluorescence and providing sufficient leisure for *Bildung* or individual creativity. Despite cultural and physical proximity, the various groups apparently retained distinct identities over long periods of time. Boas was introduced to the Northwest Coast through its art as exhibited in Europe. He was enchanted by the "flight of imagination . . . compared to the severe sobriety of the eastern Eskimo," his first fieldwork experience. He mused over the "wealth of thought" that "lay hidden behind the grotesque masks and the elaborately decorated utensils of these tribes" (Cole 1999:97). Before his first visit to the Northwest Coast, Boas already realized that traditional domains of culture (art, material culture, and myth) overlapped in practice.

His choice of field site, albeit constrained by the sponsorship of the British Association for the Advancement of Science and the Bureau of [American] Ethnology,[3] enabled Boas to explore the complexity and interconnection of cultures extending from southern Alaska to northern California. Culture was widely shared, although linguistic affiliations were wildly diverse. Joel Sherzer's monumental areal typology of Native (Indigenous in contemporary terminology) North American phonology and morphology (1976) viewed the Northwest Coast as typical of the continent's most developed (despite the undertone of evolution toward greater

complexity of organization and density of settlement) type of linguistic area, characterized by intermarriage, trade, and multilin-
gualism among relatively small and settled groups. Boas found
borrowing to be the most salient historical process.

With reference to his "Ethnological Problems in Canada," (1910)
Boas clarified the need for areal-controlled comparisons, using
the Cambridge Torres Strait Expedition and his own data from
the Jesup North Pacific Expedition as examples: "Brief reports on
local conditions were well enough when even the rough outlines
of our subject had not come into view. Since these have been laid
bare, a different method is needed. Not even exhaustive descrip-
tions of single tribes or sites fulfill the requirement of our time.
We must concentrate our energies upon the systematic study of
the great problems of each area" (1940:332).

Lévi-Strauss, in *A World on the Wane* ([1955b] 1961) and *Tristes
Tropiques* (1955a), conceptualized the culture area framework as
yielding generalizations more significant than any study he might
conceivably carry out of any single tribe:

> I planned to spend a whole year in the bush, and had hesitated
> for a long time as to where, and for what reason, I was to go. In
> the end, with no notions that the result would be quite contrary
> to my intentions, and being anxious rather to understand the
> American continent as a whole than to deepen my knowledge
> of human nature by studying one particular case, I decided to
> examine the whole breadth of Brazil, both ethnographically and
> geographically. ([1955b] 1961:237)

Indeed, the emphasis on culture area functioned positively to
distinguish American from British anthropology. British functionalism erred, in Lévi-Strauss's view, in focusing on "isolated tribes,
enclosed within themselves, each living on its own account a peculiar experience of an aesthetic, mythical, or ritual order"; populations coexisted "elbow to elbow" and deployed various "modalities
according to which each explained and represented the universe
to itself . . . elaborated in an unceasing and vigorous dialogue"
(1975:145). The ethnography of each group provided a window
to larger perspectives. Lévi-Strauss believed that his commitment
to concrete and detailed ethnographic data has been misunder-

stood. "Only those whose entire ethnological outlook is confined to the group they have studied personally are prone to overlook my almost maniacal deference for the facts" (145).

We might reformulate the question of the importance of studying the Northwest Coast: "Why did Boas move away from studying the Eskimos of Baffin Island to the people he called Kwakiutl (now known as Kwakwaka'wakw) and other cultures of the Northwest Coast?" Boas went to Baffinland, as it was then called, to decide for himself whether environment determined culture, as many of his geography professors in Germany had maintained. He returned firmly committed to the interaction of culture with an environment that played a constraining rather than a determinant role. The Central Eskimos, despite the extreme character of their environment, possessed a highly elaborated "mental" or symbolic culture. Environment thereafter held little further interest for Boas. He had moved irrevocably from questions of geography to those of ethnology, the link among his successive professions being the effect of the observer on the phenomena observed (a position deriving from his doctoral work in psychophysics on the color of sea water). If "the mind of primitive man"[4] was not set into its characteristic pattern by environment, then variability of cultures in history became, almost by default, the paradigmatic problem for anthropology. Such attention to the epistemological status of the observer applied both to the Eskimo hunter observing and taming nature or environment by culture and to the observing anthropologist. Methodology moved to the center of Boasian theory by this mentalist route.

In "The Aims of Anthropological Research," for example, Boas directly linked the inadequacy of economic determinism to the impossibility of any single historical explanation:

> Undoubtedly the interrelation between economics and other aspects of culture is much more immediate than that between geographical environment and culture. . . . Every attempt to deduce cultural forms from a single cause is doomed to failure, for the various expressions of culture are closely interrelated and one cannot be altered without having an effect upon all the others. Culture is integrated. It is true that the degree of integration is not always the same. (1940:256)

Although Boas is frequently dismissed as a mere descriptivist, he in fact practiced a deconstructive method that has come into its own with structuralism and its intellectual descendants. Diffusion provided the core concept for Boas's redefinition of "history," another heritage from his German geographical training. By identifying separate foreign elements, the analyst could trace the process of their integration into particular cultures. The method foreshadows that of Lévi-Strauss, although the explanation of distributional features was diffusion in the former case and the universal structure of the human mind in the latter.

Lévi-Strauss has on occasion acknowledged that Boas "never thought structural analysis was incompatible with ethnohistorical investigations" (1975:162). In the first volume of *Structural Anthropology*, he noted:

> In the history of structuralist thought, Boas . . . made it clear that a category of facts can more easily yield to structural analysis when the social group in which it is manifested has not elaborated a conscious model to interpret or justify it. Some readers may be surprised to find Boas's name quoted in connection with structural theory, since he has often been described as one of the main obstacles in its path. But this writer has tried to demonstrate that Boas's shortcomings in matters of structural studies did not lie in his failure to understand their importance and significance, which he did, as a matter of fact, in the most prophetic way. They rather resulted from the fact that he imposed on structural studies conditions of validity, some of which will remain forever part of their methodology, while some others are so exacting and impossible to meet that they would have withered scientific development in any field. A structural model may be conscious or unconscious without this difference affecting its nature. ([1958] 1963:281)

Boas, "the great master of modern anthropology," produces an analysis of remarkable but "mainly theoretical" "elegance and simplicity" (260). "Our analysis thus converges with that of Boas, once we have explored its sub-structure, which manifests both social and formal features" (262).

George W. Stocking Jr. (1974) has argued that the Boasian theoretical paradigm was essentially complete by 1911. Boas's two-pronged critique of classical evolution tacked between psychology and history. On the psychological front, *The Mind of Primitive Man* (1911b) denied that "primitive man" was different in kind from the anthropologists who studied him or her, while on the historical side his Introduction to the *Handbook of American Indian Languages* (1911a) analytically distinguished race, language, and culture (the title he would choose for his collected writings in 1940). In practice, however, Boas considered the psychological questions premature and called for detailed investigation of the histories of particular tribes. This research program required him to develop reliable methodologies for reconstructing the cultural histories of peoples without writing.

In "The Limitations of the Comparative Method of Anthropology" (Boas 1896, included in Boas 1911b), he wrote: "A detailed study of customs in their relation to the total culture of the tribe practicing them, in connection with an investigation of their geographical distribution among neighboring tribes, affords us almost always a means of determining with considerable accuracy the *historical* causes that led to the formation of the customs in question and to the *psychological* processes that were at work in their development" (1940:276; emphasis added). Throughout Boas's career, history and psychology remained sides of a single interpretive coin, sides that were to be examined in constant alternation:

> Understanding of a foreign culture can be reached only by analysis and we are compelled to take up its various aspects successively. Furthermore, each element contains clear traces of changes that it has undergone in time. This may be due to inner forces [psychology] or to the influence of foreign cultures [history]. The full analysis must necessarily include the phases that led to its present form. (1940:264)

Boas and Lévi-Strauss agreed that the analysis they foregrounded could not be carried out entirely from within a culture. In his Introduction to the *Handbook of American Indian Languages*, Boas insisted that "the grammar has been treated as though an intelligent Indian was going to develop the forms of his own thoughts by an analysis of his own form of speech" (1911a:70). The psychological element of the Boasian paradigm, the native point of view, however, resonated very differently for Lévi-Strauss, who was not much interested in Indigenous interpretations of cultural forms because he assumed that people did not easily articulate their unconscious understandings of cultural phenomena.

Like Lévi-Strauss, Boas was fascinated by myth variants. He wrote to George Hunt (September 1, 1906: APS) attempting to uncover the history of particular versions and to establish the "correct" version. He valued the individuality of such variable texts as a means to make the culture come alive as well as to reconstruct history through the working out of principles of rank "in the case of a number of particular men and women." These stories focused on rights to masks and dances and the stories that went with them (Boas to Hunt, April 4, 1913: APS).

In his Northwest Coast diaries, Boas emphasized the scientific value of collecting material culture objects for the American Museum of Natural History that were accompanied by the stories that made cultural sense of them (Rohner 1969:38). Reciprocally, a ceremony made no sense unless its meaning was explicated by a member of the culture. On one such occasion, Boas noted: "George Hunt was not here, and so I did not know what was going on" (188). Boas, who was determined that his students should not restrict their topics to single domains of culture, stated: "I have instructed my students to collect certain things. . . . Consequently, the results of their journeys are the following: they get [museum] specimens; they get explanations of the specimens; they get connected texts that partly refer to the specimens and partly simply to abstract things concerning the people; and they get grammatical information" (Berman 1996:270). It is a short step to the domain plasticity of Lévi-Strauss's concept of structure, with his exemplars moving freely across visual, verbal, and semantic representations.

Boas's *Primitive Art*, first published in 1927, continued to emphasize the "two principles" of psychology and history: "the fundamental sameness of mental processes in all races and in all cultural forms of the present day" and "the consideration of every cultural phenomenon as the result of historical happenings" ([1927] 1955:1). Form was constant although its meanings were variable, not only tribally but also individually, in art, mythology, and ceremonialism alike (128). Meaning "was tacked on according to the peculiar mental disposition of the individual or the tribe"[5] (129). The underlying mental processes, however, "do not take place in the full light of consciousness" (155):

> The single tribe cannot provide a reasonable perspective: There is probably not a single region in existence in which the art style may be understood entirely as an inner growth and not as an expression of the cultural life of a single tribe. Whenever a sufficient amount of material is available, we can trace the influence of neighboring tribes upon one another, often extending over vast distances. Dissemination of cultural traits that has made the social structures, the ceremonials, and the tales of tribes what they are today has also been a most important element in shaping the forms of their art. . . . Their strong individuality proves that their present distribution must be due to mutual influence among various North American cultures. We cannot determine where the pattern originated but it is quite certain that its present distribution is due to cultural contact. (176)

A long section of *Primitive Art* is devoted to the "North Pacific Coast of North America." The men's style of wood carving and painting is symbolic, distinct from the more representational designs in the women's style of weaving, basketry, and embroidery. The general features of symbolic art include "an almost absolute disregard for the principles of perspective, emphasis on significant symbols, and an arrangement dictated by the form of the decorative field" ([1927] 1955:183). The "exuberant" decorative designs have developed "only recently" (279); the Kwakiutl (Kwakwaka'wakw) now use this symbolic style for house paintings and posts and for masks (288).

Lévi-Strauss's treatment of split representation draws heavily on Boas's formulation. His sample transcended the Northwest Coast as a culture area to incorporate China, the Amur, the Neolithic, the Maori, the Eskimo, and the Amazon. His own areal work in Brazil, compared with the Northwest Coast where Boas pioneered in the anthropology of art, posed wider questions about the causes of social hierarchy and their correlation with masks and split representations.

Masks were not, for Boas in 1896, a single phenomenon, although "a few typical forms of their use may easily be distinguished" (1940:274–75). What Boas found interesting was "the intelligent understanding of a complex phenomenon" (305): "I aligned myself clearly with those who are motivated by the affective appeal of a phenomenon that impresses us as a unit, although its elements may be irreducible to a common cause" (305). "The historical development of primitive cultures" had to be "inferred" from "very inadequate material," but Boas believed this could be done, at least in part, although "the uniqueness of cultural phenomena and their complexity" probably precluded laws "excepting those psychological, biologically determined characteristics which are common to all cultures and appear in a multitude of forms according to the particular culture in which they manifest themselves" (311). In 1936, the year he retired from Columbia, Boas acknowledged that the battle against premature evolutionary generalization had been won but insisted that similar logical errors continued with "the imposition of categories derived from our own culture upon foreign cultures" (311). By this he meant not the epistemology of observation but the apparent inevitability that was belied by the subsequent revitalization of traditional cultures and languages that he called acculturation.

As early as 1895, in "The Growth of Indian Mythologies," Boas described "a dwindling down of an elaborate cycle of myths" (1940:429) in a process leaving traces of the historical movement of folklore elements. Mythologies as such were not "organic growths, but have gradually developed and obtained their present form by accretion of foreign material" that "must have been adopted ready-made" and modified "according to the genius of the people who borrowed it." Such historical inferences could not be expected to reflect "the native point of view." Rather, "explanations given by the Indians themselves were often secondary," relative to origins, and "complex" (429).

The culture area framework allowed Boas to move toward theory, or at least generalization:

The analysis of one definite mythology of North America shows that in it are embodied elements from all over the continent, the greater number belonging to neighboring districts, while many others belong to distant areas, or, in other words, that dissemination of tales has taken place all over the continent. In most cases we can discover the channels through which the tale flowed, and we recognize that in each and every mythology of North America we must expect to find numerous foreign elements. And this leads us to the conclusion that similarities of culture on our continent are always more likely to be due to diffusion than to independent development. (1940:433–34)

Boas went on to study what he called "the interesting psychological problems of acculturation," that is, "what conditions govern the selection of foreign material embodied in the culture of the people, and the mutual transformation of the old culture and the newly acquired material" (435).

In "The Decorative Art of the North American Indians" (1903), Boas suggested that borrowed motifs were assimilated "to some indigenous and familiar form" against the grain of the original "motives" (Boas 1940:557). He concluded that ceremonial objects were much more realistic than decorative objects for ordinary usage. Art styles proved to be more widely distributed than explanatory styles, demonstrating the secondary and "late" character of such explanations; interpretation and style were not necessarily correlated although they influenced one another (562). Both artistic and explanatory style were products of the particular group history. The historical explanation of customs given by the native is generally a result of speculation, not to be considered a true historical explanation (563).

"Decorative Designs of Alaskan Needle-Cases" (1908), based on museum exhibits, made the case against historical accuracy of Indigenous interpretations even more strongly: "The only satisfactory explanation lies in the theory that the multifarious forms are due to the play of the imagination with a fixed conventional form, the origin of which remains entirely obscure" (Boas 1940:588).

Boas understood the folk tale "primarily and fundamentally as a form of primitive art." Already in 1914, he considered style as a reflection of "constant play with old themes" having little to do with origins: "The explanatory element would then appear, not as an expression of native philosophy, but rather as an artistic finishing touch required for the tale wherever the art of story-telling demands it" (1940;480). Such questions of psychological reality led Boas to study of the individual in culture: "The contrast between a disorganized mass of folk-tales and the more systematic mythologies seems to lie, therefore, in the introduction of an element of individual creativeness" (482) that helps explain the contradictions in systems of myth, both within and across traditions: "These contradictory traditions are the result of individual thought in each community, and do not come into conflict, because the audience identifies itself with the reciting chief and the truth of one poetic creation does not destroy the truth of the other one" (482).

In 1916 Boas set out his method for analyzing folktales and myths, the core of his textual research program. Wide distribution of elements, however, "rarely only" provided "internal evidence" of origins or borrowing (1940:397). Nonetheless, particular forms of tales were characteristic of localized versions. These versions developed for psychological reasons:

> The artistic impulses of a people are not always satisfied with the loose connection of stories, brought about by the individuality of the hero, or strengthened by the selection of anecdotes. We find a number of cases in which a psychological connection of the elements of the complex story is sought. . . . We must infer that the elements were independent and have been combined in various ways. (401–2)

Each region, through the "imagination of the natives," selects "preponderant themes in the style of plots, and in their literary development . . . there is comparatively little material that seems to belong to any one region exclusively so that it might be considered as of autochthonous origin" (403). Ritual and social system "have been foisted upon the myths" as the variants "tend to establish harmony between mythology and social phenomena" (422). The historical vista emerging from the method he applied to the myths of the Thompson River Indians captured Boas's own imagination. In a rare rhetorical flourish, he opined: "It would seem that mythological worlds have been built up, only to be shattered again and that new worlds were built from the fragments" (424).

In 1916 Boas turned to "Representative Art of Primitive People." On the Northwest Coast, "the principles of representation of an object by means of symbols is carried to extremes" (1940:538) with little attention to realistic animal forms. Rather, "all characteristic parts" of the animal were shown conventionally. These symbols were then "squeezed" into the decorative field (538).

Lévi-Strauss brought his Boas-inspired immersion in Northwest Coast ethnology to bear on the question of mask cultures in *The Way of the Masks* (1982). Across this "vast region" peoples maintained close contacts through "migrations, wars, borrowings, commercial and matrimonial exchanges of which archaeology, traditional legends and history supply the proofs" (129). The borrowings, such as between mainland and inland or Dene and coastal peoples, have a consistent symmetrical character.

Fascinated by Northwest Coast masks from his first exposure to them in interwar New York, Lévi-Strauss acknowledged "profound respect . . . undermined by a lingering uneasiness" because "their plastic justification escaped me" (1982:10). The problem could not be resolved within the domain of art. Myths and masks were less separate objects than semantic relations: "Looked upon from the semantic point of view, a myth acquires sense only after it is returned to its transformation set" (12). Coherence involves transformation and contrast, a "restringing of the segments" (27); for example, the original mainland versions are built up logically and become less coherent as they move to the islands: "Any myth or sequence in a myth would remain incomprehensible if each myth were not opposable to other versions of the same myth or to apparently different myths, each sequence opposable to other sequences in the same or other myths, and especially those whose logical framework and concrete content . . . seem to contradict them" (56). Plastic, sociological, and semantic points of view are all needed to "articulate . . . scattered traits . . . into a system" (39). Works of art, like masks and myths, cannot contain their entire meaning. The mask domain combines myth, social or religious function, and plastic expression (57): "Hence, they will justifiably receive the same treatment." The "ideal mask" can be predicted ("described and reconstructed" on theoretical grounds) and then discovered "in reality" (59).

Both elements and wholes are integral to the structuralist position: "the relics of a common stock [provide] the elements of myths, rites, and plastic works forming this organized whole" (Lévi-Strauss 1982:189) It forms "a cultural complex" of mask types whose "traces" are found in particular tribal instantiations (189). What is finally delimited is a "semantic field" (223).

Data for such reconstructions, however, were difficult to obtain. Group styles are clearly distinguished, with the Kwakiutl taking a "hieratic, more lyrical and more violent" approach (Lévi-Strauss 1982:40). Ambiguous relations reverse at all three levels. For the Kwakiutl, "rich though they may appear when compared with others," these data are "far from exhaustive," and their distributions are not fully clear (68). The parts of such a system are transforms of one another:

> Except for stylistic differences, all the plastic characteristics of the Swaihwé masks are found in the Xwéxwé masks of the Kwak-iutl, but the latter, being avaricious instead of generous, fill a function opposite to that of the former. By contrast, the Dzo-nokwa mask (which dispenses riches like the Swaihwé and, like it, transfers its wealth from the wife's family to the husband's) has plastic characteristics which, down to the smallest details, constitute a systematic inversion of the Swaihwé mask's characteristics. (93)

This method can be extended as far as parallels are found. Alliance and exchange protect against intracommunity marriage and provide security from foreign incursion. "The coppers and the masks constituted two parallel solutions to the same problems for two different but contiguous populations" (Lévi-Strauss 1982:139).

Lévi-Strauss concludes that historical reconstruction can provide greater time depth than local explanations postulate: "I would prefer to suppose either that the existence and diffusion of the Swaihwe mask go back to a more ancient period than the various local traditions suggest, or that, in the form in which they have come down to us, the coppers and the masks perpetuate, each in its own way and in more or less parallel fashion, archaic themes" (1982:141). These forms "share the same spirit" and metaphor (143): "a mask does not exist in isolation; it supposes other real or potential masks always by its side, masks that might have been chosen in its stead and substituted for it. A mask is not primarily what it represents but what it transforms, that is to say, what it chooses *not* to represent" (144). Boas employs not the language of individual psychology but rather of culture as collectivity. It follows that style is both original and a product of borrowing and the "conscious or unconscious wish to declare itself different" (144).

The method, adapted from Boas, acknowledges that the "short-run and localized history of a people without writing eludes us by definition"; nonetheless, structural analysis can sometimes "document the concrete conjectures from which a mythic transformation has sprung" (Lévi-Strauss 1982:152). The "mechanisms" through which masks spread "by inheritance, marriage, conquest, or borrowing remain visible" (162).

In sum, then, the theoretical positions of Boas and Lévi-Strauss concur on many points and intersect significantly when viewed from the lens of the history of anthropology. Both scholars define culture and myth within the symbolic domain and apply a comparative perspective from outside the culture studied to answer larger questions of history and group interaction, if not of origins. Both take for granted what was once called the psychic unity of mankind, although Lévi-Strauss is more likely than Boas to assume that these universal products of the human mind are accessible to anthropological investigation. Boas thought that such psychological questions might be answerable sometime in the future but placed priority upon historical questions.

There is, of course, a generation of substantial duration between these two scholars and their encounters with the Northwest Coast. Without Boas's groundwork documenting the distribution of myth themes and correlating masks, ceremonials, and stories, the comparative project of Lévi-Strauss could scarcely have been formulated. He adopted both the database and the historical comparative method of Boasian Northwest Coast scholarship and deployed the method to revised theoretical purposes. The structures he compared throughout the Americas were not "historical" in precisely the Boasian sense, although their historical interactions provided evidence of universal mental processes. In this, Lévi-Strauss's approach is French, his thinking a product of an Enlightenment rationalism and universalism thoroughly alien to Boas's Germanic emphasis on the unique *Weltanschauung* (worldview) of particular cultures, including his own. That American anthropology has, for the most part, taken the Boasian direction need not preclude attention to the French side of the coin. If Lévi-Strauss was not precisely a Boasian, he built directly upon Boasian guidelines in fundamental ways that generated a productive cross-fertilization for both national traditions.

Notes

1. Originally published as "Text, Symbol, and Tradition from Franz Boas to Claude Lévi-Strauss" in *Coming to Shore: Northwest Coast Ethnology, Traditions, and Visions*, ed. Marie Mauzé, Sergei Kan, and Michael Harkin, 7–22 (Lincoln: University of Nebraska Press, 2004).

2. The terms "native" and "Indian" are problematic here but pervasive in the material analyzed, in this case by Berman. Her work of exegesis and navigation of this change in usage over time is parallel to the stance taken in this volume. [*Sic*] is implied in these usages throughout the chapter.

3. "American" was added to the "Bureau of Ethnology" in 1892, and it was known thereafter as the Bureau of American Ethnology.

4. Both "primitive" and "man" are problematic today though conventional at the time Boas wrote. The contemporary use of "Inuit" for "Eskimo" in Canada was not yet an option.

5. "Tribe" is widely used in the United States but is problematic in Canada.

References

Basso, Keith. 1979. *Portraits of "The White Man": Linguistic Play and Cultural Symbols among the Western Apache*. Cambridge: University of Cambridge Press.

Benedict, Ruth. 1934. *Patterns of Culture*. Boston: Houghton Mifflin.

Berman, Judith. 1996. "The Culture as It Appears to the Indian Himself: Boas, George Hunt, and the Methods of Ethnography." In *Volksgeist as Method and Ethic: Essays on Boasian Ethnography and the German Anthropological Tradition*, edited by George Stocking, 215–56. Madison: University of Wisconsin Press.

Boas, Franz. 1910. "Ethnological Problems in Canada." *Journal of the Royal Anthropological Institute of Great Britain and Ireland*. 40:529–39.

———. 1911a. Introduction to the *Handbook of American Indian Languages: Volume 1*, 1–83. Bureau of American Ethnology Bulletin 40. Washington DC: Government Printing Office.

———. 1911b. *The Mind of Primitive Man*. New York: Macmillan.

———. (1927) 1955. *Primitive Art*. New York: Dover.

———. 1940. *Race, Language and Culture*. New York: Free Press.

Codere, Helen. 1966. Introduction to *Kwakiutl Ethnography*, by Franz Boas, edited by Helen Codere, xi–xxxii. Chicago: University of Chicago Press.

Cole, Douglas. 1999. *Franz Boas: The Early Years, 1858–1906*. Vancouver: Douglas and McIntyre.

Darnell, Regna. 1998. *And Along Came Boas: Continuity and Revolution in Americanist Anthropology*. Amsterdam: John Benjamins.

———. 1999. "Theorizing Americanist Anthropology: Continuities from the B.A.E. to the Boasians." In *Theorizing the Americanist Tradition*, edited by Lisa Philips Valentine and Regna Darnell, 38–51. Toronto: University of Toronto Press.

———. 2000. "The Pivotal Role of the Northwest Coast in the History of Americanist Anthropology." *B.C. Studies* 125/126:33–52.

———. 2001. *Invisible Genealogies: A History of Americanist Anthropology*. Lincoln: University of Nebraska Press.

Fardon, Richard. 1990. *Localizing Strategies: Regional Traditions of Ethnographic Writing*. Edinburgh: Scottish Academic Press.

Lévi-Strauss, Claude. 1955. *Tristes tropiques*. Paris: Plon.

———. (1955) 1961. *A World on the Wane*. Translated by John Russel. London: Hutchinson.

———. (1958) 1963. *Structural Anthropology*. Translated by Claire Jacobson and Brooke Grundfest Schoeph. New York: Basic Books.

———. 1975. *The Way of the Masques*. Geneva: Editions Albert Skira.

———. 1982. *The Way of the Masks*. Translated by Sylvia Modelski. Vancouver: Douglas and McIntyre.

Mauzé, Marie, Michael E. Harkin, and Sergei Kan, eds. 2004. *Coming to Shore: Northwest Coast Ethnology, Traditions and Visions*. Lincoln: University of Nebraska Press.

Rohner, Ronald. 1969. Introduction to *The Ethnography of Franz Boas: Letters and Diaries Written on the Northwest Coast from 1886 to 1931*, edited by Ronald Rohner and Evelyn C. Rohner, 3–14. Chicago: University of Chicago Press.

Sherzer, Joel. 1976. *An Areal-Typological Study of American Indian Languages*. Amsterdam: North Holland.

Stocking, George W., Jr., ed. 1974. *The Shaping of American Anthropology, 1883–1911: A Franz Boas Reader*. Chicago: University of Chicago Press.

Valentine, Lisa Philips, and Regna Darnell, eds. 1999. *Theorizing the Americanist Tradition*. Toronto: University of Toronto Press.

8

Mind, Body, and the Native Point of View

Boasian Theory at the Centennial
of *The Mind of Primitive Man*

The Mind of Primitive Man (MPM), originally published in 1911, still stands as the primary theoretical manifesto of Boas's anthropology.[1] Reassessment is overdue for at least two reasons: First, relational or abstract thought as a universal human capacity has ceased to be recognized as common sense in public as well as anthropological discourse and thus is dismissed as ever having been a theoretical position in need of articulation and defense. Second, post–World War II positivists in North America foregrounded descriptive ethnography of a nonmentalist variety and therefore insisted that Boas was atheoretical. "Mind" was as out of fashion as "primitive" was becoming. Such self-confident empiricists as Marvin Harris (1968) and Leslie White (1963, 1966) dismissed the Boasian cultural relativism that came into its own during his anti-racist resistance to Nazi ideology, in favor of materialist and ecological perspectives that left no room for epistemological relativism in the sense of standpoint (a term Boas used alternately with "point of view"). Today, this reading of Boas as atheoretical and his mentalism as nonempirical is more often applied in archaeology and physical anthropology than in the study of culture or society. Yet Boas's argument in 1911 was grounded in the study of mental phenomena and devoted surprisingly little attention to the physical anthropology for which he was best known at the time of its writing.

The theoretical climate in anthropology since the 1960s reopens the possibility of returning to questions of what Boas called "the native point of view" (Darnell 1998, 2001; Darnell and Gleach 2002), which he understood to constitute the psychological aspects of culture and cultural experience. Anthropology, biology, geography, and psychology have all changed dramatically in the century since the appearance of *The Mind of Primitive Man*. Therefore, an exercise of deliberate historicism is required to make sense of his position today. Both "primitive" and "man" in the title of Boas's signature work should be understood in the context of their times. Despite the contemporary discordant tone, Boas's work using these terms (as well as "native" in his signature phrase "the native point of view" as distinguished from "Natives" or "Indians") held. Terms such as "primitive" and "civilized," reliance on man[kind] as generic human, and uncontextualized examples from European history all serve to obscure the prescience with which Boas argued for a theory of mind that was capable of moving move back and forth between body and mind, between the biological and the cultural. He sometimes held one constant and sometimes the other, deploying them to illuminate one another.

This chapter assesses the commensurability between Boas's ideas about the "plasticity" of human bodily form and the variability of mental or psychological forms of "abstract thinking in relation to the diversity of human cultures," and explores how this alternation allowed him to design a methodology in support of his theoretical position. Boas foreshadows here the synergy across the four subdisciplines that still constitute anthropology in the Americanist tradition. He counters the internal fragmentation of approaches to the study of humankind in the natural sciences when separated from the humanities and social sciences by reasoning analogically and comparatively across these traditional divides.

The rehabilitation of Boas as theorist has been ongoing for a long time, although the critique it counters has been remarkably impervious to evidence, such as the late Douglas Cole's biography of Boas up to 1906 (Cole 1999). George W. Stocking Jr., in selecting Boas's most significant early essays (Stocking 1974), identified 1911 as the watershed of his theorizing. In that year Boas issued dual paradigm statements: *The Mind of Primitive Man* and the Introduction to the *Handbook of American Indian Languages*. He made two interrelated claims: First, all cultures, by virtue of being human, evince functionally equivalent capacities that are manifested differently according to environment and cultural context; as a corollary, variations in human biology do not constrain this cultural potential because it operates at the species level. "Cultural relativism," although the term was introduced later by Boas's students and he never used it, follows from this position. His second point was that race, language, and culture must be understood as analytically separate, even though they sometimes coincided in practice. These two principles seem so obvious today that they are hardly considered theoretical. The corollary of combining what the evolutionists called "the psychic unity of mankind" with the historical and geographical specificities of race, language, and culture as independent variables was at the core of Boas's critique of evolution but appeared almost incidentally to his argument in *The Mind of Primitive Man*, notwithstanding that anthropology a century ago could not move forward in any interpretivist framework without such a principled rejection of preordained evolutionary hierarchies based on either culture or race. This critique stands as the third prong of Boas's theoretical edifice.

I identify the anthropology that Boas built on these foundations as "the Americanist tradition" (Darnell 1998, 2001; Valentine and Darnell 1999), distinguishing it from other anthropologies practiced in North America, including those of his latter-day critics. Boas's anthropology took for granted a symbolic rather than material definition of culture, a text-based approach to cultural knowledge through the recorded words of members of culture, and the inextricability of language, thought, and reality (i.e., the external world). This position entailed a robust standpoint-based epistemology that underwrote the later construction on Boasian foundations of culture and personality, ethnoscience, social interactionism, and other interpretivist approaches. Somewhere along the way, Boas's caveats were disarticulated in disciplinary memory from the anti-racist activism that culminated in his response to Nazi atrocities near the end of his life. The study of race, perhaps because Boas's biological studies were superseded in data and method by subsequent scientific breakthroughs, became "racism" for his intellectual heirs, and they approached it primarily through cultural analysis (Darnell 1998, 2001, 2010; Valentine and Darnell 1999). More recent scholarship has been preoccupied with Boas's interaction with the Afro-American community and his activist role in anti-Nazi critiques of race, eugenics, and genocide (Baker 1998, 2010; Hyatt 1990; Patterson 2001; Shedrich and Zumwalt 2008; Williams 1996).

To untangle the position Boas actually took in *The Mind of Primitive Man*, it behooves us to return to the details of his argument, dissolve the artificial dichotomy of mind and body, and explore how human biology provided him with a method to approach culture as its analog. Biological plasticity gave Boas a viable approach for reasoning about the apparently limitless variability of culture. A close reading of the 1911 text reveals that he foregrounded the relatively robust methods of the biological science of his day in his search for an entrée to situate mental phenomena within the broad scope he already had delineated for anthropology as the holistic science of humankind. He hypothesized a similar normal curve for "body measurements, physical phenomena [environment], and socio-economic life" (1911b:36), thereby inviting generalization of methodology and inference across these domains. Mental development had been much less studied, but he believed that it would produce "laws . . . quite analogous" to those of physical development (49). Although "actual observation" was not yet available, every explanation for differences of body and mind other than environment was rendered "improbable" by virtue of its "complexity" (64). The argument for heredity as an alternative to environment received considerably less attention.

The Mind of Primitive Man was based on a series of lectures at Boston's Lowell Institute, founded in 1836 as a family bequest to sponsor public lectures on diverse scientific and popular topics. The Lowell Institute remained firmly within the nineteenth-century institutional framework of elite learned societies of which Philadelphia's American Philosophical Society was the most distinguished. By 1911, Boas had established himself at Columbia University and already was producing a distinguished cohort of academically credentialed students who would populate the anthropology departments springing up around North America and beyond. The lectures were repeated at the National University of Mexico, where Boas had established a working collaboration with his recent PhD graduate Manuel Gamio. On the one hand, he aspired to "organize anthropological research in America" according to his own vision and under his personal control; on the other, he was deeply committed to public pedagogy, largely museum based at the time, to disseminate the anthropological point of view beyond the academy in the interests of science as "freedom from tradition" (Boas to Zelia Nuttall, May 16, 1901: APS). His pedagogical goal was to "improve human mental operations" (1911b:250).

Boas's arguments did not spring full-blown from the pages of his theoretical magnum opus. The only new material in *The Mind of Primitive Man*, reflecting his pedagogical intention and desired public audience, was an introduction on "racial prejudices" and the capacity of the anthropological standpoint to transcend them. Nor did he cease to revisit and refine these basic positions over the ensuing three decades. To appropriate the metaphor of Isaiah Berlin, Boas was more hedgehog than fox, returning to a small number of key ideas from different angles, contexts, and data sets. The 1911 preface cites six previously published articles that underpinned his arguments. None appeared in *American Anthropologist*, ostensibly the flagship journal of Boas's adopted discipline. Their titles—"Human Faculty as Determined by Race" (1894), "The Limitations of the Comparative Method of Anthropology" (1896), "The Mind of Primitive Man" (1901), "Some Traits of Primitive [*sic*] Culture" (1904), "Race Problems in America" (1909), and "Psychological Problems in Anthropology" (1910)—illustrate the complexity of these standpoints that Boas had developed sequentially but now sought to integrate into a single framework targeting a public audience in urgent need of the methods and insights of anthropological science.

Nor is it accidental that both the 1911 and 1938 editions of *The Mind of Primitive Man*, and Boas's selection of his seminal essays at the end of his career under the title *Race, Language and Culture* (RLC), still accorded with his 1911 priority of distinguishing them as independent analytic variables. In both cases, he begins with biology and moves on to culture. The structure of MPM already reflects this stereoscopic method. As we have seen, Boas's dual argument requires historicist recontextualization today because its biological thesis is largely taken for granted despite persistent vestiges of a discredited scientific racism. Conversely, contemporary studies of cultural variation are wont to remove race from its biological context to argue for human rights and identity politics and thereby also to miss Boas's synthetic intention (Darnell 2001, 2006).

Boas's discussion of "human types," his intentionally neutral term for what at the time were normally called "races," characterized "racial prejudices" as the "naive," unconscious "basis of our opinions" (1911b:1). The insights of anthropological science reveal that, due to the unique "genius of a single people," "a culture of equal value" might develop in unfamiliar times and places; indeed, several are known to have developed in the New World (7). The "vicissitudes" of the history of a people, particularly its contacts with other peoples, rather than innate biological capacity, determine the rate of its progress (9). Boas poses a high evidentiary standard for the argument that any particular "race" has less capacity for civilization given the complications introduced by diverse conditions of its contact history and geographical location. Civilization "is taken up, now by one people, now by another" (10). Ancient European societies incorporated "more primitive people" while Old World expansion introduced epidemic diseases and population decimation to the Americas (6, 11). "In short, historical events appear to have been much more potent in leading races to civilization than their faculty" (17). No single index of relative value could be determined.

"Modern biological concepts" further suggest a great divergence of humans from animals and "varying intensity" (i.e., distribution) of uniquely human features across conventional races (1911b:22). Boas contends that the anatomical peculiarities of the usual racial groupings show no necessary relationship to "mental aptitude" (19). He is far more interested in the complexity of the human central nervous system, accessible to scientific study only under experimental conditions that have yet to be met today. He aspires to compare individuals and groups "on equal terms," citing nutrition, gender, and intragroup variations as variables confounding permanent discreteness of human types (28). Multiple explanations working in tandem—including bodily measurements, "social and economic phenomena," and environment—are in his view sufficient to explain observed variability (36). "Human types" are not necessarily stable across environments (36). The degree rather than the existence of their plasticity is therefore the pressing scientific question. Bodily form cannot be permanently stable because it reflects the past history of an organism over its entire life cycle.

Despite its meaninglessness in delimiting stable racial types, Boas clings to anthropometry as a method to trace the movement of groups within a given environment over time, thus establishing a necessary albeit arbitrary proxy for the history of peoples without writing. Without some such method to access unwritten history, he would be unable to demonstrate how rate of development depended on environmental stimulus. After provisionally accepting evidence that "mental development follows laws quite analogous to those of physical development" (1911b:49), Boas turns to his own studies of immigrant head form then in progress for the U.S. Census Commission (Boas 1912). The priority he gives to the explanatory value of biological over mental variation is reflected in his choice to study head form and other anthropometric features despite the Dillingham Commission's explicit preference for research-based advice on the cultural nonassimilability of a new wave of immigrants from southern and eastern Europe, many of them Jewish ("Hebrew" in Boas's terminology). Boas excludes himself and other assimilated German Jews from these categories and unequivocally claims a personal identity as a scholar working within *our* mainstream American, white, northern European heritage; Judaism was a mere religious category to be shed along with other "trammels of culture" (Glick 1982).

Boas declines to evoke natural selection without extensive evidence from "definite families" and sets out to obtain such evidence (1911b:52). Moreover, he concludes that correlation of head form with such overtly Darwinian factors as mortality and fertility is "improbable" (51). His research in New York City provides the "good fortune" to show "direct influence of environment upon the bodily form of man[kind]" by comparing immigrants born in Europe and their American-born descendants within specific family lines (53). He describes the results as "unexpected" (54). American-born subjects developed differences in childhood that persisted through life. Sicilians, Neapolitans, Bohemians, and Hebrews (in his characteristic usage and preferred over "Jews" at the time) all changed their head form but in patterns unique to each group, thus mitigating against the existence of an emerging "uniform general type" in America (6).

After concluding that the "instability or plasticity of types" is not unlimited, Boas goes on to infer the "great plasticity of the mental make-up of human types," especially those correlated with bodily conditions and developed over the life cycle. He has "succeeded in proving that bodily changes [do] occur" and places "the burden of proof" on those who reject the parallelism that he attributes to the mental (1911b:65). The argument for the salience of environment in the emergence of plasticity is indirect and relies heavily on analogical evidence of "alternating heredity" on combinations of parental types under domestication (83). This evidence supplements the limited longitudinal data available for changes in human bodily form and justifies the inference back to the human and, for Boas, from physical to mental form.

Crucially, his argument does not identify culture as mediating between individual bodily and psychological processes. Indeed, the term "social" occurs far more frequently than "cultural." The critical influence is limited by heredity, that is, the biological rather than the cultural. Retrospective discussion of Boas on geography and environment has emphasized the limiting but also limited impact of natural environment on cultural forms. According to this reading, Boas experienced a conversion experience that caused him to reject environmental determinism during his 1883–84 fieldwork among the Eskimo of Baffin Island (now called Inuit in Canada). Stocking argues persuasively for greater complexity, with Boas combining a geographical problem and its epistemological entailments from the outset (Stocking 1968:144). As early as 1887, in "The Study of Geography," Boas already placed geography as a human science alongside history, ethnology, and cosmology (Boas 1887). His comparative method eschewed the apples and oranges of evolutionary typologies based on typological form in favor of comparing peoples with comparable livelihoods, thereby rendering environment a historically particular intersection of the natural, the social, and the technological.

The Mind of Primitive Man identifies domestication as an index of civilization and attributes the vitality of modern European and American civilizations to "their unstable population," that intensified plasticity (1911b:87). Historical conditions of intermarriage and variable origin compound the internal variability of "a people" (93). "Distinct local types" are more likely to develop "in primitive races" as exemplified by the diversity of Indigenous American cultures and adaptations to environment (89). Variation within groups is greater than across types, thereby facilitating further plasticity (94).

Reasoning "from a purely psychological point of view" necessitates "the same lines of thought" as does anatomical variability or stability (95). But psychological problems are more complex because of the requirement for the observer to transcend personal bias. In the course of fieldwork, the student must adapt to the "inner life" of the primitive (Boas 1911b:99). "Confusion" abounds in psychology, moreover, because racial and social problems, heredity and environment, can never be fully disambiguated (101). There is a chicken-and-egg character to this inextricability. Boas distinguishes the universal "organization of the mind," the species capacity or characteristic "modes of thought," from "the diversity produced by the variety of contents of the mind as found in the various social and geographical environments" (104). He predicts that the underlying mental attitudes will prove remarkably similar across time and space. Both Noam Chomsky and Claude Lévi-Strauss would appreciate the theoretical stance; the latter, like Boas, turned to local instantiations of universal products of the human mind.

Boas established the panhuman capacity by contrasting human and animal, with animality encapsulated in instinct and lacking "freedom of use," as in human inventions (1911b:97). Human minds are slippery things to study because of their "infinite variety of form," which is greater than the variety of bodily form. The investigator must set aside the assumptions of their own culture and "observe the manifestations of the mind of man under varying conditions" (98). Anthropologists are ideally situated to do this, even though no one has yet succeeded in describing "the psychological characters of races independent of their social surroundings" (100). Boas presents ethnographic evidence that such psychological character is inseparable from environmental, historical, and social context. He explores the purportedly primitive mental characteristics of fickleness of mind, inability of concentration, and lack of originality. In each case, he proposes adequate explanations other than inherent inferiority of mental process.

The observed differences are more apparent than real. Boas has observed firsthand the "mental attitude" of the "civilized philosopher" in primitive cultures (1911b:113), an argument taken up later by his student Paul Radin. The methods for the biological study of psychology, however, are necessarily different from those of the biologist: "Differences of structure must be accompanied by differences of function, physiological as well as psychological; and, as we found clear evidence of difference in structure between the races, so we must anticipate that differences in mental characteristics will be found" (115).

Boas anticipates quantitative structural differences in mental phenomena because he already has found them in physical phenomena. He laments that adequate data do not exist to specify the anatomical or mental changes accompanying civilizations, although a few cases of the same people living under different conditions can be documented. He cites Freud for evidence that some traits seem to be inherited but actually are acquired in early childhood and persist at unconscious levels. He concludes that the mental faculties of all present races of mankind are "highly developed," and all have the capacity to "reach the level of civilization represented by the bulk of our own people" (1911b:122–23).

Boas castigates Nietzsche, long before Nazi domination of Germany, for "the modern doctrine of prerogatives of the master-mind" (1911b:100) and equates the Aryan race argument with the evolutionary overtones of linguistic typology as correlated with race (124). His argument for the separation of race, language, and culture arises from his characteristic activism on behalf of privileging science over prejudice. The two theoretical manifestos of 1911 are of a piece and not discontinuous with his later and better-known politics of race (Baker 2010).

Classifications, with which the heirs of Enlightenment science are much enamored, produce artificial explanations that require empirical demonstration in particular cases. An empiricist to the core, Boas accepts that classification is necessary to the exercise of the human faculty but insists that it must be applied in self-conscious and non-ethnocentric ways. Different "points of view" inevitably produce different classifications. The argument for the mental capacity of primitive peoples as parallel to that of the "bulk of individuals" "in our own civilization," however, must proceed by inference because of the absence of direct historical evidence for the intermingling of peoples (1911b:123).

Boas relates the discreteness of race, language, and culture from the Introduction to the *Handbook of American Indian Languages* (Boas 1911a) to the contentious issues of race/biology and environment/culture. Language is part of the classificatory triad that renders mind rather than body as the centerpiece. The "genius of a people as reflected in its language" is the primary key to the "mind of primitive man" (125). This "genius" can be modified by diffusion, migration, culture contact, and other variables that "without historical evidence . . . cannot . . . be proved" but must remain a question of inference as in the case of culture (131). Documented diffusion of cultural elements constitutes the necessary "proof." By 1911 Boas had already amassed a considerable database of such evidence on the North Pacific Coast.

Boas cautions, however, that different "types" of society, beliefs, social organizations, inventions, and so on would produce different classifications and that "the general term 'culture' . . . may be subdivided from a considerable number of points of view" (1911b:139). That is, variations within races, languages, and cultures will prove at least as variable as those across them. Boas cites his early paper "On Alternating Sounds" to illustrate that familiarity guides perception "according to the classifications of our own language" (Boas 1889:139). For the member of culture "articulate speech" forms the link between the "infinitely varied" "range of personal experience" and an "underlying extended classification of experience" in the language of a people (145).

Boas assumes that change in racial type proceeds more slowly than linguistic change; ample evidence of diffusion exists. The logic of his analysis is parallel to that of Sapir's *Time Perspective in Aboriginal American Culture: A Study in Method.* (Sapir 1916; Darnell 1998, 2001). Both works cataloged extensive illustrative ethnographic details out of context to confirm a series of logical hypotheses. Archaeology, the only direct method of accessing the history of "people that have no history," could in 1911 offer little in the way of specific evidence (Boas 1911b:182–83). Comparison of civilization's own past with that of contemporary primitive peoples is a flawed method for inference because domains of culture develop independently; sequences from simple to complex develop out of order or skip stages; convergence or borrowing cannot be distinguished reliably from independent invention. Boas, citing his student Alexander Goldenweiser's analysis of totemism as a diverse set of psychological phenomena in diverse contexts, recognizes no principled reason to assume that similar surface traits of culture must reflect the same psychological processes (190–91).

The variable domains of culture must be approached "from a considerable number of points of view" (Boas 1911b:139). Particular forms always appear arbitrary from the standpoint of another language or culture. Language provides Boas with a methodological hook, a way of approaching psychological questions empirically. In culture as with language, he emphasizes universal functions, what we would now call design features of language, rather than particular forms (142). A small number of universal cultural ideas are presented by analogy from linguistic evidence, demonstrating that a few essential ideas turn up over and over. Folklore provides proof that such ideas are subject to wide transmission and adaptation. Nevertheless, Boas considers Adolf Bastian's "elementary ideas" somewhat mystical because the ideas are intangible and not accessible to empirical investigation. He also worries that the student of such mental phenomena is "compelled to think in terms of these [same] elementary ideas" (172), a telling though unacknowledged evocation of the hermeneutic circle.

Boas pulls no punches: "the evolutionary viewpoint" must yield to "unbiased research" rather than premature generalization (1911b:139). What is now called social evolution "can be understood only as an application of the theory of biological evolution to mental phenomena" (142). The whole "grand structure" rests uneasily on "our present civilization as the necessary outcome of all the activities of all the races of man[kind]" (172). Nonetheless, a very real difference begs for investigation. Here and elsewhere Boas uses the terms "civilized" versus "modern" and "primitive" matter-of-factly and without apparent irony, despite having already demonstrated the biological plasticity of human types, and extends their referents into the "psychological domain. . . . The whole classification of experience among mankind living in different forms of society follows entirely distinct lines" (198).

The classifications provided by culture come under increasing reflexive consciousness in civilizations; modern mankind, however, retains much of this inertia of bowing to forces of tradition through what Benjamin Lee Whorf would later call "habitual" thought. He argues that mythology is the conventional tool with which "primitive man as philosopher" thinks, thus anticipating both Radin and Lévi-Strauss. Although traditional elements often get in the way of logic, civilization allows more people to "free themselves from the fetters of tradition" (Boas 1911b:206). Drawing on a nonanthropological concept of culture as the property of an educated elite, Boas aspires to expand the number of his fellow citizens who achieve "freedom" from the "shackles" of tradition, to raise them above the "habitual" level of "primitive mind" (206).

Boas claims a "general theory of valuation of human activities" as anthropology's potential contribution to social thought (1911b:208), again without using the anachronistic term "cultural relativism." Differences of social etiquette must not be equated with moral lapses. What seems to us a rational explanation is highly influenced by "associated ideas" and their emotional effects (210). "Secondary explanations" ("inferences based on the general knowledge possessed by the people") do not reflect historical origins, although most of us try to "justify our standpoint" by postulating the absolute truth of our own principles (225, 226). Contact with other ways of life is in itself a method to enhance consciousness of diversity of customs (241), that is, defamiliarization. "Gradual elimination" of the irrational can never be fully successful but remains the ultimate goal of science (243). In sum, "the change from primitive to civilized society includes a lessening of the number of the emotional associations and an improvement of the traditional material that enters into our habitual mental operations" (250).

After his summary, Boas turns to the more immediate and practical question of "race problems in the United States" (1911b:262). He speaks as an American intellectual, without acknowledging his own status as immigrant, German, and Jew. Approaching the problem "from a biological standpoint" only after analysis of "the historical relations of our problem," he assumes that changes occur in both physical and mental traits (268). Nonetheless, he purports to confine himself "entirely" to the biological because "mental life is so plastic, that no hereditary inability can be assumed to exist in any of the peoples of Europe." In any case "the data of anthropology teach us a greater tolerance of forms of civilization different from our own" (278). This, rather than the impossibility of universal standards, was the essence of the now often maligned concept of cultural relativism.

Boas's motives for foregrounding the biological side of the mind-body equation return rapidly to the racial prejudices and stereotypes that began *The Mind of Primitive Man,* and he emphasizes that anthropology provides a method to transcend them. The text devotes more time to considering how environment leavens the effects of heredity than to how culture plays into the argument; the term "culture" usually appears in MPM as "culture and environment." This historical and contextual framing of the biological and the mental is, for Boas, the sine qua non for a method to access to "the native point of view," the ultimate psychological phenomenon—the individual writ large as spokesperson for the universal in one of its myriad culture-specific and empirically attested forms.

Boas felt that his 1911 synthesis stood the test of time. *Race, Language and Culture,* his collected papers (Boas 1940), took this baseline for granted and thus did not reiterate the integrated paradigmatic statements of *The Mind of Primitive Man.* Only the paper "The Limitations of the Comparative Method of Anthropology" (1886) is included. This key critique of human evolution is retitled "The Evolutionary Viewpoint." Evolution, in Boas's view, was a matter more of standpoint than of proven theory (1911b:188). The theory of evolution suffered from "lack of comparability of the data" and the "logical error" of assuming that simple phenomena inevitably developed into complex ones (195). In 1940 Boas exemplified his work in the three independent modes of anthropological classification—the biological, the linguistic, and the ethnographic or ethnological—in accordance with the respective established subdisciplines. The arrangement of papers echoes the methodology of *The Mind of Primitive Man* in beginning with physical anthropology, then looking at language, and finally turning to the fuzziest domain, that of culture. The revised edition of 1938 retained this fundamental organization.

Changes in data, method, and theory over the past century have yet to surpass Boas's challenge to anthropology to claim a key role in increasing human capacity for reflexivity and movement toward freedom, understood as individual personal fulfillment.

Notes

1. Originally published as "Mind, Body and the Native Point of View: Boasian Theory at the Centennial of *The Mind of Primitive Man*," in *Franz Boas as Public Intellectual: Theory, Ethnography, Activism*, ed. Regna Darnell, Michelle Hamilton, Susan Hill, and Joshua Smith, 3–18 (Lincoln: University of Nebraska Press, 2015).

References

Baker, Lee D. 1998. *From Savage to Negro: Anthropology and the Construction of Race, 1896–1954.* Berkeley: University of California Press.

———. 2010. *Anthropology and the Racial Politics of Culture.* Durham NC: Duke University Press.

Boas, Franz. 1887. "The Study of Geography." *Science* 9:137–41.

———. 1889. "On Alternating Sounds." *American Anthropologist* 2:47–53.

———. 1894. "Human Faculty as Determined by Race." *Proceedings of the American Association for the Advancement of Science* 43:301–27.

———. 1896. "The Limitations of the Comparative Method of Anthropology." *Science* 4:901–8.

———. 1901. "The Mind of Primitive Man" [*sic*]. *Journal of American Folklore* 14:1–11.

———. 1904. "Some Traits of Primitive Culture" [*sic*]. *Journal of American Folklore* 17:243–54.

———. 1909. "Problems in America." *Science* 29:839–49.

———. 1910. "Psychological Problems in Anthropology." *American Journal of Psychology* 21:371–84.

———. 1911a. Introduction to the *Handbook of American Indian Languages: Volume 1*, 1–83. Bureau of American Ethnology Bulletin 40. Washington DC: Government Printing Office.

———. 1911b. *The Mind of Primitive Man.* New York: Macmillan, 1911.

———. 1912. *Changes in Bodily Form of Descendants of Immigrants.* New York: Columbia University Press.

———. 1938. *The Mind of Primitive Man.* 2nd ed. New York: Macmillan.

———. 1940. *Race, Language and Culture.* New York: Free Press.

Cole, Douglas. 1999. *Franz Boas: The Early Years, 1858–1906.* Vancouver: Douglas and McIntyre.

Darnell, Regna. 1998. *And Along Came Boas: Continuity and Revolution in the History of Americanist Anthropology.* Amsterdam: John Benjamins [PB 2000].

———. 2001. *Invisible Genealogies: A History of Americanist Anthropology.* Lincoln: University of Nebraska Press.

———. 2006. "Franz Boas: Scientist and Public Intellectual." In *Visionary Observers: Anthropological Inquiry and Education,* edited by Jill Cherneff and Eve Hochwald, 1–24. Lincoln: University of Nebraska Press.

———. 2010. "Franz Boas: The Elephant in Anthropology's Room." Unpublished paper read at the Franz Boas: Ethnographer, Theorist, Activist, Public Intellectual Conference and incorporated in Darnell (2015). London ON.

Darnell, Regna, and Frederic W. Gleach, eds. 2002. Special centennial issue *American Anthropologist.*

Glick, Leonard B. 1982. "Types Distinct from Our Own: Franz Boas on Jewish Identity and Assimilation." *American Anthropologist* 84:545–65.

Harris, Marvin. 1968. *The Rise of Anthropological Theory.* New York: Thomas Crowell.

Hyatt, Marshall. 1990 *Franz Boas: Social Activist.* Westport CT: Greenwood Press.

Patterson, Thomas C. 2001. *A Social History of Anthropology in the United States.* New York: Berg.

Sapir, Edward. 1916. *Time Perspective in Aboriginal American Culture: A Study in Method.* Canada Department of Mines, Geological Survey, Memoir 90, Anthropological Series no. 13. Ottawa: Government Printing Bureau.

Shedrich, William, and Rosemary Levy Zumwalt. 2008. *Franz Boas and W. E. B. DuBois at Atlanta University, 1906.* Philadelphia: American Philosophical Society.

Stocking, George W., Jr. 1968. *Race, Culture, and Evolution: Essays in the History of Anthropology.* New York: Free Press.

———, ed. 1974. *The Shaping of American Anthropology, 1883–1911.* New York: Basic Books.

Valentine, Lisa Philips, and Regna Darnell, eds. 1999. *Theorizing the Americanist Tradition.* Toronto: University of Toronto Press.

White, Leslie. 1963. *The Ethnography and Ethnology of Franz Boas.* Austin: University of Texas Press.

———. 1966. *The Social Organization of Ethnological Theory.* Houston: Rice University Press.

Williams, Vernon J. 1996. *Rethinking Race: Franz Boas and His Contemporaries.* Lexington: University Press of Kentucky.

9

....

Franz Boas as Theorist

A Mentalist Paradigm for the Study of Mind, Body, Environment, and Culture

Franz Boas is uniformly credited as the dominant figure of American anthropology from the late nineteenth century to the Second World War.[1] His stature as a public intellectual is acknowledged to have extended far beyond the borders of the discipline he established. Nonetheless, few contemporary anthropologists actually read Boas or have a clear sense of what he wrote or thought. Sadly, little of the voluminous Boas scholarship is based on historicist engagement with his work. In the seven decades since his death, the theoretical preoccupations of anthropologists have shifted more than once. Meanwhile, the world itself has changed and the context of Boas's work now requires historicist reconstruction of his professional, personal, and culture-historical milieu.[2]

The centennial of *The Mind of Primitive Man* (MPM) in 2011 brought renewed attention to Boas's theoretical position. But few contributors delved far into the mind of Franz Boas or the degree to which he intended the book as a paradigmatic statement of his position. The cumulative stereotypes of our inherited Boas are long overdue for revision. This chapter revisits Boas's ongoing influence on anthropology, linguistics, and Native American history, identifying and debunking stereotypes where necessary and concluding that *The Mind of Primitive Man* set out already in 1911 the theoretical position that would preoccupy him for the remainder of his career. I argue that he was fully cognizant of the integration of his core ideas and that MPM, in both its 1911 and 1938 editions, constitutes a scientific paradigm statement. In this work Boas formulates both explanatory and descriptive theory and provides a systematic program for the Americanist tradition in anthropology (Darnell 1998, 2001).

The elements of this paradigm are explicitly articulated. Boas set a high standard for theory, insisting that it be based on scientifically rigorous methodology even when dealing with qualitative ethnographic or psychological phenomena. Human biological variability, more amenable to such methodology, was his starting point for the study of the mind as well as the body. Culture, in his view, was dynamic and grounded in a specific environment, operating in history. Traditional classifications of race, language, and culture were noncomparable phenomena and demanded analytic separation. Biological determinism, whether phrased as eugenics or everyday racism, was dangerous to the very existence of civilization as Boas understood it. Only science and scientific method could counter its toxicity and reveal the positive potentials inherent in human diversity. Boas predicted inevitable mixture of races over time and lamented the counterproductive blinders imposed by European American ethnic prejudice. Freedom of thought, the sine qua non of science, could be protected only by valuing racial and cultural diversity. Boas's analytic lens shifted systematically from the biological to the cultural and back again, and he refused steadfastly to consider them independently of their intersections and mutual entailments. The axioms of this paradigm worked together across subject matters and inductive or deductive methods to explore human nature, history, and "civilization" (a term that appears more frequently in this text than "culture").

One of the most persistent inherited stereotypes is that Boas was not a theorist. His legendary five-foot shelf of Kwakiutl ethnography, replete with blueberry recipes, has been ridiculed by some as the height of descriptive ethnography, a meaningless empiricism (Maud 2003; countered by Turner 2014), glossing over the significance of blueberries to the cultural practices and livelihood of the Kwakwaka'wakw (the people he called Kwakiutl). If Boas had any theoretical ideas, they have long since outlived their utility, or so goes the metanarrative (Bauman and Briggs 2003; Freed 2012; Williams 1996). In retrospect, his critique of evolution has been relegated to the past primarily because that battle has been won, at least on the fronts that Boas articulated it. He argued persuasively that the approach of the evolutionists to their own embodiment as the culmination of human civilization was based on premature generalization about both human nature and human history. Such a position might be construed merely as a theory of absence based in negation—except that Boas did not stop there. Rather, he offered a methodology, a mentalist standpoint epistemology, that entailed a fundamental rethinking of the verities of science and the purported objectivity of the scientific method (Darnell 2001). It does not follow that a mentalist theory is atheoretical, although it may be deemed nonrigorous by some when judged by the criteria of their own nonmentalist theory. Boas himself carefully avoided such reductionism.

Another facile stereotype suggests that Boas was a theorist for one shining moment in 1911 when he published both his Introduction to the *Handbook of American Indian Languages* and his monumental *The Mind of Primitive Man*. Never again, we are to assume, did he attempt to synthesize his theoretical position. The cut-off date for George W. Stocking Jr.'s compilation of Boas's writings (Stocking 1974) assumes that Boas's "theory" already was set in stone by 1911. His most comprehensive biographer at the time of original writing, Douglas Cole (1999), ends even earlier, with Boas's resignation from the American Museum of Natural History in 1906. Thereafter, Boas concentrated on consolidating his institutional leadership of American anthropology within the academy. On the subject of Boas as theorist, Cole recapitulates Stocking (1968, 1974) and the positivists without further analysis, despite substantial revisionist scholarship available at the time, and appearing since (Baker 1998, 2010; Bunzl 2004; Darnell 1998, 2001; Hyatt 1990; Jonaitis 1995; Kendall and Krupnik 2003; Stocking 1996; Vermeulen 2015; Wickwire 2019; Zumwalt 2018).

Most commentators recognize two critical ideas that emerged in the 1911 statements: The essential position of the *Handbook* introduction, that race, language, and culture are analytically independent variables, was incorporated into the methodological exegesis of MPM (Boas 1911a). In the latter, more extensive work, Boas further argued for the universality of the human mind transcending variations across geographic region, "forms of life" (i.e., subsistence pattern), and culture, regardless of the biological makeup of the societies or their individual members. These insights are now so taken for granted that they appear to be common sense rather than the theoretical breakthrough away from ethnocentrism when first formulated. Contemporary scholars and intellectual heirs too often cite these 1911 propositions as though isolated from Boas's otherwise atheoretical narrative, on the assumption that Boas was not by temperament or creative genius a theorist—even though conceding that some theoretical commitments may have been implicit in his oeuvre but left for others to draw out.

The tenor of this Boasian legacy cries out for historicist contextualization. Postwar anthropologists in North America and Britain alike engendered a turn to positivism and placed their faith in technology as the harbinger of modern progress. Mentalism was out of fashion, and that side of Boas's thought seemed increasingly old-fashioned, though he continued to be revered by generations of his students and the students of these students. Anthropologists, like high-energy physicists, wanted to be scientific (ironically, since contemporary physics increasingly challenges the parameters of linear logic and stable dimensions). Many of Boas's successors preferred to explore revitalized, presumably more nuanced and sophisticated (neo)evolutionary paradigms. Among the most vociferous critics of Boas as hindering the theoretical development of anthropology, Leslie White (1963, 1966) and Marvin Harris (1968) continue to be taken at face value by many commentators without returning to the originals.

In the interim, the theoretical pendulum of the social sciences has shifted again, back toward mentalist alternatives to formal modeling and rational actor approaches. Despite tensions between seemingly incommensurable methodologies, the former carries renewed legitimacy. In the present anthropological climate, therefore, Boas stands out as far ahead of his own time in his effort to develop a single paradigm capable of encompassing both mind and body. He called for an anthropology that was prescient in his day but remains even more robustly resonant today. He used the opportunity of his "course of lectures" delivered at Boston's Lowell Institute and at the National University of Mexico in 1910–11 to consolidate under a single umbrella the position he had been developing in a series of published papers beginning in the 1880s and lightly reworked for his synthesis. Each of these papers had worked through one or more planks of his emerging theory of mind, and in 1911 he finally was prepared to bring them together. Boas's preface listed the previously published works incorporated into his lectures. Despite the repetition of content already in the public domain and the close correspondence of chapters in MPM to these prior publications, Boas baldly asserted that the constituent pieces were "revised," "enlarged," and "embedded" in a new framework (Boas 1911b:n.p.). This embedding involved a juxtaposition adding up to more than the sum of its parts: it was intended as a paradigm statement.

"Human Faculty as Determined by Race," presented to the American Association for the Advancement of Science at the Chicago World's Fair in 1893 and published in the *Proceedings* the following year, argued that "race" was a misleading, emotionally laden, and scientifically inaccurate term for attested human variability. Two years later, in *Science*, "The Limitations of the Comparative Method of Anthropology" articulated the critique of unilinear evolution. In 1901 Boas tried out what would become the label for his developing paradigm, providing the title for his book a decade later, "The Mind of Primitive Man." This paper was delivered to the American Folklore Society, where Boas might have deemed mentalist topics particularly welcome, because folklore concerned itself with the products of mind and the histories of the communities producing them. To the same audience in 1904, "Some Traits of Primitive Culture" debunked stereotypes about the so-called primitive; the folklore audience included literary scholars for whom ethnographic folklore was unfamiliar, and a champion was needed to attest to its comparable value. By 1909 Boas's anthropometric studies were rising to prominence, and he outlined his emerging synthesis of biology and culture in "The Race Problem in America," published in *Science*, the preeminent national arbiter of professional debates on science. His intervention in the public issues of race would reach a wide audience through this venue. "Psychological Problems in Anthropology" appeared in the *American Journal of Psychology* only a year in advance of MPM. Psychology, as the science of the mental, was a critical discipline for the legitimization of mentalist anthropology. Boas (1912) also noted his use of parts of the Introduction to the *Handbook of American Indian Languages* and data from his report entitled "Changes in the Bodily Form of Descendants of Immigrants" to the United States Census Commission. The latter two works appeared virtually concurrently with MPM and were integral to the consolidation of his paradigm at this juncture in his career.

In 1911 Boas had already laid out the four-field approach that continues to hold sway in much of North American anthropology, albeit more as nostalgic norm than as uniformly reflected in departmental practices or professional identities at the time. Boas's remarkable achievement in MPM was in the first instance methodological. Because he believed that method and theory were inseparable in science, his methodological innovations, many them thought experiments based on analogy in the absence of conclusive data, allowed him to articulate his theory. This transformed everything. Boas began to talk about the "mind" of his title, "primitive" or otherwise, by talking about body, about human biological variability. He adopted this strategy because the methods of biological science were far more advanced than those for studying culture, and he was prepared to reason analogically from one to the other.

Yet another inaccurate inherited stereotype about Boas is that he was a dyed-in-the-wool culturalist and that his theory of culture was static. In MPM, however, the term "culture" rarely appears independently. The binary opposite of biology for Boas is not culture but environment (Darnell 2015, chapter 8, this volume). He wants to know why one group of people is different from another and turns to biology for explanation only as a last resort and when forms of life, including ways of gaining a livelihood, can be held constant. Boas deploys a characteristically anthropological method of defamiliarization that toggles back and forth between one set of variables and another. From the standpoint of biology, plasticity is the core of variability, and culture is held constant, with environment as its explanatory mechanism. The inductive method in the face of limited data is parallel to that employed in Darwin's original formulation of the theory of natural selection. From the standpoint of environment-culture, however, variability is rampant, and the possibility of equal "value" to "civilizations" other than our own holds constant an equal species-level capacity for mental development:

> It is somewhat difficult for us to recognize that the value which we attribute to our own civilization is due to the fact that we participate in this civilization, and that it has been controlling all our actions from the time of our birth; but it is certainly conceivable that there may be other civilizations, based perhaps on different traditions and on a different equilibrium of emotion and reason, which are of no less value than ours, although it may be impossible for us to appreciate their values without having grown up under their influence. (1911b:207)

"Value," like plasticity of bodily form, is a matrix that operates in the eye of the beholder. The predictability of biological form, cultural form, the histories of particular groups, and environmental context all potentially dissolve into a sea of multivariate complexity that broadens the desiderata of adequate theory: biology, culture, archaeology, language. Any classification is arbitrary, because variability necessarily exceeds its limits with each realignment of the beholder's classificatory lens: hence the analytic discreteness of race, language, and culture. Interestingly, the classificatory value of language is not central to MPM, although Boas developed this side of his argument further in the *Handbook* introduction and in his later work.

A final distorting stereotype comes from the reputation of the Boasian paradigm as represented by Boas's first generation of students. Despite sometimes chaffing against his institutional leadership, all acknowledged that he created a consensus for anthropology, a normal science in Kuhnian parlance. None of the students matched the breadth of Boas's own work; rather, each specialized in some part of the package (Darnell 1998, 2001): Alfred L. Kroeber attributed to Boas his own culturalist predilections for the "superorganic"; Edward Sapir pushed for history or "time perspective" based on inferences from historical linguistics as extended to encompass unwritten languages; Robert H. Lowie created typologies of social structure that did not depend on set evolutionary sequences; Paul Radin developed life history methods to capture what Boas called "the native point of view" through dialogue with the anthropologist; Ruth Benedict and Margaret Mead explored the relationship of individual personality to cultural pattern and socialization. The students concentrated on developing theory within their chosen specializations and rarely articulated the common assumptions of what became recognizable in the years following MPM as what I have called "the Americanist Tradition," that is, the Boasian paradigm.

Toward the end of his life, after his mandatory retirement in 1936, Boas turned to ensuring the legacy of his paradigm (the term "paradigm" is anachronistic, its present use stemming from Thomas Kuhn [1970] two decades after Boas's death). What the discipline remembers is Boas's late-career activism against Nazi racism and his *Anthropology and Modern Life* (Boas 1928). Crucially, however, he revised MPM in 1938 and compiled a selection of his published essays titled *Race, Language and Culture* in 1940. Taken together, these were the works he hoped to enshrine as the culmination of his life's work.

As in MPM, Boas begins *Race, Language and Culture* (RLC) with the relative methodological rigor of race/biology and ends with culture/ethnology. The final section is explicitly labeled methodology. Most tellingly, in this compendium, language has a more explicit mediating role in the analytic triad of 1911. Both historical and synchronic linguistics (extended to unwritten languages by Boas and his students) promise a methodological rigor closer to that of biology than of culture. Language is an attractive starting point because it is more akin to culture than is biology. Indeed, language is part of culture and thereby holds the potential to bring culture into greater analytic clarity on analogy to the structures of language. The logic of inference (i.e., theory) is directly parallel to that of MPM. Boas saw himself as a scientist first and foremost. The problem was to deal with mental phenomena in scientifically rigorous ways by applying insights from more fully studied or easily measured arenas of study to others until the whole succumbed to scientific method, thereby mitigating the relative fuzziness of culture considered in isolation.

The preface to the second edition emphasized that "much work has been done since 1911 in all the branches of science" engaged in the articulation of heredity, "the influence of environment upon bodily form and behavior," and the "mental attitudes of primitive man" (Boas 1938). Interestingly, "primitive" was problematized here by quotation marks, as it is not in the 1911 edition. The language of anthropological theory was changing, in good part because of the work of Boas and his students. Boas acknowledged the need to rewrite and rearrange parts of his text but nonetheless insisted that he had come to "an ever-increasing certainty of his conclusions" that "no fundamental difference in the ways of thinking of primitive and civilized men" can be identified by science (1938:v). The updated scientific results from overlapping disciplines were described as "new points of view," a position that maintained the standpoint of the scientist at the center of his epistemology. He contrasts the "logical as well as . . . biological" revisionism in which biology, psychology, and anthropology "concur" in challenging "popular prejudice based on earlier scientific and popular tradition" and further laments that science gives way to prejudice when dictators attempt to control the flow of "trustworthy science" (vi). In 1938 gathering clouds over Hitler's Europe underscored the urgency of effectively disseminating his views. He observed darkly: "The suppression of intellectual freedom rings the death knell of science" (vi).

The Argument for Mind and Body

Let us compare in more detail the consistencies and modifications in the text. The critical mass of material in both editions deals with the logic underlying the mentalist paradigm. I have elsewhere highlighted two issues: first, the reasoning by analogy from biology as rigorous and culture as less amenable to measurement and manipulation; and second, the emphasis on environment rather than culture as the methodologically preferable option (Darnell 2015, chapter 8, this volume). The foremost goal of Boas's mentalist theory is to counter biological determinism, that is, racism. The bookends that frame both editions are an introduction about race prejudice and a conclusion about the scientific incoherence of popular misconceptions of race. The work of Boas as theorist merges with the convictions of Boas as activist that science can resolve many of the dilemmas of modern society.

Boas's biological argument relies on his review of the laws of heredity insofar as they were understood in 1911 to show that variability within "races and types" far exceeds the "range of variation in each type" (1911b:94). In 1938 he notes that "heredity" in his initial treatment now is termed "genetics" (1938:54). Both editions call for the study of family lines (63) and emphasize that small, isolated populations develop relatively uniform physical characteristics because of the limited number of individual ancestors. The human type is more variable in "stable" populations with larger numbers and greater mobility. The fundamental question for Boas is demographic: "how far . . . human types are stable" and "how far variable under the influence of environment" (1911b: 40). Because we can never assume "a permanent stability of bodily form," causes of variation (e.g., environment) become crucial to explaining observed variations (41). The short time span of ethnological inquiry has precluded study of longer-range trends.

Despite the absence of conclusive evidence from the science of the day, Boas concludes that "mental development follows laws quite analogous to those of physical development" (1911b: 49). His demonstration of the plasticity of human biological types "necessarily" leads to "a great plasticity of the mental make-up of human types" (64–65). This chain of inference places the burden of proof on those who would argue for the stability (i.e., determinism) of mental forms. Boas cites his own census research (Boas 1912) with southern Italians, central Europeans, northern Europeans, and "an extended series of East European Hebrews" (54). Differences in head form and other bodily traits develop in childhood and persist throughout life. He concludes that the "advance of civilization" creates conditions for rapid response to environment with consequent instability of type, by inference mental as well as physical (75).

In 1938 Boas set up his argument about the "composition of the human race" by demonstrating the impossibility of clearly distinguishing race and culture, with culture standing alone, as it did not in 1911 (1938:35). The difficulties of maintaining a definition of race by objective biological criteria for variation based on common descent remain difficult to overcome. Unfortunately, the very "concept of type develops in our minds from general impressions" (47). However, even a purely statistical treatment cannot resolve the problem, because the types themselves are not discrete.

The 1938 edition devotes a chapter to "the morphological position of races," where Boas concerns himself particularly with the possibility of convergence or parallel development of similar traits in the absence of descent from a particular set of ancestors (1938:100). Such convergence by inference is plausible because the traits that most distinguish humans from animals are distributed across otherwise divergent groups.

In 1911 Boas reviewed "the evolutionary viewpoint" in terms of social rather than biological evolution (1911b:280). That similar forms (e.g., of religion, social organization, art) occur around the world demonstrates "the fundamental unity of the mind of all the races of man, but also of the truth of the theory of evolution of civilization" of which "our present civilization" appears as the culmination (281). Evidence is potentially available from early written history, survivals in modern civilization, and archaeology—with only the latter germane to "people that have no history" (182). Boas finds no scientific evidence that "every people in an advanced stage of civilization" must have passed through the same stages (184). Nor is it necessarily the case that the same forms result from the same causes. Further methodological problems arise because comparability of data cannot be assured. The theory of evolution assumes development from simple to complex "under more or less rationalistic impulses" (193). Many human activities, unlike technology, do not depend on reason for their development. In sum, "there is no close relation between race and culture" (196).

In 1911 the comparison of primitive and civilized mental traits begins with the comparison of animal and human mind under "varying conditions of race and environment" and quickly establishes that reason is the critical human faculty (1911b:95). Nonetheless, he maintains that the differences are more apparent than real (114). In 1938 "physiological and psychological functions of races" are grouped together (1938:116). In both cases, more complex elements are more variable. Family lines and individual variability both confound the possibility of accurately describing formal contrasts. Boas uses his own immigration data and Otto Klineberg's on the ability of Indian and white girls to reproduce beadwork patterns, concluding that social experience trumps innate ability. Posture and gesture attest that the "motor habits of groups of people are culturally determined and not due to heredity" (126). As noted above and despite some repetition, Boas declines on methodological grounds to speculate about personality: "Unfortunately, the methods of studying personality are highly unsatisfactory because the features to be investigated lack clarity" (127–28). Boas's former students, in particular, Ruth Benedict, Margaret Mead, and Edward Sapir, were developing culture and personality as a field, but none of them shared Boas's starting point of basing objective scientific measurement on the body-mind dichotomy. The tenor of culture and personality remained configurational, more ethnographic than comparative. He concluded that "the effect of civilization upon the mind has been much overestimated. . . . We should then be clear in our minds regarding the differences between the phenomena of culture themselves and the abstract concepts of qualities of the human mind that are deduced from cultural data but have no cultural meaning if conceived as absolute, as existing outside of a culture" (140–41).

"The interpretations of culture" have too often yielded to premature generalization, with Darwinian evolution as an exemplar of inadequate methodological rigor (1938:175). Boas's former student Alexander Goldenweiser's theory of totemism, foreshadowing that of Claude Lévi-Strauss, illustrates the psychological distinctiveness of ethnological patterns that render comparison of forms in isolation as meaningless. Culture is better interpreted by geographical environment than by evolution. Boas cautions, however, that geography can modify culture but is not in itself creative. "Anthropogeography" has overstated the case for determinism of cultural development. Mind is the intervening variable and draws the influence of environment into the realm of "social life" (192).

The 1938 edition glosses the question as one of "mind and progress." Boas begins with assumptions about the "advance of culture" and its relationship to "primitiveness." Because every group of people experiences foreign influences, "cultural values" cannot be taken as discrete or singular in origin (1938:198). Boas suggests that both technological innovation and "intellectual work" require leisure. Accumulation of experience and rational increase in knowledge provide an objective measure (202). Cultural achievements are not shared by all members, whether in so-called primitive or civilized cultures. Moreover, progress itself is difficult to define in such realms as social organization. Boas uses language as an example of the need for some sort of classification of experience, although diverse forms of classification might also serve this function. Languages most differ in their obligatory distinctions that must be expressed.

Boas argues that rationality has increased since whatever classifications a given language provides give rise to consciousness, which in turn allows systematization of "the whole field of knowledge" (1911b:220). In science, exemplified by the survival of the fittest, "the dominating idea determines the development of theories" (221). Science cannot progress in this mode by exploring the uniqueness of phenomena but depends on generalization. In Boas's view, progress depends on folklore, "the character of the traditional material," rather than on the individual. Despite the enormous variability of linguistic structures, the capacity of thought is not restricted in any human language (222–23).

In 1938 the chapter title expands to include language as the third typological variable, the one that would provide Boas with the title for his collected essays. Recapitulating his arguments for the instability or nonpermanence of (bodily) type, language, and culture and for their independent variability, he notes that "the Aryan problem" disintegrates when the lack of covariation is acknowledged (1938b:151). "Culture" is more in focus here than in the first edition, but Boas emphasizes that it is a "vague" term, representing developments at different times in different aspects of the life of a people (151). "Culture areas" are simply "conveniences for the treatment of generalized traits of culture" and are normally based on geography, economics, or material culture. There is no progressive series, as claimed by the evolutionary theorists (156).

In 1911 Boas frames the question of "the universality of cultural traits" as one of debunking the existence of "a lower cultural stage" (1911b:155). Observed "analogues" of cultural traits occur in contexts that have no shared historical roots (158). Environment provides inadequate explanation, because different groups in the same environment "show often marked differences" (161). Environment, at best, limits "the special forms of customs and beliefs" that themselves arise from historically determined cultural conditions (163).

In 1938 Boas begins a chapter on "early cultural traits" with a concise definition of culture as

> the mental and physical reactions and activities that characterize the behavior of the individuals comprising a social group collectively and individually in relation to their natural environment, to other groups, to members of the group itself and of each individual to himself. It also includes the products of these activities and their role in the life of the groups. The mere enumeration of these various aspects of life, however, does not constitute culture. It is more, for its elements are not independent, they have a structure. (1938:159)

Using these customary criteria, parallel animal behavior could be cited for most forms. "If we were to define culture by observing behavior alone there is little in the fundamental elements of human behavior that has not some kind of parallel in the animal world" (1938:163). But the variability of human behavior, learned through tradition, makes them different. In the case of a particular culture, folklore provides the best entrée to considering "its inner growth as well as the effect of its relations to the cultures of its near and distant neighbors" (169).

Reformulating the Paradigm for a Changing World

On the surface, Boas's most salient rationale for a revised edition was to update the biological, psychological, and ethnological database available to support his argument. The 1938 edition provides far more references to the work of others and adds a new "Historical Review" that employs the history of anthropology to debunk the views of earlier scholars. Boas states his problem not as one of biology and mind but rather as one of race and culture, whose relationship he deems "influenced too often by racial, national, and class prejudice" (1938:20). He reviews various theorists (e.g., Arthur de Gobineau, Gustav Klemm, Carl Gustav Carus, Josiah Clark Nott and George Glidden, and Houston Stewart Chamberlain) whose purported generalizations about racial type are in fact based on cultural rather than the biological grounds they claim to employ. American polygenist Samuel G. Morton is singled out for relegating Australians, Eskimos, and others to a permanent inferior "degree of civilization" (22). His arguments conveniently justify slavery in the United States. Madison Grant's "dogmatic assumption" that positive cultural characteristics must reflect otherwise unattested Nordic ancestry further illustrates the failure of such pseudoscience to ground itself in evidence. Boas takes on American eugenicists here, as the enemies close to home in America, and declines to trace a similar historical development for "modern theories" that "racial descent determines the mental and cultural qualities of the individual" (28). Having demonstrated the inadequacy of the biologically based theory of race (see Baker 2010), Boas remains willing to assume that the cultural will follow in even greater degree.

Ethnologists, not immune from disciplinary blinders, have been remiss in ignoring race and environment altogether. They gloss over actual bodily differences in an effort to "justify the assumption of a fundamental sameness of the human mind regardless of race." The ethnological paradigm assumes that "social and psychological conditions" are common to all mankind, with differences manifested through "the effects of historical happenings and of natural and cultural environment." The psychology of Wilhelm Wundt and the evolutionary sociology of William Graham Sumner err equally in paralleling social to organic evolution and in equating all peoples "on similar levels of culture." Boas concludes that ethnologists recognize a major divide between "culturally primitive man" and "civilized man" (33–34). Interestingly, this distinction perpetuates the attribution of "culture" to the primitive [sic] and reserves "civilization" for the modern. Boas's own ethnology, however, more often speaks of the "civilization" of the so-called primitive. Stocking (1968), for example, emphasized the importance of Boas's pluralization of the concept of culture and its discreteness from the elite culture of the European literati. But the extension of "civilization" to the entire human stock, as of equal mental capacity, at least in 1911, is the alternative to a rigid dichotomy between "us" and "them."

In 1911 Boas begins with "Racial Prejudices," somewhat ironically depicting the self-satisfied white race's equation of its own unacknowledged privilege with "civilization." The "naive" and "unproved" assumption of "superior aptitude" judges everything by its own standards (1911b:3). "Civilization," like "mental faculty," cannot be the exclusive possession of a single group. Rather, the history of Europe documents intermingling of cultures, each according to its own "genius" (7). If the white race is distinguished, it is because of its capacity for assimilation from myriad sources. Boas moves directly from "genius" to the potential for "equal value," citing New World civilizations as evidence and exploring reasons for the favorable "conditions for assimilation" of the white race (13). These include demographic (small population size over wide territory; degree of colonial control/settlement), geographic (isolation), historical (length of contact), medical (disease and epidemic), technological, and cultural (degree of difference in customs and physical appearance among peoples in contact). On the one hand, Mohammedans, Chinese, and Arabs have developed their own civilizations quite independently. On the other hand, obstacles to progress among the "negro race" in America can hardly be attributed to aptitude alone. In 1938 he puts it: "Several races have developed a civilization of a type similar to the one from which our own has sprung, and a number of favorable conditions have facilitated its rapid spread in Europe. Among these, similar physical appearance, contiguity of habitat, and moderate difference in modes of manufacture were the most potent. When, later on, Europeans began to spread over other continents, the races with which they came into contact were not equally favorably situated" (1938:15). We could "hardly . . . predict" Negro achievements "if he were able to live with the Whites on absolutely equal terms" (15).

Boas makes short shrift of presumed biological evidence. All human groups are vastly divided from animals, rendering bestial analogies ridiculous. Differences in the central nervous system, which in 1911 could be measured only by such indexes as brain weight and cranial capacity, are dismissed equally rapidly. The "process of evolution" still continues, and human characteristics across the species cannot be assumed to be "stable" (1911b:20). "Modern biological concepts" document the "intensity" and "varying directions" of human traits, making separate human types impossible to identify and clearly differentiate, particularly over time (22).

In 1938 Boas elaborates on the multivalence of the term "primitive" as applied to both "bodily form and culture" (1938:3). Popular stereotypes persist due to the "racial isolation of Europe and the social segregation of races in America." Reasoning by equating "higher civilization" with innate racial aptitude is based in emotion, not science. This "idea" (by which he means prejudice) of superiority is deeply rooted. Both "race" and "civilization" are terms of judgment whose relationship must be clarified before "the form and growth of culture" can be adequately studied (6). More than in 1911, Boas emphasizes the terminology in which the problems of race are delineated. Here he talks about the "germs of civilization" of the white race (10), a term adopted from the evolutionary theory of Lewis Henry Morgan. The "primitiveness" of biological differences and how they may or may not lead to permanent inferiority must be distinguished from correspondence of racial groups with "the traits of the mental and social life of those people whom we call primitive from a cultural point of view" (18).

The 1938 introduction concludes with an enlargement of the scope of the question from America to "our globe," within which diverse races and cultural forms exist (1938:17). Thus, it is ever more urgent to resolve questions of race and culture by science. As nationality replaces race in categorizing human groups, the emotional urge to rigidify artificial categories enforces an unscientific determinism on complex and as yet answerable questions. After a quarter century of further study, answers from science still fail to offer closure.

The Scope of the Race Problem

Race was the single most pressing question Boas addressed over his career. His stature as a public intellectual reflects his refusal to take up the cause of a single race subject to oppression and discrimination in a single time and place. Although he was in the first instance a specialist in the Indigenous peoples of the Americas, Boas also addressed everyday racism in the lives of Negroes and Jews in America. Science overruled personal standpoint—his theories of the relation of mind, body, environment, and culture operated the same way regardless of the group in question. Boas did not consider his Jewish background germane to his analysis of prejudice against "the Hebrews" (Glick 1982). Boas presented himself as an American and a scientist, considering his unmentioned Jewishness a question of culture that no longer applied to his personal identity (545–65). Throughout his lifetime, Boas tenaciously and publicly opposed what we now call "scientific racism," including eugenics, restricted immigration policy, forced assimilation, and all other indignities to human freedom arbitrarily imposed on grounds of group membership.

Both editions culminate with a chapter on race. This is the underlying motivation for the coalescence of anthropology's potential contribution to the often virulent and irrational public debate about race. The immediate targets of Boas's own vitriol, however, responded to then contemporary events. In 1911 he attacked the American eugenicists who opposed miscegenation, supported strict segregationist laws, and blocked Negro civil and legal rights. The everyday racism of white America was deeply embedded in the "trammels of tradition" and required vigilant attention to science rather than emotion and fear of difference. By 1938 "Race Problems in the United States" had become "The Race Problem in Modern Society," a critique both of modernity's arrogant claim to represent the pinnacle of civilization and of the dehumanization of Jews in Hitler's Europe. The structure of the argument and most of the prose are unchanged from the first edition to the second, but they are reframed in more explicitly paradigmatic terms. Anthropology could provide both moral guidance and scientific evidence.

"Our modern civilization," particularly in America, was the starting point of the 1911 argument. Boas posed the urgency of the race question in terms of the increasing heterogeneity of an immigrant nation. He asserted the relevance of anthropological knowledge while simultaneously acknowledging that key questions for political policy could not be answered "at the present time with scientific accuracy" (1911b:251). The problem was defined as a mentalist one—Boas presented "to our minds" a narrative of American history tailored by British victors. He dismissed the biological effect of Native Americans or Asians on the national gene pool (in contemporary terminology). The demographic valence of the Negro, however, had far more potential impact (251).

The "pure racial types" of the European history in which most

Americans took great pride proved to be a comfortable fiction from a scientific point of view. Processes of historical change recurrently redistributed peoples and mingled them both biologically and culturally. The "causes" of presently observed group diversity were multiple: survival from past "stock" (a more neutral term than "race"), incursion of new physical types, or environmental change. Convergent evidence from different sources might or might not enable reconstruction of the history or dominant factors in particular cases. A "peculiar selective process" in each case, involving complex intersections of race, language, and culture, precluded prediction of the direction or intensity of change across cases (1911b:257). Only the existence of change itself could be assumed. The sole feature of such multivariate processes in America was population density (but even this difference was a matter of degree because population density was growing rapidly in all modern societies). The discreteness of intermingling communities could be maintained more effectively when larger numbers permitted interaction of like groups. A small group, in contrast, would become virtually homogeneous by the fourth generation. Therefore, according to Boas's math, European communities in America could not maintain "the continuance of racial purity of our nation" even if such a state had existed in some hypothetical prior golden age (260).

Boas then turns to the potential for "degradation of type" through racial mixture, moving from historical antecedents to "a biological standpoint" (1911b:261). His own data for the 1910 Census Commission demonstrate that environment is far more significant than heredity in disrupting the stability of European types. "The most fundamental traits of the body" are subject to rapid environmental modification, even more so for bodily traits developed through maturation rather than fully present at birth (262). Therefore, Boas asserts "with a high degree of confidence that mental traits as well as physical traits will be modified by the effect of the environment" (264). The reasoning by analogy depends on the implicitly entailed plasticity of the mental relative to the physical, reinforcing the more adequately measurable phenomena. It follows that environmental factors will preclude degeneration based on original type. Boas cautions that "speculation is as easy as accurate studies are difficult," but that the fears of biological degradation are already demonstrably imaginary (268). American racial mixtures differ "only in a sociological" sense built up by "the public mind" and "by a credulous public" into a fearsome shibboleth. He sticks to the biological side of the race question, because "mental life is so plastic, that no hereditary inability [to cope with modern life] can be assumed to exist in any of the peoples of Europe." Therefore, judgments of inferiority are unjustified for the "bulk" of the white or Negro populations. Indeed, any traits that might bear on "vitality and mental ability are much less than the individual variations in each race" (269).

These questions are too important to be left to emotional speculation, especially given that good census data focused on family lines, and the relative fertility of different groups could shed light on them. Longitudinal studies over twenty or more years would be required to provide credible evidence for more explicit population modeling. Boas cautions, however, that statistics are not directly comparable from one group to another, because the circumstances of migration vary considerably (e.g., single men versus families, mobility in the new country, extended family structures). The barriers to intermixture producing rapid blending are social, not biological. "Racial cohesion" cannot be assessed based on existing data (1911b:268). Forthcoming 1910 census results would clarify many of these trends for particular groups. Boas asserts that his statistical analysis of the biology of racial mixture "is quite in accord with the result of ethnological observation" (269). The achievements of Africans in Africa stand in point. Although differences in physical and mental characteristics doubtless exist, on the basis of "an unbiased estimate of the anthropological evidence so far," they are not sufficient to "stigmatize" full participation in "our social organization" in "modern life" (272).

Boas turns his anthropological lens to the emotional "instinct and fear" embedded in European tradition and the urge to maintain "a distinct social status" to prevent mixture (1911b:274). These strong emotions lead us to "call such feelings instinctive," but they are not predetermined by biology. In sum, "the data of anthropology teach us a greater tolerance of forms of civilization different from our own" and indicate the wisdom of "a fair opportunity" for all to contribute to "cultural progress" (273). He laments the failure of governments or scientific institutions to attack the question of the American Negro but does not make explicit the sharing of popular prejudices by scientists and statesmen as a cause of the myopia.

The 1938 edition of MPM features a new introduction, broadening the issue of race beyond the internal schisms of American society. The virulent racism "of the present day" is a recent thing in Europe, becoming "a foundation of public policy" only at the turn of the twentieth century as nationality became increasingly identified with racial unity, and national characteristics were attributed to biological descent (1938:253). In Germany in 1880, for example, Jews who assimilated were acceptable. Soon after, their racial character was redefined as "definite, unalterable" (253). A parallel deterioration of racial relations occurred with the Negro in America. These increasingly impermeable social barriers run counter to the progress of science: "Serious scientists, whenever free to express themselves, . . . have been drifting away from the opinion that race defines mental status" (254). Boas gestures here to the political control of science in interwar Germany and pointedly excludes those scientists hung up on hereditary morphological determinism from his ameliorative definition of science. Sadly, too many politicians share the race prejudice of "the uninformed public." Boas's position is unequivocal; he refers to

> the errors which underlie the theory that racial descent determines mental and social behavior. The term race, applied to human types, is vague. It can have a biological significance only when a race represents a uniform, closely inbred group, in which all family lines are alike. . . . These conditions are never realized in human types and impossible in larger populations. (254)

Boas acknowledges the difficulties of measuring "the range of variation of biologically determined personalities within a race" in part because personality itself cannot be defined independently of its cultural context. He is confident in concluding that "a very general primitive attitude of mind" is reflected in "the identification of the characteristics of an individual with the supposed typical characteristics of the group" (1938:255). The sharpness of this

1938 critique is far from his 1911 optimism that Americans would rise to the challenge of accepting scientific evidence of equal capacity of races. The political policies of Nazi racism are "primitive" because they pander to the worst of public stereotypes and reflect what must surely be willful blindness to the data of science.

Boas assumes the existence of "laws" that would explain the development of particular types even though we do not yet know these laws. We do know that Europe has no pure stocks and that moral judgment is impossible based on present data for scientific probability. His review of European evidence for group intermixture over time recapitulates the1911 argument and denies any evidence of "causes for the behavior of a people other than historical and social conditions" (1938:259). We know too little about the actual movements of people to establish detailed "historical facts." Recent movements of peoples resulting from "political terrorism directed against political opponents" are trivial in population terms, however significant they may be for individuals, compared to the effects of mass migration from Europe to America (260).

As in the American case in 1911, Boas laments the still unanswerable questions about race, because "the political question of dealing with these groups of people is of great and immediate importance" and repeats in 1938 that science rather than emotion must prevail (1938:261). "Modern transatlantic migration" is far from unique; social rather than biological barriers divide so-called races. Rapid migration facilitates the breakdown and intermixture of types through environmental influence. What Boas cannot predict may be answered by "energetic" studies "on a sufficiently large scale" (266) although the recent population studies of Frank Lorimer and Frederick Osborn are especially promising. Race, language, and culture, rather than biology alone, should influence the distribution of "hereditary constitutional types into social classes." The aim of eugenics to "improve constitutional health" is "highly commendable" but unattainable in practice on both moral and pragmatic grounds (267).

"The Negro in America" reflects the same problem as the Jew in Germany: "Ethnological observation does not countenance the view that the traits observed among our poorest Negro population are in any sense racially determined." He reiterates the litany of

African achievements in Africa and the insignificance of biological and mental differences that doubtless exist. He also notes the long-standing indifference of American science to resolving these issues, citing the recent work of his former student Melville Herskovits as an exception.

To evaluate individuals on the basis of the class to which we have already assigned them is "a survival of primitive forms of thought." Whatever characteristics exist in populations are never realized in "a single individual." "Freedom of judgment," then, turns to the attested merits of individuals. We must, Boas exhorts, "treasure and cultivate the variety of forms that human thought and activity has taken, and abhor, as leading to complete stagnation, all attempts to impose one pattern of thought upon whole nations or even upon the whole world" (1938:272). In the language of science, then, Boas pleads for the application of evidence to real-world decisions, for science to be valued above the wiles of nation-states, and for the obligation of the citizen to resist emotional restriction of human potential for scientifically invalid reasons. His theory and his practice merge.

The theoretical work revisited in this chapter demonstrates Boas's concern for his own legacy. His intentions, manifested in efforts at the time of and after his formal retirement to provide a popular textbook on anthropology and modern life, a second edition of MPM, and a volume of his selected essays highlight the pieces of his paradigm that he considered pivotal. These projects were remarkably consistent over his long career but have not always been in focus for his intellectual descendants. The thread that tied them together was the emancipatory potential of anthropology as he understood it. That Boasian commitment motivates revisionist scholarship and persists into the contemporary era of anthropology despite considerable changes in the discipline and the social, cultural, and political context in which it has moved beyond modernism.

Notes

1. Originally published as "Franz Boas as Theorist: A Mentalist Paradigm for the Study of Mind, Body, Environment and Culture," in *Historicizing Identity, Theory, Nation*, ed. Frederic W. Gleach and Regna Darnell, 1–25 (Lincoln: University of Nebraska Press, 2015). Histories of Anthropology 11.

2. In line with the standards of his era, Boas used what were accepted as respectful terms although many strike a discordant tone today. Our own usage will suffer a similar fate in its turn. These usages include "primitive," "man," "man[kind]," and "American Indian(s)." Characteristic ethnonyms that will be offensive to many contemporary readers include "Negro[es]," "Negro race," "Hebrews," and "Eskimo."

References

Baker, Lee D. 1998. *From Savage to Negro: Anthropology and the Construction of Race, 1896–1954*. Berkeley: University of California Press.

———. 2010. *Anthropology and the Racial Politics of Culture*. Durham NC: Duke University Press.

Bauman, Richard, and Charles Briggs. 2003. *Voices of Modernity: Language Ideologies and the Politics of Inequality*. Cambridge: Cambridge University Press.

Boas, Franz. 1911a. Introduction to the *Handbook of American Indian Languages*. Bureau of American Ethnology Bulletin 40. Washington DC: Government Printing Office.

———. 1911b. *The Mind of Primitive Man*. New York: Macmillan.

———. 1912. *Changes in Bodily Form of Descendants of Immigrants*. New York: Columbia University Press.

———. 1928. *Anthropology and Modern Life*. New York: W. W. Norton.

———. 1938. *The Mind of Primitive Man*. 2nd ed. New York: Macmillan.

———. 1940. *Race, Language and Culture*. New York: Free Press.

Bunzl, Matti, ed. 2004. Special issue, *American Anthropologist* 106 (3).

Cole, Douglas. 1999. *Franz Boas: The Early Years: 1858–1906*. Vancouver: Douglas and McIntyre.

Darnell, Regna. 1998. *And Along Came Boas: Continuity and Revolution in Americanist Anthropology*. Amsterdam: John Benjamins.

———. 2001. *Invisible Genealogies: A History of Americanist Anthropology*. Lincoln: University of Nebraska Press.

———. 2015. "Mind, Body and the Native Point of View: Boasian Theory at the Centennial of the Mind of Primitive Man." In *Franz Boas as Public Intellectual: Theory, Ethnography, Activism*, edited by Regna Darnell, Michelle Hamilton, Robert L. A. Hamilton, and Joshua Smith, 3–17. Lincoln: University of Nebraska Press.

Freed, Stanley. 2012. *Anthropology Unmasked: Museums, Science and Politics in New York City*. Wilmington OH: Orange Frazer Press.

Glick, Leonard B. 1982. "Types Distinct from Our Own: Franz Boas on Jewish Identity and Assimilation." *American Anthropologist* 84:545–65.

Harris, Marvin. 1968. *The Rise of Anthropological Theory*. New York: Thomas Crowell.

Hyatt, Marshall. 1990. *Franz Boas, Social Activist: The Dynamics of Ethnicity*. New York: Greenwood.

Jonaitis, Aldona, ed. 1995. *A Wealth of Thought: Franz Boas on Northwest Coast Art.* Seattle: University of Washington Press.

Kendall, Laurel, and Igor Krupnik, eds. 2003. *Constructing Cultures Now and Then: Celebrating Franz Boas and the Jesup North Pacific Expedition.* Washington DC: Arctic Studies Center, National Museum of Natural History, Smithsonian Institution.

Kuhn, Thomas S. 1970. *The Structure of Scientific Revolutions.* Chicago: University of Chicago Press.

Maud, Ralph. 2003. *Transmission Difficulties: Franz Boas and Tsimshian Mythology.* Vancouver: Talonbooks.

Stocking, George W., Jr. 1968. *Race, Culture, and Evolution: Essays in the History of Anthropology.* New York: Free Press.

———. 1974. *The Shaping of American Anthropology, 1883–1911: A Franz Boas Reader.* New York: Basic Books.

———, ed. 1996. *Volksgeist as Method and Ethic.* Madison: University of Wisconsin Press.

Turner, Nancy. 2014. *Ancient Pathways, Ancestral Knowledge.* 2 vols. Montreal: McGill-Queens University Press.

Vermeulen, Han. 2015. *Before Boas: The Genesis of Ethnography and Ethnology in the German Enlightenment.* Lincoln: University of Nebraska Press.

White, Leslie. 1963. *The Ethnology and Ethnography of Franz Boas.* Bulletin of the Texas Memorial Museum 6. Austin: Museum of the University.

———. 1966. *The Social Organization of Ethnological Theory: Monograph in Cultural Anthropology. Rice University Studies* 52:1–66.

Wickwire, Wendy. 2019. *At the Bridge: James Teit and an Anthropology of Belonging.* Vancouver: University of British Columbia Press.

Williams, Vernon J. 1996. *Rethinking Race: Franz Boas and His Contemporaries.* Lexington: University of Kentucky Press.

Zumwalt, Rosemary. 2018. *Franz Boas: The Emergence of an Anthropologist.* Lincoln: University of Nebraska Press.

10

The Powell Classification
of American Indian Languages

A linguistic classification requires a theoretical model.[1] Although linguists regularly deal with objective evidence of past changes in languages that reflect historical relationships, interpretation of the facts of historical linguistics is a less certain matter. Particularly when the linguist deals with unwritten languages, multiple interpretations may be useful for different purposes and, in particular contexts, equally correct. It is impossible to give a simple answer to the question "How many languages are there in Native America north of Mexico?" Linguistically serious, that is, defensible, answers have ranged from six to fifty-eight. Such divergent answers reflect different conceptions of the nature and function of a linguistic classification. The Americanist linguist is forced to evaluate the problem at hand and adapt the classification to best suit their purposes.

American "folk linguistics," a term provisionally adopted in parallel to the "oral tradition" shared among practitioners, has juxtaposed the fifty-eight unit classification of John Wesley Powell and the Bureau of Ethnology in 1891 with the six-unit classification of Edward Sapir in 1929. These are accepted as the conservative and bold extremes. In between lie a number of efforts at compromise. The fifty-eight unit classification has been reified as cautious, as though this makes it somehow more real. Rarely has choice of any classification been backed up by reference to the completeness or theoretical nature of the evidence on which it was based. A philosophical position for or against consolidation of stocks has been common and has obscured the interpretation of constantly growing evidence for particular genetic relationships. The controversy seems to have been guided by the imagery of the map of North America and the number of colors needed to fill it in. Powell's map was presented along with the 1891 classification and maintained by the bureau for ensuing research. Edward Sapir's presentation of his tentative grouping into only six major stocks was also accompanied by a map. The recent Voegelin and Voegelin map again presents colors on a map. Sapir appears to have been the only party to the dispute who clarified his position and acknowledged the arbitrariness of the number of units. His famous classification actually consisted of two distinct classifications: the first consisted of twenty-three units, those which had been clearly demonstrated; the second was the consolidation into six stocks that he realized would require further demonstration.

Examination of the evidence for Powell's classification—which still forms the conservative baseline for American Indian linguistics—will clarify some of the issues that still plague contemporary linguists in their assignment of genetic relationship among American Indian languages and the relation of this linguistic picture to understanding the prehistory of the continent. Untangling this will require detailed attention to the social context of the bureau classification, the design of the project, the allotment of tasks among the bureau staff, the purposes for which that classification was intended, the state of knowledge of American Indian languages in 1891, and the development of anthropology as a professional discipline in America. These are the factors that determined the character of a classification that is now interpreted independently of the context of its development, often to the detriment of open-minded and accurate assessment of the presently available evidence.

Forerunners

Although the Powell classification was the first to fill the blank spaces on the map of North America, it did not arise in a vacuum. Rather, Powell drew heavily on his predecessors and developed his own classification gradually over a number of years. As with most events singled out in retrospect by historians as marking an important occurrence, the year of publication is an almost incidental representation of the culmination of a more gradual emergence.

Speculation on the character and origin of American Indian languages[2] began with the discovery of the continent and the attempts of explorers and colonists to communicate with the Indians (Haas 1969; Hallowell 1960). Most early discussions underestimated the diversity of North American languages and concentrated on the easily recognizable relationships of the languages of the Northeastern U.S. and Canada. Such scholars as Peter Stephen Du Ponceau and John Pickering held that all American languages shared "a wonderful organization": a statement that referred more to national character than to linguistic structure. The implicit theoretical framework of this work assumed "folk psychology" would determine language typology in an era before the variables of language, race, and culture were clearly separated (see Boas 1911). When Thomas Jefferson insisted that linguistic diversity would prove greater than had been previously realized, he was drawing on nativist pride rather than a European philosophical perspective, regardless of surface similarities.

With such a prevailing attitude, problems of genetic classification of the Indigenous languages of North America were unlikely to emerge. Emphasis on grammar rather than vocabulary obscured evidence of close connection among languages. Techniques developed in Europe to deal with the history of Indo-European languages were not applied to American languages because they were unwritten. Although William Dwight Whitney suggested the value of such an approach, there were no European-trained scholars who specialized in American languages. As a result, study of these languages and their genetic relationships proceeded outside the developing framework of European linguistics and depended heavily on observation of obvious lexical cognates. The purposes of such classifications were more practical than philosophical.

From the beginning, explorers, missionaries, and traders collected vocabularies from the Indian peoples they visited. The resulting vocabulary lists, although not formally standardized, tended to overlap in many of their basic items so that comparison among languages could be made at later dates. Over the course of the nineteenth century, such items were standardized into questionnaires that covered all aspects of Indian cultures (Fowler 2011).

The first tentative effort at systematic genetic classification came from Albert Gallatin, primarily a statesman and diplomat, at the request of Alexander von Humboldt. This classification did not receive much publicity, and Gallatin is better known for its revision in 1836. Gallatin, like Jefferson, was interested in classifying the languages of the various tribes so that government agents could deal more effectively with them. The Gallatin classification presented comparative vocabularies, drew explicitly on Indo-European linguistics to interpret the results of comparison representing a number of genetic groupings, and noted that the similarities were insufficient to make common origin of the languages a virtual certainty. The 1836 revision was incomplete because of the data available to Gallatin: it dealt almost exclusively with the languages of the Northeast that were already relatively well known.

Two further revisions of the classification took place in 1848 and 1954. Their greater coverage resulted from data brought back by Horatio Hale from the Wilkes Expedition on the American Northwest Coast.

Another step toward standardization took place with the appearance of George Gibbs's vocabulary lists that were circulated through the Smithsonian Institution, founded in 1847, to everyone in contact with the Indians. By the time Powell turned to the problem of genetic classification in the 1870s, the Smithsonian manuscript collection included 670 vocabularies that were turned over to him in 1877 as director of the Geological Survey of the Rocky Mountain Region. Powell, a trained geologist, turned away from "pure" geology to study human use of the environment under different cultural conditions and thus to the study of ethnology. In 1877, two years before the founding of the Bureau of Ethnology (the "American" was added in 1892), Powell published the first edition of "An Introduction to the Study of American Indian Languages." In the same year, he added an appendix to the Smithsonian publication of Stephen Powers's *The Tribes of California*. The latter consisted entirely of thirteen vocabulary lists without comment on recognized cognates.

Powell's Contribution

The "Introduction" was intended to systematize the collection of future vocabularies beyond anything previously possible; it was designed for use by untrained observers. Powell revisited the Gibbs vocabulary and suggested a new alphabet. He also devoted himself to increasing the circulation of the standardized forms.

His staff checked lists of individuals working on American languages and noted those who had not advanced too far to change their system of recording. Manuscripts received by the bureau were frequently returned to be revised in accordance with the accepted alphabet. The alphabet also served within the bureau to guide Powell's staff in their work. Because of the bureau's unparalleled resources for publication and comparative work, many observers were eager to cooperate.

The questionnaire was intended to provide "just enough information" [*sic*; in original] to specify linguistic affiliation. Gibbs (BAE MS; see also Gibbs 1963) had already realized that "more remote affinities must be sought in a wider research, demanding a degree of acquaintance with their languages beyond the reach of transient visitors." The immediate problem was the genetic classification, and Powell, whatever his intentions, was unable to pursue more detailed research on particular languages; only in Siouan did he attempt subclassification within a major language family. Powell's goals did become more general; the 1880 edition of the "Introduction" included more information on morphology and signaled interest in the development of languages as well as listing lexical similarities. In practice, however, expediency prevailed; in the introduction to the 1891 classification, Powell stated:

> The author has delayed the present publication somewhat, expecting to supplement it with another paper on the characteristics of those languages which have been most fully recorded, but such supplementary paper has already grown too large for this place and is yet unfinished, while the necessity for the speedy publication of the present results seems to be imperative. The needs of the Bureau of Ethnology in directing the work of the linguists employed in it, and especially in securing and organizing the labor of a large body of collaborators throughout the country, call for this publication at the present time. (1891:216)

Powell was an applied scientist, and standardization was more important to him than completeness. Obtaining more data was the priority.

Powell was not entirely unaware of the difficulties of standardization. Faced with the need for an alphabet, he consulted an expert, William Dwight Whitney of Yale University, a noted oriental and Indo-European philologist. Although Whitney realized that any phonetic system would be arbitrary, Powell failed to foresee the objections of his staff. Whitney reminded him that "you have no good reason for regarding and treating me as an authority in these matters, . . . questions of alphabetizing are questions of expediency and compromise" (July 25, 1877: BAE). The staff, however, attributed the rigidity to Whitney rather than Powell and did not take into account the intensity of Powell's determination to have complete and comparable results for all languages. Albert Gatschet wrote to Powell:

> Professor Whitney is an excellent orientalist, but knowing nothing of the phonetics of American languages he could not be expected to draw up an alphabet settling all requitements in this line. There is perhaps nobody in world now living who could do it. (Gatschet to Powell, August 3, 1879: BAE)

Gatschet's fieldwork with particular languages had convinced him that changes would have to be made in the abstract scheme; he also objected to the insistence on using symbols acceptable to the government printing office, another practical consideration that was necessarily of great importance to Powell.

The linguistic classification, based on all these preliminary labors, was formulated in a series of stages. The 1877 annual report of Powell's Geological Survey noted that "a tentative classification of the linguistic families of the United States has been prepared." In 1880 the Tenth United States Census referred to Powell's linguistic classification, which "had been in tentative outline for several years" (quoted in Stegner 1954:268). The first effort to systematize a classification for the entire continent was a privately printed manuscript in 1885 entitled "Linguistic Families of the Indian Tribes North of Mexico, with a Provisional List of the Principal Tribal Names and Synonyms." The authors were listed as James Mooney, responsible for the synonymy, also part of Powell's plan to summarize existing knowledge of North American Indians, and Henry W. Henshaw, responsible for the linguistic classification. Few changes were made in the 1885 classification before it appeared in print in 1891 under Powell's name. Most of the changes (see table 1) resulted from fieldwork by the bureau staff and their reevaluation of evidence from the Smithsonian manuscripts and newly filled-out questionnaires. Although Gatschet had proposed the connection of Catawba and Siouan in 1881, Powell was convinced only when Dorsey reexamined the evidence between 1885 and 1891 (Powell 1891:188). Kwakiutl[3] and Nootka were combined into Wakashan on the basis of Franz Boas's fieldwork on the Northwest Coast, sponsored at different times by the bureau and the British Association for the Advancement of Science. Natchez and Taensa were merged into Natchesan presumably in response to Daniel Garrison Brinton's exposure of the Taensa language as an elaborate forgery in 1888. Powell's source for classifying Aleut as an unintelligible dialect of Eskimo (called Inuit in Canada) was probably William H. Dall, whose work on Eskimo (now known as Inuit and their language as Inutitut) was sponsored and published by the Smithsonian.

The two cases where Powell separated previous families both resulted from Henshaw's 1888 fieldwork in California. Henshaw confirmed Jeremiah Curtin's opinion that Esselenian and Salinan, Costanoan and Moquelumnan (Miwokan) were distinct (Powell 1891:139, 148). The latter decision was in opposition to Gatschet. In any case, Powell was at that time focused on lexical correspondences and accepted Henshaw's more conservative opinion. Gatschet, who was inclined to favor grammatical evidence, expressed his opinion, but it was rejected in the 1891 classification.

Four new stocks were added to the 1885 classification before 1891. The distinctness of Beothukan emerged from Gatschet's articles in the late 1880s (Powell 1891:133–40). Chimarikan was separated from Pomo on the basis of the Curtin vocabularies. Karankawan was separated from Attakapan in the absence of sufficient evidence for connection and the failure of the bureau to locate surviving speakers; Gatschet's 1884 vocabulary was considered inconclusive. Tunica was defined as an independent family on the basis of Gatschet's 1886 vocabularies, but his earlier connection with Caddoan was rejected. Powell also rejected Gatschet's suggestion, previous to this fieldwork, that Tunica, Shetimacha, and Atakapa might be related.

TABLE 1. The Powell classification

Powell stock	Recognition as distinct	BAE changes	Powell's rejections	Later connections
1. Adaizan	Gallatin 1836	In 1903 bureau accepted Gatschet 1887 joining to Caddoan	Powell noted Gatschet 1887 but rejected	Sapir 1929 put in Iroquois-Caddoan branch of Hokan-Siouan
2. Algonquian	Gallatin 1836			Sapir added Wiyot-Yurok and Beotuk within Algonquian-Wakashan
3. Athabascan	Gallatin 1836; Gatschet adds Gallatin's Kinai of 1854			Sapir put Athabascan-Tlingit-Haida in Na-Dene
4. Attakapan	Gallatin 1836		Related to Chitimachan in 1885 by Gatschet and to Karankawan by Sibley	Sapir put Tunican-Attakapan with Chitimachan under Tunican (Hokan-Coahuiltecan in Hokan-Siouan)
5. Beotukan	Latham thought distinct; Gatschet separated	Gatschet distinguished from Algonquian between 1885 and 1891	Gatschet 1887 put with Adaizan	Sapir left unclassified in 1921, but placed in Algonquian-Wakashan by 1929
6. Caddoan	Gallatin 1836	Independent of Tunican in 1886.	Powell noted proposed Chimarikan and Kulanapan (Pomo)	Sapir 1929 put it in Iroquois-Caddoan under Hokan-Siouan

7. Chimarikan	Powell 1891	Curtin vocabularies separated from Pomo; Powell and Gatschet united in 1877		Sapir placed in Northern Hokan under Hokan-Siouan
8. Chimakuan	Gibbs 1855 but named by Gatschet			Mosan or Wakashan-Salish in Sapir's Hokan-Siouan
9. Chimmesyan (Tsimishian)	Latham 1848			Sapir placed in Oregon Penutian under Penutian
10. Chinookan	Gallatin 1836		Powell follows Gallatin and Gatschet in rejecting Natchez connection	Sapir's Oregon Penutian in Penutian
11. Chitimachan	Gallatin 1836			Sapir placed Tunican in Hokan-Coahuiltecan under Hokan-Siouan
12. Chumashan	Latham 1856			Sapir's Salinan-Seri under Hokan-Coahuiltecan in Hokan-Siouan
13. Coahuiltecan	Orozco y Berra 1864 and Gatschet			Sapir's California Penutian in Penutian
14. Copehan (Wintun)	Latham 1856; Gatschet			Sapir's California Penutian in Penutian

15. Costanoan	Latham 1856	1885 classification accepted Gatschet's 1882 Mutsun; 1891 rejected from Henshaw field work in 1888 and Curtin vocabularies	Powell noted proposed Mutsun with Moquelumnan (Miwok)	Sapir's Miwok-Costanoan in California Penutian under Penutian
16. Eskimauan	Gallatin 1836	Aleut added between 1885 and 1891, probably by Dall's Smithsonian sponsored field work		Sapir's Eskimo-Aleut
17. Esselenian	Latham 1856	Curtin and Henshaw separated from Salinan in 1888	Powell noted possible relationship to Salinan	Sapir placed in Salish in Wakashan-Salish (Mosan) in Algonquian-Wakashan
18. Iroquoian	Gallatin 1836; Cherokee added by Hale, Hewitt			Sapir's Iroquois-Caddoan in Hokan-Siouan
19. Kalapooian	Gallatin 1848			Sapir's Oregon Penutian under Penutian
20. Karankawan	Gatschet 1886		Powell thought perhaps Attakapan	Sapir put in Coahuiltecan under Hokan-Siouan

21. Keresan	Powell and Gatschet accepted Turner 1856		Sapir left as an isolate in Hokan under Hokan-Siouan
22. Kiowan	Gallatin 1853; Turner 1856	Powell thought maybe related to Comanche	Sapir placed in Tanoan-Kiowan branch of Aztec-Tanoan
23. Kitunahan (Kutenai)	Hale 1846; Gallatin 1848; Latham 1856		Sapir put in Algonquian-Ritwan in Algonquian-Wakashan
24. Koluschan (Tlingit)	Gallatin 1836	Powell cited Boas for unclear boundary with Haida	Sapir placed with Athabascan and Haida in Na-Dene
25. Kulanapan (Pomo)	Gibbs 1853		Sapir's Northern Hokan in Hokan in Hokan-Coahuiltecan in Hokan-Siouan
26. Kusan	Gatschet 1882		Sapir's Coast Oregon Penutian in Oregon Penutian
27. Lutuamian (Klamath-Modoc)	Hale 1846; Gatschet	Powell rejected Hewitt's Waiilatpuan and Sahaptian connection	Sapir placed in Plateau Penutian with Hewitt's Waiilatpuan and Sahaptian
28. Mariposan (Yokuts)	Latham 1856; Powell and Gatschet 1877		Sapir's California Penutian in Penutian
29. Moquelumnan (Miwok)	Gibbs 1853	1885 classification accepted Gatschet's 1882 Mutsun; Powell realized might prove related to Costanoan	Sapir's Miwok-Costanoan in California Penutian in Penutian

Group				
30. Muskhogean	Gallatin 1836	Bureau accepted Natchez connection in 1903	Brinton merged with Natchez in 1863; Powell accepted Gatschet's rejection	Sapir's Natchez-Muskhogean in Eastern group of Hokan-Coahuiltecan in Hokan-Siouan
31. Natchesan	Gallatin 1836	Gatschet said Taensa distinct; Brinton proved forgery	Powell accepted Gatschet's rejection of Brinton's 1863 connection to Muskhogean	Sapir's Natchez-Muskhogean in Eastern group of Hokan-Coahuiltecan in Hokan-Siouan
32. Palaihnihan (Achomawi)	Hale 1846; Gallatin 1848	Bureau accepted Shasta-Achomawi in Sastean in 1903	Powell rejected Gatschet's joining of Sastean	Sapir's Natchez-Muskhogean in Northern group of Hokan-Coahuiltecan in Hokan-Siouan
33. Piman	Latham 1850		Brinton, Gatschet and Buschmann had already connected to Nahuatl	Sapir placed in Uto-Aztecan under Aztec-Tanoan
34. Pujunan (Maidu)	Latham 1856			Sapir's California Penutian in Penutian
35. Quoratean (Karok)	Gibbs 1853			Sapir's Northern Hokan in Hokan-Coahuiltecan in Hokan-Siouan
36. Salinan	Latham 1856; Powell 1877	1885 classification joined with Esselenian; Henshaw separated	Powell didn't mention Esselenian connection, but once thought Chumashan related	Sapir joined Salinan and Chumash in Salinan-Seri under Hokan in Hokan-Coahuiltecan in Hokan-Siouan

Family	Source		Powell	Sapir
37. Salishan	Gallatin 1836		Powell noted Boas and Gatschet joined to Palaihnihan	Sapir placed in Wakashan-Salish or Mosan in Algonquian-Wakashan
38. Sastean	Hale 1846; Gallatin 1848	In 1903 bureau accepted connection to Palaihnihan	Powell rejected Gatschet's Palaihnihan	Sapir's Northern Hokan in Hokan-Coahultecan in Hokan-Siouan
39. Shahaptian	Hale 1846; Gallatin 1848		Powell rejected Hewitt's connection with Lutuamian and Waiilatpuan	Sapir put Hewitt's Shahaptian-Lutuamian-Waiilatpuan together as Plateau Penutian in Penutian
40. Shoshonean	Gallatin 1836		Powell rejected Buschmann's Nahuatl connection	Sapir placed in Uto-Aztecan within Aztec-Tanoan
41. Siouan	Gallatin 1836; Gatschet and Dorsey added Catawba, Gatschet added Biloxi and Gale Tutelo			Sapir placed in Siouan-Yuchi in the Eastern group of Hokan in Hokan-Coahuiltecan in Hokan-Siouan
42. Skittagetan (Haida)	Gallatin 1848		Powell rejected Boas's connection with Tlingit in Koluschan	Sapir placed Haida and Tlingit together (along with Athabascan) in Na-Dene
43. Takilman (Takelma)	Gatschet 1882		Powell thought some further connections would emerge	Sapir placed in Oregon Penutian in Penutian

Family	Reference	Notes	Sapir's placement
44. Tanoan	Powell 1878	Powell thought might prove Shoshonean but accepted Gatschet's rejection	Sapir placed in Tanoan-Kiowa under Aztec-Tanoan
45. Timuquanan	Smith 1853; Brinton 1859; Gatschet 1877, 1884	Both Gatschet and Brinton related to Carib	Sapir raised the question of placing it with Natchez-Muskhogean in Eastern group of Coahuiltecan in Hokan-Coahuiltecan in Hokan-Siouan
46. Tonikan (Tunican)	Gallatin 1836	Gatschet's 1886 vocabularies separated from Caddoan	Sapir placed in Coahuiltecan in Hokan-Coahuiltecan in Hokan-Siouan
47. Tonkawan	Gatschet 1876		Sapir's Coahuiltecan in Hokan-Coahuiltecan in Hokan-Siouan
48. Uchean (Yuchi)	Gallatin 1836	Powell rejected Hewitt's connection with Lutuamian and Shahapatian	Sapir's Siouan-Yuchi in Eastern group of Coahuiltecan in Hokan-Coahuiltecan in Hokan-Siouan
49. Walilatpuan (Cayuse-Molale)	Hale 1846; Gallatin 1848		Sapir placed Hewitt's three families together as Plateau Penutian in Penutian
50. Wakashan (Kwaqiutl and Nootka)	Gallatin 1836; Boas 1887	After 1885 Powell accepted Boas's Wakashan	Sapir's Wakashan-Salish was placed in Algonquian-Wakashan

51. Washoan	Gatschet 1882		Sapir's Hokan in Hokan-Coahuiltecan in Hokan-Siouan
52. Weitspekan (Yurok)	Gibbs 1853; Gatschet 1877		Sapir's Ritwan (with Wiyot) in Algonquian-Ritwan in Algonquian-Wakashan
53. Wishoskan (Wiyot)	Gibbs 1853; Powell and Gatschet 1877		Sapir's Ritwan (with Yurok) in Algonquian-Ritwan in Algonquian-Wakashan
54. Yakonan	Hale 1846; Gallatin 1846	Powell accepted Dorsey's joining of Siuslaw and Alsea on Gatschet's work	Sapir's classification separated the two but placed both in Oregon Coast Penutian in Penutian
55. Yanan	Powers 1877 on Curtin vocabulary		Sapir placed in Northern Hokan in Hokan-Coahuiltecan in Hokan-Siouan
56. Yukian	Powell 1877		Sapir left as an independent branch of Hokan-Siouan
57. Yuman	Turner 1856; Latham 1856	Powell followed Hewitt separating from Serian; Gatschet and Brinton had already related; Powell notes proposed connection to Piman	Sapir placed Esselen-Yuman in Hokan in Hokan-Coahuiltecan in Hokan-Siouan
58. Zunian	Turner 1856	Powell and Gatschet agree isolate	Sapir placed tentatively in Aztec-Tanoan

Nor was the 1891 classification put forth as a finished product. For each stock, Powell listed the history of previous work, often indicating that additional connections had been suggested, with the implication that further research might clarify some of the problems. One can almost identify a second 1891 classification best described as a prospectus for the future (see table 1). The connections of Moquelumnan and Costanoan, Esselenian and Salinan, Chimarikan and Kulanapan (Pomo), Shetimachan and Attakapan, and Karankawan and Attakapan have been discussed above. Adaize and Caddoan, Shasta and Achomawi were noted as possible relationships; both were united in the bureau's 1903 revision of the classification. The only other revision accepted within the bureau itself—the uniting of Natchez and Muskhogean suggested by Daniel Garrison Brinton in 1863, was dismissed by Gatschet in 1880s. Powell noted two connections proposed by Boas—Haida and Tlingit, Salish and Wakashan—but considered both tentative. He also rejected Brinton's connection of Piman and Nahuatl and noted the possible relationship of Tanoan and Shoshonean. Both of these relationships have considerable time depth, making the units identified much more general than the others in Powell's scheme. Gatschet had attributed the similarities between Kiowa (Tanoan) and Shoshonean to "long association of these peoples" (Powell 1888:xxv) (i.e., nongenetic relationship through recent borrowing or language mixture), and Powell had avoided forming "a decided opinion" (Powell 1891:198). Finally, Powell suggested that Natchez and Chitimacha, Timuquana and Carib might eventually prove to be related. Although this possibility of a second classification has not been recognized by later students, it must be seen as part of the conception and implementation of the bureau enterprise.

Although the 1891 classification appeared under Powell's name, he consistently described it as a cooperative task. The question of authorship does not seem to have been an important one to Powell's staff. It became an issue later for linguists and anthropologists attempting to understand the background of the classification. Depending on the definition of authorship, at least three parties may be held responsible: Powell himself, Henry Wetherby Henshaw, and the two linguists, Albert S. Gatschet and John Owen

Dorsey. Examination of the particular contributions of each will clarify the matter further.

Most of the fieldwork was done by Dorsey and Gatschet. Gatschet clearly considered himself a coauthor, and Powell acknowledged his debt to the two bureau linguists for the preparation of his comparative lists. In reviewing the development of American linguistics in 1914, Pliny Earle Goddard attributed the classification to them (1914:559). To Powell himself, however, collection of the evidence was an objective rather than an analytical task. For example, Powell was not careful to assign his staff to tasks with which they had any previous acquaintance. He rejected Gatschet's separation of Siuslaw and Yakonan (1891:210) on the basis of a brief trip to Oregon by Dorsey. Only the ready-made vocabularies from Powell's "Introduction" were available as evidence. Although Dorsey recognized the absurdity, Powell clearly did not. In the words of Sturtevant, reevaluating the bureau's linguistic contribution:

> For this sort of relationship, publication of the evidence was hardly necessary. . . . Powell was quite careful to give credit for the collection of vocabularies and for work on etymology and mapping but he tended to pass over the actual comparisons without giving specific credit. . . . The difficult matter was to obtain the vocabularies; once these were in hand, simple juxtaposition was all that was required and this could have been done by almost anyone, and certainly was done in different instances by almost all the early staff of the Bureau. (1959:198)

Henshaw was responsible for the administrative work involved in compiling the classification. He was listed as the author of its 1885 version and was responsible for deciding what fieldwork was still necessary; all letters of inquiry about American Indian languages were referred to him. Alfred L. Kroeber, in reviewing the background of the classification, concluded that Henshaw's biological training was the source of the principles of synonymy and priority of nomenclature that guided the bureau project. He described Powell's role:

> It is well known that Powell did not carry out the work of this undertaking. Another hand, that of a scholar-administrator, was

necessary for the fulfillment and realization of the plan. That he was not by training or profession an anthropologist will make his distinction all the greater. But it was Powell's mind that first conceived the idea of a classification . . . and it was Powell's will and character that held to the idea. (1905:580)

However, the bureau apparently did not consider this an accurate estimate of Henshaw's contribution:

Many thanks for calling attention to the passage at the beginning of my paper on nomenclature. I am not so situated here as to find out definitely anything as to the real authorship of Powell's work. I had always understood that the man who was responsible for the work was Henshaw and he himself has since stated this to me quite explicitly. If I am correct, the work was done by a number of men, including Henshaw himself, under Henshaw's directions according to the general plans of Powell which he [Powell] had not been able to carry out, with an understanding that the acknowledged responsibility for the work was to be entirely Powell's. I understand, for instance, that while the general idea of a classification was Powell's, it was Henshaw who was really responsible for the principles of nomenclature whoever may have collaborated with him in the actual work of compiling the paper. (Kroeber to Hodge, November 9, 1905: ALK)

Hodge's reply apparently did not satisfy Kroeber, since he referred later to Powell's classification "which, as is well known, was largely the result of the labors of H. W. Henshaw" (Kroeber 1913:390).

Principles of Classification

The actual classification, then, was a practical enterprise. Problems of ethnological classification (ultimately of reservation policy and congressional approval) were more salient than the complexities of historical linguistics. As Kroeber noted: "What Powell did was to seize clearly the conception of the necessity of some classification, and of the inevitability of this being on a linguistic basic, and then to carry through his purpose rigorously, systematically and completely" (Kroeber 1905:579); or, as Sturtevant has stated,

Powell stresses "the accumulation of data, rather than any problems of comparative linguistics" (1959:196). Powell saw the linguistic classification as a step toward compilation of a synonymy of all the Indian tribes. Distant genetic relationships were of little interest for such purposes. Swadesh has even suggested that the bureau staff "did not ordinarily set down the points of contact they noted between one and another language" (1967:281). Powell himself wrote:

> To establish connection between languages, it is necessary to compare extensive vocabularies, to study the phonetic systems and to analyze roots of words. To limit comparison to a large number of languages having no possible affinities can lead to no beneficial results and tends only to confuse and mislead. (Powell to Faris, April 12, 1888: BAE)

Powell was quite clear about the principles upon which the 1891 classification was based. His text listed six postulates designed to elucidate the history and laws of development of both language in general and languages in particular (Powell 1891:216):

1. The classification was deliberately conservative;

2. There were many cases of doubtful assignment;

3. All languages contained borrowed material;

4. There had probably been more languages in primitive times;

5. All languages had diverse histories;

6. Primitive languages change slowly.

These postulates, taken together, constituted a reasonably coherent philosophy of language, but one that would not be accepted in its entirety today by any serious scholar. The implications of this framework for Powell's decisions must be part of any contemporary effort to evaluate the utility of the 1891 classification as a conservative baseline for further research.

Powell intended his classification to be based entirely on lexical evidence. He believed that the original character of a language was preserved in its vocabulary, whereas the grammar was subject to change:

Grammatical similarities are not supposed to furnish evidence of cognation, but to be phenomena in part relating to state of nature and in part adventitious. . . . Grammatic structure is but a phase or accident of growth and not a primordial element of languages. The roots of a language are its most permanent characteristics, and while the words which are formed from them may change so as to obscure their elements or in some cases even to lose them, it seems that they are never lost from view but can be recovered in large part. The grammatic structure or plan of a language is forever changing, and in this respect the languages may become entirely transformed. (1891:88)

This statement was fully consistent with Powell's acceptance of the notion of Du Ponceau, Pickering, and others that American Indian languages fell into "a class entirely distinct from any others in the world" (Powell to Morris, April 28, 1896: BAE). The argument was really an evolutionary one. Grammar was indicative of the stage of development reached by a particular group of people. Because such changes could occur fairly rapidly, grammar could not be used for classification of tribes. Grammar was a feature of all American Indian languages by which they could be compared to languages found in other parts of the world. Powell took for granted that he knew the evolutionary sequence by which human languages developed to their ultimate efficiency in English. However, the complexity and variability of his data necessitated a philosophy that could incorporate exceptions. He seized upon the notion of a mixed language caused by the inherent instability of grammatical forms:

The languages are very unequally developed in their several parts. Low gender systems appear with high tense systems, highly evolved case systems with slightly developed mode systems, and there is scarcely any one of these languages . . . [W]hich does not exhibit archaic devices in its grammar. (1891:139)

Given the possibility of mixed languages, Powell believed that although details of his classification might be modified, the number of units would probably remain constant. Some families would fuse in the future, but no new linguistic families remained to be discovered in North America. Assuming "the present methods of linguistic analysis" (1891:102), drastic changes seemed unlikely. Powell ignored the innovations within particular languages and thus most of the insights of historical linguistics as developed in Europe. Rather, he stressed divergence of related languages through borrowing from unrelated neighbors and envisioned each of his fifty-eight stocks as a composite resulting from a complex history. Linguistic classification reflected social evolution in the sense that borrowing occurred with incorporation into progressively larger political units. Languages began in pristine isolation and became more similar through absorption from contiguous tribes (141). Indeed, differentiation of dialects into languages was directly comparable to organic specialization and biological differentiation, since a language spoken over a wider area was deemed to be superior (Powell to Taylor, February 23, 1881: BAE). Culture growth through blending was described by Powell:

> But the conspicuous fact of the aboriginal [Indigenous in contemporary terminology] American tongues is their diversity, a diversity so wide as to imply essentially independent development. . . . the present tendency is toward diffusion through imitation, and this tendency is so far preponderant that the vast collections of records of aboriginal languages are little more than records of linguistic blending; so that the well-ascertained course of linguistic development is toward interchange and thence to ultimate union. (Powell 1898:xxxv).

Powell's theory of political organization was formulated to apply to social structure in the tradition of Lewis Henry Morgan and only incidentally applied to language. Under Powell's direction, J. N. B. Hewitt applied the mechanism of blending to his studies of Iroquois cosmologies (Powell 1899:xliv); originally independent myths had blended more often than they had become differentiated, "so that myth, like the speech in which it is crystallized, is a composite of many elements."

In spite of its roots in evolutionary theory, this view of the difficulties of preparing a linguistic classification that would accurately reflect culture history was startlingly similar to that of Franz Boas, formulated a generation later in methodological caution to the efforts of his students to define more distant relationships of linguistic stocks. Like Powell, Boas was interested in linguistics primarily as a tool for ethnology; again, like Powell, he preferred a conservative classification. He even stressed the areal diffusion of grammatical traits, arguing that resulting similarities between two languages could not be distinguished from those that were genetic. Boas's critique of evolutionary generalization and call for study of the culture history of particular peoples thus led him to a position surprisingly similar to the evolutionary one he attacked. He did not participate in the classificatory work of his students, spearheaded by Sapir, during the first two decades of the twentieth century to revise the Powell classification by demonstrating that the presence of sound correspondences by definition reflected common origin. Boas did not, of course, stress the evolutionary implications of Powell's work, and his critique has been effectively forgotten in the realm of social theory.

The Brintonian Alternative

Powell had considerable choice in procedure and theoretical basis in planning his classification. A comparison to the other major linguistic classification of the late nineteenth century will illustrate the alternatives. In the same year as Powell's famous classification, Daniel Garrison Brinton, an independent scholar from Philadelphia (see Darnell 1988), presented a classification of the languages of North and South America in *The American Race* (Brinton 1891). Brinton was committed in principle to the priority of grammatical factors in identifying genetic affiliation of languages. He omitted the evolutionary arguments entailed in Powell's discussions of grammar:

> Wherever the material permitted it, I have ranked the grammatic structure of a language superior to its lexical elements in deciding upon relationship. In this, I follow the precepts and example of students in the Aryan and Semitic stocks, although the methods have been rejected by some who have written on American tongues. As for myself, I am abidingly convinced that

the morphology of any language whatever is its most permanent and characteristic feature. (1885:x)

In practice, however, the data forced Brinton to use lexical evidence in the absence of adequate grammatical evidence. It is probable that his stress on grammar was in part a deliberate attempt to differentiate his work from that of Powell and the Bureau of [American] Ethnology. His disclaimer, in spite of its effect on the results presented throughout the volume, appears only in the appendix of lexical lists for little-studied languages of South America:

> The linguistic classification of American tribes is at present imperfect in many regions on account of the incomplete information about their tongues. A proper comparison of languages or dialects includes not merely the vocabulary, but the grammatical forms and the phonetic variations which the vocal elements undergo in passing from one form of speech to another. In some respects, the morphology is more indicative of relationship than the lexicon of tongues; and it is in these grammatical aspects that we are peculiarly poorly off when we approach American dialects. Yet it is also likely that the tendency of late years has been to underestimate the significance of merely lexical analogies. The vocabulary, after all, must be our main stand-by in such an undertaking. (1891:344)

On the whole, the Brinton classification (see table 2) is less satisfactory than Powell's, although Brinton was less conservative than Powell in principle. His thirteen major units for North America involve a number of consolidations that Powell was unwilling to accept. He combined Gallatin's Pawnee and Caddoan, joined Catawba to Yuchi, Natchez, Chetimacha, and Adaize, and was the first to relate Chontal, Seri, and Hokan (for which Kroeber presented detailed evidence in 1907). Brinton even considered the possibility that Kiowa and Shoshonean were related but concluded that the evidence was insufficient; this relationship was proposed again by John P. Harrington a number of years later. Brinton accepted the connection of Nahuatl and Shoshonean that had been suggested by Buschmann's extensive studies.

TABLE 2. The Brinton Classification

By linguistic stocks	By language families
A. North Atlantic	1. Eskimos and Aleutians
	2. Beothuks
	3. Athabascans
	4. Algonkins
	5. Iroquois
	6. Chahta-Muskokis
	7. Taakapas, Carankaways, Tonkaways, Coahultecans, Maritans, Catawabas, Yuchis, Timucuas, Natchez, Chetimachas, Tonicas, Adaize
	8. Pawnees (Caddoes)
	9. Dakotas (Sioux)
	10. Kioways
B. North Pacific	1. Northwest Coast and California: Tlingit, Haidahas, Salish, Sahaptins, etc.
	2. Yumas
	3. Pueblos: Kera, Tehua, Zuni
C. Central Group	1. Uto-Aztecan
	a. Ute (Shoshonean)
	b. Sonoran
	c. Nahuatl
	etc. . . . (Mexican languages not included by Powell)

Other comparisons were less fortunate. Brinton was more willing to accept superficial similarities when the classification made sense geographically, indicating that he, like Powell, saw linguistic classification as a means to organize the ethnographic diversity of North America. Several of Brinton's categories are geographical and cultural rather than linguistic, such as the Pueblos, the Northwest Coast, and California. Each of these groups includes considerable linguistic diversity in the Powell classification and crosses several major stocks in the six-unit Sapir classification. Brinton noted explicitly that the fifty-nine stocks of the bureau classification were separated into five geographic groups "for convenience" (1891:57).

Despite the reduction in number of stocks, therefore, Brinton's classification did not increase the overall time depth inherent in the classification of American Indian languages. Brinton's major claim to priority in the classification is his recognition Uto-Aztecan. He was intrigued by this language family because it included the range of cultural development within the American continent— from the root-digging Utes to the Nahuatl empires of Mexico. His willingness to accept this connection was consistent with his belief that the American continent comprised a single cultural and political type in an evolutionary sequence. Johann Carl Eduard Buschmann, using his data only to demonstrate the northern origin of the Aztecs, did not outline the full extent of the family, but Brinton could easily extend his interpretation. Powell rejected the primarily grammatical evidence on which Brinton's identification of Uto-Aztecan was based. In fact, he apparently never examined the original German since he did not realize that Buschmann had not himself connected Nahuatl to the other languages of the stock. Unfortunately, Brinton presented little evidence for the connection, and skepticism by later workers was not unjustified:

> A short comparative wordlist was given in support of the relationship of the languages. It was much too short to offer convincing evidence, and since Powell's work was on the whole more careful than Brinton's those who consulted only Powell and Brinton could hardly be blamed if they rejected the Uto-Aztecan stock. (Lamb 1964:120)

The Powell and Brinton classifications can profitably be juxtaposed as evidence of the institutional development of American anthropology in the late nineteenth century. Powell headed the first major organization for anthropological research; Brinton, although he technically held the first American professorship in anthropology, was outside the developing institutional framework of the discipline. His primary scholarly affiliation was with the American Philosophical Society in Philadelphia, and he did not have access to the results of a corps of scholars. None of his data was drawn from personal fieldwork.

Brinton attempted to use the results of the bureau while their classification was in progress. As early as 1885, he requested "the current Bureau classification of tribes," whether "by linguistic stocks or otherwise" (Brinton to Pilling, June 12, 1885 BAE). Pilling's reply excluded Brinton from access to the unpublished materials of the bureau:

> I regret to have to say that the linguistic classification is still unfinished—indeed, in so unsatisfactory a condition that it would scarcely be intelligible to those not engaged in its compilation. It is a slow affair, as you may well imagine, and I fear it will be some time yet before it is available for use. (Pilling to Brinton, June 13, 1885: BAE)

In 1890 Brinton wrote to Henshaw several times inquiring about details of classification. He was at this time preparing a series of lectures for the Academy of Natural Sciences of Philadelphia that served as the basis for his 1891 book. Brinton's published classification acknowledged Henshaw's aid with the Northwest Coast material (through the work of Boas for the bureau) and for "various other suggestions" (Brinton 1891:xii). He then indicated that he had been denied access to the bureau classification.

This, however, is not entirely accurate. In November 1890 Brinton had asked to see the proofs of the bureau classification. On learning that the project was not so far along, he voluntarily withdrew his request in order not to be accused of basing his own work unfairly on that of the bureau (Brinton to Henshaw, November 15, 1890: BAE):

> I am much obliged to you for the courteous offer . . . about the map, etc. At first I was inclined to come on and look it over; but on second thoughts, I think I had better not. The information I wish to gain could be made public soon in my lectures, and perhaps in printed reports from them, and this, I can readily see, might not be agreeable to the Bureau. It would, for this reason, be better for me not to see the map, as even if I confined my publication to matters already in my possession, some members of the Bureau might think I had learned them by the facilities you offer, and I had refrained from giving credit. There are, in fact, only a few points in the ethnology of the United States area about which I am much in doubt.

It must have been at this time that Brinton resolved to place his own work in direct competition with that of the bureau. Although his optimism was somewhat unrealistic, his efforts do provide a point of departure for evaluating the post-1891 Powell classification in terms of its original historical context. Powell intended to extend and correct the classification on the basis of further research by the bureau and its collaborators, but the 1891 results formalized previous knowledge of American Indian languages so systematically that the classification itself became the starting point for future work. The bureau (see table 1) accepted only three further reductions in the number of stocks (Adaize-Caddoan, Natchez-Muskhogean, and Shasta-Achomawi). After Powell's death in 1902, the bureau lost its central role in American anthropology and did not participate actively in the next wave of fieldwork, which concentrated on California and the Northwest Coast, producing further revisions by Sapir, Kroeber, Radin, and others (Darnell 1971, chapter 11, this volume).

Notes

1. Originally published as "The Powell Classification of American Indian Languages," *Papers in Linguistics* 4 (1971): 71–110.

2. The term "American Indian" is used consistently by disciplinary convention among linguists in discussions of classification and by many of their sources. I have changed this to "Native American" or "Indigenous" when speaking in my own voice. Other terms that are problematic today include "Native American (languages)," "Indian (languages)," "Amerindian (dialects or tribes)," and even more problematically "primitive languages" and "primitive tribes." I use the language of my sources so as not to distort the discourse that is the subject of this chapter.

3. Now known as Kwakwaka'wakw but cited in this chapter as "Kwakiutl" for ease of reading.

References

Boas, Franz. 1911. *The Mind of Primitive Man*. New York: Macmillan.

Brinton, Daniel Garrison. 1885. "American Indian Languages [*sic*] and Why We Should Study Them." *Pennsylvania Magazine of History and Biography* 9:15–35.

———. 1891. *The American Race: A Linguistic Classification and Ethnographic Description of the Native Tribes of North and South America*. New York: N. D. C. Hodges.

Darnell, Regna. 1971. "The Revision of the Powell Classification." *Papers in Linguistics* 4:233–56.

————. 1988. *Daniel Garrison Brinton: The "Fearless Critic" of Philadelphia.* University of Pennsylvania Publications in Anthropology no. 3. Philadelphia: Department of Anthropology, University of Pennsylvania.

Fowler, Don D. 2011. "Notes on Inquiries in Anthropology: A Bibliographic Essay" In *Toward a Science of Man*, edited by Timothy H. H. Thoresen, 15–32. Berlin: De Gruyter Mouton.

Gibbs, George. 1863. *Instructions for Research Relative to the Ethnology and Philology of America.* Smithsonian Miscellaneous Collections 160. Washington DC: Smithsonian Institution.

Goddard, Pliny Earle. 1914. "The Present Condition of Our Knowledge of North American Indians." *American Anthropologist* 16:555–601.

Haas, Mary. 1969. "Grammar or Lexicon? The American Indian Side of the Question from Duponceau to Powell." *International Journal of American Linguistics* 35:239–55.

Hallowell, A. Irving. 1960. "The Beginnings of Anthropology in America." In *Selected Readings from the American Anthropologist, 1888–1920*, edited by Frederica de Laguna, 1–99. Evanston IL: Row, Peterson.

Kroeber, Alfred L. 1905. "Systematic Nomenclature in Ethnology." *American Anthropologist* 7:579–93.

————. 1913. "The Determination of Linguistic Relationship." *Anthropos* 8:389–401.

Lamb, Sydney. 1964. "The Classification of the Uto-Aztecan Languages: A Historical Survey." In *Studies in Californian Linguistics*, edited by William Bright, 106–25. University of California Publications in Linguistics 34. Berkley: University of California Press.

Powell, John Wesley. 1888. *Sixth Annual Report of the Bureau of Ethnology to the Secretary of the Smithsonian Institution, 1884–85.* Washington DC: Government Printing Office.

————. 1891. "Indian Linguistic Families of America North of Mexico." In *Seventh Annual Report of the Bureau of Ethnology to the Secretary of the Smithsonian Institution, 1885–86*, 7–139. Washington DC: Government Printing Office.

————. 1898. *Seventeenth Annual Report of the Bureau of Ethnology to the Secretary of the Smithsonian Institution, 1895–96.* 2 vols. Washington DC: Government Printing Office.

————.1899. *Eighteenth Annual Report of the Bureau of Ethnology to the Secretary of the Smithsonian Institution, 1896–97.* 2 vols. Washington DC: Government Printing Office.

Sapir, Edward. 1929. "Central and North American Languages." *Encyclopedia Britannica* 5: 138–41.

Stegner, Wallace. 1954. *Beyond the Hundredth Meridian: John Wesley Powell and the Second Opening of the West.* Boston: Houghton Mifflin.

Sturtevant, William C. 1959. "The Authorship of the Powell Classification." *International Journal of American Linguistics* 25:196–99.

Swadesh, Morris. 1967. "Linguistic Classification in the Southwest." In *Southwestern Ethnolinguistics*, edited by Dell Hymes, 281–309. The Hague: Mouton.

11

....

The Revision of the Powell Classification

The Powell classification of 1891 emerged gradually from ongoing research and was almost immediately subjected to revisionary pressures.[1] Although collection of vocabularies and tentative efforts at classification began much earlier, the classification that is still accepted today as the conservative baseline for American Indian linguistics is the one that resulted from the cooperative effort of the Bureau of Ethnology founded by John Wesley Powell in 1879 (Darnell 1969, 1971a).[2] Powell systematized the knowledge accumulated by his predecessors, drawing particularly on the successive classifications of Albert Gallatin in 1836, 1848, and 1854 and the standardized vocabulary list prepared by George Gibbs in 1863. His staff supplemented the vocabularies and grammars already collected by the Smithsonian Institution with carefully chosen fieldwork in a systematic effort to determine the linguistic affiliation of every North American language and dialect.[3]

Powell's aims were not primarily linguistic. In the late nineteenth century, the American Indian[4] was still the major foreign policy problem of the United States government. The need was urgent for a classification of tribes that would permit intelligent administration and settlement of Indians. Other projects envisioned by Powell in his efforts to "organize anthropological research in America," particularly the synonymy that eventually became the Introduction to the *Handbook of American Indians*, presupposed a linguistic classification. Powell's classification was the first to omit all blank spaces on the map of North America. It was deliberately conservative, having been designed as a guide to ethnographic inquiry rather than as an extension of the limits of linguistic inference.

Powell's successors tended to consider the fifty-five stocks he identified as units whose existence had been clearly demonstrated and could be taken for granted. Those who shared his agenda of using linguistic classification as a means to ethnographic ends were satisfied with this formulation. Because it was the first complete classification, Powell's heuristic classification was reified as a convenient baseline against which to evaluate later suggestions of genetic relationship.

Major changes were afoot in American anthropology at the end of the nineteenth century. Franz Boas, the preeminent figure of early twentieth-century American anthropology, began his Northwest Coast fieldwork partially under the auspices of the Bureau of Ethnology. Initially, he accepted the bureau's emphasis on the need for broad-scale classification of languages and tribes. The Powell classification drew on his own fieldwork and that of his staff. Boas had suggested in 1888 that Haida and Tlingit were related. Because the preliminary evidence was grammatical rather than lexical, Boas expressed his opinion cautiously, and Powell concluded that the relationship remained unproven. The 1891 classification, however, listed the connection as a subject for further research. Powell did accept Boas's joining of Wakashan (Kwakiutl[5] and Nootka). By 1849 Boas was proposing genetic relationships as the appropriate explanation for the similarities, primarily grammatical, between Athabascan, Tlingit, and Haida as well as Salish, Chemakuan, and Nookta (now known as Nuu Chah Nulth). He noted with regard to Tlingit and Haida that this similarity of structure becomes the more surprising if we take into account that not one of the neighboring languages shows any of the peculiarities enumerated here. The structural resemblances of the two languages and their contrast with the neighboring languages can be explained only by the assumption of a common origin. The number of words which may possibly be connected by etymology is small, and the similarities are doubtful. Nevertheless the structural resemblance must be considered final proof of a historical connection between the two languages (Boas 1894).

Boas was prepared to go beyond Powell in combining evidence from grammar with that of vocabulary to assign genetic relationship. The larger relationships were not, however, widely accepted at the time, and Boas did not pursue genetic questions after his summary of linguistic diversity on the Northwest Coast (Boas 1894). During the course of the 1890s, Boas turned away from ethnographic and linguistic surveys and toward folklore studies as he acquired more intimate acquaintance with several Northwest Coast cultures. He was struck by the obvious diffusion and repatterning of folklore elements and assumed that linguistic and narrative traits spread in a similar manner. Because he treated language as a part of culture, Boas expected linguistic change to form a limited case of cultural process in general. He even came to believe that it was impossible to separate the effects of "diffusional cumulation" and "archaic residue" (Swadesh 1951). Because genetic problems could not be definitively solved, they should be put aside.

Boas's position became progressively more conservative in response to the work of his former students, particularly in the period between 1910 and 1920 when extensive new relationships were proposed, and Boas became increasingly skeptical even about his own earlier statements of genetic relationship on the Northwest Coast. In 1911 he suggested:

> Under the circumstances we must confine ourselves to classifying American Indian languages in those linguistic families for which we can give a proof of relationship that cannot possibly be challenged. Beyond this point we can do no more than give certain definite classifications in which the traits common to certain groups of languages are pointed out, while the decision as to the significance of these common traits must be left to later times. (Boas 1911:54)

A few years later, he took the view that although phonetics, morphology, and lexicon were not "necessarily" distinct, they did not always coincide in particular cases. He took this as evidence that "acculturation" influenced language histories to be point where a single common ancestor could not be assigned for each modern language:

> In other words, the whole theory of an "Ursprache" for every group of modern languages must be held in abeyance until we can prove that these languages go back to a single stock and

that they have not originated, to a large extent, by the process of acculturation. (Boas 1920:274–75)

To the extent that languages behaved like cultures, as typified by folklore elements that could be abstracted and compared statistically, similarities (particularly in grammar) might be due to multiple causes.

Boas's interests turned, in the early part of the twentieth century, to problems of structural description and psychological characterization of particular languages. His willingness to bypass problems of genetic relationship implicitly testified to the success of the Powell classification in precluding further tinkering. Boas's choice of Haida, Tlingit, and Athabascan for inclusion in the Introduction to the *Handbook of American Indian Languages* (Boas 1911, 1922) demonstrates that he retained some interest in distinguishing the effects of borrowing from those of internal change. He did not, however, accept Swanton's evidence for genetic connection of these languages, because phonetic, lexical, and grammatical features did not fully corroborate one another.

Although he was extremely conservative in accepting proof of genetic relationship, Boas contributed importantly to the development of more rigorous descriptive standards in American Indian linguistics that would reflect the unique internal organization of each language. The *Handbook* set out a standardized format for such descriptive grammars; most of its sketches were prepared by Boas's students or former students. The effort to increase the pool of available data and raise its level of professional quality and comparability parallels Powell's intentions for his linguistic classification and model for collecting vocabularies (Darnell 1971b, chapter 10, this volume).

Although Boas referred to "large unities" based on "similarity of the psychological foundations of languages" instead of phonetic features reflecting genetic unity (Boas to Woodward, quoted by Stocking [1974]), Boas never found a way to formalize the results of the psychological investigations. The section of the *Handbook* that was to summarize this work remained unwritten. Carried to its logical extreme, Boas's position meant that historical linguistics, as traditionally understood, was impossible. He believed that similarities among languages could be adequately described without their causes being known.

Boas criticized Edward Sapir for his emphasis on phonetics (Boas to Hodge, February 8, 1910: BAE) and failed to recognize the difference in methods between cultural anthropology and historical linguistics. Sapir, in contrast, believed that the comparative method, as developed for Indo-European languages, could be applied to unwritten languages. There was a recognizable structural distinction between genetic and borrowed features of language in that systematic sound changes were by definition genetic. The difference was an important one. Boas complained that Sapir overstressed phonetics and included too much detail in his grammars. For example, Sapir's grammatical sketch of Takelma was omitted from the first volume of the Introduction to the *Handbook of American Indian Languages* because it was too long. Sapir, predictably, was disturbed by Boas's treatment of historical problems:

> I must confess I have always had a feeling that you entirely overdo psychological peculiarities in different languages as presenting insuperable obstacles to genetic theories, and that, on the other hand, you are not sufficiently impressed by the reality of the differentiating processes, phonetic and grammatical, that have so greatly operated in linguistic history all over the world. (Sapir to Boas, July 10, 1918: APS)

Boas's lack of interest in problems of linguistic classification posed a dilemma for his students who worked in areas where the basic survey work among linguistic families had not yet been carried out. For example, Alfred L. Kroeber confronted the linguistic diversity of California, where twenty-two of Powell's fifty-five stocks were found. His changing understanding of the causes of similarity among the California languages illustrates the sea change in American Indian linguistics from domination by Boas, who in spite of his great descriptive contributions was not by training or inclination primarily a linguist, to Sapir, who aspired to develop a linguistic science independent of anthropology.

The description of California languages in the early years of the twentieth century was a cooperative enterprise. Roland Dixon worked on Chimariko and postulated its connection to Shastean in 1910. John P. Harrington joined Chumash and Yuman in 1913. At the University of California, Berkeley, Kroeber confirmed the unity of Chantal, Seri, and Yuman (as proposed by Brinton) in 1914. J. Alden Mason worked on Salinan, and John Swanton studied groups in the American Southwest that Sapir believed to be related to California languages. Sapir himself worked on Yana, joining it to Hokan in 1917. Sapir, Dixon and Kroeber, and Harrington all worked on Washo and concluded independently that it was related to Chumashan.

The California funding of Kroeber's studies made it almost inevitable that attention would be restricted to the single state even if its boundaries proved arbitrary for the definition of Indigenous linguistic groups. By 1903, it seemed possible to consolidate the results and attempt to place the languages of the State in a general perspective. Dixon and Kroeber compared sixteen California stocks and placed them in three structural types: Central Californian, typified by Maidu; Northwestern California, typified by Yurok; and Southwestern California, typified by Chumash. They noted that linguistic diversity extended into Oregon but did not suggest particular connections. The classification was explicitly nongenetic:

> It must be clearly understood, however, that the classification that has been attempted deals only with structural resemblances, not with genetic relationships; that we are establishing not families but types of families. . . . The classification here proposed is really one of another order from that used by Powell, for structure and not lexical content is made the basis on which all comparisons are made. (Dixon and Kroeber 1903:2–3)

Kroeber had privately considered the possibility of genetic connection when he examined the lexical materials but had dismissed this explanation of observed similarities:

> You may be interested to hear that on comparing vocabularies recently I found an unexpectedly larger number of words common to two or more languages. . . . I do not know quite what to make of the case; I think there has been extensive borrowing, but it is by no means impossible that many of the languages will turn out to be related. Curiously enough the lexical similarities

seem to be confined mainly to the group of simple languages of which Maidu is a type. In the northwestern group, I know of no cases of words common to two languages. (Kroeber to Boas, April 24, 1903: ALK)

Boas's assumption that lexical and morphological information might provide different classifications was accepted without qualification. In line with Boas's work on the Northwest Coast, Dixon and Kroeber started from an areal-typological perspective rather than a genetic one. Like Powell, Kroeber and his colleagues at the University of California pointed out linguistic similarities without committing themselves to genetic relationship.

Dixon and Kroeber continued to examine their data on California languages from an areal-typological point of view and were increasingly struck by the anomalies. They still defined the problem in Boasian terms as one of separating the effects of borrowing from those of genetic differentiation, but they differed from Boas in believing the problem worth solving and designed an elaborated methodology to shed light on it in terms of the particular cultural histories that were Boas's most cherished source of data and inference:

> The relations between the languages of the different stocks are being examined more closely than heretofore. Where the languages have been regarded as unrelated, efforts are being made to determine their roots for comparison instead of relying on words. Where there appears to have been borrowing, the geographical distribution of the borrowed words, their nature and the causes of their being borrowed are studied. Within each linguistic family the dialects are examined to determine the nature of the changes occurring in them and the character and causes of their differentiation, since it is thought that a knowledge of these developments may make clearer the processes that may have been in operation in a division of prehistoric Californian languages into what now appear to be distinct families. (Kroeber 1904:29–30)

By 1910 Kroeber was at work on a systematic comparative vocabulary for the entire set of California languages, since direct comparison of only two languages at a time did not reveal the full extent of lexical and grammatical similarities. The initial results had indicated that almost every California stock shared at least a few words with neighboring or even more distant languages, but these similarities were attributed to diffusion. The consistency of lexical and grammatical evidence ultimately convinced Dixon and Kroeber that genetic relationship was the only legitimate explanation of the same similarities they had long been noting. Both were convinced of the essential conservatism of their conclusion, since they had been led to it gradually and unwillingly as a result of their evidence (1913:225).

After analysis of the collected information (comparison of two hundred stem words) had progressed beyond a certain point, it became apparent that the only satisfactory explanation of the resemblances between certain languages was genetic relationship. On the basis of these indications, the grammatical information extant on the same languages was reexamined, and in every instance the grammatical information extant on the same languages was reexamined and in every instance was found strongly confirmatory. Lexical and structural similarities coinciding and being found relatively abundant, true relationships have been accepted as established.

Dixon and Kroeber proposed three new *genetic* stocks: California Penutian, Hokan, and Ritwan (Wiyot and Yurok). The evidence for the new stocks was not published until 1919 because of Dixon's fieldwork in the Orient. The authors again stressed their conservatism; they had "proceeded, not impetuously, but rather reluctantly, and step by step." They recalled their "baffled impotence" at the failure of geographical contiguity to explain similarities and considered their 1919 paper a reinterpretation rather than a new classification.

In retrospect, Dixon and Kroeber justified their conservatism by the fact that by the time the evidence reached print, Sapir had already joined the languages in their Hokan and Penutian stocks to even larger units that extended beyond the boundaries of California.

The chronology of these developments makes it clear that something had changed between 1903 and 1913 when genetic unity had become an acceptable explanation for linguistic similarity. Much of this change must be attributed to Kroeber's almost constant contact with Edward Sapir during the intervening decade about questions of genetic relationship of California languages and their extension to the rest of North America.

Sapir complained of the quality of much of the California field-work but accepted all the connections Kroeber proposed. Kroeber had been concerned primarily to find an adequate classification of California languages for ethnographic purposes, that is, at a shallow time depth, and he did not follow Sapir in the search for wider grouping. Sapir, in contrast, never assumed that the California languages were a bounded unit that would provide the closest cognates within larger groupings and attempted internal reconstruction within his larger Hokan-Coahuiltecan.

From about 1910 to 1920, more and more of Boas's former students turned to the "reduction" of linguistic stocks. This, of course, meant consolidation of stocks as their genetic relations became demonstrable—which in turn resulted in a reduction of the number of stocks or colors on the map of North America. The imagery of a progressively more simplified map appears in most discussions of this period. People seem to have thought in terms of the number of colors necessary to represent the linguistic stocks of North America on a map. Both the Powell and Sapir classifications were accompanied by a map. Although the independence of race, language, and culture had been established in scientific anthropology, in practice linguistic relationships were still used for ethnographic classification. There was little alternative in the days before archaeological stratigraphy; linguistic classification offered the most accurate indication of time depth in Native American culture history (Sapir 1916).

No one knew what the final irreducible classification would look like, although estimates of fifteen to twenty stocks were common. In several cases, the same people worked on the same languages or linguistic relationships and came to similar conclusions. The new perspective spearheaded enthusiastic searching for linguistic groupings that would reflect culture history.

Sapir found the Powell classification "tantamount to a historical absurdity" and sought to deal with the "actual historical current" of particular languages. He was repulsed by the Powell classification because its units could not be linked in any meaningful way to culture history. Kroeber wrote to Sapir: "We seem at last to have got Powell's old fifty-five families on the run, and the farther we can drive them into a heap, the more fun and profit" (June 30, 1913: ALK). A Sapir version is: "I have, like you, lost my love for an unlimited number of stocks" (Sapir to Kroeber, January 28, 1914: ALK). Harrington, Radin, Leo Frachtenberg, and others expressed similar enthusiasm. Most of these individuals were committed in principle to consolidation or conservatism prior to examining the data:

> At last analysis these controversies boil down to a recognition of two states of mind. One, conservative intellectualists, like Boas (and his camp-followers, Goddard and Reichard for instance), who refuse absolutely to consider far-reaching suggestions unless they can be demonstrated by a mass of evidence. . . . Hence, from an over-anxious desire to be right, they generally succeed in being more hopelessly and fundamentally wrong, in the long run, than many more superficial minds who are not committed to "principles." . . . The second type is more intuitive and, even when the evidence is not as full or theoretically unambiguous as it might be, is prepared to throw out tentative suggestions and to test as it goes along. . . . I have no hope whatever of ever getting Boas and Goddard to see through my eyes or to feel with my hunches. I take their opposition like the weather, which might generally be better but which will have to do. (Sapir to Speck, October 2, 1924: APS)

Sapir was convinced that American Indian linguistics had to turn away from mere description and toward scientific linguistics for which standards were developing elsewhere (Sapir to Kroeber, November 28, 1930: ALK). Boas's pioneering attitude of rescuing knowledge of dying languages was no longer enough to qualify him as a linguist.

Although many individuals contributed to the fieldwork, the period of intensive research on American Indian languages was summarized by Sapir. His effort at genetic classification, like that of the Bureau of Ethnology in 1891, resulted from more than a decade of accumulating evidence and working toward a theoretical framework that would accommodate it. The famous six-unit classification that Sapir published in the *Encyclopedia Britannica* (Sapir 1929) was preceded by paper read at the annual meetings of the American Association for Advancement of Science in 1920 and published the following year in *Science* (Sapir 1921).

Throughout the preceding decade, Sapir had grown progressively more enthusiastic about the possibilities that consolidation of linguistic stocks would produce a classification capable of accurately reflecting culture history. He wrote to Frank Speck:

> It is becoming fairly clear that the great stock of North America is Hokan-Yuchi-Siouan-Muskhogean-Tunican-Coahuiltecan, probably with further affiliations southward. Na-dene, Penutian (as extended by me), Algonquian-Yokuts-Wiyot, Wakashan Salish-Chemakuan stand apparently apart but even now there are some suggestive connections visible here and there. Getting down to brass tacks, how in the Hell are you going to explain general American n-"I" except genetically? It's disturbing I know but (more) non-commital conservatism is only dodging after all, isn't it? Great simplifications are in store for us, but we must be critical and not force our evidence. Besides we must try to work out genealogically degrees of relationship. Only so will fascinating perspectives appear. It seems to me that only now is American linguistics becoming really interesting, at least in its ethnological bearings. (Sapir to Speck, August 1, 1918: APS)

In the period just before the presentation of his 1920 paper, Sapir wrote to friends and colleagues about his new ideas, making it clear that his evidence was both morphological and lexical. He even considered the possibility that relationships might be discovered among the six units, which were not directly comparable in time depth. Na-Dene was highly specialized, Hokan-Siouan the basic American type. Penutian ultimately perhaps developed from Hokan-Siouan; Uta-Aztecan was a mixture of Hokan-Siouan and Penutian; Algonquian-Wakashan had perhaps developed out of Penutian.

Attempting to explain his position to Boas, Sapir noted that the classification grew out of his "feel" for the languages. He stressed possible proto-American traits and suggested that Boas felt such connections better than anyone else and was merely hesitant to interpret them genetically. Moreover, Boas's interest in psycho-

logical similarities across languages led him to compare typolog-
ically languages that Sapir believed to be genetically related. For
example, Boas had cited parallels between Iroquois and Pawnee
(Caddoan) in his Introduction to the *Handbook of American Indian
Languages* in 1911. In the same year, Sapir had cited these same
languages in a paper on noun incorporation. By 1920 Sapir was
willing to identify this similarity as genetic, although evidence for
the connection was yet to be presented.

The 1920 classification was admittedly tentative. Several languages were omitted (Waiilatpuan, Lutuamian, Sahaptian, Zuni,
and Beothuk). Sapir included the connections suggested by his
colleagues, and his synthesis was meant primarily for them. Reac-
tions toward the classification were based primarily on Sapir's reputation as a linguist. The period was one of intellectual isolation
for Sapir. He wrote to Ruth Benedict:

> It fills me with something like horror and melancholy both to
> see how long and technical the road I must travel in linguistic
> work, how fascinating its prospect, and how damnably alone I
> must be. There is practically no one to turn to for either assis-
> tance or systematic interest. (Sapir to Benedict, June 25, 1922;
> Mead in Benedict 1959)

Boas was not the only one of Sapir's colleagues to remain skeptical. Kroeber believed without understanding the evidence. Truman Michelson objected to the connection of California Wiyot
and Yurok to Algonquian. Pliny Earle Goddard refused to consider
Athabascan relationships to Sapir's wider Na-Dene. No one took
seriously the connection of Na-Dene with Indo-Chinese. Frachtenberg thought Sapir's extended Penutian too tenuous, although
his own work had enabled Sapir to connect Takelma, Coos, and
other Oregon languages to California Penutian as defined by Dixon
and Kroeber. The bureau retained a rigid adherence to the Powell classification despite repeated overtures of collaboration from
Boasian linguists, particularly Kroeber.

The 1929 classification was a more nearly finished product. The
languages omitted in the initial formulation were now included,
although Sapir had done no firsthand work on any of them in the
interim. Moreover, the classification was presented in two parts.

The six units appeared side by side with another classification—this time including twenty-three units. Sapir listed twelve sets of connections that he believed were accepted by most of his colleagues (see table 3 and table 4) and stated, "The following reductions of linguistic stocks which have been proposed may be looked upon as either probable or very possible" (1929:171–72).

TABLE 3. Sapir linguistic classification by number of stocks

Sapir 1929—A	Sapir 1929—B	Powell 1891
I	1	1
II	3	8
III	2	3
IV	5	14
V	9	24
VI	3	5
Total	Total	Total
6	23	55

Together with the isolates from the Powell classification, the fifty-five stocks of 1891 were now reduced to twenty-three. Although this classification provided a choice for conservative linguists and anthropologists, it has been virtually ignored in the history of American Indian linguistics. Sapir himself would not have accepted the simple dichotomy between fifty-five units and six units; yet his very boldness in seeking new kinds of meaning for linguistic classification forced this polarization on the growing discipline.

TABLE 4. Sapir linguistic classification by language families

Sapir 1929—A	Sapir 1929—B	Powell 1891
I. Eskimo Aleut	Eskimo	Eskimo
II. Algonquian-Ritwan	*Algonquian-Ritwan	Algonquian, Beothukan, Wiyot, Yurok
	*Mosan	Wakashan, Chemakuan, Salish
	Kootenay	Kootenay

III. Na-Dene	*Tlingit-Athabascan	Haida, Tlingit, Athabascan
	Haida	
IV. Penutian	*California Penutian	Miwok, Costanoan, Yokuts, Maidu, Wintun
	*Oregon Penutian	Takelma, Coos (-Siuslaw), Yakonan, Kalapuya
	*Plateau Penutian	Waiilatpuan, Lutuamian, Sahaptin
	Chinook	Chinook
	Tsimshian	Tsimshian
	(Mexican Penutian)	—
V. Hokan-Siouan	*Hokan	Karok, Chimariko, Salinan, Yana, Pomo, Washo, Esselen, Yuman, Chumash
	*Coahuiltecan	Tonkawa, Karankawa, Coahuiltecan
	*Tunican	Tunica, Atakapa, Chitimacha
	*Iroquois-Caddoan	Iroquois, Caddoan
	Yuki	Yuki
	Keres	Keres
	Timucua	Timucua
	Muskhogean	Muskhogean
	Siouan	Siouan, Yuchi

VI. Aztec-Tanoan	*Uto-Aztecan	Nahuatl, Pima, Shoshonean
	*Tanoan-Kiowan	Tanoan, Kiowa
	Zuni?	Zuni

* Twelve units that Sapir considered as accepted by most of his colleagues. The reduction from 23 to 6 units he felt to be his own work.

Examination of a few of Sapir's postulates in greater detail will elucidate the state of the art at the time of his formulations. The most controversial was perhaps the connection of Wiyot and Yurok in California to the widespread Algonquian family of the eastern United States and Canada. The relationship was clearly a remote one, but geographical distance and cultural content made it totally unacceptable to many. Sapir, however, was willing to trust his sound correspondences despite his surprise when confronted with evidence of the relationship. Sapir wrote to Kroeber: "This, of course, was one of my strong pieces. It is laughably obvious" (August 6, 1913: ALK).

Although Kroeber eventually came to share Sapir's enthusiasm, Michelson, the country's major Algonquianist, was bitterly skeptical. Like Sapir, he had been trained in Indo-European linguistics, but he was unwilling to accept genetic relationship by divergence of stocks from a common ancestor in the case of languages not recorded through time. This, of course, made historical linguistics as traditionally understood virtually impossible. Michelson had little interest in distant relationships and resented Sapir's encroachment on his territory. He was himself unable to formulate sound correspondences for divergent languages within Algonquian as conventionally understood, and Sapir's addition of still more languages further incensed him. Michelson did, however, accept Sapir's Na-Dene, for which he had presented detailed sound correspondences (Swadesh 1951). His conservatism was based less on opposition to any consolidation of the Powell stocks than to his defensiveness of gatekeeper status in matters Algonquian.

Sapir's Na-Dene raised other hornets' nests. Boas and Swanton both preferred a more conservative interpretation, and the recognized specialist on Athabascan, Goddard, refused to take seriously any explanation for similarity other than borrowing. Goddard had long planned a comparative study of Athabascan and felt justified in avoiding additional comparative generalization in his grammars of single languages. Sapir described Goddard to Kroeber as "absolutely without vision as to be older drift of Athabascan" (October 1, 1921: ALK).

Sapir believed that Na-Dene was a recent intrusion into North America that held the key to the relationship of American Indian languages to those of Asia. When he came to compare Na-Dene to Indo-Chinese, however, virtually no one took him seriously. Sapir remained undaunted in the face of his evidence, writing to Kroeber:

> It is all so powerfully cumulative and integrated that when you tumble to one point a lot of others fall in line. I am now so thoroughly accustomed to the idea that it no longer startles me. For a while I resisted the notion. Now I can no longer do so. I do not feel that Na-Dene belongs to the American languages. I feel it as a great intrusive band that has ruptured an old Eskimo-Wakashan-Algonquian continuity. And I decidedly feel the old quasi-isolating base. Then there is tone, which feels old. . . . I am all but certain that Athabascan and Haida are like Tlingit as to tone. In short, do not think me an ass if I am seriously entertaining the notion of an old Indo-Chinese offshoot into Northwest America. . . . Am I dreaming? (Sapir to Kroeber, October 1, 1921: ALK)

For Sapir, the effort to attain a long-range perspective on culture history through linguistic evidence led logically to the Asiatic origin of some major American language grouping(s). Few of his contemporaries were willing to accept such postulates, regardless of the evidence. In fact, American anthropologists at the time were unwilling to consider any sort of Asiatic relationships. Physical anthropology and archaeology were equally restricted to the American continent. Much of this ingrained attitude was a response to previous purely conjectural speculation about Old World origins;

lack of time depth in archaeology made comparisons to the longer sequences of the Old World difficult. Moreover, the struggle of American anthropology for recognition as an autonomous and relatively self-contained discipline mitigated against acceptance of evidence linking its established subject matter to the Old World.

Sapir's work on Penutian is interesting in comparison to that of Frachtenberg. For the most part, the two worked independently, reaching similar conclusions about genetic relationships at about the same time. Although Sapir had connected Dixon and Kroeber's Penutian to Oregon languages before 1918, his first published commentary came in response to Frachtenberg (Hymes 1957). Sapir went on to add more genetic connections, drawing heavily on Frachtenberg's descriptive fieldwork with Penutian languages.

The relationships involved in many of these connections were too broad for a single scholar to have worked on each language directly. Sapir was unique in the number on which he actually did work firsthand (seventeen between 1907 and 1920). Historical insight and descriptive contribution were inextricably linked. Although Sapir is often remembered for his broad connections of linguistic stocks, he was also important in setting rigorous standards for proof of relationships. His work on Uto-Aztecan was among the first applications of the comparative method in North America and the first effort at reconstruction of the phonemic system of a proto-language.

From a question of proving genetic relationship to exist, Sapir had redefined the effort as one of cataloging the histories of individual languages in great detail and incorporating time depth.

At the opposite extreme, Sapir realized that a different kind of evidence was necessary for relationships of great time depth. He assigned Subtiaba, a language of Nicaragua, to the Hokan stock because of anomalous morphology that provided evidence for very ancient stages of the language:

> The most important grammatical features of a given language
> and perhaps the bulk of what is conventionally called its gram-
> mar are of little value for remote comparison, which may rest
> largely on submerged features that are only of minor interest to

descriptive analysis. Those who find this a paradox think descriptively rather than historically. (Sapir 1925:492)

The "morphological kernel" of a particular language was its oldest layer that could be reconstructed and contained features that had become archaic in the present language. ("Deep structure" in more recent terminology is almost directly opposite conceptually in that it purports to be universal and is thus useless for assessment of genetic relationship.)

Sapir turned to other problems after 1929. Just as Boas had attempted to mold anthropology into a professional discipline at the beginning of the century, Sapir turned to the training of linguists and the development of professional standards for the description of American Indian languages. Emphasis on genetic relationships shifted toward structural problems just as it had done in the years following the Powell classification.

Renewed work on genetic classification has, indeed, been quite recent in American Indian linguistics. Number of stocks recognized has often been of more concern than amount or quality of evidence for particular relationships, with individual scholars taking a position of general conservativism or general boldness and failing to consider the differences in kind among the consolidations proposed since the Powell classification in 1891.

Notes

1. Originally published as "The Revision of the Powell Classification," *Papers in Linguistics* 4, no 2 (1971): 233–57.

2. "American" was inserted into the Bureau of American Ethnology only in 1892.

3. Because this chapter and the preceding one appeared separately in nonconsecutive numbers of *Papers in Linguistics*, a degree of repetition is necessary to frame them independently.

4. The terms "Indian" and "the American Indian" are pervasive in linguistic discussion. To substitute "Native American" or "Indigenous" would distort the discourse that this chapter revisits. Variants include "American Indian languages" and "linguistics."

5. Now known as Kwakwaka'wakw, to be so understood throughout this chapter. Linguists tend to be less sensitive to changes in terminology than anthropologists or some Indigenous peoples. They are also more likely to use specific ethnonyms rather than such generic terms.

References

Benedict, Ruth. 1959. *An Anthropologist at Work: Writings of Ruth Benedict.* Edited by Margaret Mead. Boston: Houghton Mifflin.

Boas, Franz. 1894. "Classification of the Languages of the North Pacific Coast." *Memoirs of the International Congress of Anthropology,* edited by D. Stanisland Wake, 339–46. Chicago: Schulte.

———. 1911. Introduction to the *Handbook of American Indian Languages.* Bureau of American Ethnology Bulletin 40. Washington DC: Government Printing Office.

———. 1920. "The Classification of American Languages." *American Anthropologist* 22:267–76.

———. 1922. *Handbook of American Indian Languages: Vol. 2.* Washington DC: Smithsonian Institution.

———. 1940. *Race, Language and Culture.* New York: Free Press.

Darnell, Regna. 1969. "The Development of American Anthropology, 1880–1920: From the Bureau of American Ethnology to Franz Boas." PhD diss., University of Pennsylvania.

———. 1971a. "The Powell Classification of American Indian Languages." *Papers in Linguistics* 4:71–110.

———. 1971b. "The Professionalization of American Anthropology." *Social Science Information* 83–103.

Dixon, Roland, and A. L. Kroeber. 1903. "The Native Languages of California." *American Anthropologist* 5:1–26.

———. 1913. "Relationship of the Indian Languages of California." *Science* 37:225.

———. 1919. *Linguistic Families of California.* University of California Publications in American Archaeology and Ethnology 16, 48–118. Berkeley: University of California.

Hymes, Dell. 1957. "Some Penutian Elements and the Penutian Hypothesis." *Southwestern Journal of Anthropology* 13:69–87.

Kroeber, Alfred. L. 1904. "The Languages of the Coast of California South of San Francisco." *University of California Publications in American Archaeology and Ethnology* 2:29–80. Berkeley: University of California Press.

Mead, Margaret, ed. 1959. *An Anthropologist at Work: Writings of Ruth Benedict.* Boston: Houghton Mifflin.

Powell, John Wesley. 1891. "Indian Linguistic Families North of Mexico." *Seventh Annual Report of the Bureau of Ethnology to the Secretary of the Smithsonian Institution, 1885–86.* 7–139. Washington DC: Government Printing Office.

Sapir, Edward. 1916. *Time Perspective in Aboriginal American Culture: A Study in Method.* Department of Mines, Geological Survey of Canada Memoir No. 90, Anthropological Series no. 13. Ottawa: Government Printing Bureau.

———. 1921. "A Bird's Eye View of American Languages North of Mexico." *Science* 54:408.

———. 1925. "The Hokan Affinity of Subtiaba in Nicaragua." *American Anthropologist* 27:402–35, 491–527.

———. 1929. "Central and North American Languages." *Encyclopedia Britannica* 5:138–41.

Stocking, George W., Jr. 1974. "The Boas Plan for American Indian Languages." In *Essays in the History of Linguistics: Traditions and Paradigms*, edited by Dell Hymes, 454–84. Bloomington: Indiana University Press.

Swadesh, Morris. 1951. "Diffusional Cumulation and Archaic Residue as Historical Explanation." *Southwestern Journal of Anthropology* 7:1–21.

12

Désveaux, Two Traditions of
Anthropology in Mirror

American Geologisms and French Biologism

On National Traditions and Metaphors of Science

Emmanuel Désveaux, in addition to his argument about the particular traditions of American and French anthropologies in their formative periods, has raised highly significant issues about the importance of national traditions in the understanding of anthropology as a discipline, both historically and at the present time.[1] Transnational conversations among anthropologists of various theoretical persuasions have often produced unrecognized and unintended miscommunications because of different underlying presuppositions about the nature and scope of the science (or social science) of humankind.[2] Désveaux suggests parallel but independent invention of anthropological traditions.[3] I agree that national traditions constitute a critical variable in the desirable history of anthropology but at the same time caution attention to the unforeseen pitfalls of cross-connection and mutual fertilizations. No major national tradition is fully autonomous. Moreover, the American and the French traditions are difficult to interpret seriously without attention at least to their British and German counterparts.

The anthropologies arising from the former colonies of these anthropology-producing nations and those of Indigenous peoples outside European nation-states or colonial states raise further questions I will largely pass over here, although they merit reflexive historiographic attention. National tradition is of necessity closely related to national character and to the wider relationships among nation-states. Location in Canada has led me to muse on how Canadian anthropology intersects with the encounters of the three founding nations (British, French, Indigenous) as well as with the anthropology of the monolithic (as it traditionally represents itself) state to the south. The result is a highly self-conscious, although not necessarily self-confident, hybrid positioning potentially poised to mediate translation across national traditions. I assume a similar standpoint of national context for the uniqueness of Russian anthropology where the invitation to prepare this commentary arose (see Vermeulen 2015).

Désveaux focuses on his own French tradition and the American one with which his career has also produced extensive familiarity as the rhetorical poles or mirror images of anthropology.[4] His reading of the two traditions is both polar and reflective of his own standpoint.[5] That they differ "*sensiblement*" does not entail the absolute separability of these traditions, merely their contrast in emphasis and situated context. He assumes that the disciplinary linkages of American and French anthropology have emerged differently and that their roots remain below the level of consciousness for most practitioners. Nonetheless, he hypothesizes enduring contemporary effects without specifying causes.

I accept the principle if not the absolute persistence of continuity, with the caveat that national traditions are far from homogeneous over time. It is a long way from Paul Broca to Claude Lévi-Strauss, though both are French insofar as they assume a universalist or species-wide commonality beyond an ethnographic diversity that might even be dismissed as trivial in relation. Désveaux considers a cross-disciplinary Enlightenment heritage of rationality to be fully coherent in a biologist framework, at least insofar as culture is equated with the ethnographically diverse and biology with the universal. This definition of biologism entails an evolutionary progression to modern European civilization in which the subject matter of anthropology coheres less for its own sake than to validate foundations of the investigators' presuppositions.

Désveaux grounds the roots of American anthropology in geology, the discipline of its first key institutional leader, John Wesley Powell, founder of the Bureau of [American] Ethnology[6] in 1879. Powell moved from geology to ethnology as a result of his mapping of the so-called arid lands of the American Southwest, modeling land use as an intersection of culture, technology, and environment. His brief fieldwork with the Ute and Shoshone Indians who exploited this challenging environment with minimal technology may indeed parallel the geographic (as opposed to geological) conversion of Franz Boas from environmental determinism to the discovery of cultural complexity even among the Eskimo (today called Inuit in Canada) of Baffin Island. His ensuing choice of a second field site, the Northwest Coast, eliminated environment as a cause of cultural diversity and turned to the mutual borrowings among peoples whose linguistic and cultural variation persisted although they exploited similar environments. Boas came to his views by way of a very different anthropological and geographical tradition. Powell's self-taught skills in surveying and exploration of physical territory during American geographical expansion and the settlement of Indigenous populations on reservations contrast sharply with Boas's German university training in psychophysics and geography. His Americanist relativism constitutes a break from Powell's geology. His turn to ethnology engaged a mentalism in constructing culture and environment that was not native to American science. Indeed, the very debate about the nature of science was different. For Boas, science encompassed both materialist science and history/geography/cosmology. Inductive and deductive, scientistic and interpretive (what he called "the native point of view") were equally valid in their own domains. Geography remains significant in this formulation because territory bounds the groups whose cultures coalesce as worldviews. *Weltenschauung*, worldview, arises from the German romanticism of Herder and von Humboldt rather than from an American politics of manifest destiny.

Another source of geology/geography/space in the American anthropological tradition arises from the four subdisciplinary structure conventionally attributed to Boas, but perhaps more accurately traced to Powell's contemporary, Harvard archaeologist Frederic Ward Putnam. Material environment and the distribution of cultures are engaged here in a way that is absent in the French tradition. The third nineteenth-century leader in anthropology, Daniel Garrison Brinton, was a linguist and interpretivist in an idealist, incipiently structuralist manner that contrasts to the mainstream that Désveaux highlights, partly because of his immersion in European, especially German, scholarship.

I am not persuaded that the environmental anthropology of Julian Steward, Leslie White, and the Marxist neo-evolutionists in cultural anthropology has ever been the dominant American tradition—although it is indeed easy to attach some continuity to this research focus in the work of Powell and some of that of Boas. The core Boasians (including in my view Robert Lowie, Alfred Kroeber, Edward Sapir, Alexander Goldenweiser, Paul Radin, Ruth Benedict, and Margaret Mead) were all on the social, cultural, and idealist side of this question (Darnell 2001).[7] They aspired to describe cultures in their own terms before turning to historically particular comparisons.

Powell's anthropology, sponsored by the American government, was necessarily "applied." Boas and his students, in contrast, moved to academic locations where "useful knowledge" was not the immediate or direct goal. Institutional constraints determine the options for both.

Désveaux makes much of the distinction between "society" in the French tradition and "culture" in the American. Lévi-Strauss is a key figure for Désveaux and leads him to the title of his essay.[8] It is useful, I think, to recall that British social anthropology acquired this distinction from French sociology in its Durkheimian vein. The paramount ethnographer among the Durkheimians, Marcel Mauss, particularly in his later work, passionately opposed reference to "primitive" societies, preferring to look at expressive culture (religion, art, language, the reciprocity of "*le don*" [the gift) rather than economics or technology as the basis of comparing societies. This move brings him closer to the Boasian cultural construction of "the native point of view." In my view Lévi-Strauss is closer to the Durkheimian position, although he shares with Boas the comparison of cultures at a level of abstraction not accessible to the member of culture.

In any case the Boasian culture concept largely follows Edward B. Tylor's definition adopted from the British tradition, but he elaborates Tylor's construction of culture as a symbolic form having psychological reality for members of a culture. As Boasian anthropology increasingly turned to what came to be called culture and personality after about 1910, Benedict's aesthetic notion of cultural pattern allowed comparisons of cultures as wholes, largely independently of their environmental roots.

Désveaux suggests in passing that the British tradition, by which he now means British social anthropology, coheres around "law" rather than society or culture. This is an intriguing entreé to understanding the mid-twentieth-century British concern with what I might call "negative ethnography" (in which social institutions are characterized by what they lack in familiar European terms, e.g., stateless societies in Africa). Yet, the legal emphasis arises through German routes (e.g., Bachofen), rather than being native to the British Isles or the anthropology of the British Empire.

Désveaux properly emphasizes the emergence of anthropological paradigms in the vacuum left by theology with the rise of science across Europe. Exploration involved cataloging everything from geological features to languages and cultures. Geology and biology were undoubtedly the primary contenders for classificatory categories in early ethnographic work. Indeed, Darwinian evolution, building on static taxonomies from Buffon to Linneaus, depended directly on the already existing uniformitarian geology of Charles Lyell. Processes observable in the present operated also in the past. Archaeological stratigraphy and cultural evolution drew with parallel logic on such analogies adapted across what are now separate disciplines.

I reformulate Désveaux's attributing the disorder and refusal of origins to American messianic attitudes. To be sure, there was rejection of unwritten history among American Indians (the term Désveaux uses), especially during efforts to expropriate their lands and assimilate their cultures. To the extent that Powell's anthropology was evolutionist, I am unpersuaded that this derived from geological metaphors. Désveaux considers the classification of American Indian languages as a chaotic process of dealing with their diversity. This describes Powell's effort to provide administrative and political clarity but omits the homogeneity entailed by Du Ponceau's largely German-derived continental "polysynthetic" hypothesis (see Darnell 1971, chapter 10, this volume). In this version of European linguistics, European languages were, if anything, less homogeneous than those of the Americas.[9] The question of contemporary or coeval status does not seem to me attested in either French or American treatments of "the primitive" until at least the work of Boas and Mauss. Lewis Henry Morgan's evolutionary anthropology follows a much more biological than geological framework, although it was adopted by the geologist Powell as the theoretical foundation for the Bureau of American Ethnology. Désveaux correctly notes that evolutionary reductionism failed to encompass the cultural and linguistic diversity of North America.

Désveaux does not explicitly address the degree to which the mirror contrast of his title is based in metaphor. The move from geological erosion to acculturation, or culture as a mineral inclusion, or society as an organic body, are suggestive as metaphors; but it is important to remember that they are not metaphors used by the parties to these debates. Thus I find them of limited utility in understanding the emergence of these national traditions; the history of science seems to require causes operative at the time of events, whatever may be made of them by commentators in retrospect.

More interestingly, Désveaux ties his universalist argument to the metaphor of light in the French tradition. I am intrigued by the parallel he draws of geology to metonymy and of biology to metaphor. Such images may capture the imagination of individual anthropologists as well as national traditions to explore potential synthesis and cross-fertilization. I concur with this argument and aspiration.

I have less to say about the French tradition because I come to it less directly, both in professional affiliation and historical research. I would like to think more about the theoretical breakthrough that Russian formalists such as Vladimir Propp modeled for French anthropology, especially whether this served as a corrective to biological reductionism. On the other hand, origins in an evolutionary theory translate all too easily to racism and discrimination from an Americanist point of view.

In terms of contemporary American anthropology, Désveaux reads what I have called "the Americanist text tradition" as an interpretive challenge of infinite regress and thus interpretive nihilism (though I overstate his argument, of course).[10] I would not equate Geertzian interpretivism with postmodernism or with the committed engagement of many American anthropologists with the political conditions of power that inevitably constrain the ethnographic enterprise. In any case, both of these trends are a long way from any geological disciplinary bedrock.

Notes

1. Originally published as "On National Traditions and Metaphors of Science" [O national'nykh traditisiiakh I metaforakh nauki], *Etnograficheskoe Obozrenie* 5 (2007): 3–18.

2. Difficulties of translation precluded inclusion of Désveaux's full response. I could not translate without incorporating my own point of view, and he declined to respond in English to the nuance involved. I saw his commentary only in a bad machine translation from the French and never read his rebuttal or the comments of the other reviewer, Claude Blankaert. An expanded version in Désveaux (2007a) supersedes the original. Excerpts from his commentary in my translation appear in footnotes throughout the text and convey its flavor.

3. "We are here in the presence of these two traditions of anthropology . . . geology for the American and biology for the French."

4. "Cultural environmentalism constitutes the language made commonplace by the classical age of American anthropology. . . . The theoretical bedrock of the French anthropology is a fixed idea of the unique origin to the social thing."

5. "The Americans in the first half of the nineteenth century represent themselves as the only origin [of their ideas]. They reject in effect the civilization of old Europe as well as deny an Indigenous history under the pretext that they are ignorant of writing." In contrast, "The French tradition is more difficult to allocate to an origin because of an uninterrupted production of new ideas in Europe for the nineteenth century."

6. "American" was added to the "Bureau of Ethnology" in 1892, and it was known thereafter as the Bureau of American Ethnology.

7. With reference to the purported postmodernism of Clifford Geertz: "The anthropology which implicates the ground appears as one loophole, otherwise as a case in philosophy, free because speculative."

8. "Lévi-Strauss represents this essential social link, sometimes through the gift, sometimes through exchange of women. This social link has a quasi-mystical character in Durkheim. . . . The unsaid confers its significance on the thought of Durkheim through the universal charm of light."

9. "This geological comprehension of the American domain sees itself reinforced by the linguistic works of Du Ponceau then Gallatin, which throws into relief with an acuteness always more lively given the extreme diversification of the languages of the New World whereas Indo-European fills this role in terms of genetic diversification and morphophological homogenization."

10. "The objective is not a purpose of knowledge as such but rather the proof of the validity of a quasi-philological method that reveals traces of cultures that have subsequently disappeared."

References

Blankaert, Claude. 2007. "Le premier 'terrain' des anthropologues a propos des styles nationaux de la science." *Etnograficheskoe Obozrenie* 5:3–18.

Darnell, Regna. 1971. "The Powell Classification of American Indian Languages." *Papers in Linguistics* 4:71–110.

———. 2001. *Invisible Genealogies: A History of Americanist Anthropology*. Lincoln: University of Nebraska Press.

Désveaux, Emmanuel. 2007a. *Spectres de l'anthropologie: Suite nord américaine*. Paris: Aux lieux-d'être ("Sciences contemporaines").

———. 2007b. "Two Traditions in Anthropology: American Geologism vs. French Biologism" [Dve traditsii v antropologii: Amerikanskii geologizm i fransuzskii biologism]. *Etnograficheskoe Obozrenie* 5:3–18.

Vermeulen, Han. 2015. *Before Boas: The Genesis of Ethnography and Ethnology in the German Enlightenment*. Nebraska: University of Nebraska Press.

Rationalism, the (Sapir-)Whorf Hypothesis, and Assassination by Anachronism

Linguistic theory, when it considers disciplinary history at all, has tended until quite recently to rewrite it as a handmaiden to subsequent theoretical concerns.[1] While interest in the subject is growing increasingly prominent, and there are many fine exemplars today, especially due to the efforts of Konrad Koerner and John Benjamins Publishers, many such efforts have minimized what intellectual ancestors actually said and the context in which they proposed their ideas in terms of their own theoretical perspectives. This approach misrepresents insights from previous work that would enable contemporary work to build on prior insights in dialogue with them, whether in emulation or critique. Historical topics remain of legitimate interest because of their relevance to present practice, but a historian of science would insist on also addressing the original intellectual context as the starting point for evaluation of present relevance. As a historian of American anthropology and linguistics, I illustrate by revisiting one such reevaluation of the long-controversial work of Benjamin Lee Whorf that raised my ire at the time of its original appearance and served to focus my attention on the questions discussed below (Darnell 1974); other exemplars could equally well have been chosen. Although Whorf's notions of how linguistic categories influence the structure of habitual thought require reformulation to meet present standards of scholarship, it does not follow that we must jettison the baby with the bathwater.

Noam Chomsky's *Cartesian Linguistics* (1966) typifies a mainstream approach that inspired a series of reassessments in a similar present-oriented vein. I pursue the critique based on Richard

Ogle's "Aspects of a Rationalist Critique of the Whorf Hypothesis" (Ogle 1973). After examining its claims about Whorf's views and their relationship to then current transformational and generative theory, I frame the context in which Whorf's views were formulated, thereby allaying some of Ogle's one-sidedness. According to Ogle, Whorf's argument challenged "the structuralist orthodoxy" (325) prevalent in America at the time, but he neglects to point out that Edward Sapir, Whorf's teacher and mentor in linguistics, also operated in fundamental opposition to orthodox structuralism. Sapir is not such an easy target and gets a free pass that Whorf does not.

Ogle admires Whorf's notion of "cryptotype," the abstract form underlying linguistic categories and his concern for the psychologically real, hence with mentalism. Ogle stresses that Whorf's insights can be restated easily in terms of "modern" semantic theory. For example, Whorf recognized that a speaker's knowledge, by which he meant how grammatical categories function to organize experience, operated below the level of consciousness but was nonetheless real. In this sense Whorf was an important forerunner of later insistence on a psychological starting point for the description of what speakers know.

Ogle proceeds as though his critique of Whorf were the only point at issue. Although Whorf indeed was concerned to establish mentalist approaches to the writing of grammars, his psychological concepts were never subjected to rigorous exposition in distributional terms. Ogle castigates him for not documenting the role of linguistic categories in cognition, an anachronism given that neurolinguistics had not and still has not progressed to the point of definitive proof. Ogle further laments that Whorf restricts his primary attention to linguistic relativity rather than specifying the exact nature of the link between language and thought.

Whorf's thought is analyzed logically rather than historically. For example, Whorf "may well have reasoned something along the following lines" (Ogle 1973:326). The discussion that follows presents no evidence for what Whorf actually said in justification of his methods and procedures. In apparent contradiction, Ogle then notes that in an era of behaviorism in American psychology, no mentalistic explanation was available to Whorf except on the basis of linguistic concepts (326), that is, concepts internal to language. The historically appropriate question would be what did Whorf do with the concepts available to him rather than a critique of what he was not able to do and therefore did not do.

The core of Ogle's argument is that because Whorf and Chomsky both focus on abstract constraints on meaning, they must be conceptual confreres. To Whorf, these constraints are culturally variable whereas Chomsky defines them as universal and a priori, proceeding from nonlinguistic principles of cognition (329). In practice, an adequate linguistic theory must address itself to both the universal and the language-specific properties of language. Ogle's claim that Whorf's psychological principles were culture-specific and thus could only be acquired through socialization is a misreading of Whorf's relationship to the emergent "school" of Americanist linguistics and anthropology built on Boasian foundations. Whorf insisted that the immediacy of the culture-specific was necessary to ground the search for universals in the study of other languages and cultures by those who approached them from experience of growing up in a different cultural and linguistic universe. The innate knowledge of universals that Ogle sees as underlying "the traditional generative paradigm" (331) was also implicit in Whorf's theory. The claim that there is little "richness" of "cognitive mechanisms" (331) again reflects the state of knowledge of the period rather than marking a culpable weakness in Whorf's thinking. This is what I refer to as "assassination by anachronism." Ogle is adamant that universals exist and seems to assume that Whorf would have disagreed. He cites examples of time and space concepts and the capacity to name objects:

> In the majority of cases, of course, the relationship between modes of cognition and the semantic structure of language could not be as direct as in the case of the constraint on the nameability of objects. Were this so, the logical result would be that all languages would have identical semantic structure, which is naturally not what is being claimed. Rather, the features which . . . represent cognitive dispositions provide the basic inventory of elements out of which language-specific concepts may be elaborated. (337)

That is, Whorf wanted to understand the variable portion of semantic systems in a narrowly linguistic way, particularly in the contrast between Hopi and English (generalized as what he called Standard Average European [SAE]). Ogle praises Whorf's discussion of the Hopi categorization of "clouds" as animate. Today, largely as a result of the cross-cultural tolerance propounded by Boasian anthropology and widely disseminated in America between the two world wars, this categorization can no longer be dismissed as a mere failure to perceive the physical reality of clouds. Rather, the Hopi have a different way of understanding what it means to be alive. Ogle concedes: "If we readmit a degree of relativism, even in the form of variations in the values of features, we thereby to the same extent reopen the case for Whorf" (338).

The theory of cognition that emerges is "relative and language-dependent" (338). Again, Ogle seems to assume that Whorf would not have accepted the universality of something like a category of animate-inanimate despite expecting that languages would map the content of this category uniquely. Whorf did not address this issue because he did not see it as a problem but rather took it as embedded in the phenomena under investigation.

Ogle deems Whorf's theory nonviable because it is deterministic. That is, neo-Cartesian (by which he meant modern transformational) linguistics sees linguistic relativity as a habitual aid to organizing the environment, not as "the primary organizing power of the mind" (340). Despite some strongly deterministic statements in Whorf's writings in rhetorical support of an argument (see Ridington 1999), the qualifier *habitual* was ubiquitous in his evocative prose. Translation between widely divergent languages and cultures was possible although hardly easy or wholly satisfactory. John B. Carroll, the psychologist who was largely responsible for rehabilitating Whorf's reputation, came to Whorf's work by way of his own discipline of psychology rather than linguistics. He quotes Whorf (in Carroll 1956):

In order to describe the structure of the universe according to the Hopi, it is necessary to attempt—insofar as it is possible—to make explicit this metaphysics, properly describable only in the Hopi language, somewhat inadequately it is true, yet by availing ourselves of such concepts as we have worked up into relative consonance with the system underlying the Hopi view of the universe. (58)

For Ogle, Whorf's determinism is directly contradicted by the data in his examples. He discusses Boas's argument that Indigenous Americans develop new concepts as they become necessary under conditions of culture contact (341–44). Whorf himself already took for granted that culture rather than language was responsible for developing new concepts. Emphasizing that Einsteinian physics can be described in Hopi more concisely and elegantly than in English, he expresses no surprise that English speakers rather than Hopi speakers formulated the Einsteinian paradigm. There is no necessary relationship between the two assertions, and they do not constitute a syllogism. In Whorf's words:

> Thus the worldview of modern science arises by a higher specialization of the basic grammar of the Western Indo-European languages. Science of course was not CAUSED by this grammar; it was simply colored by it. It appeared in this group of languages because of a train of historical events that stimulated commerce, measurement, manufacture, and technical invention in a quarter of the world where these languages were dominant. (Whorf, qtd. in Ogle 1974:221–22)

Whorf's identification of diverse "fashions of speaking" (Ogle 1973:158) characteristic of specific cultures does not preclude the possibility that an outsider could learn to understand another world. Multilinguals do this all the time, and it is, after all, the task of anthropology. The relationship between culture and linguistic categories was not one of direct "correlations or diagnostic correspondences between cultural norms and linguistic patterns" (159).

Ogle's final potshot charges untenable determinism at the same time he criticizes Whorf's linguistic colleague Harry Hoijer for his less tidy effort to balance the intuitive truth of Whorf's presentation with the need for increased rigor in further study. He adopts a weaker version of the Whorf hypothesis that is in fact close to the points on which Ogle has conceded that Whorf was correct (Ogle 348–49). Ogle's contention that Whorf offers no magic key to free oneself from the categories of one's natal language fails to recognize that the pursuit of linguistics and anthropology was itself the exemplar and provided a testable pragmatics on which to build a cultural and linguistic relativism.

Ogle's skewed reading obscures many potentially useful insights Whorf may still offer to contemporary linguistics. Examining Whorf's contribution in historical perspective is complicated by the fact that many of his most basic concepts are now superseded as his insights because they have since been adopted by all linguists who deal with unwritten languages. That grammatical categories and cultural norms are relative is now trivial. When Whorf wrote, Americanist linguists trained by Boas and Sapir still were struggling to escape the reliance of the linguistic discipline on Greek and Latin analytic categories. Boasian students of language and culture rejected the evolutionism that enshrined Victorian man [*sic*] as the pinnacle of human civilization with lurking implications embedded in the hierarchical assumptions of comparative linguistic typologies. Boasian linguists aspired to describe phenomena in American Indigenous languages for which there were no terms in their inherited scientific lexicon. The problems of translation and habitual thought were constant and poignant. They did not have to be argued explicitly. The validity and prestige of each language could not yet be taken for granted in the Indo-European scholarship that had invented the science of linguistics as a product of the Western world. Americanist fieldwork-based data necessitated new theories and methods that linguistics would have to incorporate if it were to sustain its claim to be a science of language as a whole. Whorf's conviction that translation was possible allowed him to address the variables that would have to be translated in the alternations that emerged in moving between and among cultures and languages.

This framework is a necessary prelude to considering the state of the art in American anthropology and linguistics during the interwar years. Sapir's "The Psychological Reality of Phonemes" appeared in French in 1925 but was not translated into English until 1933. Sapir expanded the theoretical implications of Boas's argument that "alternating sounds" are a result of the sounds habitually perceived in the native language (Boas 1889) and added the important proviso for linguistics that the sounds of a given language are not themselves arbitrary but form a phonemic grid structure unique to that language. In the period just preceding Whorf's earliest writings, Boas argued in *The Mind of Primitive Man* (1911), in opposition to the claims of behaviorism in psychology and cultural Darwinism in the social sciences, that anthropology was ultimately a psychological science, a tenet elaborated by his students during the 1920s and 1930s in what is now called "culture and personality." Sapir, the teacher and mentor of Whorf, was central to this intellectual circle of Boas students that also included Ruth Benedict, Margaret Mead, Alexander Goldenweiser, and Alfred L. Kroeber among others (Darnell 2001). All were cultural anthropologists who adopted as axiomatic the application of this comparative framework beyond linguistics in the narrow sense.

Benedict provided the key metaphor for the anthropology of the period in *Patterns of Culture* (Benedict 1934). Her "arc" of cultural potentials accounted for the patterning, by which she meant the nonrandom selection, of culture traits by each human group. Linguistic pattern and culture pattern were treated analogously by the Boasian cohort over successive generations reaching to Whorf and beyond. Whorf inherited this genealogy through Sapir. Following the analogy further, it is not inconsistent with a rationalist and universalist position. Segments of the arc may differ for each culture, but all potential points on its circumference are drawn in relation to a single central point, which is the universal core of all human culture and language.

To more recent tastes in concepts and format of presentation, the Boasian emphasis on data collection may seem obsessive. Theoretical perspectives were shared and thus tended to be taken for granted, but their reconstruction from a present-day perspective through deliberate historical consciousness reveals their critical role as evidence for what was then an urgently needed paradigm shift. Benedict, for example, began with a dissertation, written over a decade before *Patterns of Culture*, on the Plains Indian vision quest. Using the insights of Sigmund Freud and Gestalt psychology, she moved from listing of traits to culturally based explanations of why certain traits were grouped together in particular cultures. Boas himself tended to stop with the trait list, but his students in the culture and personality school talked explicitly about "pattern" (Benedict) and "configuration" (Kroeber). Even Wissler, the quintessential data advocate, postulated that universal categories of culture were a necessary starting point to arrangement of material artefacts in museum collections into culturally relevant patterns.

In sum, the Boasians, including Whorf, were primarily concerned with enhancing the likelihood of effective communication across cultural boundaries. They understood all anthropology as translation in the broad theoretical sense. Habitual thought had to be reconciled with the creativity of mankind [*sic*] and with the obviously documented human potential for semantic change and cultural adaptation. Language provided an entrée to these questions for many Boasians. Sapir is often linked to the Whorf or Sapir-Whorf hypothesis, and many of his statements were as deterministic as Whorf's. Elsewhere, Sapir's major interests included other aspects of linguistic description as well as rationalism and universalism (see Leavitt 2010 for a sophisticated explication of the significance of linguistic relativity). Despite the hypothetical danger in a rationalist linguistic theory that the universal might obscure or even obliterate the language-specific and the detail of actual life, translation is still necessary, and linguists remain obligated to account for both the differences and the similarities between languages and cultures.

Notes

1. An earlier form of this chapter appeared in "Rationalist Aspects of the Whorf Hypothesis," *Papers in Linguistics* 7 (1974): 41–50. It is a dramatic reworking, using Ogle as a methodological exemplar rather than criticizing his argument as though it were contemporary, a strategy that made more sense at original date of publication.

References

Boas, Franz. 1889. "On Alternating Sounds." *American Anthropologist* 2:47–53.
———. 1911. *The Mind of Primitive Man*. New York: Macmillan.
Benedict, Ruth. 1934. *Patterns of Culture*. Boston: Houghton Mifflin.
Carroll, John B. 1956. "Introduction to Whorf." In *Language, Thought and Reality: Selected Writings of Benjamin Lee Whorf*, edited by Lisa Philips Valentine and Regna Darnell, 1–34. Cambridge MA: MIT Press.
Chomsky, Noam. 1966. *Cartesian Linguistics*. New York: Harper and Row.

Darnell, Regna. 1974. "Rationalist Aspects of the Whorf Hypothesis." *Papers in Linguistics* 7:41–50.

———. 2001. *Invisible Genealogies: A History of Americanist Anthropology.* Lincoln: University of Nebraska Press.

Leavitt, John. 2010. *Linguistic Relativities: Language Diversity and Modern Thought.* Cambridge: Cambridge University Press.

Ogle, Richard. 1973. "Aspects of a Rationalist Critique of the Whorf Hypothesis." *Papers in Linguistics* 6:317–50.

Ridington, Robin. 1999. "Theorizing Coyote's Cannon: Sharing Stories with Thomas King." In *Theorizing the Americanist Tradition,* edited by Lisa Philips Valentine and Regna Darnell, 19–37. Toronto: University of Toronto Press.

14

The Structuralism of Claude Lévi-Strauss

Sources of Lévi-Strauss's Structuralism

The structuralism of Claude Lévi-Strauss (1908–2002), based in France but widely practiced beyond its place of origin, dominated the intellectual landscape of the 1960s and 1970s in a range of disciplines beyond his own anthropology.[1] Intersecting webs of intellectual influence cross national borders, disciplinary boundaries, and personal trainings, making it a daunting historiographic task to trace the route of particular scholars in the construction of their characteristic positions. Conventional wisdom in the history of anthropology has it that Lévi-Strauss's core concept of structure owes much to linguistics, by way of his intense interaction during their mutual exile from the perils of wartime Europe with Prague School linguist Roman Jakobson (1896–1982) in New York. This puts Lévi-Strauss firmly within the purview of the history of linguistics.

Paradoxically, however, Lévi-Strauss has little to say about language. The almost total absence of attention to language in his argument about structural universals and human cognition seems very strange to a linguist. This puzzling omission also pervades the work of Emile Durkheim (1858–1917) and French sociology more generally. Like Durkheim, Marcel Mauss (1872–1950) and other members of the *L'Année sociologique* school, Lévi-Strauss approaches ethnography comparatively rather than through detailed fieldwork based on participant observation in a particular society. This renders his work fundamentally alien to the empiricist mainstream of Anglo-American anthropology. For example, Clifford Geertz (1988:27) refers to "my own admitted skepticism toward the structuralist project as a research program and my outright hostility to it as a philosophy of mind."

When Lévi-Strauss does cite ethnographers, he relies on the work of the early students of Franz Boas (1848–1942). Boas worked in the Americas, insisted on the inseparability of linguistics and ethnology, and defined culture in terms of the symbolic forms uniquely encoded in each language. In this relationship also, the New York interlude of the 1940s was the formative catalyst. Definitive reconstruction of Lévi-Strauss's intellectual biography is a complex and tentative exercise, lacking closure almost by definition. Much of the evidence for the theoretical roots of his biography, however, lies in the public domain and in the oral tradition within which linguists and anthropologists draw (or do not draw) upon his published works. The pieces of the enigma include:

1. the legacy of the sociologists around Durkheim;

2. the migration of Prague School structuralism to North America when Jakobson and other European intellectuals fled Europe in the prelude to and during the Second World War;

3. the role of Boas and other anthropologists in assisting many of these emigrés to settle in the New World;

4. how Lévi-Strauss himself read the main tenets of structuralism and defined his career in terms of them.

These issues clarify the context of how Lévi-Strauss's structuralism provides a baseline to define the parameters of the ensuing interdisciplinary critique loosely glossed as poststructuralist or postmodern. Tentative answers may be found in the biographical trajectory of Lévi-Strauss's career and what he has said in print at various times about his intentions and positions. Geertz (1988:25) observes that "structuralism became an international movement." Through Lévi-Strauss, structuralism brought a new and heady "sense of intellectual importance" to the discipline of anthropology; indeed, there was a "wholesale invasion of neighboring fields" (25) by what had previously been one of the smallest and least fashionable of the social and human sciences. Despite its "apparent origination in France" (Sturrock 1986:ix) around the work of Lévi-Strauss in anthropology, the structuralist movement also included Michel Foucault (1926–84) in the history of ideas,

Roland Barthes (1915–80) in literary criticism, Louis Althusser (1918–93) in political science, and Jacques Lacan (1901–81) in psychoanalysis. Not all of the core figures were French. Ferdinand de Saussure (1857–1913) was Swiss; Jakobson, Mikhail Bakhtin (1896–1984) and Count Nikolaj Trubetzkoy (1890–1938) were Russian; Louis Hjelmslev (1899–1965) was Danish; and Charles S. Peirce (1839–1914), Edward Sapir (1884–1939), and Noam Chomsky (b. 1928) were American.[2]

Brazilian Interlude: The Escape from Durkheimian Sociology

Lévi-Strauss defined his version of structuralism as an ambitious young man in self-imposed exile from the French academy, which French intellectuals automatically understand to be the center of the world. Lévi-Strauss's disciplinary identity was ambiguous; he had studied law, philosophy, sociology, and anthropology, none of which were then at the core of French intellectual life. When he went to Brazil (1934–37), geographically at the periphery of the known world for the French intelligentsia, he knew virtually nothing about linguistics. But already he was self-consciously searching for a disciplinary niche to carve out for his own.

Anthropology was particularly appealing to Lévi-Strauss because Brazil could be constructed as a chosen place to do fieldwork rather than a space of exile, even though it had been the only place where he could obtain a teaching position. Participant-observation fieldwork in exotic, isolated, so-called primitive cultures had been privileged by Bronislaw Malinowski (1884–1942) on similar grounds during the First World War. After this rite of passage, the anthropologist who did such fieldwork was expected to return to the universities of Europe or North America to interpret the exotic for stay-at-home colleagues in the humanities and social sciences (see Stocking 1983). A teaching position that facilitated fieldwork in Brazil could be rationalized as a temporary condition in the attainment of professional credentials as an anthropologist. Sociology was not a realistic option because that professional niche was already occupied in Brazil, as it was back in France. Lévi-Strauss was critical of the Durkheimian sociologists in Brazil for what he perceived as employing their positivist social science in the ideological service of the Brazilian ruling class (Pace 1983:31). He resisted this linkage and chose to identify himself instead with the Sao Paulo of the immigrants and small landowners, a position consistent with his superficial adherence to French Marxism at this early stage of his career.

Lévi-Strauss spent his academic holidays on what appear in retrospect to have been rather superficial safaris into the Amazon jungle. Oral tradition in anthropology suggests that his survey ethnography made little permanent contribution to the empirical database of ethnology; at the time, however, it was considered significant in light of limited ethnographic knowledge of interior South America. Lévi-Strauss was a respected contributor to the *Handbook of South American Indians* edited by latter-day Boasian Julian Steward (1902–72) for the Bureau of American Ethnology (BAE) in Washington DC.

Whatever its long-range impact, however, there can be no question that fieldwork experience served as a rite of passage for the young anthropologist and irrevocably changed his views of the cultural difference reflected in the gulf between "civilized" and "primitive."[3] In *Tristes tropiques* ([1955] 1975), virtually alone among his writings, Lévi-Strauss recorded his despair and alienation from civilization as he personally knew it alongside his compassion for the plight of the oppressed and impoverished Indigenous peoples of Brazil. He wrote as a man suffering from culture shock. *Tristes tropiques* is a tour de force, a book combining multiple genres: travelogue, ethnography, philosophy text, "reformist tract" directed to indictment of Western civilization, and "symbolist literary text" structured around an encounter of superficially chaotic sensory imageries (Geertz 1988:39, 41). The narrative becomes a myth of quest, with the anthropologist as its hero (Sontag 1961).

Part of Lévi-Strauss's quest, heroic at least in his own eyes, from alienation to confident professional identity as a structuralist resonates with the biographical experience he brought to the encounter. His birth in Belgium made him an outsider to France, although he embraced French intellectual culture wholeheartedly. He rarely constructed himself as a Jew but was the grandson of a rabbi. His escape from France to New York in 1941, chronicled in *Tristes tropiques*, created a kind of "transcendental homelessness," a second exile from the civilization with which he identified regardless of events in wartime Europe (Torgovnick 1990:218). On shipboard, Lévi-Strauss described his alienation and loss of distinctiveness as an individual. Perhaps for the first time, he associated himself with the lower class, feeling himself "subject to extermination" as were the so-called primitive tribes he had met in Brazil (212). Insofar as the issue exceeds the biographical, Torgovnick suggests that Lévi-Strauss saw Jewish exile as a mediating third term between the endangered "primitive" and the endangered modern civilized intellectual (288). Throughout his career, Lévi-Strauss distanced himself from his research subjects; he continued to identify with the French intelligentsia as the "us" to which the primitive cultures of Brazil and elsewhere were the contrastive "them" or "other." He was interested in the generic nature of the primitive rather than in the cultural features of particular primitive groups.

Tristes tropiques proposes several mediating terms between primitive South America and civilized France that Torgovnick (1990:215) reads as representing alternative imaginable futures for humankind. The violence and limitation of space for the vast population of modern India prefigure, for Lévi-Strauss, a fearsome but far from implausible postwar global monoculture swallowing up local knowledges and forms of life, while Islam "severs" the traditions of East and West, precluding the possibility of their blending (215–16). Lévi-Strauss's position seems to be that each society chooses its way of living in such a way that the observer has no matrix within which to compare or evaluate those choices. It is a relativism rooted in passivity, a paralysis arising from moral positioning. Yet there is a countervailing thread of utopian wistfulness in which Buddhism represents for Lévi-Strauss the lost opportunity for global philosophical integration quite alien to the mainstream West. Although science provides no firm criterion of value, the scientist cannot but regret the loss of naive commitment to their own version of civilization. Torgovnick (214) suggests that Lévi-Strauss's obsession to reach deep structures of cognition beyond the particulars of history arises from his effort to transcend personal alienation.

Lévi-Strauss's later theoretical writings privileged a more disengaged authorial authority. Sanche de Gramont (in Hayes and Hayes 1970) laments the absence of the impassioned response to the cross-cultural experience of *Tristes tropiques* in structuralism as Lévi-Strauss later practiced it: "With Lévi-Strauss, the whole humanist tradition goes down the drain. Instead of a free spirit, responsible for its decisions, we have a man [*sic*] responding to programmed circuits called structures. The individual conscience is no longer relevant" (7). By implication, the Indigenous peoples of Brazil are helpless in the face of cultural genocide and environmental destruction. The anthropologist becomes an elegist for a nostalgic "primitivism" rather than an advocate for the preservation of diverse lifeways still viable in the contemporary world.

Retrospectively, Lévi-Strauss's conversations with Didier Eribon (1926–84) (Lévi-Strauss and Eribon [1988] 1991) claimed that he aspired to be an anthropologist even in those early days and insisted that the boundaries between anthropology and sociology "had not been fixed" when he was in Brazil (16). He distanced his own position from the "modernized positivism" of Auguste Comte (1798–1857), filtered through Durkheim, and emphasized that Brazil wanted "sociology" (20). Whatever Brazil received from Lévi-Strauss's brief sojourn there, it was not sociology. With the benefit of hindsight, he claimed that, already in Brazil, he preferred the Americanist fieldwork tradition of the early Boasians about which he knew little at the time to the sociological theories of his homeland. Arriving in New York in 1941, Lévi-Strauss found that the newly transplanted European intellectuals fleeing Hitler's Europe shared with the less recently immigrant Boasians (most of whom were German or Jewish or both in the early generations) a rejection of the rationalist positivist tradition of French sociology. Lévi-Strauss's characterization of the arts in New York in the 1940s applies equally well to the Boasians. Indeed, in New York at that time, "anthropology was part of the decor of avant-garde art and writing" (Clifford 1988:243). "The surrealists were attuned to the irrational and sought to exploit it from an aesthetic standpoint" (Lévi-Strauss [1983] 1985:266).

In any case, Lévi-Strauss remained an exile from his homeland when he went to New York, and the Durkheimians remained firmly in control of what remained of French sociology after the devastation of the First World War. This context limited his choices, and it is not surprising that he rejected Durkheim and embraced the American anthropological tradition.

In the second volume of his collected papers, *Anthropologie structurale*, Lévi-Strauss included his essay "What Ethnology Owes to Durkheim," originally published in 1960. According to Lévi-Strauss's reading, Durkheim began by mistrusting ethnology because its data about other cultures were "superficial" ([1958] 1963:44). By 1912, in *Les formes élémentaires de la vie religieuse*, however, Durkheim attempted an abstract formulation of the simplest *forms* of religious thought. These were transformed into *structures* in Lévi-Strauss's revisionist human science of structuralism.

Lévi-Strauss remarks somewhat acidly that Durkheim was "protected by his rationalism" from the "rambling" character of ethnographic data ([1958] 1963:47). "Elementary forms" could not be derived from study of the complex modern societies on which positivist sociology was otherwise based. For Durkheim, the elementary forms were prior in chronology and subordinate in evolutionary origin to the "non-primitive" data. In a flourish of apparent magnanimity, surprising in light of his previous critique, Lévi-Strauss acknowledged (48): "The first generation formed by Durkheim would have yielded field workers, had it not been decimated by World War I." That is, they might have become anthropologists and thereby provided themselves with the data that could have circumvented Lévi-Strauss's critique. That Durkheim's "elementary forms" were already structuralist, however, escapes notice in Levi-Strauss's reading. He deliberately distances himself from the positivist tradition of Durkheimian sociology so that he can claim a more innovative status for his own self-labeled "Structural Anthropology." The parallelism of titles between Durkheim's *Les Formes élémentaires de la vie religieuse* and Lévi-Strauss's own *Les Structures élémentaires de la parenté* in 1949, however, suggests self-conscious intellectual continuity, whether or not he perceived it at the time of writing. Discontinuity may have loomed larger in retrospect.

In other contexts Lévi-Strauss spoke positively about the (largely abortive and therefore nonthreatening) ethnological program of Durkheim's students. In an introduction to the work of Mauss, written in 1950 but not translated into English until 1987, Lévi-Strauss emphasized the "modernity" of Mauss's explication of the relationship of individual and group ([1950] 1987:3), an argument adapted from Durkheim. Lévi-Strauss praised the determined subordination of the psychological to the sociological, the necessarily collective character of the symbolic, and the careful sifting of data to identify their underlying commonality (12).

In an argument to which he would often return, Lévi-Strauss asserted that no society was "fully symbolic," although language, matrimonial rules, economic relations, art, science and religion were all inherently symbolic systems ([1950] 1987:16–17). He elaborated to Eribon: "The idea that structural analysis can account for everything in social life seems outrageous. It has never occurred to me. . . . In this vast empirical stew . . . where disorder reigns, are scattered small islands of organization" (Lévi-Strauss and Eribon [1988] 1991:102). When Eribon suggested (99) that *Les structures élémentaires de la parenté* might be read as an expansion on Mauss's *Essai sur le don* (*The Gift*) ([1924] 1954), Lévi-Strauss responded laconically: "If you like." Mauss's expansion of the Trobriand Islands ethnography of Bronislaw Malinowski (1884–1942) in terms of an abstract model of reciprocity and exchange paralleled his own quest for the "islands of organization" or universal cognitive structures in the data of kinship and, later, myth. The organization rather than the subject matter was significant.

Meaning, for Lévi-Strauss, intersects with the substantive categories of culture. In *La voie des masques*, for example, he argued that masks were like language in that "each one does not contain within itself its entire meaning" ([1975] 1982:56). Versions of a myth or types of masks form complementary series "functionally bound together" (57) in complementary distribution with "other real or potential masks that might have been chosen in its stead and substituted for it" (144). "Logical operations" (147) rather than plastic or verbal surface form were at stake.

Lévi-Strauss's introduction to Mauss aligned his own position with the ethnography of the Durkheimian sociologists as the "inspirer of a new humanism" in which all human societies "taken together" could explicate "the subject's capacity to objectify himself [*sic*] in practically unlimited proportions" ([1950] 1987:32). Cultural particulars were encompassed in larger generalizations. It was a "tragic risk" to confuse subjective understanding of Indigenous peoples with the need for distanced analytic attention to the unconscious collective construction of social facts (33–34). Anthropology from the point of view of the native(s) was not Lévi-Strauss's project. By this point in the essay, his focus had moved rhetorically from the priorities of Mauss to those of his emergent structuralist framework.

In sum, Lévi-Strauss was eager to associate himself with the Durkheimian tradition insofar as he could present his own version of structuralism as its culmination. His historiographic strategy, therefore, was to marginalize the structuralist strain within the Durkheimian tradition, thereby enhancing the originality of his own contrastive formulation. From greater historiographic distance, however, the incipient structuralism of Durkheim and Mauss laid the groundwork for Lévi-Strauss's seminal appropriation of the methodology of Prague School structuralism from linguistics and his felicitous positioning to recognize that it could be applied not only to language but also to the symbolic systems whose structures constituted the part of culture that interested him.

The Appropriation of Boasian Ethnography

This latent structuralism from Durkheimian sociology was already in place when Lévi-Strauss arrived in New York. After meeting Jakobson in New York, he superimposed it on the Boasian ethnographic tradition that was firmly ensconced in his new homeland at the time. Although his North American residence proved to be temporary, the realignment of Lévi-Strauss's thinking about culture and ethnography was permanent.

In "The Work of the Bureau of American Ethnology and Its Lessons," included in the second volume of *Anthropologie structurale*, Lévi-Strauss waxed ecstatic about American ethnography, eulogizing the "sacrosanct" volumes of the BAE bulletins and annual reports that he had purchased from a New York collector because they would preserve the "fundamentals of mankind" from irretrievable loss "when the last primitive culture will have disappeared from the earth" ([1973] 1976:50, 51). This is the rhetoric of *Tristes tropiques*, although its intent also is consistent with the Boasian commitment to the urgent need for ethnology and linguistics that Lévi-Strauss encountered between his Brazilian interlude and the writing of his complex ethnographic memoir.

Interestingly, Lévi-Strauss never distinguished clearly between the work of the Bureau of American Ethnology and that of the Boasians. In practice, although the contest had been conceded to the Boasians for two decades when Lévi-Strauss first arrived in North America, Boas had struggled from the late 1880s until about 1920 to replace the amateur research method and outdated evolutionary theory of the BAE ethnology with a professional anthropology based in universities and committed to a historical and psychological perspective derived from fieldwork geared toward providing counterexamples to premature generalization (Darnell 1969, 1998).

For Lévi-Strauss, these differences were not important. He coveted the American data as grist for his theoretical mill and illustration for his structuralist principles. The ethnographies "would form the authentic ethnographic material from which structuralism's metacultural orders were constructed" (Clifford 1988:245). For anyone working in the American context, however, the crucial paradigm shift occurred between the Bureau of American Ethnology and the Boasians, to the extent that the enduring documentary value of prior work was eclipsed in Boasian rhetoric (e.g., Boas 1904; Darnell, 1990, 1998).

Lévi-Strauss went on to predict, in a lyrical tone reminiscent of the underlying sentiment, if not the rhetoric, of the Americanist, particularly Boasian, tradition that the anthropology of the future would involve members of formerly "primitive" societies describing themselves. His prognostication contrasts sharply to latter-day Americanist dismissals of early work by the BAE as *merely* descriptive whereas his own were sophisticated and scientific. Several tenets of Boasian anthropology, as it contrasted with earlier North American work centered in the Bureau of American Ethnology, were extremely attractive to Lévi-Strauss in developing a structuralism distinct from French sociology. He particularly admired Boasian work in social structure by Robert H. Lowie (1883–1956) and Alfred L. Kroeber (1876–1960). But the theoretical approach shared by all of the early Boasians emanated from the work of the master himself (Darnell 2001). Lévi-Strauss's structuralism adopted at least three of its basic premises:

1. Boas defined the pressing theoretical problems of anthropology as historical and psychological. For Lévi-Strauss, the field of the psychological, what an older theory referred to as

"the psychic unity of mankind," provided justification for cognitive structures of relational thought as the basis for ethnological generalization.

2. Boas provided a mechanism for generalization about psychological categories of human thought. His concept of "secondary rationalization" postulated that the underlying forms of culture are not accessible to the consciousness of members of those cultures. Thus, the insights of the analyst, as opposed to those of "psychological reality" (Sapir [1933] 1949), were privileged. The distance of Lévi-Strauss's structures from the perceived world of "primitive" individuals was theoretically justifiable on these grounds.[4]

3. The historical particularism that Boas substituted for unilinear evolution mapped specific borrowings and subsequent integrations of cultural traits. Diffusion, particularly of folklore elements, provided him with data to reconstruct the histories of Indigenous North Americans. Most systematically in the four volumes of *Mythologiques* ([1964] 1969; [1966] 1973; [1968] 1978; [1971] 1981), Lévi-Strauss traced abstract variants of the same myth across South and North America. Although his argument stressed universal structures, his handling of the data retained much of the Boasian diffusional methodology and controlled comparison within particular culture areas.

When Lévi-Strauss acknowledged his debt to the Boasians, he emphasized ethnographic database over theoretical grounding. Pieces of the Boasian argument that he did not appropriate saliently included the emphasis on the individual in relation to culture and the foregrounding of language and text as tools of cultural analysis (Darnell 1991, 1992). These omissions distinguish Lévi-Strauss's structuralism from Boasian historical particularism despite substantial incorporation into the new framework of what he acquired from the Boasians he met in New York during the Second World War.

Surrealist Fieldwork in New York City

In volume three of his collected papers, *Le regard eloigné* ([1983] 1985), Lévi-Strauss describes "New York in 1941."[5] The French exile who had survived the jungles of Brazil was once again in culture

shock. New York was as alien to him as Brazil. It was "an anthropologist's dream, a vast selection of human culture and history" (Clifford 1988:237). Like the Amazon rainforest so powerfully evoked
in *Tristes tropiques*, the city became one among rare "moments of
intelligible human order and transformation surrounded by the
destructive, entropic currents of global history" (237). His was a
"redemptive metahistorical narrative" (215) of civilization as represented in the kaleidoscope that was New York in 1941.

Lévi-Strauss evoked Alice stepping through the looking glass,
describing the "immense horizontal and vertical disorder attrib-
utable to some spontaneous upheaval of the urban crust," and
his "sense of oppression every time I revisit New York" but also its
exoticism and the "curious shapes" of "beauty" within it (1985)
1988:261, 258. Like the surrealist art fashionable in New York emigré circles, Lévi-Strauss conceived the human mind as "implicitly
surrealistic" (Clifford 1988:140) in its creative capacity to encompass chaos and diversity. Lévi-Strauss's New York consisted of art
museums, libraries, and curio shops. He was curiously caught up
by the material representation of New York's cosmopolitan culture. Clifford (1988:236) reads this searching out of collector's
artifacts of primitive and modern art as a chronotype for "modern
art and culture collecting," for the encapsulation of the primitive
and exotic apart from the mainstream of modern life.

Colleagues among his fellow refugees were necessary to Lévi-
Strauss's American experience. This was his second fieldwork culture. Paul Radin (1883–1959) spoke of "primitive philosophers,"
the intellectuals to be found in any culture to whom anthropologists gravitated for their theories and interpretations. Clifford
(1988:238) identifies those with whom he debated his ideas: André
Breton (1896–1966), Roman Jakobson (1896–1982), Max Ernst
(1891–1976), André Masson (1896–1976), Georges Duthuit (1891–
c.1965), and Yves Tanguy (1900–1955). They were not Americans.

Jakobson and Structuralism without Language

Despite his profession of adherence to the Americanist tradition
of fieldwork and empiricist theory, Lévi-Strauss was far more profoundly influenced by the structuralism he borrowed and transformed from Roman Jakobson than by anything he learned from

Boasian historicism. The four ambitious volumes of *Mythologiques* and *La voie des masques* draw their voluminous data largely from Boasian fieldwork, but Lévi-Strauss did not work with these materials in an Americanist way. The Boasian database is texts in the words of native speakers of American Indigenous languages. Lévi-Strauss, however, uses these texts in a singularly unlinguistic manner alien to the spirit of their collectors. What Lévi-Strauss appropriates from the Boasians is myth elements and plot structures, abstracted from both their social context and the original languages that render them comparable across time and space. The expressive and connotative meaning of myth and myth narration is swallowed up by the analytic language of structural oppositions that Lévi-Strauss repurposed from Jakobson. The Jakobson valorized by Lévi-Strauss was not the same Jakobson who wrote about the poetic functions of language or about language in its literary instantiations. The latter Jakobson was the one with whom the Boasians found sympathetic common ground.

Lévi-Strauss always maintained that structuralism is a method, not a theory. As a method, according to his reading of Jakobson, structuralism has nothing, or at least very little, to do with language. Like Durkheim, Lévi-Strauss failed to address the contention of historical linguistics that the comparative method provided the closest thing to a *scientific* method attainable to the social sciences. The paradox, then, is that Lévi-Strauss borrowed his most essential claims for structuralism from linguistics, a discipline whose subject matter—language—failed to engage his imagination.

The encounter with Jakobson was critical to Lévi-Strauss's reorientation of his career in the early 1940s. "Moreover, the application of linguistic methods to anthropological problems not only seemed to offer enormous advantages to anthropology, but it must also have appeared as an excellent road to professional fame for a relatively young and ambitious person such as Lévi-Strauss" (Pace 1983:154). Jakobson was a prestigious mentor who did not challenge Lévi-Strauss's own field of expertise because he was not interested in the ethnography of the exotic. He was twelve years older than Lévi-Strauss and already well established in European intellectual circles that did not overlap with French sociology. Jakobson as linguist posed no threat to Lévi-Strauss's decision to identify himself professionally as an anthropologist.

Further, Lévi-Strauss called upon the common plight of war-time refugees from the European intelligentsia to claim Jakobson as a peer, not as someone who had taken a junior scholar under his wing in a new country. Lévi-Strauss reports attending Jakobson's lectures on sound and meaning in New York, while Jakobson, reciprocally, attended his own on kinship (Lévi-Strauss and Eribon [1988] 1991:42). Lévi-Strauss attributes his own brand of structuralism to the impact of this intellectual exchange. He recalled to Eribon (41) that when he met Jakobson, his own views were not fully formed; he was "a kind of naive structuralist, a structuralist without knowing it." Jakobson advised him to write about kinship, but Lévi-Strauss thought that his creative contribution would lie in the application of the structuralist method beyond linguistics (99): "I didn't apply his ideas; I became aware that what he was saying about language corresponded to what I was glimpsing in a confused way about kinship systems, marriage rules. and more generally, life in society" (99).

Lévi-Strauss did not move instantly from kinship to myth to all products of the human mind as the appropriate domains of structural anthropology. As early as "The Structural Study of Myth," written in the 1950s and included in the first volume of *Anthropologie structurale* in 1963, Lévi-Strauss stated the principle on which each of his later books would "recursively . . . [train] the constant, unchanging, structuralist gaze on one or another domain of anthropological research; a huge rotating searchlight, lighting up first this dark corner, then the next" (Geertz 1988:31).

Across the domains of conventional ethnography, it was necessary to "restate the thought of those societies in another language which is intelligible to us" (Pace 1983:143). All products of the human mind reflected "the formal play of the human intellect" (Geertz 1988:30). Again, language, as understood by linguists, disappeared from the definition of the structuralist method. The label "structural anthropology seemed obvious. I have found [that] I was doing structuralism as the linguists did. . . . I simply meant that I placed myself in the same intellectual province as Saussure, Troubetzkoy, Jakobson, Benveniste" (Lévi-Strauss and Eribon [1988] 1991:68). Later, however, Lévi-Strauss would reject the very term "structuralism" as " besmirched," "degraded," and

"deceptive" (68, 91, 72). He claimed no ambition to have spearheaded a fad and rejected identifying his own intellectual commonality with others labeled as structuralists. He preferred to see
himself as part of the "intellectual family" of Emile Benveniste
(1902–76) and Georges Dumézil (1898–1986) to association with
Michel Foucault (1926–84), Jacques Lacan (1901–80), or Roland
Barthes (1915–80) (91–92). By the 1970s the competition was for
the role of reigning guru of Paris. Lévi-Strauss was never fond of
competition and once again rewrote his intellectual genealogy to
his own taste.

In *La pensée sauvage* ([1962] 1966), which initiated the vogue
of structuralism, Lévi-Strauss appropriated considerable terminology from linguistics. It was his ace in the hole in his debates with
Jean Paul Sartre on the nature of history. To Eribon (Lévi-Strauss
and Eribon [1988] 1991:42), Lévi-Strauss explicitly denied that his
intentions were linguistic in any technical sense. Rather, linguistics

> provides precious notions, such as that of binary opposition, of
> marked and unmarked terms. But that is more the vocabulary
> of relational thought. The nature and importance of my bor-
> rowings from linguistics have been misunderstood. They boil
> down to the role of unconscious mental activity in the produc-
> tion of logical structures. (43)

Lévi-Strauss reiterates that he was simply seeking confirmation from
another discipline for his preexisting claim that component elements are meaningful only in their relation or position: "I don't
believe I have asked anything else from linguistics, and Jakobson,
during our conversations, was the first to recognize that I was making an original use of these notions in another area" (43). Jakobson
never disputed Lévi-Strauss's assertion that he had taken nothing of importance from linguistics. Indeed, Lévi-Strauss probably
realized that Jakobson would have been threatened only had his
French protégé attempted to become a linguist. Their friendship
continued until Jakobson's death forty years later.

Perhaps unsurprisingly, Lévi-Strauss made no effort to follow
the development of linguistics after his intense period of interaction with Jakobson and linguistic structuralism. "Linguistics
has become so involved and complicated that I no longer feel

capable of following it. The discipline as practised by Jacobson enthralled me like a detective story" (Lévi-Strauss and Eribon [1988] 1991:114). He dismissed contemporary linguistics as "arid and tedious" and professed himself bored by transformational grammar (114).

The word "language" has a different meaning for Lévi-Strauss than it does for a linguist, regardless of theoretical persuasion. For example, the comparative method in structural anthropology grounds its theory in multiple cases, converting them into a "common language" that is a language of structures, of organizations; it is linguistic only in the most metaphorical of senses. Identical "tactics" are employed for "sociological facts" in Durkheim in *Les structures élémentaires de la parenté*, for religious facts in Le *potière jalouse* ([1985] 1988), and for mythological facts in *Mythologiques* (1969, 1973, 1978, 1981) and *La voie des masques* ([1975] 1982:129, 141). "But the underlying question doesn't change. . . . [There is] an underlying order, a deep structure" (129). Although Chomsky's transformational grammar introduced the term "deep structure" and popularized the term "transformation"[6] at about the time Lèvi-Strauss's work was becoming known in France, this is almost certainly a case of independent invention as a result of a Zeitgeist shared across diverse disciplines.[7] Lèvi-Strauss's concept of "transformation" is grounded somewhere between Boas, Jakobson, and Marx, by way of Hegel; it is an analyst's rule of historical interpretation.

In "Language and the Analysis of Social Laws," published in the *American Anthropologist* in 1951 and included in the first volume of *Anthropologie structurale*, Lévi-Strauss claims to analyze the different features of social life at a "deep enough level [. . .] to cross from one to the other; or to express the specific structure of each in terms of a sort of general language, valid for each system separately and for all of them taken together" ([1958] 1963:62). Language and culture are the results of fundamentally similar activities and may be taken as equivalent in their status as representations of the human mind itself. Oddly enough, Lévi-Strauss has never shown much interest in neuropsychology or neurolinguistics as potential sources of independent confirmation for his universal structures.

Conclusion: Bricoleur Par Excellence

Lévi-Strauss, finally, emerges as the master weaver, more bricoleur than systematic analyst, his tapestry incorporating threads from the disciplines of sociology, anthropology, philosophy, and linguistics, and from French, Slavic, and North American versions of social science theory and method. His gift for outrageous formulation of hypotheses and his prodigious capacity to sort through and impose order on ethnographic data guarantee him a lasting place in the histories of all of these sciences, including linguistics. His own version of the history within which these linkages emerged, however, cannot be taken as canonical.

Since the heyday of structuralism as an international and interdisciplinary movement in the 1960s and 1970s, subsequent fashions of intellectual thought have come and gone. After the student revolts in Paris in 1968, those who sought political engagement turned away from structuralism. The most devastating critique of Lévi-Strauss came from Jacques Derrida (1930–2004), whose *Of Grammatology* in 1974 (cited by Torgovnick 1990:221–23) emphasized the elaborate and illusory formalism of structuralism's purported universalist edifice.

Notes

1. Originally published as "The Structuralism of Claude Lévi-Strauss," *Historiographia Linguistica* 22 (1995): 217–34.

2. Although Chomsky explicitly rejected the label of structuralism, in practice his critique was addressed primarily to the Bloomfieldian version thereof (Hymes and Fought 1975). In the larger context of structuralism as an international intellectual movement, Chomsky's transformational grammar is structuralist in its basic assumptions.

3. The discourse of "primitive," "primitive culture," and "primitivism" as a movement in the arts is unproblematic in France and in the connotations of the terms themselves. Embedded assumptions of romanticized nostalgia may jar the sensibilities of some North American readers. "Native(s)" appear with similar resonance.

4. The countercurrent in Boasian anthropology, centered in the work of Edward Sapir, Ruth Benedict, and Margaret Mead, leading to what came to be called "culture and personality," failed to engage Lévi-Strauss's attention.

5. The original French title of "New York post-et-préfiguratif better conveys the tension and perhaps even anxiety of Lévi-Strauss's New York years" (Clifford 1988:236).

6. The term "transformation" was used beginning in the 1940s in the work of Chomsky's teacher, Zellig S. Harris (1909–92).

7. In anthropology, componential analysis and ethnoscience reflected parallel intellectual trends in searching for universals but failed to appreciate the complexity of Lévi-Strauss's method of assembling his evidence without linguistics. In any case, his work constitutes a necessary baseline for the successors of structuralism regardless of their discipline.

References

Boas, Franz. 1904. "The History of Anthropology." *Science* 20:513–24.

Clifford, James. 1988. *The Predicament of Culture*. Cambridge MA: Harvard University Press.

Darnell, Regna. 1969. "The Development of American Anthropology, 1879–1920: From the Bureau of American Ethnology to Franz Boas." PhD diss., University of Pennsylvania.

———. 1990. *Edward Sapir: Linguist, Anthropologist, Humanist*. Berkeley: University of California Press.

———. 1991. "Franz Boas, Edward Sapir and the Americanist Text Tradition." *Historiographia Linguistica* 17:129–44.

———. 1992. "The Boasian Text Tradition and the History of Anthropology." *Culture* 12:39–48.

———. 1998. *And Along Came Boas: Continuity and Revolution in Americanist Anthropology*. Amsterdam: John Benjamins.

———. 2001. *Invisible Genealogies: A History of Americanist Anthropology*. Lincoln: University of Nebraska Press.

Derrida, Jacques. 1974. *Of Grammatology*. Baltimore: Johns Hopkins University Press.

Durkheim, Emile. (1912) 1961. *Elementary Forms of the Religious Life* [*Les formes élémentaires de la vie religieuse*]. New York: Collier.

Geertz, Clifford. 1988. *Works and Lives: The Anthropologist as Author*. Stanford: Stanford University Press.

Hayes, Nelson, and Tanya Hayes, eds. 1970. *The Anthropologist as Hero*. Cambridge MA: MIT Press.

Hymes, Dell, and John Fought. 1975. "American Structuralism." In *Current Trends in Linguistics 10: Historiography of Linguistics*, edited by Thomas A. Sebeok, 903–1176. The Hague: Mouton.

Lévi-Strauss, Claude. (1949) 1969. *The Elementary Structures of Kinship* [*Les structures élémentaires de la parenté*]. Boston: Beacon.

———. (1950) 1983. *Introduction to the Work of Marcel Mauss*. London: Routledge.

———. (1955) 1975. *Tristes tropiques*. New York: Aetheneum.

———. (1958) 1963. *Structural Anthropology* [*Anthropologie structurale*]. Vol. 1. New York: Basic Books.

———. (1962) 1966. *The Savage Mind* [*La pensée sauvage*]. Chicago: University of Chicago Press.

————. (1964) 1969. *Mythologiques 1: The Raw and the Cooked* [*Le cruet et le cuit*]. New York: Harper and Row.

————. (1966) 1973. *Mythologiques 2: From Honey to Ashes* [*Du miel auxcendres*]. New York: Harper and Row.

————. (1968) 1978. *Mythologiques 3: The Origin of Table Manners* [*L'origine des manières de table*]. New York: Harper and Row.

————. (1971) 1981. *Mythologiques 4: The Naked Man* [*L'homme nu*]. New York: Harper and Row.

————. (1973) 1976. *Structural Anthropology* [*Anthropologie structurale*]. Vol. 2. New York: Basic Books.

————. (1975) 1982. *The Way of the Masks* [*La voie des masques*]. Vancouver: Douglas and McIntyre.

————. (1983) 1985. *The View from Afar* [*Le regard eloigné*]. New York: Basic Books.

————. (1985) 1988. *The Jealous Potter* [*Le potière jalouse*]. Chicago: University of Chicago Press.

Lèvi-Strauss, Claude, and Didier Eribon. (1988) 1991. *Conversations with Claude Lèvi-Strauss*. New York: University of Chicago Press.

Mauss, Marcel. (1924) 1954. *The Gift* [*Essai sur le don*]. London: Cohen and West.

Pace, David. 1983. *Claude Lèvi-Strauss: The Bearer of Ashes*. London: Routledge and Kegan Paul.

Sapir, Edward. (1933) 1949. "La realité psychologique des phonèmes." *Journal de Psychologie Normale et Pathologique* 30:247–65. Reprinted in English translation as "The Psychological Reality of Phonemes." In *Selected Writings of Edward Sapir in Language, Culture and Personality*, edited by David G. Mandelbaum, 46–60. Berkeley: University of California Press.

Sontag, Susan. 1961 "The Anthropologist as Hero." In *Against Interpretation*, 69–81. New York: Farrar, Straus & Giroux.

Stocking, George W., Jr., ed. 1983. *Observers Observed: Essays on Ethnographic Fieldwork*. Madison: University of Wisconsin Press.

Sturrock, John. 1986. *Structuralism*. London: Paladin.

Torgovnick, Marrianna. 1990. *Gone Primitive: Savage Intellects, Modern Lives*. Chicago: University of Chicago Press.

Fig. 1. Frederica de Laguna (1906–2004). Courtesy of the American Anthropological Association.

15

Obituary for Frederica de Laguna (1906–2004)

Frederica de Laguna, a leading ethnographer of the Northwest Coast and one of the last students of Franz Boas, died on October 6, 2004.[1] She served as president of the American Anthropological Association (1967–68), receiving its Distinguished Service Award in 1986. She and Margaret Mead were the first women elected to the National Academy of Sciences, in 1975. In that year she retired from Bryn Mawr College as the William R. Kenan Jr. Professor Emerita of Anthropology, but she continued her research and writing for another twenty-nine years. De Laguna studied "the geographic and cultural hinge" (Guédon 2004:53) between the Northwest Coast and the Aleutian-Eskimo, employing a combination of archaeology, linguistics, ethnohistory, and ethnography. She was fascinated with the circumpolar connections posed by Boas's Jesup North Pacific Expedition, and her early work in Greenland allowed her to extend this regional complex even more broadly.

Frederica (Freddy) Annis Lopez de Leo de Laguna was born in Ann Arbor, Michigan, on October 3, 1906. She was homeschooled until she was nine. Both of her parents, Grace Mead Andrus and Theodore Lopez de Leo de Laguna, were philosophy professors at Bryn Mawr College. Freddy's life experience was more international than that of most Americans of the time, beginning with her parents' European sabbaticals in England and France in 1914–15 and 1921–22. She returned to the United States feeling alienated from the isolationism of the interwar years.

Freddy attended Bryn Mawr College, where she majored in economics and politics, graduating summa cum laude in 1927. She delayed acceptance of Bryn Mawr's prestigious European fellow-ship to complete a year of graduate coursework in anthropology at Columbia University. As she later reflected (de Laguna 2004:29), she was bored by the already completed Boasian critique of cultural evolution, enjoyed courses with Ruth Benedict and Gladys Reich-ard, thrived on hearing periodic reports of fieldwork in weekly seminars, and found Boas's linguistic field methods course "not clearly organized."

The postponed fellowship supported a year of contacts with European archaeologists and ethnologists, notably Abbé Bréuil, Marcellin Boule, and Paul Rivet in France, and Charles Gabriel Seligman, William James Perry, and Bronislaw Malinowski at the London School of Economics. She found Malinowski arrogant, and she resented his anti-Americanism and his displacement of dislike for Boas onto her, a hapless (female) student.

But it was her museum tour of Scandinavia that set de Laguna on her ethnographic life course.[2] At the First International Con-gress of Anthropological and Ethnological Sciences in Copenha-gen in 1928, Freddy met Therkel Mathiassen and Kai Birket-Smith. Mathiassen invited her to Arctic Greenland as his assistant on a field exploration of Eskimo-Norse contacts. The trip expanded to six months in the field (de Laguna 1977). In North America at that time, such an opportunity would have been closed to a sin-gle young woman.

Boas chose her dissertation project, a comparison of Upper Paleolithic and Eskimo (called Inuit in Canada) art styles. Although she never demonstrated the hypothesis (proposed by Boas) that Paleolithic hunters had moved north with reindeer herds at the end of the Pleistocene, the project foreshadowed the cir-cumpolar scope and time depth of her later research. She was awarded her doctorate in 1933 for the dissertation with its neg-ative conclusion.

De Laguna had not yet completed her dissertation when Birket-Smith invited her to assist him in excavations at Prince William Sound, Alaska. When he fell ill, the University of Pennsylvania Museum authorized a survey of potential sites, also encompass-ing Cook Inlet. She went to Cook Inlet alone in 1931 and 1932 and returned with Birket-Smith to Cook Inlet and Prince William Sound in 1933, supported by the museum and the National Research Council. A coauthored work on Eyak appeared in 1938; Birket-Smith's Chugash (Eskimo) ethnography was published in 1953, and her Chugash prehistory in 1956. The University of Pennsylvania Museum published her archaeological work on Cook Inlet in 1934. A 1935 search for Paleo-Indians in interior Alaska, integrating ethnography and more recent archaeology, produced results spanning a more modest time depth.

During the Depression, de Laguna divided her interests between northern culture history and the cultural patterning of individual lives. With limited job prospects, she concentrated on writing up her Yukon work (although publication was delayed until 1947 because of World War II). She wrote a historical novel for youth and two detective stories (1937, 1938) to finance her research, arguing that "the ethnographer should know enough about a culture to . . . use it as the setting for a novel" (2004:50). She recalled her "confusion" between Scandinavian and U.S. methods at this time (39).

In 1935 de Laguna became a soil conservationist for the Bureau of Indian Affairs on the Pima Reservation. With her mother, she toured southwestern archaeological excavations, seeking background to teach U.S. archaeology (a course I took with her nearly thirty years later). They returned to the area for several summers thereafter. Her fieldwork was a family enterprise; after her father's death in 1930 while she was in the field, her mother and younger brother Wallace often joined her on research trips. During 1936–37 a National Research Council fellowship allowed de Laguna to continue studying Eskimo archaeology, to learn practical linguistics, and to visit various Northwest Coast cultural groups. As in her European travels, she carefully established contacts with local experts.

De Laguna's professional career at Bryn Mawr College began in 1935 with a single course. She became an assistant professor of anthropology in 1938, associate professor in 1949, and professor in 1955 within the Sociology and Anthropology Department. She chaired the joint department from 1950 until it divided in 1967,

and she chaired anthropology from that time until her mandatory retirement at age sixty-five. Although a joint major nominally existed, sociology and anthropology were utterly separate
in practice, at least during the early 1960s. In 1941 de Laguna
led a student field excavation near Flagstaff, Arizona. A year later
she joined the U.S. Naval Reserve, teaching codes and ciphers
to women midshipmen at Smith College. In 1943 she moved to
Naval Intelligence in Washington DC, retiring as a lieutenant com-
mander. Although de Laguna recalled her work in the navy as
"often vague and unimportant" and found the chauvinism "frustrating and ignominious" (2004:45), she later took great pride
in her naval service.

A Rockefeller fellowship subsidized a year in northern Arizona
that enabled her to retool in her profession before returning to
teaching. She then undertook an ambitious research project to
trace the archaeology, history, and ethnography of the Tlingit
through time. The fieldwork began at Yakutat in 1949 and culminated with the three-volume *Under Mount St. Elias* in 1972. In
her thirteen trips to Alaska, with collaborators including Catharine McClellan and Marie-Françoise Guédon, she explored the
distinctive cultural growth of the coastal Tlingit (at Yakutat and
Angoon) and their links to the interior Upper Tanana and Copper River Athabascans (McClellan 1989:40).

Although de Laguna staunchly declared herself to represent
a blend of European and U.S. traditions, insisting that Boas was
uninvolved in her formational Danish collaborations (2004:35),
I found her the quintessential Boasian. She was an obedient student who revered her mentor and displayed his picture above
her computer. Boas assigned her dissertation topic. When he
told her not to pursue Eyak linguistics because the language was
not then endangered (Guédon 2004:61), she went on to other
projects. De Laguna spoke wistfully of the days when Indians
eagerly passed on to anthropologists what their own descendants
no longer wished to learn, and she took pride in the fact that
her work had become a resource to the communities she studied. She was invited to return to Yakutut in 1986, at the age of
eighty, to examine archaeological sites threatened by the advanc-

ing Hubbard Glacier. Films by Laura Bliss recorded the potlatch held in her honor there and documented her return to the Eyak at Angoon in 1996.

De Laguna revisited the same communities through multiple generations of "informants," learning local languages and customs. Her ethnographic present was longitudinal, incorporating all four subdisciplines of anthropology. Anthropology was a way of life for her. Her website records the "joy" of fieldwork "because it meant one could meet others" (de Laguna 2005). Like Boas, she rarely spelled out theories, but they were implicit in her work. For example, she emphasized the role of the observer in the observation long before this became fashionable. Without overt feminist rhetoric, she held—and conveyed to her students—"a deep contempt for institutions unable to recognize the potential of women" (de Laguna 2005). She never married (and broke an engagement during her Greenland expedition), feeling that her work precluded marriage.

In the manner of her generation and despite her collaborative research commitments, de Laguna held firmly to the authority of the anthropologist. Recording disappearing cultures was an urgent calling. She deplored a political climate in which Native American identity politics could sway the course of science, for example, by forestalling the study of human skeletal remains and repatriating ceremonial objects, which was characteristic of her generation. Deeply embedded in the museum milieu of her mature career, de Laguna envisioned anthropology as "a vast, capacious cabinet with multiple cubbyholes and shelves . . . [with] a place for everything" (2004:52), a metaphor of stasis that few would employ today. As president of the American Anthropological Association (AAA) in the politically tumultuous mid-1960s, she remained adamant that personal political positions should hold no place in a professional organization.

Although Freddy deplored the loss of Bryn Mawr's graduate program and the modern interdisciplinary thrust of recent anthropology there, the continuing "robust" anthropological tradition (Philip Kilbride, email to author, January 20, 2005) at the college owes much to her commitment to "rigorous" undergraduate teaching (Richard Davis, email to author, January 26, 2005), fieldwork, a holistic four-field discipline with a historical focus, museum curation, and the reading of original sources. Since 1983 the department has produced over two hundred senior seminar fieldwork papers (Kilbride, Goodale, and Ameisen 1990).

Each of Freddy's students has her own memories, but some of mine are perhaps shared by others. I did not realize at the time that Danish pedagogy (Guédon 2004:57) surfaced in her first-year requirement that reading notes be handed in. I acquired a lifetime habit of automatically recording page numbers and full references that has saved me countless hours. She sent the first-year class to the University of Pennsylvania Museum to write about any exhibit; I chose Samuel Noah Kramer's on cuneiform script, acquiring another lifelong habit of reading the placards in museum cases. For years I could rattle off the harpoon head sequence of St. Lawrence Island Eskimo [*sic*] cultures. I changed my major from English to a double major with anthropology because her stories about women friends in Tlingit fishing villages leavened the solemnity and isolation of the ivory tower. I remember especially her description of cajoling informants to provide Rorschach profiles by playing this "game" alongside them.

Although Freddy maintained a degree of formality with her students, we shared vicariously her contagious commitment to the life of the mind. In my undergraduate days, her mother gave several lectures and was always present at (rare) social occasions at their home on the edge of the campus. I participated, at a distance, in the intellectual ferment created between Freddy, her mother Grace, Pete (A. Irving) Hallowell, and Maude (Frame) Hallowell at the intersection of culture and personality. Freddy never lost track of her students who went on in anthropology. Years later, after a very late AAA party, I met her while carrying my shoes en route through the hotel; with a twinkle in her eye, she murmured, "and some things never change."

Freddy battled escalating health problems with uncompromising determination. I was invited to tea at her retirement home only weeks after her double hip replacement; using a walker, she apologized for not managing dinner. In response to her increasing blindness, caused by hereditary macular degeneration, Freddy's final Christmas newsletter proposed the type size and font to be used in replies. She could be something of a martinet.

Katharine Woodhouse (email to author, January 20, 2005) remembers her dictating, "sitting alongside me at the computer," as they worked together on her later projects. In the 1990s Freddy edited and annotated George Thorton Emmons's Tlingit work (de Laguna [with George Thornton Emmons] 1991) and wrote two books of "tales" on her Dena (de Laguna 1937) and Tanaina fieldwork (de Laguna 1938). At the time of her death, three days after her ninety-eighth birthday, Freddy was planning a book on the animals in her life, a biography of a Tlingit woman, and a Northern Encounters series for students (de Laguna 2005). Her legacy includes Frederica de Laguna Northern Books and a research center at the University of Ottawa with Marie-Françoise Guédon as executor. De Laguna's ethnographic materials are located at the Alaska State Library Archives, where they are accessible to descendants and their communities. Her professional papers and correspondence are at the National Anthropological Archives at the Smithsonian Institution.

Notes

1. Originally published as "Frederica de Laguna," *American Anthropologist* 107 (2005): 742–44.

2. Some of the language that de Laguna used has changed since: "Eskimo" (called Inuit in Canada) appears in various hyphenated terms, cf. "paleo-Indian." "Indian" is still the preferred term in some Indigenous communities, but "Indigenous" is preferred as a cover term.

References

Birket-Smith, Kai. 1953. *The Chugash Eskimo.* Copenhagen: Nationalmuseets Skrifter, Etnografisk Raekke 6.

Birket-Smith, Kai, and Frederica de Laguna. 1938. *The Eyak Indians of Copper River Delta, Alaska.* Copenhagen: Levin and Munksgaard.

de Laguna, Frederica. (1934) 1975. *The Archaeology of Cook Inlet, Alaska.* Philadelphia: University of Pennsylvania Museum. Reprint, Fairbanks: Alaska Historical Society.

———. 1937. *The Arrow Points to Murder: The Crime Club.* New York: Doubleday Doran.

———. 1938. *Fog on the Mountain: The Crime Club.* New York: Doubleday Doran.

———. 1947. *The Prehistory of Northern North America as Seen from the Yukon.* Memoirs from the Society for American Archaeology, 3. Menasha WI: Society for American Archaeology.

———. 1956. *Chugash Prehistory: The Archaeology of Prince William Sound, Alaska.* University of Washington Publications in Anthropology, 13. Seattle: University of Washington Press.

———. 1972. *Under Mount St. Elias: The History and Culture of the Yakutat Tlingit.* 3 vols. Smithsonian Contributions to Anthropology, 7. Washington DC: Smithsonian Institution Press.

———. 1977. *Voyage to Greenland: A Personal Initiation into Anthropology.* New York: Norton.

———. 1991. *The Tlingit Indians.* With George Thornton Emmons. New York: American Museum of Natural History.

———. 2004. "Becoming an Anthropologist: My Debt to European and Other Scholars Who Influenced Me." In Mauzé, Harkin, and Kan, *Coming to Shore,* 23–52.

———. 2005. *Northern Books.* Electronic document, http://www.fredericadelaguna.com (no longer functional). Accessed April 26, 2005.

Guédon, Marie-Françoise. 2004. Crossing Boundaries: Homage to Frederica de Laguna. In Mauzé, Harkin, and Kan, *Coming to Shore,* 53–62.

Kilbride, Philip, Jane Goodale, and Elizabeth Ameisen, eds. 1990. *Encounters with American Ethnic Cultures.* Montgomery: University of Alabama Press.

Mauzé, Marie, Michael Harkin, and Sergei Kan, eds. 2004. *Coming to Shore: Northwest Coast Ethnology, Traditions and Visions.* Lincoln: University of Nebraska Press.

McClellan, Catharine. 1989. Frederica de Laguna and the Pleasures of Anthropology. *American Ethnologist* 16:766–85.

16
....

Obituary for Dell Hathaway Hymes (1927–2009)

Dell H. Hymes, whose unique combination of contributions to the ethnography of speaking, ethnopoetics, Amerindian linguistics, and the discipline's political engagement personified linguistic anthropology over the course of his career, died in Charlottesville, Virginia, on November 13, 2009.[1] At the time of his death, he was professor emeritus at the University of Virginia.[2]

Dell Hymes was born on June 7, 1927, in Portland, Oregon. He grew up in a middle-class neighborhood in Portland and chose to attend Reed College because he could commute across town. After one year, he was drafted into the army and served two years as a clerk in Korea. A side trip to Hiroshima indelibly impressed him with the capacity of war to devastate a people through overreaching greed, a parallel on which he would draw repeatedly throughout his life in relation to the Chinookan "Sun's Myth." After the war he returned to Reed on the GI Bill. He quickly joined what would become the long-term research project of Reed anthropologists David French and Kay (Story) French and their students at nearby Warm Springs Reservation, which saw the "emergence of a cosmopolitan intellectual elite" coalescing around "abstract art, modern literature and or the sciences, non-western (i.e., Asian or Indigenous) religions, and progressive (usually Marxist) politics" (Moore 2008:12). Linguistics, Eastern philosophy, poetry, and politics were the cornerstones of Hymes's 1950 BA in literature and anthropology. He especially loved poetry, which he continued to write throughout his life.

Together with his friend and former roommate Gary Snyder, Hymes began graduate school at Indiana University with its unique

Fig. 2. Dell Hathaway Hymes (1927–2009). Courtesy of the American
Anthropological Association.

amalgam of linguistics, anthropology, and folklore. Snyder soon reoriented their shared commitments toward community immersion, Buddhist philosophy, and poetry, while Hymes pursued his PhD, receiving it in 1955 with a grammar of Kathlamet Chinook based on texts collected by Franz Boas (Hymes 1955a). In 1954 he married Virginia Dosch Wolff, with whom he would raise four children, and for the next thirty years the couple continued research and fieldwork at Warm Springs (Dell on Wasco and Virginia on Sahaptin), spending summers at their cabin in Rhododendron, Oregon. The study of an American Indian[3] language, he mused, "stays with you; you feel responsible for it in a way that you might not feel for Greek or Azerbaijani" (Hymes 1980a:209).

Hymes's career remained interdisciplinary around his established and inextricably linked core commitments, including those to the people of Warm Springs and the landscape of the Pacific Northwest. He taught linguistics at Stanford in 1954–55, hoping to study anthropology with Harry Hoijer, but instead he devoted himself to completing his Indiana dissertation quickly to take up a five-year appointment in Harvard's Department of Social Relations (1955–60). During a year at Stanford's Center for Advanced Studies in the Behavioral Sciences in 1957–58, he was influenced by Boasian anthropologist Alfred Kroeber and literary polymath and activist Kenneth Burke. At Harvard he explored Penutian historical linguistics, supplementing lexicostatistics with "positional analysis" of grammatical categories (1955b, 1956, 1957, 1960). He failed to obtain tenure at Harvard, which he attributed to his political activism (1999:ix), and spent the next five years at Berkeley (1960–65), noting five was "the pattern number for the Chinook" (1980a:209). He thrived alongside Berkeley colleagues linguist John Gumperz, sociologist Erving Goffman, educational psychologist Susan Ervin-Tripp, and language philosopher John Searle. Reflecting anthropology's broader turn to meaning, he and Gumperz called for an "ethnography of communication," opening an ethnographic space between the formal structures studied by linguists, increasingly isolated from linguistic behaviorism in Chomskyan linguistics, and the equally patterned use of language in actual speech communities (Gumperz and Hymes 1962). Hymes came to speak almost interchangeably of the ethnography of communication and the ethnography of speaking, which he saw as mediating social theory and behavioral detail.

Hymes moved to the University of Pennsylvania in 1965, where he taught anthropology, folklore, sociology, and linguistics. He served for twelve years as dean of the Graduate School of Education, where he embedded linguistics in the curriculum and engaged the school with innovative inner-city education in Philadelphia (Cazden, John, and Hymes 1972; Hymes 1980b). With Goffman and folklorist John Szwed, he established the Center for Urban Ethnography, drawing in William Labov from linguistics, Kenneth Goldstein from folklore, and Sol Worth from the Annenberg School of Communication. Hymes's essays of this period are collected in *Foundations in Sociolinguistics* (1974a). His "Models of the Interaction of Language and Social Setting" in *Directions in Sociolinguistics* (Gumperz and Hymes 1972) provided a preliminary theoretical framework. As described elsewhere in that volume (Sherzer and Darnell 1972), Hymes's Penn research team (including, in addition to myself, Michael Foster, Helen Hogan, Virginia Hymes, Judith T. Irvine, Elinor [Ochs] Keenan, Susan U. Phillips, Sheila [Dauer] Seitel, and K. M. Tiwari) documented the variability of language use in the ethnographic literature, which had been consigned to virtual invisibility because its patterned nature was not singled out for explicit attention. This first generation of ethnographers of speaking went on to carry out exemplary fieldwork along these lines (Bauman and Sherzer 1974).

Hymes's "running guerilla warfare" (1980b:206) against Noam Chomsky's exclusion of the social from the study of language underlay his revisionist concepts of "communicative competence"—structured adherence to the usages socialized within a speech community—and "breakthrough into performance." These concepts reflected his emphasis on the abstract nature of actor knowledge, alongside and of equal importance with grammatical competence, necessary to live in society. Hymes reformulated the Sapir-Whorf hypothesis in "Two Types of Linguistic Relativity" (1964a), arguing that culture-specific communicative economies predispose habitual ways of thought as powerfully as do grammatical categories. He was less interested in "formal problems of language" than in "a language I wanted to know about"

(1980b:205), and he emphasized the emergent patterns of social order and discourse cohesion in recorded texts—what he would later call "ethnopoetics."

Hymes had a talent for discerning in advance where the field might move next and for gathering colleagues around a topic of interest and synthesizing the results of their dialogue. He turned to pidgin and creole languages (1971), for example, with the assumption that their processes of formation would not differ from those of language in general, either in structure or in social use. In a surprisingly contemporary-sounding introductory essay on the use and usefulness of computers in anthropology, he assessed the relative merits of digital and analog models and identified the challenge to "explicate one's own processes of analysis, whether the result is couched mathematically or not," all while maintaining "a primary commitment to ethnographic data" (1965b:24). "Humanely channeled" computer use, consistent with his more overtly political work, promised "a democratic and decentralized effect" (1965b:27) that evoked "the logic and practice of quantitative and qualitative analysis, and the forms of cooperation and integration needed to make our stores of data systematic, comparable, accessible to each other and to theory" (1965b:31).

Hymes persistently worried about how things got to be the way they are. He first turned to the histories of anthropology and linguistics to establish the nature of his personal genealogy in the Americanist tradition of Boas, Kroeber, and Edward Sapir (Hymes 1983). He traced the proliferation of national traditions in linguistics despite the ethical constraints of postcolonial relevance, and he lamented the implicit hegemony of "paradigms," favoring instead the more inclusive concept of "traditions" (1974b). In a magisterial revisioning of American structuralism, Hymes and John Fought (1975) defined a First Yale School around Sapir's commitment to structuralist method, the autonomy of linguistics, the preservation of "disappearing" languages (today called "endangered," a term that leaves space for responsive agency), the genetic relationship of Amerindian languages, and the extension of linguistic insight across the social sciences and humanities (997). All but the last carried over to the Second Yale School that crystalized around Leonard Bloomfield after Sapir's death. Hymes's intellectual histories emphasized continuity rather than radical disjuncture.

Linguistics in anthropology, the study of unwritten languages as a necessary part of fieldwork training, emerged in Hymes's work as distinct from both of its constituent disciplines. He delimited a broad intellectual scope for generations of linguistic anthropology students with his reader *Language in Culture and Society* (1964b) and the widely interdisciplinary range of *Language in Society*, the journal that he founded in 1972 and edited for twenty-one years. His leadership was widely sought across the several disciplines of his practice. He served as president of the American Folklore Society (1973–74), the Council on Anthropology and Education (1977–78), the Linguistic Society of America (1982), the Consortium of Social Science Associations (1982–84), the American Anthropological Association (1983), and the American Association of Applied Linguistics (1986) (Handler 2002:267).

Hymes believed that it was possible—indeed necessary—to be interested in many things, a capacity he brought to the generosity and inclusiveness of his teaching and collegiality as well as to his scholarship. In a moment of reflexive musing, he wrote: "I seem to have an internal mechanism that always allows me to move to the margin from any center" (personal communication, March 21, 1987). The range of his professional involvements was breathtakingly broad. His University of Virginia webpage described his diverse body of work this way: "So much of it has depended and depends on circumstances. . . . I have often written about ideas, and spent a fair amount of time hanging around Indians" (n.d.). The subjects that intrigued him were not centered exclusively in either theory or ethnography and included "the use of language, oral narrative, and poetry, the history of anthropology and linguistics, Native Americans, theology. . . . What's interesting is real work. I am always interested in combating elitism and narrowness . . . at the expense of the rest of the world" (University of Virginia n.d.).

Hymes's acute political engagement during the Vietnam years, tempered by his coming of intellectual age under the McCarthyism of the Cold War, is reflected in *Reinventing Anthropology* (1972). His original introduction, "The Use of Anthropology: Critical, Political, Personal," articulates an innovative manifesto still germane to contemporary disciplinary reflexivity. The label and vested interests of "anthropology" remain secondary to interest in other peoples and inclusion of ourselves in the analysis (11). Elsewhere, however, he worried about maintaining "the liberal, social, moral passion" behind linguistics (1980b:212). Synthesizing Karl Marx and Boas, Hymes foreshadowed a method built around the emergence of culture in particular ethnographic contexts. The "true coherence" (1972:47) of anthropology is personal: each practitioner reinvents a genealogy and must ask of himself or herself, as of the discipline, "responsiveness, critical awareness, ethical concern, human relevance, a clear connection between what is to be done and the interest of mankind" (7). He envisioned a "socialist humanism" that would attack structures of power as well as defend the powerless and recommended the capacity of "ethnographic relationship" for "enlarging of the moral community" (53).

When Hymes moved to the University of Virginia in 1987 as Commonwealth Professor of English and Anthropology, he agonized over his right to abandon politics for poetics. Nonetheless, he returned to textual and theoretical work on Chinookan languages begun much earlier (e.g., Hymes 1965a), focusing on poetic structures of line and verse that proved to carry over to other Northwest Coast languages and that he came to believe were universals of narrative competence that had been obscured by lack of attention to the expressive form and poetic skill of narrators such as Wasco and Wishram Chinookan speakers Charles Cultee, Philip Kahclamat, and Hiram Smith in their own languages. This work appears in three volumes of essays (1981, 1996, 2003). "Verse analysis" restored the imagination and artistry of the originals "predicated explicitly on concerns of justice and equality" (Moore 2008:30). Revealing the original poetic structure of such narratives constituted for Hymes a new kind of repatriation; he took pride that his early work on Wasco sound and letters was still used at Warm Springs (1999:xxi). His dictionary of Wasco (Kiksht), however, remains unfinished, and only three speakers remain.

At a seminar honoring his retirement in 1998, Hymes came full circle, performing the Chinookan "Sun's Myth" both in its original language, out of respect for the traditional knowledge it encodes, and in his own ongoing retranslation, which reflected the meaning this allegory brought to his own life. What he envisioned as "the full universalization of anthropology proceeds slowly and not without significant resistance" (1999:xx). He deplored postmodernist claims that rejection of reality precluded serious work and was therefore "inimical to the interests of oppressed peoples and to the tradition to which I subscribe, namely that accurate knowledge of the world can be in the service of liberation" (xxv). Hymes predicted the survival of anthropology, through bringing its distinctive ethnographic and comparative imagination into collaboration with other disciplines. He left generations of students to carry forward the implications of his complex and humanitarian interdisciplinarity. He produced not disciples but an open-ended web of influence and connection among colleagues whom he invited to share his vision of anthropology, linguistics, folklore, education, politics, poetics, and the many other interests that came together in his oeuvre.

Dell Hymes's professional papers are housed at the American Philosophical Society. He is survived by his wife Virginia (deceased 2015), four children, five grandchildren, and two great-grandchildren.

Notes

1. Originally published as "Dell Hathaway Hymes," *American Anthropologist* 113 (2011): 192–95.

2. At the time of this writing, Hymes was facing serious charges of long-term sexual harassment that did not fit my experience. Many of his students were women. I acknowledge the pain revisiting this obituary may cause some colleagues but believe that the genre of flagship journal obituary has a stature beyond the momentary. I would write it differently today, if at all. See the acknowledgments for chapter 16 and the introduction for a more general discussion of this slippery slope.

3. The terms "American Indian," "Indians," and "Amerindian" are used appropriately for the time at which Hymes did his fieldwork.

References

Bauman, Richard, and Joel Sherzer, eds. 1974. *Explorations in the Ethnography of Speaking*. Cambridge: Cambridge University Press.

Cazden, Courtney, Vera John, and Dell Hymes, eds. 1972. *Functions of Language in the Classroom*. New York: Teachers College Press.

Gumperz, John, and Dell Hymes, eds. 1962. Special Issue, "The Ethnography of Communication." *American Anthropologist* 66 (6), Part 2.

———. 1972. *Directions in Sociolinguistics: The Ethnography of Communication.* New York: Holt, Rinehart and Winston.

Handler, Richard. 2002. "Dell Hymes." In *Celebrating a Century of the American Anthropological Association: Presidential Portraits,* edited by Regna Darnell and Frederic W. Gleach, 255–58. Lincoln: University of Nebraska Press.

Hymes, Dell. 1955a. "The Language of the Kathlamet Chinook." PhD diss., Indiana University.

———. 1955b. "Positional Analysis of Categories: A Frame for Reconstruction." *Word* 11:10–25.

———. 1956. "Na-Dene and the Positional Analysis of Categories." *American Anthropologist* 58:624–38.

———. 1957. "Some Penutian Elements and the Penutian Hypothesis." *Southwestern Journal of Anthropology* 13:69–87.

———. 1960. "Lexicostatistics So Far." *Current Anthropology* 1:3–44.

———. 1964a. "Two Types of Linguistic Relativity: Some Examples from American Indian Ethnography." In *Sociolinguistics,* edited by William Bright, 114–67. The Hague: Mouton.

———, ed. 1964b. *Language in Culture and Society.* New York: Harper and Row.

———. 1965a. "Some North Pacific Poems: A Problem in Anthropological Philology." *American Anthropologist* 67:316–41.

———, ed. 1965b. *The Use of Computers in Anthropology.* Mouton: The Hague.

———, ed. 1971. *Pidginization and Creolization of Languages.* Cambridge: Cambridge University Press.

———, ed. 1972. *Reinventing Anthropology.* New York: Pantheon.

———. 1974a. *Foundations in Sociolinguistics: An Ethnographic Approach.* Philadelphia: University of Pennsylvania Press.

———, ed. 1974b. *Studies in the History of Linguistics: Traditions and Paradigms.* Bloomington: University of Indiana Press.

———. 1980a. "In Five-Year Patterns." *In First Person Singular: Papers from the Conference on an Oral Archive for the History of American Linguistics (Charlotte, N.C., 9–10 March 1979),* edited by Boyd H. Davis and Raymond K. O'Cain, 203–13. Amsterdam: John Benjamins.

———. 1980b. *Language in Education: Ethnolinguistic Essays.* Washington DC: Center for Applied Linguistics.

———. 1981. *In Vain I Tried to Tell You: Essays in Native American Ethnopoetics.* Philadelphia: University of Pennsylvania Press.

———. 1983. *Essays in the History of Linguistic Anthropology.* Amsterdam: John Benjamins.

———. 1996. *Ethnography, Linguistics, Narrative Inequality: Toward an Understanding of Voice.* Critical Perspectives on Literacy and Education. London: Taylor and Francis.

————. 1999. Introduction to *Reinventing Anthropology*, edited by Dell Hymes, v–xlix. Ann Arbor: University of Michigan Press.

————. 2003. *Now I Know Only So Far: Essays in Ethnopoetics*. Lincoln: University of Nebraska Press.

Hymes, Dell, and John Fought. 1975. "American Structuralism." In *Current Trends in Linguistics*, vol. 13: *Historiography of Linguistics*, edited by Thomas A. Sebeok, 903–1176. The Hague: Mouton.

Moore, Robert E. 2008. "Listening to Indians—The Warm Springs Project: Reed Anthropology in the Postwar Moment." *Reed Magazine* (Winter): 12–17, 30. http://web.reed.edu/reed_magazine/winter2008/features/listening_to_indians/index.html. Accessed August 30, 2010.

Sherzer, Joel, and Regna Darnell. 1972. "An Outline Field Guide to the Ethnographic Study of Speech Use." In *Directions in Sociolinguistics: The Ethnography of Communication*, edited by John Gumperz and Dell Hymes, 548–54. New York: Holt, Rinehart and Winston.

University of Virginia. n.d. *Dell H. Hymes*. http://www.virginia.edu/anthropology/dhymes.html (no longer functional). Accessed August 30, 2010.

17

....

Obituary for George W. Stocking Jr. (1928–2013)

George W. Stocking Jr., who presided over the professionalization of the history of anthropology as a subfield within the discipline and dominated its reception for five decades, died on July
13, 2013, in Chicago, Illinois.[1] He called for the "refamiliarization"
of anthropologists with their own past, insisting that such critical
self-reflexivity must be grounded in the rigorous methods of historicism. Stocking spoke from the standpoint of a historian. The
history of anthropology always remained for him a historical rather
than primarily an anthropological problem, although his openness
to anthropology students responsive to his position mellowed this
stance considerably. From his first pronouncements on, his relativist stance to the changing meanings of events and the actions
of their primary actors challenged anthropologists to respond to
the history of anthropology as an anthropological problem.

Stocking was born in Berlin on December 8, 1928, where his
father, George Ward Stocking Sr., a distinguished economist, was
on sabbatical from the University of Texas. His father's English
Puritan roots warred with his socialist leanings and government
service under Franklin Roosevelt's New Deal. His mother, née Dor-
othea Amelia Reichart, reflected the more emotive and humanistic idealism of the failed German revolution of 1848. George Jr.
struggled to find a balance between these parts of his heritage.
His younger brother, Myron, who later became a psychoanalyst,
and two adopted younger sisters, Sybil and Ashley, completed the
family. Austin, Texas, was their home base through George's childhood, but because the family traveled extensively to accommodate

Fig. 3. George W. Stocking Jr. (1928–2013). Courtesy of Carol Stocking.

George Sr.'s research, he attended several high schools, graduating from Horace Mann-Lincoln School in New York in 1945.

Stocking described himself as a haphazard and uninspired undergraduate at Harvard, where his creative energies were channeled into politics. Nonetheless, he graduated cum laude in English in 1948. He married Wilhemina (Mina) Davis the following year, and they had five children together. Stocking was a member of the Communist Party from 1949 to 1956. The couple undertook factory work, and George dabbled in union organization. Throughout his life, he framed this early political activism as fundamental to his personal and professional identity. In his autobiography he took great pride in reconstructing his FBI file from the McCarthy era (Stocking 2010:29)

Stocking considered his return to graduate school at the University of Pennsylvania as a move from Oedipal rebellion back to his "liberal academic patrimony" (2010:68). Entering an interdisciplinary program in American civilization that reflected the postwar optimism of America as the pinnacle of history and positivism as the method of science, Stocking combined the quantitative methodology of social historian Murray Murphey with anthropological subject matter mediated through cultural anthropologist

A. Irving Hallowell. His 1960 dissertation, "American Social Scientists and Race Theory, 1890–1915," was a content analysis not of race itself but of social scientists studying race. Stocking was already turning to a more interpretive and relativistic approach, with Franz Boas emerging as the "permanent reference point," a fulcrum for the development of modern race thought (2010:93). Though he never again employed this quantitative methodology, the work provided an empirical database for the problematic of race that would never cease to preoccupy him on moral as well as intellectual grounds.

Despite the increasingly qualitative bent of his work and his radical political background, Stocking managed to skirt the loyalty oath in place at the time and was hired at the University of California, Berkeley as a social historian. Considerable debate ensued over his failure to meet departmental expectations of a unified book, but he received tenure at Berkeley in 1966. In retrospect, he identified his then anthropology colleague Dell Hymes as his primary mentor and advocate. Stocking found himself increasingly torn between his disciplinary training in history and the primarily anthropological audience for his scholarship. His self-proclaimed stature as the exemplary historian of anthropology dates to a 1962 Social Science Research Council conference on the topic.

Stocking's first book, *Race, Culture, and Evolution: Essays in the History of Anthropology* (1968), brought together seminal essays of the previous decade. His reading of Boas's move from physics to ethnology by way of geography, his attribution of the methodologies of historicism to historians and presentism (or Whig history) to anthropologists, and the pluralization of the term "culture" in the work of Edward B. Tylor remain particularly salient. Although his research focus up to this point had been primarily on Boas and the concept of race, Stocking simultaneously laid the groundwork for a move across the Atlantic to the roots of British social anthropology and the professionalization and diversification of the social sciences in Europe and North America.

Race, Culture, and Evolution established Stocking as the master of the vignette, despite its failure to meet persistent calls of some critics for a "unified book." He referred to his chosen genre as the "narrowly focused miniature," the "revelatory microcosm," or the "juicy bits" from which he could tease out the influence of "major canonical figures" and the context of events (2010:125, 147, 73). Historicism and presentism represented methodological antitheses that Stocking believed were necessary to critique nonrigorous and ideologically motivated readings of the history of anthropology that were widely accepted at face value by anthropologists in the 1960s. Once that battle was won, Stocking's views became more nuanced, acknowledging that anthropologists could learn the methods of historicism and that assessment of "influence" necessarily involved presentism of a sort. Increasingly, his students and major intellectual interlocutors were anthropologists whose engagement with their own past rested on contemporary relevance.

Stocking's restlessness, accentuated by the breakup of his marriage, culminated in a research Wanderjahr in 1967–68, supported by the National Science Foundation, to enhance his professional engagement with anthropology. He spent the first semester at the University of Pennsylvania harboring aspirations to write a biography of Boas, but the magnitude of the task quickly confounded him. Rather, he chose to edit *The Shaping of American Anthropology, 1883–1911: A Franz Boas Reader* (Stocking 1974); its introduction explored the anthropology of the interwar years (reprinted in Stocking 1992). Like other ambitious synthetic projects envisioned over his career, the Boas biography was never completed.

The die was cast the following semester at the University of Chicago when in Stocking accepted a joint appointment in the Departments of Anthropology and History in 1968, with the major impetus coming from the anthropologists. His new colleagues emphasized culture as a system of symbols, introduced him to British social anthropology, and drew him into a department he considered to be the center of the discipline. The same year he married Carol Bowman.

When the Chicago history department balked at the absence of a unified book to justify promotion to professor, he moved to the Department of Anthropology full-time in 1974. Stocking held a unique niche in the department. He never came to think of himself as fully an anthropologist, noting that his "fieldwork" was archival and his methodology resolutely historical. He was more comfortable with texts than oral sources, especially as his topics neared the present and potentially compromised his objectivity. At Chicago he trained several generations of social and cultural anthropology students to think historically about their profession. Those who have contributed actively to the history of anthropology include Ira Bashkow, Matti Bunzl, Frederic W. Gleach, Richard Handler, Michael Harkin, and Sergei Kan, and he was an active mentor to many more. Student parties at the Stockings' cottage in Beverly Shore, Indiana, were legendary.

Although Stocking initially envisioned producing a history of the social sciences at Chicago, what seemed a straightforward, manageable project quickly overflowed its bounds. His only published work on this topic was an exhibition catalogue tied to the fiftieth anniversary of the anthropology department (Stocking 1979). His subsequent shift of focus to the British national tradition encouraged Stocking to return to the vignette form he had already mastered. *Victorian Anthropology* (Stocking 1987) brought together essays on British precursors of professional anthropology, with that on James Cowles Pritchard being particularly notable. The essays in *After Tylor: British Social Anthropology, 1888–1951* (Stocking 1995) traced the story through to the professionalization of a separate discipline of anthropology. Taken together, these essays constitute a systematic reading of the emergence of British social anthropology as a national tradition.

Stocking's editorial work further developed the analytic method of the interpretive essay as the core genre of his history of anthropology. He was the principal founder of the *History of Anthropology Newsletter* (HAN) in 1973. HAN sustained a network of scholars interested in disciplinary history without identifying as specialists. Stocking chose to establish a monograph series titled simply History of Anthropology (HOA) rather than a journal under his editorship, initially intending it to appear annually. He edited eight thematic volumes on issues he considered essential to creating contemporary anthropology: fieldwork, functionalism, museums and material culture, culture and personality, biological anthropology, anthropology's romantic sensibility, colonial contexts, and the German roots of Boasian anthropology. Stocking personally contributed chapters structuring the central problematic of six of these. Several were among the essays collected and reprinted in Stocking 1992 and 2001. He was an activist editor, carefully tailoring the mostly invited papers to his vision of each volume as a whole. The same contributors tended to appear in multiple volumes and to have ties to Chicago anthropology, although Stocking nominally recognized the dangers of a closed community of anthropological historians. He worried about criticisms that he was a harsh gatekeeper for the history of anthropology but was in his own eyes open to divergent methods and topics. At the same time, he weighed this intention against a perceived responsibility to enforce historicist standards as he understood them.

Four additional volumes of HOA, including Stocking's autobiography (Stocking 2010), were edited by his former student, Richard Handler. Stocking's final effort at synthesizing his view of anthropology's past examined the postwar anthropology of the 1950s, the decade in which he had come to know the discipline and to mature as a scholar. Though his later years were plagued by declining health, each of his biographical essays, appearing in HOA 9–11 (Stocking 2000, 2004, 2006), provided a distinctive lens on the political engagement of key anthropologists and the personal cost of their activism: the engaged government service of his Chicago colleague Sol Tax contrasted with the "liberal" engagement of Robert Redfield; the "disengaged" internally contained anthropology of his teacher A. I. Hallowell; and the McCarthy-era exclusion from the disciplinary fold of Chicago-trained anthropologist and political activist George Gelston Armstrong. Stocking considered Dell Hymes part of this cohort but excluded him from the project because he was then still living. At the time of his death, Stocking was working on an essay about Clyde Kluckhohn and how government collaboration damaged his anthropological reputation (2010:139).

Stocking's own career, both political and academic, seemed to him part of the story of what he glossed as "anthropology yesterday." In this sense the "self-deconstruction" of his autobiography in HOA 12 (Stocking 2010) brings the series full circle and situates him within the history he recounted. It was the closest he came to writing about contemporary anthropology and opened him up to sharp criticism from others who had known his biographical subjects and read their lives and careers differently. In characteristic Stocking style, however, the context of individual careers was framed in terms of its larger social and political context, the social networks of the scholar in question, and the institutional infrastructure within which these seminal anthropologists pursued their work. His interpretations of both himself and others tend to the psychological if not quite the psychoanalytic.

Stocking was recognized by numerous awards. He was a Guggenheim fellow in 1984–85, a Getty Scholar in 1988–89, and a fellow at the Princeton Institute of Advanced Studies in 1992–93. In 1990 he was elected to the American Academy of Arts and Sciences and appointed a Distinguished Service Professor at Chicago. He received the Huxley Medal of the Royal Anthropological Institute in 1993 and the Franz Boas Exemplary Service Award of the American Anthropological Association in 1998, the highest honors given by the paramount national professional associations of British and U.S. anthropology, respectively.

George Stocking's legacy in anthropology as the discipline's quintessential historian forms an ongoing baseline for the history of anthropology into the future. His professional papers are held at the Special Collections Center, University of Chicago.

Notes

1. Originally published as "George Ward Stocking, Jr.," *American Anthropologist* 116 (2014): 712–14.

References

Stocking, George W., Jr. 1960. "American Social Scientists and Race Theory, 1890–1915." PhD diss., University of Pennsylvania.

———. 1968. *Race, Culture, and Evolution: Essays in the History of Anthropology*. New York: Free Press.

———, ed. 1974. *The Shaping of American Anthropology, 1883–1911: A Franz Boas Reader*. Chicago: University of Chicago Press.

———. 1979. *Anthropology at Chicago: Tradition, Discipline, Department*. Chicago: Regenstein Library.

———. 1987. *Victorian Anthropology*. New York: Free Press.

———. 1992. *The Ethnographer's Magic and Other Essays in the History of Anthropology*. Madison: University of Wisconsin Press.

———. 1995. *After Tylor: British Social Anthropology, 1888–1951*. Madison: University of Wisconsin Press.

———. 2000. "'Do Good Young Man': Sol Tax and the World Mission of Liberal Democratic Anthropology." In *Excluded Ancestors: Essays toward a*

More Inclusive History of Anthropology, edited by Richard Handler, 171–264. History of Anthropology 9. Madison: University of Wisconsin Press.

———. 2001. *Delimiting Anthropology: Occasional Inquiries and Reflections.* Madison: University of Wisconsin Press.

———. 2004. "A. I. Hallowell's Boasian Evolutionism: Human Irrationality in Cross-Cultural Evolutionary, and Personal Context." In *Significant Others: Interpersonal and Professional Commitments in Anthropology*, edited by Richard Handler, 196–260. History of Anthropology 10. Madison: University of Wisconsin Press.

———. 2006. "Unfinished Business: Robert Gelston Armstrong, the Federal Bureau of Investigation, and the History of Anthropology at Chicago and in Nigeria." In *Central Sites, Peripheral Visions: Cultural and Institutional Crossings in the History of Anthropology*, edited by Richard Handler, 99–247. History of Anthropology 11. Madison: University of Wisconsin Press.

———. 2010. *Glimpses into My Own Black Box: An Exercise in Self-Deconstruction.* History of Anthropology 12. Madison: University of Wisconsin Press.

18

Review of *Glimpses into My Own Black Box:*
An Exercise in Self-Deconstruction,
by George W. Stocking Jr.

It is fitting that the twelfth and final volume of the University of
Wisconsin's thematic series History of Anthropology (HOA), should
record the autobiographical musings of its distinguished founder
George W. Stocking Jr. (1928–2013).[1] The narrative is not systematic and poses an awkward contrast to the avowed methodology in
the body of his work. Stream of consciousness, vagaries of memory, and retrospective readings of his past or present self-image
thus fulfill the title's promised mere "glimpses" of the "black box"
of influences and opportunities. It is an ambivalent swan song for
both the series and Stocking's distinguished career.

A prologue, including reproduced Freedom of Information Act
documents, traces Stocking's Communist Party and trade union
activism from 1949 to 1956 after a desultory career at Harvard. The
first and longest section is devoted to personal biography; space
precludes summarizing details. Stocking's engagement with anthropology emerged during his graduate program in American civilization at the University of Pennsylvania where he absorbed Murray
Murphy's historical method and learned anthropological content
from anthropologist A. Irving "Pete" Hallowell. His unpublished
dissertation, a quantitative analysis of race relations in America,
was his sole foray into counting things. Stocking obtained employment at Berkeley despite his McCarthy-era political record and
stayed long enough to get tenure before moving to Chicago (via
a semester interlude back at Penn in the anthropology department, glossed over in his memory but seminal for this reviewer's
training in history of anthropology). At Chicago he reoriented
his focus from Franz Boas to British social anthropology, deploy-

ing the reputation of the Chicago department to assure his entrée among his new colleagues.

Section II, "Historiographic Reflections," documents how Stocking's career reflects changes in the discipline and hence in how disciplinary history was both written and read thereafter. *Race, Culture, and Evolution* (Stocking 1968) collected his essays written over the previous decade in a self-conscious effort to set a standard for the emerging subdiscipline and grounded its audience, although not its methodology, within anthropology. He distinguished "historicism" as a method belonging to historians from the self-serving "presentism" of what he called Whig history. Over the four ensuing decades, Stocking's views mellowed considerably as he acknowledged that some anthropologists could master the historian's hermeneutic capacity to frame things initially in their own terms and only afterward to consider them in relation to potentially useful continuities for contemporary work. This moderated presentism served to attract an audience in the discipline of his readership.

Stocking (2010) approaches HOA from what he considers to be its unequivocal institutional center at the University of Chicago and implicitly presents himself as its gatekeeper. He focuses on "canonical figures," viewed from "a privileged institutional position," while characterizing himself as an "interpretive bricoleur" who leaves much of the work of interpretation to readers (154). Chicago's postmodernist turn in the 1990s encouraged Stocking to experiment with the "relativist ambivalence" (148) that underwrote an increasingly personal and presentist focus on the 1950s anthropology with which he remained most comfortable. His "Anthropology Yesterday" project had produced, as of 2010, essays on Sol Tax, Hallowell, Robert Gelston Armstrong, and Clyde Kluckhohn (under construction at the time of his death). Paradoxically, Stocking professed himself unable to write about near contemporary questions by virtue of his closeness to them while simultaneously choosing to focus on the intimacy of his own anthropological encounter.

This professional autobiography is heavy on contextualizing research projects and scholarly output. Stocking obsesses about his career-long pattern of uncompleted works and unpacks their underlying impasses. He embraces his personal alternative to the historian's usual monographic oeuvre, the "revelatory microcosm" (74) as a turning point in HOA. He declares himself puritanical, anxious, and self-critical, with a lingering "neo-evolutionary positivism" (176) tempered by liberal conscience. He admits to considerable "anxiety of influence" (111) about his legacy and rues the changing face of the discipline that leaves him feeling isolated and unable to communicate effectively with a new generation of anthropology graduate students. Hence, perhaps, this excruciatingly honest testimonial to explain himself in his own terms.

Section III, "Octogenarian Afterthoughts," and an epilogue on deteriorating health and increasing pessimism about anthropology and the world add little new but consolidate the continuity of a major scholar's reflection on his life in relation to his work. Stocking rejects charges that his editorial role as HOA's gatekeeper opposed political relevance and reiterates as evidence his undeniable activist credentials in the 1950s. Nonetheless, he exhibits no false modesty about exercising his self-assigned role as doyen of HOA. On a rare diversion from the Chicago narrative, Stocking relegates to a footnote (173–74n30) the "implicit adjectival dig" at his series in Nebraska's *Histories of Anthropology Annual* and Critical Studies in HOA series. As founding editor of both series, I emphasize the deliberate intention to serve as foil and supplement to Stocking's Wisconsin series, thereby filling a gap in the literature by loosening the editorial control and broadening the range of contributors. During the years of their coexistence, these publications functioned as complementary enterprises and, as Stocking goes on to acknowledge, built on his own methods and exemplars bridging the disciplines of history and anthropology.

HOA will continue to evolve, as scientific paradigms inevitably do. Stocking's autobiography challenges his successors and protégés to articulate his legacy in relation to the methodological terms he pioneered. This will remain a crucial document in the historiography of HOA.

Notes

1. Originally published as "Review of Stocking 2010, *Glimpses into My Own Black Box: An Exercise in Self-Destruction," Journal of Anthropological Research* 67, no. 3 (2011): 450–51.

References

Stocking, George W., Jr. 1968. *Race, Culture, and Evolution: Essays in the History of Anthropology.* New York: Free Press.

———. 2010. *Glimpses into My Own Black Box: An Exercise in Deconstruction.* History of Anthropology, vol. 12. Madison: University of Wisconsin Press.

19
....

Obituary for Anthony F. C. Wallace (1923–2015)

Anthony ("Tony") Francis Clarke Wallace died on October 5, 2015, in Ridley Park, Pennsylvania.[1] Tony Wallace obtained all of his professional degrees from the University of Pennsylvania, receiving the doctorate in anthropology in 1950. He remained in Philadelphia throughout his career, at the University of Pennsylvania and at the Eastern Pennsylvania Psychiatric Institute. His work bridged the overlapping fields of psychology and history (including both ethnohistory and historical anthropology). He was a perceptive ethnographer and archivist of contemporary and historic Indigenous populations and a theorist of note in testing the relationship between individual and culture, devising empirical methods for the study of memory and cognition, and searching for universal principles of value and meaning. An able administrator, he served as president of the American Anthropological Association (AAA) in 1971–72.

Wallace explored anthropological and public discourses as superficially diverse as Native American[2] ethnohistory, historical anthropology, culture change and technology, biocultural evolution, psychological anthropology, warfare, religion, and kinship. These varied perspectives coalesced in a single lifelong ethical preoccupation with creating a better world through rigorous investigation and reflection on the ongoing implications of past and contemporary events and the personalities that created them. Science and humanism, ethnography and archive, application and theory marched apace in his lucid, thoughtful prose. Although colleagues tend to know only the parts of his work that correspond to their own interests, in Wallace's own eyes these diverse topics

Fig. 4. Anthony F. C. Wallace (1923–2015). Courtesy of the American Anthropological Association.

followed a trajectory without perceived contradiction of emergent and overlapping questions and contingent answers (Wallace, personal communication with author, November 2014).

Tony Wallace was born on April 15, 1923, in Toronto, Canada, and retained a lifelong temperamental affinity to the country of his birth. He grew up in Annville, Pennsylvania, near Lebanon Valley College, where his father, Paul A. W. Wallace, taught history and literature with forays into Native American traditions and histories, especially Delaware and Iroquois. Young Tony was his father's assistant and eventual colleague in these ventures and later acknowledged this family legacy as his lodestone and single most important career influence. His mother, Dorothy Eleanor Clarke, was British. He had one brother, David. Tony entered Lebanon Valley College in 1941 to study history and physics but soon enlisted. After a year's Army Specialized Training in electrical engineering, he served with the Fourteenth Army Division in Germany and participated in the liberation of Dachau, an experience that indelibly impressed him with the horrors of war.

After the war he returned to the University of Pennsylvania, where he completed his BA in history in 1948, switching to anthropology for his MA in 1949 and PhD in 1950. He had married Elizabeth Shillot, and the couple had two sons, Daniel and Anthony Jr., by the time he completed the doctorate. His mentors, Frank Speck and Speck's former student, A. Irving Hallowell, were building a Boasian four-field department emphasizing the ethnographic study of Native Americans, especially in New England and southern Canada. Wallace's MA research produced his first published book, a psychobiography of eighteenth-century Delaware chief Teedyuskung (1949). His dissertation research, based on two summers among the Tuscarora, sought a rigorous scientific method to measure degree of "acculturation" based on Rorschach profiles then considered a culture-free research tool (Wallace 1952). Following the lead of Cora DuBois, Wallace moved from a monolithic view of the relation between culture and personality and a more empirical "modal personality type" that located intracultural variability at a given time and place as a cultural norm with standard deviations. Although Tuscarora profiles varied in the intensity of the patterns found in the most conservative and isolated communities, the continuity of traditional patterns was remarkably consistent and thus demonstrated the inadequacy of the binary acculturation model.

Wallace would develop these ideas more fully in *Culture and Personality* (1961), distinguishing an essentialist "replication of uniformity" or basic personality type shared by all culture members and transmitted as a whole, from the more precise and dynamic "organization of difference." He developed the concept of "mazeway," each individual's personal amalgam of experience and temperament forming a unique integration of potentials drawn from the cultural environment. Individuals varied in degree of consciousness of their own behavioral patterns. Consequences for the culture as a whole also varied considerably. In a festschrift for Hallowell, for example, Wallace described the complexity of what he had to know to drive to work (Wallace 1965). Cognitive "nonsharing" was critical at both individual and cultural levels.

Seminal papers on mazeway resynthesis (1956a) and disintegration (1957) characteristically combined Native American and mainstream North American exemplars of resynthesis after cultural trauma. Wallace identified the "revitalization movement" (1956b) led by Seneca prophet Handsome Lake in an ethnohistoric foray into the potential of religion for cognitive transformation later elaborated in *The Death and Rebirth of the Seneca* (1970). Two North American community studies contrasted the successful integration of a Pennsylvania mill town in *Rockdale: The Growth of an American Village in the Early Industrial Revolution* (1978) with a failed industrial experiment in *St. Clair: A Nineteenth-Century Coal Town's Experience with a Disaster-Prone Industry* (1987). When *Rockdale* won the Bancroft Prize for American History, Tony, with characteristic modesty, wryly admitted he had never heard of the prize until he won it (Wallace, personal communication with author, November 2014); *St. Clair* won the Dexter Prize from the Society for the History of Technology. Several significant essays generalizing the "social context of innovation" appeared separately (Wallace 1982).

Despite other opportunities, Wallace chose to spend his entire career in or around Philadelphia. He lectured in sociology at Penn from 1948 to 1955. After completing his doctorate, he worked at various projects in applied anthropology. As a researcher for the Indian Claims Commission, his analysis for the Fox-Sauk explored the traumatic legacy of the Black Hawk War and dovetailed with his disaster preparedness study of a recent tornado in Worcester, Massachusetts, to reveal general conditions of community and individual responses to disaster. From 1955 to 1980, Wallace served as senior research associate at the Eastern Pennsylvania Psychiatric Institute (EPPI). He underwent training analysis at the Philadelphia Psychoanalytic Institute. From 1955 to 1960, he also served as visiting associate professor of anthropology at the University of Pennsylvania. He became director of clinical research at EPPI in 1960–61 but resigned to become professor and chair of anthropology at the University of Pennsylvania, a position he held for the next decade. There, he proved himself a gifted administrator and spearheaded the construction of an academic wing for the Penn Museum.

Wallace's search for an empirical method that could capture what Franz Boas called "the native point of view" led him to distinguish the "structural" and "psychological" adequacy of alternative analyses of kinship terms. He emphasized the cognitive nature of semantic systems and their psychological reality for individuals. Religion shared with such formal systems what he understood to be a universal tendency toward cognitive integration (Urban 2016:11). *Religion: An Anthropological View* (1966), a creative and underappreciated reflection, developed this position in comparative terms (Darnell 2002). Cognition, for Wallace, was a biocultural phenomenon. His work at EPPI facilitated studies of Arctic hysteria, schizophrenia, prophetic experience, and nutritional deficiency, demonstrating how factors of history, environment, and cultural values mediate the expression of biological inheritance. During my own graduate years at Penn (1965–69), he was the only cultural anthropologist who raised questions about the integration of culture and biology.

Amid the turmoil of the 1960s, Tony and Betty adopted four more children, two Vietnamese-born (Samuel and Sun-Ai) and two Native American (Cheryl and Joseph). Honors began to accumulate. He was elected to the American Philosophical Society in 1969 and to the American Academy of Sciences in 1973. In 1971–72 he served as president of the American Anthropological Association, a compromise candidate who attempted to mediate the polarization of traditional scholarship versus activism (epitomized by American engagement with counterinsurgency movements in Latin America and Southeast Asia) and to preserve a space within the AAA for rational debate across these divides. His presidency also acknowledged the increasing specialization of the discipline by overseeing reorganization into the interest groups that later became "sections."

After his retirement as university professor emeritus in 1988, Wallace's work reflected on the meaning of his six-decade career and returned to Native American exemplars, this time emphasizing the unequal power relations that had devastated tribal communities. *The Long, Bitter Trail* (1993) traced the ignoble legacy of Cherokee removal under Andrew Jackson. *Jefferson and the Indians* (1999) presented a poignant portrait of the idealistic spokesman for the new American republic whose ambivalent vision left no room for the First Peoples. That such an alternative vision was possible emerged in Wallace's final book, *Tuscarora: A History* (2012). After Betty's death in 2003, Tony returned to Tuscarora Nation, Lewistown, New York, the site of his first fieldwork, and lived there for the next decade, participating in a local history group, portraying the community as contemporary Tuscarora members saw their own emerging future within (post)modernity, and apologizing for the patronizing objectification implicit in his early work. By implication, his personal position indicted the systemic consequences of the discipline's methodologies, however well intentioned. His Tuscarora colleagues Wendy and Jim Bissell and Deborah Holler are part of the family he leaves behind. Among his academic progeny, Raymond Fogelson, Robert S. Grumet, Sol Katz, and Regna Darnell are particularly salient.

A final reflexive tendril returned to the troubled topic of war, a longtime preoccupation now writ large. The full manuscript remains unpublished, but part of the introduction appeared in the University of Nebraska's Histories of Anthropology Annual series edited by Darnell and Gleach (Wallace 2018). Wallace weaves together the strands of his own World War II experience with his reflections on Iroquois warfare, characteristically seeking a universal cognitive model of human sociality. Wallace was a hedgehog, returning to and deepening his analyses of a few recurrent themes, a self-contained scholar who did not follow academic fads. Robert S. Grumet suggests that he was most comfortable with the supra-personal perspective of archival documents that also simplified ethical issues around invasion of privacy (Grumet 1998, 109). His seminal theoretical papers eventually produced books giving fuller evidence and comparative reflection. Grumet has edited a selection of these papers (Wallace 2003, 2004) that conveys the broad range of the subjects that engaged his curiosity. His work instantiated the "useful knowledge" envisioned by Benjamin Franklin when founding the American Philosophical Society in 1743 and enshrined in the society's motto. This oeuvre stands as a monumental achievement of Wallace's generation and anthropology's legacy.

Wallace donated his personal papers to the American Philosophical Society and organized the Wallace Family Papers there, incorporating with his own papers those of his father, Paul A. Wallace, and grandfather, Francis Hurston Wallace.

Notes

1. Originally published as "Anthony F. C. Wallace," *American Anthropologist* 119 (2017): 785–87.

2. The terms "Native" and "Native American" are problematic in some contexts, although they are conventional usage in the United States.

References

Darnell, Regna. 2002. "Anthony F. C. Wallace." In *Celebrating a Century of the American Anthropological Association: Presidential Portraits,* edited by Regna Darnell and Frederic W. Gleach, 221–24. Lincoln: University of Nebraska Press.

Grumet, Robert S. 1998. "An Interview of Anthony F. C. Wallace." *Ethnohistory* 45:103–7.

Urban, Greg. 2016. "Anthony F. C. Wallace, 1923–2015: A Biographical Memoir." *Biographical Memoirs: National Academy of Sciences:* 1–17.

Wallace, Anthony F. C. 1949. *King of the Delawares: Teedyuscung, 1700–1763.* Philadelphia: University of Pennsylvania Press.

———. 1952. *The Modal Personality Structure of the Tuscarora Indians as Revealed by the Rorschach Test.* Smithsonian Institution, Bureau of American Ethnology Bulletin 150. Washington DC: U.S. Government Printing Office.

———. 1956a. "Mazeway Resynthesis: A Biocultural Theory of Religious Inspiration." *Transactions of the New York Academy of Sciences* 18:626–38.

———. 1956b. "Revitalization Movements." *American Anthropologist* 58:264–81.

———. 1957. "Mazeway Disintegration: The Individual's Perception of Socio-cultural Disorganization." *Human Organization* 16:23–27.

———. 1961. *Culture and Personality.* New York: Random House.

———. 1965. "Driving to Work." In *Context and Meaning in Cultural Anthropology,* edited by Melford Spiro, 277–92. New York: Free Press.

———. 1966. *Religion: An Anthropological View.* New York: Random House.

———. 1970. *The Death and Rebirth of the Seneca.* New York: Alfred A. Knopf.

———. 1978. *Rockdale: The Growth of an American Village in the Early Industrial Revolution.* New York: Alfred A. Knopf.

———. 1982. *The Social Context of Innovation: Bureaucrats, Families and Heroes in the Early Industrial Revolution as Foreseen in Bacon's New Atlantis.* Princeton NJ: Princeton University Press.

———. 1987. *St. Clair: A Nineteenth-Century Coal Town's Experience with a Disaster-Prone Industry.* New York: Alfred A. Knopf.

———. 1993. *The Long, Bitter Trail: Andrew Jackson and the Indians.* New York: Hill and Wang.

———. 1999. *Jefferson and the Indians: The Tragic Fate of the First Americans.* Cambridge MA: Harvard University Press.

———. 2003. *Revitalization and Mazeways.* Edited by Robert S. Grumet. Lincoln: University of Nebraska Press.

———. 2004. *Modernity and Mind.* Edited by Robert S. Grumet. Lincoln: University of Nebraska Press.

———. 2012. *Tuscarora: A History.* Albany: State University of New York Press.

———. 2018. "Guns and Ivy: An Anthropologist's Memoir." In *Tracking Anthropological Engagements,* edited by Regna Darnell and Frederic W. Gleach, 249–66. Vol. 12 of Histories of Anthropology Annual. Lincoln: University of Nebraska Press.

INDEX

Berman, Judith: "the culture as it appeared to the Indian himself," 118–19

Bildung or individual creativity, 120

biography, definition of, 49

biomedicine, 35, 36–37

biomonitoring, 36

Birket-Smith, Kai: as European cohort of Frederica de Laguna, 264–65

Blackhawk War, 297

Bliss, Laura: as recorder of Frederica de Laguna, 267

blueberry recipes (Kwakwaka'wakw/ Kwakiutl), theoretical value of, 152

Boas, Franz: "alternating sounds," 145; "anthropogeography," 162; "the Aryan Problem," 163; "civilized philosopher in primitive cultures," 144; cohort of "civilizations other than our own," 156–57, 170–71; cohort of core Boasians, 228; cohort of first-generation students, 48, 157; cohort of former students, 162; cohort of racist critics, 154–60; "cultural relativism," 48, 51, 137–38, 147; "forms of life," 153–54; "genius," 166; "genius of a people with reference to its language," 145; "germ of the civilization of the white race," 167; "heredity," 160; "history," 123; "human types," 140–41; "idea" as racial prejudice, 167; "language," 147; "laws," 172; "linguistic classification," 198–202, 206–7; "man," 136; "the mind of primitive man," 122; "the native point of view," 6–7, 43, 48, 78, 92, 94, 95–96, 108–9, 118–19, 127, 135–36, 228, 297; "the negro race in America," 166; "organize anthropological research in America," 138–39; paradigm statements of, 136; "plasticity," 136, 160, 167; "primitive," 135–36, 139, 159; "primitive man," 124; "psychic unity of mankind," 48, 132, 137; as public intellectual, 138–39, 151; "race," 169; "racial prejudices" 165–66; reaction to Sapir six-unit classification, 220; "secondary rationalization," 253; "speculation," 169–70; "tolerance for forms of civi-

lization other than our own," 170–71; on universal products of human mind, 143; "value to civilizations other than our own," 15–17. *See also* Chomsky, Noam; Lévi-Strauss, Claude

—Works: *Anthropology and Modern Life*, 158; "The Decorative Art of the North American Indians," 128; "Decorative Designs of Alaskan Needle Cases," 128; Introduction to the *Handbook of American Indian Languages*, 79, 124, 136, 145, 153, 156, 205, 208, 209, 216; "The Limitations of the Comparative Method of Anthropology," 124, 135, 139, 148, 155; *The Mind of Primitive Man*, 124, 135–49, 151, 153, 155–58, 171, 173, 239; "On Alternating Sounds," 145; *Primitive Art*, 125–26; *Race, Language and Culture*, 139, 148, 158; "Representative Art of Primitive People," 130; "The Study of Geography," 110, 142

Borofsky, Robert: collaboration, high standard of evidence for, 103

Boule, Marcellin: as European cohort of Frederica de Laguna, 264

Bourdieu, Pierre: in contrast to Claude Lévi-Strauss, 169–70

Breton, André: as cohort of Claude Lévi-Strauss, 254

Bréuil, Abbe: as European cohort of Frederica de Laguna, 264

bridging: history of anthropology, disciplines of, 291

Brinton, Daniel Garrison, 198–203; *The American Race*, 198; as discontinuous link to Frank Speck at University of Pennsylvania, 90; as incipient structuralist, 227; influence of German scholarship on, 227. *See also* learned societies

British social anthropology, 25; influence of, on Marcel Mauss, 228; influence of Durkheimians on, 228; law as core of (Désveaux), 229; on our science as universal, 11

Broca, Paul: in French national tradition, 226

Bureau of American Ethnology (BAE),

79, 120, 177, 180, 205, 214–15, 227, 246,
281–82
"the bureau" [of American Ethnology], 192
Burke, Kenneth: as cohort of Dell H.
Hymes, 273; "representative anecdote," 40
Burnaby, Barbara: as cohort of Regna
Darnell, 31
Buschman, Johann Carl Eduard, 199;
and northern origin of Aztecs, 201

calibration of knowledge traditions, 66
Canadian Anthropology: distinction
between Native American and First
Nations, l; relative to three founding
nations, 225–26
Canadian organizations and institutions: Aboriginal Healing Foundation,
73; Canadian Anthropology Society
(CASCA), 21, 22–23, 23–24, 39; Canadian Ethnology Society (CES), 22;
Canadian Sociology and Anthropology
Association (CSAA), 23; CIHR (Canadian Institutes of Health Research),
24–25; Indian Association of Alberta,
30–31; Musgamakw Dzawada'eneux
Tribal Council, 40–41; National Film
Board of Canada, 109; National
Museum of Canada (now Canadian
Museum of History), 23; Social Sciences and Humanities Research Council of Canada (SSHRC), 24–25, 283;
University of Alberta, 31; University
of British Columbia, 31; University of
British Columbia Museum of Anthropology, 22; University of Victoria, 40–
41; Walpole Island First Nation, 34;
Western's Interfaculty Program in Public Health (MPH), 37; Western University's Schulich School of Medicine
and Dentistry, 37; York University
(Toronto), 21
capacity building, 31, 34, 41–42
Cardinal, Harold: at Indian Association
of Alberta, 30–31
Carpenter, Brian: at Center for Native

American and Indigenous Research,
42
Carroll, John B.: critique of Sapir-Whorf
hypothesis, 236–37; "Introduction to
Whorf," 236–37
Carus, Carl Gustav: and Franz Boas
cohort of racist critics, 164–65
Chamberlain, Houston Stewart: and
Franz Boas cohort of racist critics,
164–65
Chamberlain, Ted: "ceremonies of
belief," 65
Chomsky, Noam: "butterfly collecting," 104; as cohort of Claude Lévi-
Strauss in structuralism, 244–45;
"competence," 104; "description" and
"explanatory adequacy," 107; as foil
for Dell H. Hymes, 274; "mere performance," 104; on universal products of
human mind, 143
—Works: *Cartesian Linguistics*, 233
civilization, definition of, 75
civilizations (Boas) of Mohammedans,
Chinese, and Arabs, 166
Codere, Helen: "five-foot shelf of Kwakiutl ethnography," 119. *See also* blueberry recipes (Kwakwaka'wakw/
Kwakiutl), 152
"cognition and culture" (Wallace), 297
cognitive science, 104
Cole, Douglas: as biographer of Franz
Boas, 153; critique of Franz Boas as
theorist, 136–37
collective sovereignty, 75
Colwell-Chanthaphonh, Chip (and T. J.
Ferguson): *History Is in the Land*, 9–10
community-based research, xxi
comparative method of classical evolutionism, 47–48
Comte, Auguste: as foil for Claude Lévi-
Strauss, 248
convergent evidence on modes of history making, 9
Coon, Carleton: as cohort of Anthony
F. C. Wallace, 94–95; inherent racism
of, 99n4
Cruikshank, Julie, 3–4, 4–5
—Works: *Do Glaciers Listen?*, 5

cultural Darwinism in social sciences, 239

cultural pattern: aesthetic definition of (Benedict), 228

cultural relativism: Boas students' introduction of, as term, 136–37

cultural studies as discipline, 43–44, 45–46

culture: according to Boasians, 49, 228; concept of, 152, 163–64; definition of, 61

culture and personality: in A. Irving "Pete" Hallowell, 91; in Anthony F. C. Wallace, 91, 95; cohort of former Boas students in, 162; in Frederica de Laguna, 268; in Margaret Mead, 95; in Ruth Benedict, 95

culture vs. civilization, definition of, 5

cumulative stereotypes about Franz Boas, 152–53

Curtin, Jeremiah: as source for Henry Wetherbe Henshaw on linguistic classification, 183

Dall, William H.: as source for John Wesley Powell on linguistic classification, 183

Darnell, Regna: "an accordion model of Algonquian social organization," 15, 75; alternatives to George W. Stocking Jr., xxi–xxii; "Americanist," 78–79; "Americanist text tradition," 137, 230; "Americanist tradition," 47, 97, 118, 151–52, 158; "anthropological concept of culture," 45; anthropology as anthropological problem, 7–8; "assassination by anachronism," 235; Canadian grafting of A. Irving "Pete" Hallowell, 90; cohort at University of Pennsylvania, 58–59, 89; as cohort of Anthony F. C. Wallace, 288; as cohort of Dell H. Hymes, 274; cohort of last students of A. Irving "Pete" Hallowell, 86; "collaborative anthropology," 30–31; as editor of Franz Boas Papers series, xxi; as founder of Ecosystem Health Program, 34–35; "generic narrative," 4, 40; "how to think like an anthropologist," 29; "nomadic legacies," 14–15, 53; "prehistory," 6–7; public health cohort of, 29; "standpoint-based archival eth-

nography," 7–8; theoretical cohort of, 119. *See also* Bend, Jack; Canadian organizations and institutions: Western's Schulich School of Medicine and Dentistry; Trick, Charlie

—Works: *Historicizing Canadian Anthropology*, 22–23

Darwin, Charles: and natural selection, iv

defamiliarization of anthropological fieldwork, 106; as explanatory mechanism, 156

de Laguna, Frederica: cohort at Bryn Mawr College, 268; as cohort of Regna Darnell, 119, 268; European cohort of, 264; Northern Books series, 269; scope of work of, 268; "a vast capacious cabinet with multiple cubbyholes and shelves . . . and a place for everything," 267

—Works: *Under Mount St. Elias*, 266

Deleuze, Gilles, and Felix Guattari: "the human mind is more like a grass than a tree," 105; "pragmatics," 105; "rhizomatic," 105

Derrida, Jacques, critique of Claude Lévi-Strauss, 259

de Saussure, Ferdinand: as cohort of Claude Lévi-Strauss in structuralism, 244–45

dialogue on return from field, 66

Dillingham Commission, 141. *See also* U.S. Census Commission

Dixon, Roland: as co-author on linguistic classification of California languages, 209–10, 211, 212–13; as cohort of Edward Sapir and Alfred L. Kroeber on linguistic classification of California languages, 209–10

Dollard, John: as neo-Freudian cohort of Margaret Mead and Ruth Benedict, 95

Dorsey, James Owen: on authorship of 1891 linguistic classification (Powell), 192–93. *See also* American Philosophical Society (APS); Gatschet, Albert

Dumézil, Georges: as cohort of Claude Lévi-Strauss in structuralism, 257

Du Ponceau, Peter Stephen: as cohort of

early commentators on unity of American languages, 179, 196; cohort of founders of American Philosophical Society, 27; polysynthetic hypothesis, 229. *See also* American Philosophical Society (APS); Gallatin, Albert; Jefferson, Thomas; Pickering, John

Durkheim, Emile: as influence on Claude Lévi-Strauss, 243; *Les formes élémentaires de la vie religieuse*, 249

Duthuit, Georges: as cohort of Claude Lévi-Strauss, 254

Eggan, Fred: as cohort of Anthony F. C. Wallace on cognition and culture, 96–97; on social structure, 96–97

Einsteinian paradigm as analogy to Hopi, 237

Eiseley, Loren: as cohort of Anthony F. C. Wallace, 94–95

Emmons, George Thorton: as edited by Frederica de Laguna, 269

emplacement of the anthropologist, 66

Enlightenment science, role of classification in, 144–45

epistemological relativism, 60

Erikson, Erik: as neo-Freudian cohort of Margaret Mead and Ruth Benedict, 95

Ernst, Max: as cohort of Claude Lévi-Strauss, 254

Ervin-Tripp, Susan: as cohort of Dell H. Hymes, 273

ethical stance of nondisclosure, 32–33

"ethno" as prefix, 93–94

"ethno-ecology" (Wallace), 95–96

"ethno-ethnohistory" (Fogelson), 87–88

ethnographic evidence: uses of (Boas), 143–44

ethnographic intuition, 106

ethnographic present: Indigenous, 6; as longitudinal (de Laguna), 267

ethnographic writing, 80–81

ethnography: appropriation of, in cultural studies, 48; in cultural studies, dismissal of, 102; definition of, 114; paralysis of, 47

ethnological classification: as aid to res-

ervation policy (Powell), 194–95; ethnological paradigm, 165

ethnologists: disciplinary blinders of (Boas), 165

ethnonationalism, 45

ethnopoetics (Hymes), 275

ethnoscience: in 1960s anthropology, 104–5; in Regna Darnell, 96

ethnosemantics, 88–89

eugenics, 137, 151, 168, 172

Evans-Pritchard, E. E.: on Azande rational thought, 118; on social construction of science, 111

everyday racism: as biological determinism, 152; of white America, 168

evidence necessary at great time depth (Sapir), 221

expeditions: Cambridge Torres Straits Expedition, 121; Jesup North Pacific Expedition, 121, 263; Wilkes Expedition of the American Northwest Coast, 180

Fabian, Johannes: on seeking and applying knowledge as aesthetic moment, 29

Fardon, Richard: area-specific attitudes around the globe, 119

Ferguson, T. J. (and Chip Colwell-Chanthaphonh): *History Is in the Land*, 9–10

Ferris, Neal: "deep history," 16; definition of "territory," 15–16

field site: choice of, constrained by funding, 120

fieldwork: archival (Stocking), 284; Brazil as chosen place of (Lévi-Strauss), 245; as rite of passage, 70; scope of (de Laguna), 268

Fogelson, Raymond: cohort at Chicago, 89, 90; as cohort of Anthony F. C. Wallace, 298; cohort of last students of A. Irving "Pete" Hallowell, 86; as cohort of Regna Darnell, 89; "epitomizing events," 87–88; "ethno-ethnohistory," 16–17, 93–94; "Gardez le Foi," 85; "historical consciousness," 94; "history," 92–93; "Indian sovereignty," 98–99 folk linguistics as oral tradition, 177

folklore: as best entree to "inner growth of a particular culture," 164

folklore elements on Northwest Coast, 206–7

folk psychology, 179

Foster, Michael: as cohort of Dell H. Hymes, 274

Foucault, Marcel: as cohort of Claude Lévi-Strauss in structuralism, 244–45

Fought, John: as co-author with Dell H. Hymes, 279–80

Frachtenberg, Leo: as Edward Sapir interlocutor on language classification, 213–14; on Penutian, 216, 221; reaction to Sapir six-unit classification, 214

Franklin, Benjamin: as American Philosophical Society founder, 27, 89–90. *See also* American Philosophical Society (APS); Du Ponceau, Peter Stephen; Gallatin, Albert; Jefferson, Thomas; Pickering, John

Freedom of Information Act, 289

freedom of thought as sine qua non of science, 152

Freeman, Derek: critique of Margaret Mead and Ruth Benedict, 95

French, David, and Kay (Story) French: as cohorts of Dell H. Hymes, 271

French anthropology: influence of Vladimir Propp on, 230; as national tradition, 226

French Marxism, early ties of Claude Lévi-Strauss to, 245

Freud, Sigmund, 95

Gallatin, Albert: as American Philosophical Society founder, 27, 89–90; cohort of John Wesley Powell in authorship of linguistic classification, 179–80; cohort of John Wesley Powell in classification of American Indian languages, 205. *See also* American Philosophical Society (APS); Du Ponceau, Peter Stephen; Franklin, Benjamin; Jefferson, Thomas

Gamio, Manuel: as Franz Boas cohort in Mexico, 138–39; and National University of Mexico, 138–39, 154–55

gatekeeper: George W. Stocking Jr. as, 286, 291

Gatschet, Albert: on authorship of Powell classification, 179–80, 182, 183, 192

Geertz, Clifford: on Claude Lévi-Strauss, 244–45; "eye/I witnessing," 111; "local knowledge," 8–9; on philosophy of mind, 243; "redemptive historical narrative," 254. *See also* Malinowski, Bronislaw

"genius," 4: Alfred L. Kroeber on, 49; with reference to Edward Sapir (Boas), 166

genres of writing: annual meetings, 2, 21; archives, 8; collaboration with publisher, xx–xxi; commentary, 101; at conferences or professional associations, xix; obituaries, xxii–xxiii; presidential address to American Society for Ethnohistory, 1, 3; reviews, xx; standardized questionnaires, 179–80

German romanticism, 227. *See also* von Humboldt, Wilhelm

Gibbs, George: and authorship of linguistic classification, 180; as cohort of John Wesley Powell, 205

Gleach, Frederic W.: as co-editor of Histories of Anthropology Annual series, xxi

Glidden, George: as racist critic of Franz Boas, 164–65

globalization, 43, 60

Gobineau, Arthur de: as racist critic of Franz Boas, 164–65

Goddard, Pliny Earle: on Indo-European, 86; as interlocutor of Edward Sapir, 216; negative reaction to Sapir six-unit classification, 213–14, 216

Goffman, Erving: as cohort of Dell H. Hymes, 274, 275; "impression management," 105–6; "presentation of the self in everyday life," 105–6; "stigma," 105–6; as teacher of Regna Darnell at University of Pennsylvania, 105; "tie-signs," 105–6

Goldenweiser, Alexander: "civilization,"

history: emergent characteristics of, 6; metalinguistic nature of, 1

history of anthropology: as handmaiden to linguistic theory, 233

Hjelmslev, Louis, as cohort of Claude Lévi-Strauss in structuralism, 244–45

Hogan, Helen: as cohort of Dell H. Hymes, 274

Hoijer, Harry: as cohort of Dell H. Hymes, 275; critique of Sapir-Whorf hypothesis, 237–38

home: as reference point to home territory, 75

homeplace, 35–36, 75

Hong, Keelung: and Murray-Hong Family Trust, xxi

honors: of Anthony F. C. Wallace, 297–98; of Dell H. Hymes, 276; of Edward Sapir, 90; of Frederica de Laguna, 263; of George W. Stocking Jr., 289, 297; Weaver-Tremblay Award, 21, 22, 23–24

Horney, Karen, as neo-Freudian cohort of Margaret Mead and Ruth Benedict, 95

Hymes, Dell H.: "breakthrough into performance," 274; cohort at Berkeley, 275; cohort at Center for Urban Ethnography, 274; cohort at University of Pennsylvania, 274; as cohort of Anthony F. C. Wallace, 94–95; as cohort of Regna Darnell, 89; "communicative competence," 70, 274; "competence for performance," 70; "ethnography of communication," 273–74; "ethnography of speaking," 273–74; "ethnopoetics," 275; and First Yale School, 275; as mentor of George W. Stocking Jr., 283; personal genealogy of, in histories of anthropology and linguistics, 275; and Second Yale School, 274–75; "traditions," 275
—Works: *Directions in Sociolinguistics*, 274; *Foundations in Sociolinguistics*, 274; *Language in Culture and Society*, 276; *Language in Society*, 276; *Reinventing Anthropology*, 276; "Two Types of Linguistic Relativity," 274

Hymes, Virginia: as cohort of Dell H. Hymes, 274

Indian Claims Commission, 9, 296–97

"Indian Englishes," 33

"Indian sovereignty" (Fogelson), 98–99

"Indian [*sic*]-white relations" (Hallowell), 95–96

Indigenous actors: Handsome Lake (Seneca), 296; Nanabush (Anishinaabeg), 63–64; Popul Vuh (Mayan), 1–2; Teedyuskung (Delaware), 92, 295; Wisahketchak (Cree), 30, 31, 38, 42

Indigenous collaborators: Albert Alvarez (Papago, now Tohono O'odham), 78–79; Angela Sidney (Yukon), 4–5; Annie Ned (Yukon), 4–5; Charles Cultee (Wasco and Wishram), 277; Charles Henry (Western Apache), 5, 14; Chief William Berens (Ojibwe), 195–96; Deborah Holler, 298; Freda Ahenakew (Cree), 3; George Hunt (Kwakiutl [Kwakwala]), 125; Hiram Smith (Wasco and Wishram), 277; Jim Kâ-Nîpitêhtêw, 3; J. N. B. Hewitt, 197; Kitty Smith (Yukon), 4–5; Philip Kahclamat (Wasco and Wishram), 277; Wendy and Jim Bissell, 298

Indigenous knowledge: emergence of a discipline of, 17; persistence of, 5

Indigenous terms, 3–4, 6, 12, 13–14, 16, 81, 133, 207–8, 227

Indigenous writers: Bryan Louks, 16; David Maracle, Kanatawahkon (Mohawk), 68–69; Drew Hayden Taylor, 64–65; Eli Baxter (Anishinaabemowin, Ojibwe), 68–69; Farley Mowat, 72; Gerald Vizenor (Anishinaabeg), 73; Neal McLeod (Cree), 76–77; Thompson Highway (Cree), 64–65; Tom King, 64–65

Indo-Chinese (Sapir): link to Na-Dene, 220

interdisciplinary social science, 22, 54, 112. *See also* Sapir, Edward; Sullivan, Harry Stack

interpretive community (Darnell), 15

intertextuality, 96–97

intracultural variability, 106–7

introspection as method, 106

Irvine, Judith T.: as cohort of Dell H. Hymes, 274

Jakobson, Roman: as cohort of Claude Lévi-Strauss in structuralism, 244–45, 254, 255; "near-universals," 110

Jefferson, Thomas: as cohort of American Philosophical Society founders, 27, 89–90; as cohort of early commentators on unity of American languages, 179. *See also* American Philosophical Society (APS); Du Ponceau, Peter Stephen; Franklin, Benjamin; Gallatin, Albert; Pickering, John

Jewishness of Franz Boas, 168

Jews: dehumanization of, 168; in Franz Boas, 141

Judaism, 141

Jung, Carl: *Psychological Types*, 91

Katz, Sol: as cohort of Anthony F. C. Wallace, 298

Keenan, Elinor (Ochs): as cohort of Dell H. Hymes, 274

Keetowah Society (Cherokee), 98–99

King, Tom: "the truth about stories," 65

kinship, 89; adaptive significance of, 94

kinship system: changes in (Hallowell), 96

Kleinberg, Otto: on immigration data, 161; and social experience trumping innate ability, 161

Klemm, Gustav: as cohort of racist critics of Franz Boas, 164–65. *See also* eugenics

Kramer, Samuel Noah: at University of Pennsylvania Museum (cited by Frederica de Laguna), 268

Kroeber, Alfred L., 49, 50, 53; on California language myth and diversity, 209, 210–11; as cohort of core Boasians, 47, 48, 228, 239; as cohort of Dell H. Hymes, 273; as cohort of Edward Sapir on California linguistic classification, 209–10, 211–12; as cohort of first-generation Boas students, 157–58; as commentator on authorship of Powell classification, 193–94; "configuration," 240; and culture and history, 82; and culture genuine and spurious, 55–56, 57, 60, 112; as interlocutor of Edward Sapir, 216, 219–20; on native speaker intuitions; "sui generis," 52; "superorganic," 49, 50

Kuhn, Thomas: and "paradigm" as term

anachronistic for Boas, 158; reliance of George W. Stocking Jr. on, xxii

Labov, William: as cohort of Dell H. Hymes, 274

Lacan, Jacques: as cohort of Claude Lévi-Strauss in structuralism, 244–45

land acknowledgements, 66

later commentators on Brinton classification: Alfred L. Kroeber, 199, 203; John P. Harrington, 199; Sydney Lamb, 201

Latour, Bruno: on Janus faces of science, 29

learned societies: cohort at APS in Philadelphia, 138

Leavitt, John: critique of Sapir-Whorf hypothesis, 240

legal acts: Canadian Constitution Act (1982), 73; Delgamuukw' decision of 1991, 9; James Bay and Northern Quebec Agreement (1975), 74–75; NAGPRA (Native American Graves and Repatriation Act [1990]), 10; Royal Commission on Aboriginal Peoples (1996), 4, 73; Truth and Reconciliation Commission (2015), 4, 73

Lévi-Strauss, Claude: Auguste Comte as foil for, 258; as bricoleur, 259; on British functionalism, 121–22; cohort in New York, 254; cohort in structuralist movement, 244–45, 256, 257; debates with Jean-Paul Sartre, 257; "deep structure," 258; disciplinary niche, search for, 245; and emigres to new world, role of Franz Boas in, 244; on Enlightenment rationalism and universalism, 132–33; fieldwork, Brazil as chosen place for, 245; and French Marxism, early ties to, 246; and French national tradition, 226; intellectual biography of, 244; interdisciplinary critique of, poststructuralism as, 244; and Jacques Derrida, 259; "logical operations," 250; on Prague school structuralism, 244; self-imposed exile of, 245; "transformation," 130, 258; "a view from afar," 109–10; on universal products of human mind, 143

—Works: *Anthropologie Structurale*, 249, 251, 256, 258; *Handbook of South American Indians*, 246; *La pensée sauvage*, 257; *La voie des masques*, 250, 255, 258; *Les Structures élémentaires de la parenté*, 249; *Mythologiques*, 253, 255, 258; *Tristes Tropiques*, 121, 246–48, 251, 254; *The Way of the Masks*, 130; *A World on the Wane*, 121

lexicostatistics, 273

liberation of Dachau (Wallace), 295

linguistic classification: as geographical and cultural (Brinton), 200–201; nature and function of, 177; as reflected in social evolution, 196–97; subclassification only in Siouan (Powell), 181

linguistic inference, limits of, 205–6

linguistics as tool for ethnology, 197–98

longitudinal data: on bodily form in Boas, 142

longitudinal studies, need for, 170

Lorimer, Frank, 172

Loucks, Bryan, 16

Lowie, Robert H.: as cohort of core Boasians, 228; as cohort of first-generation Boas students, 47, 51, 57–58

Lyell, Charles: uniformitarian geology of, 229

MacEachern, Justice Allan: in Delgamuukw' 1991, 39

Malinowski, Bronislaw: as European cohort of Frederica de Laguna, 264; in history of anthropology (Hallowell), 87; "imponderability of everyday life," 78; and role of fieldwork, 245

Mannheim, Bruce, 65

map of North America, 213; blank spaces in, 205–6; Voegelin and Voegelin, 177–78. *See also* Powell, John Wesley; Sapir, Edward

Marx, Karl: as influence on Dell H. Hymes, 277

mask cultures (Lévi-Strauss), fascination with, 130

mask designs (Lévi-Strauss), 109

masking complex, 93

masks: Claude Lévi-Strauss's first exposure to, 130; as "cycle of myths" (Boas), 127; social hierarchy correlated with, 126

Mason, J. Alden: as cohort of Alfred L. Kroeber, Edward Sapir, John P. Harrington, John Swanton, and Roland Dixon in linguistic classification of California languages, 209–12; as cohort of Anthony F. C. Wallace, 94–95

Masson, André: as cohort of Claude Lévi-Strauss, 254

Mathiassen, Therkel: as European cohort of Frederica de Laguna, 264

Mauss, Marcel: influence of British social anthropology on, 228; as influence on Claude Lévi-Strauss, 120, 245

McClellan, Catherine: as cohort of Frederica de Laguna, 266

McDougall, Allan: as collaborator with Lisa Phillips Valentine and Regna Darnell, 33

McGregor, Gaile: on Canadian mindset of Erving Goffman, 106

McKinley, Gerald: as cohort with Regna Darnell in Master of Public Health teaching, 37

McLeod, Neal: "Cree narrative memory," 76–77

Mead, Margaret: on Canada as hardest country to study, 73–74; as cohort of core Boasians, 228, 239; as cohort of first-generation Boas students, 157–58; as cohort of former Boas students in culture and personality, 162; columns in *Redbook* magazine, 112; "culture and personality," 95; neo-Freudian cohort of, 95

media: audio and video tapes, 72–73; nontraditional technologies, 77–78; video tape, 71

medicine wheel as heuristic device, 14

mental life as plastic (Boas), 170

metaphor, double meaning implicit in, xxiii–xxiv

Michelson, Truman: as gatekeeper of Algonquian language family, 219; reaction to Sapir six-unit classification, 216, 219

"microhistories" (Bernardini), 11–13

"microhistory," 8–9

migration: "histories" and "pathways" (Bernardini), 11

Mooney, James: as co-author of "Linguistic Families of the Indian Tribes of Mexico," 182–83; as cohort of John Wesley Powell on authorship of Powell classification, 192–93

Morgan, Lewis Henry: "germs of civilization," 167; as influence on evolutionary anthropology, 229–30; as source for John Wesley Powell in linguistic classification, 197

Moritz, Sarah: as cohort of Canadian research team, 41

Morton, Samuel G.: as cohort of racist critics of Franz Boas, 164–65

Mowat, Farley: on Inuktitut, 72; *People of the Deer*, 72

multiculturalism, 43

Murphy, Murray: as cohort of George W. Stocking Jr., 282–83, 289

Murray, Stephen O.: as co-editor of Critical Studies in History of Anthropology, xxi; and legacy of Murray-Hong Family Trust, xxi

museum curation in Frederica de Laguna, 268

myth as composite of many elements, 197

myth variants: Claude Lévi-Strauss and Franz Boas fascinated by, 125. *See also* masks

national character (Benedict), 225. *See also* Mead, Margaret

nationality in categorizing human groups, 167

national tradition in relation to national character, 225

Newton, Isaac: view of science, 29

Nietzsche, Friedrich: on Aryan race (cited by Boas), 144

Noble, Brian: as cohort of Canadian research team, 41

North Pacific Coast, 145

Northwest Coast: importance of, for Franz Boas, 226–27; as laboratory for controller comparison, 120; as microcosm for history of anthropology, 117

Nott, Josiah Clark: as cohort of racist critics of Franz Boas, 164–65

Nuttall, Zelia: as Franz Boas cohort in Mexico, 139

Ogle, Richard: critique of Sapir-Whorf hypothesis, 233–34; "neo-Cartesian," 236

Oppenheim, Robert: as co-editor of Critical Studies in the History of Anthropology series, xxi

Osborn, Frederick, 172

"the Other," 46, 55, 59

"Others" (Boasians), 45, 59

paradigms: of historical particularism and structuralism, 117; of revolution and discontinuity, 11

paradigm statements of Franz Boas, 136–37, 151–52, 155

participant observation, 60

Peirce, Charles S.: as cohort of Claude Lévi-Strauss in structuralism, 244–45

peoples that have no history, archaeology as only access to, 145–46

peoples without writing, proxy for, 141

Perry, William James: European cohort of Frederica de Laguna, 264

personality defined in cultural context, 171

Philadelphia institutions: Academy of Natural Sciences of Philadelphia, 202; Center for Native American and Indigenous Research, 42; Center for Urban Ethnography, 274; Eastern Pennsylvania Psychiatric Institute (EPPI), xxiii, 293, 297; Graduate School of Education, 274; Philadelphia Psychoanalytic Institute, 297; University of Pennsylvania, 38–39, 88, 89, 90, 91, 92, 96, 274, 282, 289, 293, 295; University of Pennsylvania Museum, 264–65, 297

Phillips, Susan U.: as cohort of Dell H. Hymes, 274

Rivet, Paul: as European cohort of Frederica de Laguna, 264

Rorty, Richard, 78: on "edifying conversations," 113–14; on "mirror of nature," 113

Russian anthropology: as national tradition, 225–26

Sapir, Edward, 177: as cohort in critique of Kroeber's superorganic, 31, 53; as cohort of Alfred L. Kroeber and Roland Dixon in classification of California languages, 209–10, 212–13; as cohort of Claude Lévi-Strauss in structuralism, 244–45; as cohort of core Boasians, 228, 239; as cohort of first-generation Boas students, 47, 157–58; as cohort of former Boas students in culture and personality, 162; on comparative method for unwritten languages, 209; critique of Sapir-Whorf hypothesis, 254; "culture, genuine and spurious," 54–55, 55–56; "feel" for languages, 215–16; fieldwork languages, 209–10; "genuine," 55, 60; "the impact of culture on personality," 102; "morphological kernel" as archaic in present language, 222; on poetry and the aesthetic, 57; "psychological reality," 128–29, 253, 258; response to Powell classification, 213–14; and superorganic, 51, 52, 57, 157. See also interdisciplinary social science; Sullivan, Harry Stack
—Works: "Culture, Genuine and Spurious," 55, 57, 112; "The Psychological Reality of Phonemes," 238; Time Perspective in Aboriginal American Culture, 145

Sapir-Whorf hypothesis: critique of, 233–34; in Dell H. Hymes, 274; in John B. Carroll, 236. See also Hoijer, Harry; Leavitt, John; Ogle, Richard; Sapir, Edward

science: arising from vacuum left by theology (Désveaux), 229; importance of, for Franz Boas, 227; in interwar Germany, 171

sciences: Chinese, Indian, and Arabic, 111

scientific racism: as target of critique (Boas), 139–40, 169

Searle, John: as cohort of Dell H. Hymes, 275

Segal, Dan, 102–3

Seitel, Sheila (Dauer): as cohort of Dell H. Hymes, 274

Seligman, Charles Gabriel: as European cohort of Frederica de Laguna, 264

Sherzer, Joel: on areal typology, 120; as cohort of Dell H. Hymes, 274

Smith, Joshua: as cohort of Canadian research team, 41

Snyder, Gary: as cohort of Dell H. Hymes, 271–72

socialization, professional. See professional socialization

Social Science Research Council (SSRC), 283

Social Sciences and Humanities Research Council of Canada (SSHRC), 24–25; Partnership Grant, 40–41

Sontag, Susan: "a myth of quest," 246

sound correspondences, 198, 219

Speck, Frank: as cohort of A. Irving "Pete" Hallowell, 88; as cohort of Anthony F. C. Wallace, 295; as interlocutor of Edward Sapir, 214

speculation, 179; interpretive, as exegesis, 4–5; on time depth in archaeology (Sapir), 220–21

Spier, Leslie: as cohort of first-generation Boas Students, 47

Spiro, Melford: as cohort of Anthony F. C. Wallace in culture and cognition, 96–97; as cohort of Raymond Fogelson, 89

standardization of linguistic format for grammars, 181–82

standards of evidence, social constructivist, 43

statistical treatment: inadequacy of, 160–61

Stephenson, Peter: as cohort of Canadian research team, 41

Stocking, George W., Jr.; "anthropology yesterday," 290–91; and British social anthropology, 284, 289–90; cohort at University of Pennsylvania, 289; as cohort of Dell H. Hymes, 283; as cohort of Raymond Fogelson, 90; as cohort of Regna Darnell, 38–39; as editor, xxi, 282; FBI file of, 282; fieldwork of, archival, 284; as founder of history of anthropology subdiscipline, xxi–xxii; as gatekeeper, xxii–xxiii, 286, 290, 291; on hermeneutic apparatus of Thomas Kuhn, xxii; honors, 287; and presentism and historicism, xxii, 284, 289; "refamiliarization," 281; "revelatory microcosm," 283, 291; uncompleted works, pattern of, 290

—Works: *After Tylor*, 285; *Race, Culture, and Evolution*, 283, 290; *The Shaping of American Anthropology, 1883–1911*, 284

Stoler, Ann: on field notes and archives, 8

structural resemblance and assumption of common origin, 206

Sturtevant, William: as later commentator on authorship of Powell classification, 191–92, 193

Subtiaba, evidence at great time depth and (Sapir), 221

Sullivan, Harry Stack, 54. *See also* interdisciplinary social science; Sapir, Edward

Sumner, William Graham: evolutionary sociology of, 165

surrealist art in New York emigré circles, 254

Swadesh, Morris: "diffusional cumulation" vs. "archaic residue," 206–7; as later commentator on authorship of Powell classification, 191–92

Swanton, John: on cohort of California linguistic classification, 209–10; reaction to Sapir six-unit classification, 220

symbolic anthropology (Darnell), 93, 95

symbolic interaction, 59–60

Szwed, John: as cohort of Dell H. Hymes, 274

Tanguy, Yves: as cohort of Claude Lévi-Strauss, 254

Tedlock, Barbara, and Dennis: "the dialogic emergence of culture," 65–66

Tedlock, Dennis, 1–2

—Works: *The Spoken Word and the Work of Interpretation*, 1–2

theory of culture as cross-cultural research methodology (Sapir), 55

theory of history (Western Apache), 13–14

Tiwari, T. K.: as cohort of Dell H. Hymes, 274

Torgovnik, Marianna: "transcendental homelessness," 246

totemism: in Alexander Goldenweiser, 146

transportable knowledge, xxiv, 34

Tremblay, Marc-Adélard, 21–22, 23–24

Trick, Charlie: as founder of Ecosystem Health Program, 34–35; as public health cohort of Regna Darnell, 29. *See also* Bend, Jack; Canadian organizations and institutions: Western's Schulich School of Medicine and Dentistry; Darnell, Regna

Trubetzkoy, Count Nikolaj: as cohort of Claude Lévi-Strauss in structuralism, 244–45

"two-eyed seeing" (some Indigenous scholars), 64

Tylor, Edward B.: influence of British social anthropology on, 228

unwritten languages, multiple interpretations equally correct for, 177

U.S. Census Commission, 141, 156

"useful knowledge" (cited by John Wesley Powell), 228. *See also* American Philosophical Society (APS)

Valentine, Lisa Philips: as collaborator with Regna Darnell and Allan McDougall, 33

validity, 5–6

variability, 58

Vizenor, Gerald: "survivance," 73

von Humboldt, Wilhelm, 179–80

Waldram, Jim: interventions in public policy by, 24–25

Wallace, Anthony F. C.: "cognition and culture," 97; cohort at University of Pennsylvania, 298; as cohort of A. Irving "Pete" Hallowell, 88; as cohort of Regna Darnell, 88–89; cohort on cognition and culture, 97; commitment to northeastern ethnography, 91–92; "culture and personality," 91; disaster preparedness, 297; "ethno-ecology," 95–96; "mazeway," 91; "modal personality type," 295; "organization of difference," 296; "organization of diversity," 91, 106–7; professional papers, location of, 299; range of topics studied by, 293; and religion as cognitive integration, 297; "replication of uniformity," 106–7, 296; "revitalization movement," 91–92, 296

—Works: *Culture and Personality*, 94, 96, 296; *Death and Rebirth of the Seneca*, 296; *Jefferson and the Indians*, 298; *Rockdale*, 296; *St. Clair*, 296; *Tuscarora*, 298

Wallace, Paul A. W.: as son of Anthony F. C. Wallace, 91–92, 295

Washburn, Sherwood, 97

Weaver, Sally Mae, 21–22, 23, 23–24

Weiser, Conrad: as influence on Anthony F. C. Wallace and Paul A. W. Wallace, 91–92

White, Hayden, 2, 8

White, Leslie: as critic of Boas evolutionary paradigm, 154; dismissal of epistemological relativism, 136

Whitney, William Dwight, 179; as collaborator of John Wesley Powell on alphabet for linguistic classification, 182

Whorf, Benjamin Lee: "cryptotype," 234; "fashions of speaking," 234; "habitual thought," 80, 147, 233; "linguistic relativity," 234, 236, 240; "multilingual awareness," 113; Standard Average European (SAE), 80, 113

Wierzbicka, Anna: methodological contrast of Polish, English, and various Aboriginal Australian languages, 105–6; "semantic primitives," 104–5

Williams, Raymond: on "selective tradition," 15–16

Witthoft, John: as cohort of Anthony F. C. Wallace, 95

Wolf, Eric: and "extreme" cultural elaborations, 113; "relations of power," 113

Wolfart, H. C., 3

"wondering" as method, 32

workload, academic: allotment to teaching, research, service, xx, 3; double bind of forty-hour work week, xx

World Health Organization (WHO), 37

Worth, Sol: as cohort of Dell H. Hymes, 274

Wundt, Wilhelm: psychology of, paralleling social to organic evolution, 165

Yanagisako, Sylvia, and Dan Segal: "unwrap the sacred bundle," 102–3

In the Critical Studies in the History of Anthropology series

Invisible Genealogies: A History of Americanist Anthropology
Regna Darnell

The Shaping of American Ethnography: The Wilkes Exploring Expedition, 1838–1842
Barry Alan Joyce

Ruth Landes: A Life in Anthropology
Sally Cole

Melville J. Herskovits and the Racial Politics of Knowledge
Jerry Gershenhorn

Leslie A. White: Evolution and Revolution in Anthropology
William J. Peace

Rolling in Ditches with Shamans: Jaime de Angulo and the Professionalization of American Anthropology
Wendy Leeds-Hurwitz

Irregular Connections: A History of Anthropology and Sexuality
Andrew P. Lyons and Harriet D. Lyons

Ephraim George Squier and the Development of American Anthropology
Terry A. Barnhart

Ruth Benedict: Beyond Relativity, Beyond Pattern
Virginia Heyer Young

Looking through Taiwan: American Anthropologists' Collusion with Ethnic Domination
Keelung Hong and Stephen O. Murray

Visionary Observers: Anthropological Inquiry and Education
Jill B. R. Cherneff and Eve Hochwald
Foreword by Sydel Silverman

Anthropology Goes to the Fair: The 1904 Louisiana Purchase Exposition
Nancy J. Parezo and Don D. Fowler

The Meskwaki and Anthropologists: Action Anthropology Reconsidered
Judith M. Daubenmier

The 1904 Anthropology Days and Olympic Games: Sport, Race, and American Imperialism
Edited by Susan Brownell

Lev Shternberg: Anthropologist, Russian Socialist, Jewish Activist
Sergei Kan

Contributions to Ojibwe Studies: Essays, 1934–1972
A. Irving Hallowell
Edited and with introductions by Jennifer S. H. Brown and Susan Elaine Gray

Excavating Nauvoo: The Mormons and the Rise of Historical Archaeology in America
Benjamin C. Pykles
Foreword by Robert L. Schuyler

Cultural Negotiations: The Role of Women in the Founding of Americanist Archaeology
David L. Browman

Homo Imperii: A History of Physical Anthropology in Russia
Marina Mogilner

To order or obtain more information on these or other University of Nebraska Press titles, visit nebraskapress.unl.edu.

CPSIA information can be obtained
at www.ICGtesting.com
Printed in the USA
LVHW101913070522
718181LV00002B/113